W9-BWV-866

7/14

DATE DUE

APR 11 2005		

GAYLORD   PRINTED IN U.S.A.

Nebraska Symposium on Motivation 1986

Volume 34

University of Nebraska Press
Lincoln and London 1987

Nebraska Symposium on Motivation 1986

Alcohol and Addictive Behavior

Richard A. Dienstbier   *Series Editor*

P. Clayton Rivers   *Volume Editor*

Presenters

Peter E. Nathan   *Henry and Anna Starr Professor of Psychology and Director of Alcohol Studies, Rutgers University*

Robert A. Zucker   *Professor of Psychology and Director of Clinical Training, Michigan State University*

Richard W. Wilsnack   *Professor of Sociology, University of North Dakota*

Sharon C. Wilsnack   *Professor and Director of Preclinical Curriculum in Psychiatry and Behavioral Science, University of North Dakota School of Medicine*

Theodore Jacob

Associate Professor of Psychology and Psychiatry, University of Pittsburgh

Shirley Y. Hill

Associate Professor of Psychiatry, University of Pittsburgh School of Medicine, and Director of the Substance Abuse Program and Alcoholism Research Program, Western Psychiatric Institute and Clinic

Timothy B. Baker

Associate Professor of Psychology, University of Wisconsin–Madison

Nebraska Symposium on Motivation, 1986, is Volume 34 in the series on CURRENT THEORY AND RESEARCH IN MOTIVATION

"The Library of Congress has cataloged this serial publication as follows:"
Nebraska Symposium on Motivation.
  Nebraska Symposium on Motivation. [Papers] v. [1]–1953–
  Lincoln, University of Nebraska Press.
    v. illus., diagrs. 22 cm. annual.
  Vol. 1 issued by the symposium under its earlier name: Current Theory and Research in Motivation.
  Symposia sponsored by the Dept. of Psychology of the University of Nebraska.

  1. Motivation (Psychology)

BF683.N4   159.4082   53-11655

Library of Congress

Preface

*T*his volume of the *Nebraska Symposium on Motivation* focuses on addictive behavior, particularly addiction and abuse of alcohol.

The volume editor for this 34th volume is Professor P. Clayton Rivers. He has assumed the major responsibility for successfully drawing together the contributors and for overseeing their production of these chapters. My thanks to him for his efforts and his patience in seeing the volume through to its final conclusion.

The *Symposium* series is supported largely by funds donated in the memory of Professor Harry K. Wolfe to the University of Nebraska Foundation by the late Professor Cora L. Friedline. This volume, like those in the recent past, is dedicated to the memory of Professor Wolfe, who brought psychology to the University of Nebraska. After studying with Professor Wilhelm Wundt, Professor Wolfe returned to this, his native state, to establish the first undergraduate laboratory of psychology in the nation. As a student at Nebraska, Professor Friedline studied psychology under Professor Wolfe. The editors are grateful to the late Professor Friedline for her bequest and to the officers of the University of Nebraska Foundation for their continued interest in and support of this series.

RICHARD A. DIENSTBIER
Series Editor

Contents

Introduction

P. Clayton Rivers

University of Nebraska–Lincoln

*T*here has been a rapid expansion of research on alcoholism in the past 15 years— so rapid that it is easy to forget that only a short time ago it would have been difficult to collect enough scholarly work in the field to fill a volume of this type. This explosion of thinking and research made choosing specific topics for this book very difficult. On the one hand, several lines of programmatic research are well established, and several have been widely reported in the literature. Selecting material from these established lines of inquiry has the advantage of presenting well-documented research by recognized scholars whose work has clearly contributed to the field. But this approach to a scholarly area frequently produces a volume that simply reiterates what has already been published elsewhere. Another approach is to select programmatic research that is still in progress, usually by less well known scholars whose impact on the field must await the unfolding of history.

The papers chosen for this volume reflect a synthesis of these alternatives. The lead authors have all established themselves as outstanding researchers on alcoholism. However, the work reported here represents new conceptualizations or new programmatic research, much of it still in progress.

We also attempted to choose topics that were emerging as key issues in research on alcohol and drugs. This selection strategy produced a diverse group of papers that, as the reader will see, overlap somewhat despite their differences in focus. They range from broad subjects, such as what social scientists know about alcoholism, to questions about developmental issues and special groups, such as women and families, whose alcohol use and abuse are currently of major concern. There are chapters that home in on factors of long-term interest in the alcohol and drug field. For example, there is a chapter on genetic markers that adds to our information about the influence of heredity on alcoholism. Finally, one of the most central and continuing questions regarding alcohol and drugs is why people crave alcohol and use it to extremes and why there is such a high relapse rate for those attempting to maintain sobriety. The paper on drug urge offers new experimental data and a new way of conceptualizing this long-standing and frustrating puzzle. Despite their differing foci, the essays do share some broadly equivalent concerns about the etiology, treatment, prognosis, and prevention of alcoholism. There are also some specific overlaps that will be pointed out where appropriate.

The ordering of the papers was based on a somewhat arbitrary principle—moving from broader field and subpopulation considerations to new conceptualizations and research on genetic markers and drug urge. This arbitrary arrangement means that here the contributions are organized in a different way than they were originally presented at the symposium. (Nathan, Hill et al., and Baker et al. originally presented their papers in the fall session 1985, and the remaining papers were given in the spring session 1986.)

The first chapter, by Nathan, compares and contrasts what we knew about alcoholism 50 years ago (1935, the year Alcoholics Anonymous was formed) with what we know today. This broad overview of our progress covers four main areas: behavioral pathology, etiology, treatment, and prevention. Regarding behavioral pathology, Nathan notes that we no longer view behavioral tolerance as deriving from some culturally and morally deviant life-style in which alcoholics were reared; we now recognize that heavy alcohol intake increases the rate at which the abusive drinker produces the enzyme alcohol dehydrogenase. Another factor found to be important is the role of Pavlovian conditioning in reducing the effects of drugs such as alcohol. The concepts of craving and loss of control have also changed dramatically in the past half-century. In the face of data pointing to environmental and expectancy factors in the behavior of the alcoholic, Nathan notes that craving and loss of control, as well as the disease model itself, have come to be regarded by many as metaphors rather than literal truths. The paper by Baker et al., outlined below, will look at the craving issue in more modern terms.

The moral insanity concept of the 1930s has disappeared, and there has also been a change in the way we view alcohol and depression. Alcoholics are now viewed as a heterogeneous group, not as morally flawed individuals. Depression and alcoholism are seen as reciprocal—that is, each disorder can cause the other. The 1930s perception, drawn from psychoanalytic thinking, that alcoholics were commonly depressed no longer prevails. Finally, alcoholism is no longer seen as a disease of men. Although we still know too little about alcoholism in women, we now know that the problem affects both sexes, even though the traditional stigma borne by female alcohol abusers kept this from being revealed until recently. Nathan notes that we still have little information on the role alcohol plays in women's lives or on how we should treat or prevent alcoholism in this subpopulation. (The reader will not be surprised to find that the paper by Wilsnack et al. focuses on alcohol use and abuse in women and gives us more information on factors that may contribute to alcohol abuse by females.)

In terms of etiology, Nathan points out the important roles that both psychoanalytic theory and the disease model of Alcoholics Anonymous played during the 1930s. The early behavioral clinicians highlighted the idea that alcohol was the way the alcoholic had chosen to deal with anxiety. In the 1980s a genetically determined predisposition to alcohol has been generally accepted. The precise mechanism of this genetic transmission is unknown, however, although the best guess is that it is mediated by the central nervous system. Hill and her coauthors look at one way of obtaining information about genetic contributions in their chapter on genetic markers.

Even more elusive is the exact role learning plays in etiology. Nathan suggested that an interaction between classical and operant conditioning and modeling may be involved. Whatever the underlying causative factors, the recent longitudinal studies suggest it is not early childhood factors like inadequate child rearing or emotional deprivation that are directly tied to later alcoholism.

Treatment availability and diversity have changed markedly since the thirties. Instead of treatment in psychiatric facilities with moral reeducation as a central theme, there is recognition of alcoholism as a chronic, remitting, recurrent disease, with treatment provided in a variety of freestanding alcohol treatment centers. Alcoholics Anonymous is now a central component of treatment. There has also been an attempt to match treatment to the individual. Despite these more sophisticated methods, there is no evidence that any single approach to alcoholism is best. Nor has it been found that recovering alcoholics are better therapists than other counselors.

Nathan does not see us making as much progress in prevention as in the other three areas over the past 50 years. In the 1930s (after repeal of Prohibition) an attempt was made to control alcohol use through higher liquor taxes and legislating drinking age. Authorities were very punitive toward the alcoholic. Although the ineffectiveness of punitive interventions has led to a modification of those laws, there have been few changes in our current approach to preventing alcohol abuse. With the exception of the focus on alcohol education in the 1980s, Nathan sees us as using many of the same prevention strategies utilized in the mid- to late 1930s.

Zucker has long advocated developing theoretical models that are not alcohol specific but are useful with both normal and abnormal behavior. His contribution develops a rationale for conceptualizing four types of alcoholism. To achieve this he reviews several sets of literatures and presents preliminary results from the early stages of a developmental study of high-risk families currently in progress. Zucker and his research group are particularly interested in isolating potential risk factors for alcohol problems and alcoholism even before alcohol is introduced. To see if this might be possible, they are mounting a longitudinal study focused upon high-risk families. A particular interest is male children (beginning at 4 years of age) of fathers arrested for driving while intoxicated with high alcohol levels. Zucker sees these boys as being at high risk. He also believes they may show biological, psychological, and social characteristics early in life that may differ from those of a normal comparison group. Over time one may be able to isolate individual differences that will give clues to the etiology of alcohol abuse.

Zucker and his colleagues see drinking patterns as resulting from an interactive process between cultural/situational, familial, and individual differences influences. To illustrate how these factors might be isolated, Zucker summarizes preliminary findings of differences between young children of alcoholics and their yoked controls in his longitudinal study. For example, children of alcoholics tend to be retarded in social and cognitive development, and their parents show more antisocial and aggressive behavior than do nonalcoholic parents.

Zucker and his colleagues see their longitudinal data as supporting a continuity model of alcoholism etiology. Using these data and data from completed longitudinal studies, they reach the following conclusions:

1. Early observations of poorer personal and social development can be linked to later childhood antisocial behavior and alcoholism.

2. Early developmental influences in cognitive functioning

appear to predict differences later observed in achievement-oriented activity.

3. Heightened parental marital conflict in the prealcoholic child's preschool years is substantiated by parent self-report data. Parent-child interpersonal difficulties in these high-risk families have not been well documented. However, Zucker's clinical observations of early childhood oppositionalism fit with other researchers' observations of less dependency in later life in some children of alcoholics.

4. These inadequacies and differences can be identified in preschool children.

From the data above and from related studies, Zucker develops a "probabilistic risk etiology framework for clinical disorders." He sees the terminology for this framework as developmental in nature, with various risk factors ebbing and flowing throughout the life span. The implication from the model is that the notion of a progressive disease process needs to be questioned—for example, people may move out of a set of symptoms as well as becoming more pathological over time. The latter fits the traditional conception of alcoholism.

Using this framework as a base, Zucker develops four models of alcoholism. The first model (and the one most frequently studied, according to Zucker) is antisocial alcoholism. It occurs more frequently in males, has an early onset, and may be signaled by early antisocial behaviors. The second type, which cuts across sex and social class, is called developmentally cumulative alcoholism. There is less antisocial involvement with this type of alcoholism, but adult-child interactions are likely to be harsher than for nonalcoholic individuals. These early relationship problems lead to a greater likelihood of peer, career, and marital difficulties. The third type, developmentally limited alcoholism, has been labeled by others as heavy drinking. It is somewhat more common in men and cuts across social classes. A pattern of heavy drinking peaks early in life, probably as a function of life changes (employment, starting a family) that lead drinkers to a more conventional life-style. In this group, the largest proportion of abusive drinkers show a sharp drop-off in drinking in their mid-twenties. The final type, negative-affect alcoholism, occurs primarily in females and is significantly related to a family history of affective disorders.

These types indicate that alcoholism is no longer an appropriate term. They also suggest differing paths to a common phenotype in terms of overt symptoms. The types, if sustained by future longitudinal research, suggest diverse etiological paths and, down the road, may suggest new strategies of prevention, intervention, and treatment.

The Wilsnack, Wilsnack, and Klassen chapter deals with a major research project currently being undertaken. The authors report findings from the first national household survey of drinking and drinking problems among women. As noted above, Nathan has highlighted the need to know more about drinking patterns in women. This nationwide survey (N = 900) asked women about their drinking behavior and about personal, social, and life experience characteristics that might be causes or consequences of drinking. Although the study failed to find any dramatic increases in women's drinking over the past decade (1971–1981), it did establish that some women were at higher risk for alcohol problems. Those falling into the higher-risk group include younger women (ages 21–34), divorced or separated women, unmarried women cohabiting with men, and women unemployed and looking for work. Depression, husbands or partners that drink, and sexual reproductive problems were also related to alcohol abuse.

The path analysis these researchers utilized highlights the complexity of alcohol problems in women. For example, this analysis reveals that factors influencing women to drink were not the same as those that influenced women to become dependent upon alcohol. Access to alcohol and moral judgments were the major factors in whether women used alcohol at all. Heavy drinking was most likely to occur if women had the frequent companionship of drinkers privately in the home and if they had an open and trusting marital relationship.

Lesser family role responsibilities or reductions of normal role responsibilities in the family owing to events such as the husband's involuntary unemployment or the recent departure of the last child led women to increase their alcohol consumption. Drinking-related problems and alcohol dependence developed not only because women drank heavily but also because they expected alcohol to make them feel better. In addition, social and psychological problems led women to seek help from alcohol. A finding related to the increased drinking rates of women noted above is that women were not at great risk because they were required to play multiple roles. In fact, women were more likely to become problem drinkers if they had too few roles rather than too many. Women with multiple responsibilities such as housekeeping, child rearing, and earning an income tended to reduce their level of drinking, thus protecting themselves from drinking problems. Another interesting finding that might not have been anticipated was that binge or party drinking (consuming a large amount of alcohol on a single occasion) did not cause as many problems for women as routine, everyday drinking.

Some factors that were not present in the path analysis are also important. For example, subjects' recall of maternal or paternal drug use was not related to alcohol dependence. However, parental love and praise had strong indirect effects reducing the likelihood of symptomatic drinking. Thus, both genetic history and parental nurture may have to be taken into account when predicting alcohol dependence in women. Another surprise was that the number of drugs women currently used was not related to any of the behaviors measured, though a history of drug use "did affect drinking patterns in several ways." This finding suggests that it is not necessarily what the woman is currently doing that is most predictive; historical events can affect drinking more than current issues. It is for this reason that the Wilsnacks plan to look at longitudinal changes in their sample beginning in 1986.

Jacob's contribution on how family patterns disrupt or maintain alcohol use offers a new perspective on the role alcohol plays in family life. He views alcohol as having multiple possible effects on family interaction and stability. For example, he suggests that aspects of family relationships can weaken family structure and stability and can promote or maintain abusive drinking patterns. These drinking patterns can make offspring more vulnerable to psychosocial and alcohol-related difficulties.

Although he reviews alcohol-related family studies, the bulk of Jacob's chapter focuses on his own research, which is an attempt at a more rigorous and programmatic examination of the alcoholic family than any accomplished in the past decade. His research includes a diagnostically homogeneous subgroup of alcoholics as well as a psychiatric control group (depressed mates). The key issue addressed in Jacob's research is the impact alcoholism can have on the process and structure of family life. In particular, he is concerned with the role family processes play in maintaining alcohol abuse. For example, he is concerned with how different patterns of family interaction increase or inhibit the development of alcoholism.

The data for the paper come from observations of marital interaction in the laboratory. One of the key findings was that alcoholic couples were much more negative in their interactions during laboratory sessions where ad-lib drinking occurred. This was true when these ad-lib drinking sessions were compared with those of normal and psychiatric comparison groups of couples who were allowed free access to alcohol. Further analysis of Jacob's results highlighted the importance of drinking style and location. These findings suggest that alcohol may have some adaptive consequences for families. The findings are particularly relevant when comparing steady day-to-day drinkers with binge drinkers. The family's response to episodic drinkers (binge as well as weekend drinkers) is clearly different from the response to the in-home drinker. In the laboratory setting, if the alcohol abuser was a steady-state drinker, couples became more problem focused and instrumental in the drinking situations. The opposite was true for the binge drinkers and their wives. The reduction in problem solving was due to the binge drinker's spouse, who greatly decreased her task-related activity during the session where ad-lib alcohol was available to the couple. The findings suggest that alcohol can play both supportive and negative roles in family interaction depending upon the pattern of use and abuse.

Hill and her fellow researchers have used the vulnerability model to merge biological and psychosocial factors of alcoholism. While the proposed model is new, it is actually an "old" idea in the alcohol field, and the authors give credit to Jellinek for his earlier proposal of this type of model. Their proposed model is based upon the work of Zubin, one of the coauthors, in schizophrenia research. It differs from the schizophrenia model, however, in the characteristic of constant risk. In the alcohol model, unlike the schizophrenia model, the individual must be exposed to alcohol to be vulnerable; vulnerability is lifelong in schizophrenia.

To clarify this presentation, Hill and her colleagues review possible conceptions of etiology—for example, biological and environmental models. These include the genetic, ecological, and developmental etiology models. A limitation of these existing models is that each fails to explain why one individual becomes alcoholic and another does not. Since all current models share this weakness, the present writers merged all the conceptions into a "supermodel" to explain alcoholism.

The vulnerability model of Hill and her associates combines these ideas into a framework that, they maintain, has greater explanatory and predictive utility. The model is similar to that Zubin proposed earlier for schizophrenia. The vulnerability model incorporates relevant findings from both biological and psychosocial domains. It is a move away from the disease model, since it does not see alcoholism as a continuous disorder but does view vulnerability as constant (this would allow people to move in and out of alcoholism but still maintain their vulnerability). The model suggests that individuals who are vulnerable may or may not succumb, depending upon the level of stress they experience and the coping resources available to help them endure stress without drinking. Vulnerability is gauged by measuring various indicators that cushion a potential precipitating variable. Such indicators include degree of vulnerability, triggering event, and moderating variables. The advantage of the model is that it allows predictions where people are at greater risk to develop alcoholism even though they currently do not have alcohol problems.

To identify the people at risk for alcoholism, we need to find indicators or markers for performance (e.g., neuropsychological test responses), measures of psychosocial functioning (e.g., participation in social and family networks), or other characteristics (e.g., profiles on personality tests) that may predict vulnerability to alcoholism. In all cases, the ideal marker would be one that occurs only in alcoholics and not in normal control subjects. Such a marker should also be present in high-risk individuals, such as blood relatives, who do not suffer from the disorder.

Hill and her colleagues suggest several possible markers but are careful to distinguish between episode markers, which are related to factors associated with abusive drinking and occur during the drinking period, and vulnerability markers, which are present before alcoholic drinking and during recovery. These markers range from behavioral factors to personality and ecological factors. Although only preliminary results are available, Hill's group does have some illuminating data on their multiplex families and markers. In a multiplex family, one affected member is detected, at least one other sibling is affected, and one sibling is not affected by the alcoholism. This allows partialing out the acute effects of the illness using a cross-sectional design. Responses to the MMPI, a test widely used in alcohol treatment, constitute one of the markers they have found potentially useful. On the MMPI, high-risk individuals had elevated profiles on both the Psychopathic Deviate and Schizophrenia scales compared with normals. These findings may indicate that these types of responses are "markers" in the broader definition of the term used by these researchers.

A second possible marker reported by Hill and her colleagues comes from the authors' multiplex family research. Event-related potential differences across control and at-risk groups provided a possible marker—a longer brain potential latency for the at-risk groups (both alcoholics and their nonaffected siblings) than for the control group. Liver-enzyme tests on nonalcoholic siblings eliminated the possibility that they could have been drinking at heavy levels, further supporting the idea that brain potential might be a marker.

Research based on the vulnerability model suggests it may eventually be possible to isolate people at risk for alcoholism by developing ways to measure vulnerability. These measurements would allow a greater focusing of prevention and therapeutic efforts and perhaps reduce the rate of occurrence. At least it would allow early intervention and a better focus of treatment efforts.

One of the factors that may be a key to both etiology and prognosis in drug addiction is a better understanding of "craving," or the reasons a person seeks out drugs. Baker and his fellow researchers review several areas of research and point out some of the consistencies and inconsistencies of data and various conceptual models of drug urges.

In reviewing urge data for alcohol, opiates, and nicotine, they isolate several interesting factors. For example, from relapse data it is apparent that self-reported drug urge can predict relapse and that most relapses follow stressors. However, a significant number of reported relapses occur while the person is in a positive affective state. In fact, when closely examined, several factors are related to drug urge—for example, withdrawal symptoms, negative affects, and positive affects. Depending on the particular drug used, different factors may be important in determining drug urge. For example, heavy drinkers are especially likely to associate alcohol use with withdrawal symptoms.

Several models have been developed to help conceptualize what is occurring in drug urge. The authors critically review these models, pointing out their strengths and weaknesses. These conceptual frameworks, including the withdrawal, compensatory, and opponent-process models, are seen as homeostatic. Baker views these homeostatic models as inconsistent with data suggesting that drug urge can be elicited by and during positive affective states. The authors review other research and use their own work with cigarette smokers to show that in active and withdrawing smokers drug urge is set by different and distinct events. Only those smokers in withdrawal show responses consistent with predictions from the homeostatic model. Individuals continuing to smoke show positive responses to the anticipation or intake of nicotine. When these findings are paired with addict reports of having drug urge in a state not compatible with withdrawal, and with reports of relapse by addicts while in a positive affective state, then the need for a new model of drug urge that will incorporate both appetitive and nonappetitive drug urge is established.

Baker and his colleagues suggest a two-affect model of drug motivation. Their model posits two types of drug networks, positive and negative. The positive-affect network is elicited by appetitive stimuli (those that make the person feel good and enhance the pursuit of the drug). These appetitive drug actions increase, among other things, pursuit of more of the drug. The positive-affect network operates so that the drug establishes a positive feedback loop. This positive feedback loop may account for some of the most salient aspects of addiction, such as that once a drug is tasted relapse probability increases, and that drug addicts attain such high blood levels of the drug when they use it.

These researchers see the "negative-affect" network as characterized by punishment, by signals of punishment, and by withdrawal and signals of withdrawal. This network is activated by things like withdrawal symptoms and signs, negative affect, and drug seeking. The authors caution that their model does not adequately account for all drug-use behavior. Its failure to explain why some drug users do not become addicted is a shortcoming shared by other theories of drug addiction.

Despite these limitations, this model may have some important implications for etiology, treatment, and prognosis. For example, in establishing etiology using this model, it would be important to have a history of benefits of the drug, something not emphasized in most treatment centers. This understanding of the source of drug urge might be useful in treatment planning. It might require that we "coach" people on how to get natural highs and help them identify potentially risk-laden positive-affect states. The way the individual handles positive affect at the beginning and end of treatment might also have important ramifications for prognosis. At present, work dealing with drug use focuses almost entirely on those factors called "negative affect" by Baker and his coauthors. If this theoretical position can be shown to be widely applicable to several varieties of drug taking, it may well point to newer, more effective ways to ensure reduced relapse rates for alcoholics and other addicts.

The papers summarized above are potentially useful in thinking about etiology, intervention, therapy, and prognosis with alcohol-addicted people. Although new ideas about alcohol treatment should be incorporated cautiously, we hope this volume will help narrow the gap between what we know and what we do when working with addictive behavior in general and alcoholics in particular.

What Do Behavioral Scientists Know—and What Can They Do— about Alcoholism?

Peter E. Nathan

Rutgers, the State University

*T*he fellowship of Alcoholics Anonymous (AA) was founded 50 years ago in Toledo, Ohio. In reflecting on my contribution to the Nebraska Symposium on Motivation, I realize that AA's special anniversary has had an impact. What changes have taken place in what we know about alcoholism, I began to wonder, between 1935, the year AA was founded, and 1985, the year this symposium held sessions devoted to Alcohol and Drug Use and Abuse? How much more do behavioral scientists know now about how alcohol affects behavior? What have we learned about etiology? Are we more effective in our treatment efforts? And can we more readily prevent alcoholism? These are the questions that came readily to mind as I wondered what effect five decades of work have had on these issues. What follows represents my best effort to answer them.

Not only is 1985 the golden anniversary of the founding of one of the most influential treatment systems in the field of alcoholism, it is also the 50th anniversary of the founding of the Center of Alcohol Studies at Yale, an institution whose creation lent great scientific respectability to alcoholism research. And not long after the Center of Alcohol Studies came into being, some of its faculty members launched the *Journal of Studies on Alcohol*, then and now the premier journal in the field. Many alcoholism workers date the beginning of serious efforts to treat alcoholism to the founding of Alcoholics Anonymous; and they link the first concerted scientific efforts to understand the actions of alcohol and the antecedents and consequences of alcoholism to the founding of the Center of Alcohol Studies and the *Journal of Studies on Alcohol*. Accordingly, 1985 seems a

fine year to assess progress in understanding, treating, and preventing alcoholism over this active 50-year span.

It is patently impossible to chronicle all the advances in the varied
disciplines that have contributed to knowledge about alcohol, alcoholics, and alcoholism. Instead, I shall confine my efforts to two sufficiently difficult tasks: determining what behavioral scientists
knew about alcohol abuse and alcoholism—and what they could do
about them—in 1935, and presenting what they know and can do
now, in the mid-1980s. The domains of knowledge chosen have met
three criteria: they are important to the clinical enterprise; they are
objects of serious scientific study; and behavioral scientists have
been extensively involved in them. My four areas of inquiry include
behavioral pathology, etiology, treatment, and *prevention.*

Behavioral Pathology

BEHAVIORAL TOLERANCE—1935

Alcohol tolerance was well recognized in 1935. Heavy drinkers, including alcoholics, can usually drink more alcohol than lighter
drinkers, usually continue to function at blood-alcohol levels that
would disable others, and at times actually seem to function better
when intoxicated than when they are sober. All of these behaviors
are hallmarks of behavioral tolerance, a common consequence of
heavy drinking and chronic alcoholism.

In 1935 and for almost three decades afterward, the ability of alcoholics to consume substantially more alcohol than others without
the expected impairment in functioning was presumed to reflect
two factors on which alcoholics and nonalcoholics differed: a learning history that provided more than enough experience to compen-
sate for alcohol-induced behavioral impairment, and a familial and
cultural milieu that provided equally extensive experience with parents and others who often drank heavily but did not always demonstrate profound impairment. These explanations for tolerance, not
empirically derived for the most part, reflected a prevailing societal
view that alcoholics tend to beget alcoholics by perpetuating for
their children a morally and culturally deviant lifestyle. They were
associated with a surprising paucity of research on tolerance formation and maintenance in human beings that has lasted virtually to

this day (Jellinek & Jolliffe, 1940; Jellinek & McFarland, 1940; Tabakoff & Rothstein, 1983).

Some commentators at the time were convinced that alcohol affects alcoholics differently from nonalcoholics; this view grew much more influential with AA's advocacy of what came to be called the disease model of alcoholism. Nonetheless, it remained unclear how differences in reaction to alcohol directly enhanced understanding of tolerance. Even in the face of the growing influence of the disease model, many continued to view tolerance as primarily a function of cultural and personal experience with alcohol rather than as a pharmacologic matter.

In reviewing the 1930s literature on tolerance, I was surprised that both the ubiquity of tolerance and its potential role in the diagnosis of alcoholism were generally unacknowledged several decades ago other than by a few pharmacologists (e.g., Mirsky, Piker, Rosenbaum, & Lederer, 1940; Newman, 1941); those who diagnosed and treated alcoholics rarely had much to say about an effect that vastly complicated treatment but could have aided their diagnostic efforts.

BEHAVIORAL TOLERANCE — 1985

Behavioral tolerance to alcohol has been studied, written about, and understood much more fully in the 1980s than in the 1930s. Most biobehavioral scientists, for example, now recognize that as people drink more and more, they increase their capacity to metabolize ethanol. The most common mechanism is an increase in production of the alcohol-metabolizing enzyme alcohol dehydrogenase, which has been shown to speed up the oxidation of ethanol to acetaldehyde *in vitro* (Li, 1983). To the earlier view that tolerance is entirely a function of learning and environment there has been added an empirically derived biophysiological explanation.

Also, after prolonged and very heavy drinking, perhaps found only in alcoholics, individuals may develop an alternate pathway for metabolizing alcohol. The microsomal ethanol oxidizing system (MEOS) is a membrane-associated electron transport system that, in the presence of NADPH and oxygen, oxidizes ethanol to acetaldehyde. Some (e.g., Lieber, 1980) have claimed that MEOS can account for as much as 20% to 25% of the rate of ethanol oxidation in the liver, whereas others consider its contribution insignificant (e.g., Berry, Fanning, Grivell, & Wallace, 1980).

Of greater interest to behavioral scientists are data reported during the past decade strongly suggesting that ethanol and drug tolerance are importantly influenced by Pavlovian conditioning as well as physiological processes. Research on tolerance to morphine in rats led Siegel (1975) to hypothesize that cues routinely paired with morphine become conditioned stimuli eliciting a conditioned response that tends to be opposed—antagonistic—to the direct effects of morphine. With repeated pairings of environmental cues and drug, the conditioned response becomes stronger, leading to a decrease in drug effects. Tiffany and Baker (1981), among others, have confirmed Siegel's initial demonstration, and Crowell, Hinson, and Siegel (1981) have done so for ethanol tolerance in rats. Just recently, Shapiro and Nathan (1986) reported data indicating that human drinkers also learn to anticipate the effects of ethanol on behavior and, via a Pavlovian conditioning mechanism, demonstrate the compensating behavior we call tolerance.

CRAVING AND LOSS OF CONTROL—1935

It was widely believed during the 1930s, 1940s, 1950s, and before that alcoholics will always choose to drink as much alcohol as they can for as long as they can. This belief reflected the assumption that the loss of control that still is generally thought to characterize problem drinking is so strong and so invariant that it is a central component of the behavior of all drinking alcoholics. This view, current before the founding of Alcoholics Anonymous, was reinforced by the AA philosophy's strong advocacy of the disease model of alcoholism. A correlative assumption is that every alcoholic craves alcohol when sober and that it is this craving that causes the return to alcohol after a period of sobriety. What was assumed to be responsible for these behaviors in 1935? Speculation had it that the alcoholic's personality, interacting with a debauched life-style, yielded an inability to postpone gratification or do without pleasure (Fleeson & Gildea, 1942; Lewis, 1940). The advent of AA added the conviction that craving and loss of control were somehow mediated as well by a biophysiological mechanism unique to the alcoholic—that some unidentified lesion in the central nervous system was responsible for these two hallmarks of the disease model of alcoholism.

CRAVING AND LOSS OF CONTROL—1985

A great deal of research on craving and loss of control, most of it by behavioral scientists, has taken place during the 1960s, 1970s, and 1980s. This research has revealed the following:

1. Contrary to the view still current among those who strongly advocate the disease model of alcoholism, convincing evidence that alcoholics can and do moderate their drinking has been reported since the 1960s. Alcoholics have demonstrated this capacity in the experimental laboratory when reinforcing stimuli support either termination or moderation of drinking for varying periods (Bigelow, Cohen, Liebson, & Faillace, 1972; Mendelson & Mello, 1966; Nathan, Titler, Lowenstein, Solomon, & Rossi, 1970), as well as in the natural environment, where virtually every alcoholic has periods of controlled consumption, abstinence, and abusive drinking (Davies, 1962; Pattison, Sobell, & Sobell, 1977). It now seems abundantly clear that loss of control in drinking is neither an invariable nor a defining accompaniment of chronic alcoholism.

2. Data on craving gathered during the past decade, like the evidence on loss of control reviewed above, are contrary both to the views of those who support the disease model of alcoholism and to widespread general belief. These data demonstrate convincingly that craving for alcohol is not necessarily either consistent or the most important threat to sobriety for the recovering alcoholic. Research on expectancies completed during the past decade indicates instead that craving may be largely a function of the alcoholic's belief that once a "priming dose" of alcohol has been consumed craving will ensue, rather than being a pharmacologic action of alcohol as the disease model presumes (Cutter, Schwaab, & Nathan, 1970; Marlatt, Demming, & Reid, 1973).

Also relevant is the work of Marlatt and his colleagues on relapse. They consider the likelihood of relapse far greater if the sober alcoholic thinks craving and loss of control are inevitable and also believes in the abstinence violation effect—that a single drink will invariably lead to uncontrolled, abusive drinking. By contrast, Marlatt and his colleagues write, it is necessary to help the recovering alcoholic to see that relapse is an unwelcome but inevitable feature of recovery, to view a single "slip" as an unpleasant but not necessarily disastrous signpost on the road to recovery, and to develop skills for coping with the effects of relapse. If this is done, the recovering alcoholic will be more likely to put craving and loss of control into

6
NEBRASKA SYMPOSIUM ON MOTIVATION, 1986

context and to realize that a drink or two will not lead to a return of abusive drinking (Marlatt, 1978; Marlatt & Gordon, 1985).

3. The earlier view saw craving and loss of control, central to the disease model of alcoholism, as consequences of an actual physical lesion. In the face of strong evidence for the role of environmental and expectancy factors in the behavior of the alcoholic, many have come to regard craving and loss of control, as well as the disease model itself, as metaphors rather than literal descriptions. Even though the disease model (as well as craving and loss of control) implies a cause primarily though not exclusively internal to the organism—either a physical or a psychological lesion—environmental and cognitive mediators are still involved, and so the model can be incorporated comfortably into the empirical data set now extant.

ALCOHOLISM AND MORAL INSANITY—1935

Through the centuries, up to and beyond the 1930s, it was widely thought that alcoholism leads to antisocial and psychopathic behavior—moral insanity—and that moral insanity causes alcoholism. In its extreme, this residual of the moralistic beliefs of temperance workers also required the conviction that poverty, immorality, ignorance, and atheism cause alcoholism and that alcoholism causes poverty, immorality, ignorance, and atheism.

Reviewing a sixteenth-century classic of the alcohol literature, *On the Horrible Vice of Drunkenness*, written by the historian and philosopher Sebastian Franck, E. M. Jellinek observed that:

> Franck, however, was much more interested in the ethical deterioration of the chronic alcoholic than in bodily ailments. The blunting of emotion, the economic irresponsibility, the untruthfulness, brutality and loss of interest in all the finer aspects of life were the factors which Franck regarded as the greatest perils of habitual inebriety. (Jellinek, 1941)

ALCOHOLISM AND MORAL INSANITY—1985

The enormous diversity of alcoholics—rich and poor, white and black, male and female, young and old, bright and stupid, moral and immoral, believers and unbelievers, presidents, kings, professors, and the Skid Row homeless—has become generally recognized. Accordingly, no longer do most of us believe, as was the case 50 years ago, that alcoholics come largely from the ranks of the poor, the ignorant, and the morally degenerate.

Vaillant's report (1983) on two 40-year longitudinal studies of normative samples of men, some of whom became alcoholics, is widely cited as evidence of the heterogeneity of present-day alcoholics. One of Vaillant's samples, originally a control group in the Glueck and Glueck (1950) study of juvenile delinquency, was composed largely of lower SES male alcoholics who had first been studied between 1940 and 1944 while they were students in Boston inner-city schools. As boys this group demonstrated an average IQ of 95; only 33% of their parents had attended high school; 49% of these subjects fell into social classes IV or V (the lowest) as adults. The other group of alcoholic males was originally a portion of a sample of normal Harvard College students first studied in 1938 (Heath, 1946; Hooten, 1945). In contrast to the Boston inner-city group, this group of men came predominantly (98%) from social classes I and II (the highest). Average IQ was between 125 and 140; 94% of this group's parents had attended high school.

Another influential source of data on the heterogeneity of alcoholics in this country comes from the studies of Cahalan and Room (1974). Exploring the nature and frequency of problem drinking among a large, normative sample of men, these investigators concluded that alcohol problems were ubiquitous in all strata of American society. A recent series of papers by Wiens and his colleagues reporting on treatment outcomes from a private alcoholism hospital in the Pacific Northwest (Wiens & Menustik, 1983; Wiens, Montague, Manaugh, & English, 1976) makes essentially the same point: alcoholics in this country are drawn from every walk of life. These data support the contemporary view that alcoholics and prealcoholics are not likely to fit the old stereotypes that portray them as morally insane—as morally, economically, socially, and interpersonally deteriorated. While some may fit this stereotype, so do some nonalcoholics. And while some nonalcoholics function well in the face of serious disease, so do some alcoholics.

ALCOHOLISM AND DEPRESSION — 1935

The psychoanalytic view of alcoholism, extremely influential in the 1930s and 1940s, sees alcoholism as deriving from strong unmet oral dependency needs left over from actual or symbolic loss during early childhood (e.g., Schilder, 1941). Alcoholism is seen as an effort, ultimately unsuccessful, to recover these lost objects—generally parents. Since psychoanalytic theorists also consider depression a consequence of early loss, it was not surprising that alcoholism and depression were believed to share common determinants—and that alcoholics were viewed as commonly depressed.

ALCOHOLISM AND DEPRESSION—1985

The marked diminution in the acceptance of psychoanalytic views on alcoholism in the past two decades has been paralleled by increasing recognition that the links between alcoholism and depression are reciprocal. Simply stated, it is now generally recognized that alcoholism often causes depression because of the enormous personal, vocational/professional, and interpersonal losses the alcoholic suffers owing to abusive drinking. Alcoholism also causes depression from the pharmacologic effects of ethanol, a sedative drug; only when the body has fully metabolized the ethanol and returned to a stable baseline do the depressive effects of alcohol disappear. And reciprocally, depression frequently causes alcoholism when, for example, the depressed individual uses alcohol to temper dysphoria. In this context, preliminary data suggesting an empirically supported link (Goodwin, 1985; Winokur, Reich, Rimmer, & Pitts, 1970) between antisocial behavior in male relatives, depression in female relatives, and alcoholism in probands deserve elaboration.

ALCOHOLISM AS A DISORDER OF MEN—1935

Fifty years ago alcoholism was generally acknowledged to be virtually the exclusive province of men. Men were considered more likely than women or youths to demonstrate the antisocial behavior, immorality, and criminality that also characterized alcoholism (and were, in fact, assumed to be important in its development). Alcoholic men also came to public attention—and condemnation—by seeking treatment in much higher numbers than women. Moreover, the few women alcoholics seen by clinicians were considered even more deviant than alcoholic men and were thus more severely condemned. It is little wonder that women alcoholics revealed themselves as such only when they had absolutely no choice (Bacon, 1945; Dollard, 1945).

ALCOHOLISM AS A DISORDER OF MEN — 1985

For at least two decades, alcoholism has been recognized to afflict both women and men at high rates. At the same time, it is true that even in 1985 male alcoholics are more visible than females, in part because they are more likely to come to, remain in, and benefit from treatment than are female alcoholics (Braiker, 1982; Lex, 1985). Most observers have believed this difference in treatment access exists because treatment facilities are oriented mainly to the values and expectations of males in treatment for alcoholism (Nathan & Skinstad, in press). Another consequence of these treatment differences is uncertainty whether rates of alcoholism for men and women are strictly comparable or only roughly so.

Unhappily, research on the behavioral consequences of alcoholism in women, on women in treatment, and on strategies for preventing alcoholism in women continues to be scarce, for reasons that are not entirely clear. Questions such as whether men and women metabolize ethanol at different rates, whether the behavioral consequences of intoxication are the same for men and women at comparable blood-alcohol levels, whether they become alcoholics for the same reasons, whether they would benefit most from different or similar treatment programs and therapists remain unresolved—and largely unstudied—in 1985 (Nathan & Skinstad, in press).

Etiology

ETIOLOGY — 1935

Through the 1930s and for several centuries before, the etiology of alcoholism was principally assumed to involve a weak will, sinfulness, and bad moral character. People became alcoholics because for some unknown, perverse reason they chose to flout society's rules.

With the founding of Alcoholics Anonymous, and with its growing influence in the years thereafter, the disease model, however it was variously interpreted, became influential in shaping views of what caused alcoholism. Unfortunately, the absence of data to flesh out the disease model made it a target for attack from every quarter, in part because it was simply misunderstood. Basically, the position of AA appears to be that alcoholism is the product of an unidentified, otherwise unspecified lesion somewhere in the body that is responsible for crucial differences in how prealcoholics and others respond to alcohol challenge. Environment, personality, and psychopathology all can influence the form alcoholism takes, but central to every alcoholic is this inborn inability to drink alcohol as normal drinkers do.

As I have already noted, it was during the 1930s that the influence of the psychoanalytic view of the causes of alcoholism reached its peak. That view stated that alcoholism is a consequence of excessive deprivation or gratification of dependency needs during the oral stage of infantile psychosexual development. During the following decades, until the early 1970s, the psychoanalytic view was second in influence only to the disease model advocated by the fellowship of Alcoholics Anonymous.

Other etiological theories saw alcoholism as the burden—and consequence—that some of the children of alcoholics carry because they live with alcoholic parents. It was not clear why living with alcoholic parents increased the likelihood of developing alcoholism, though many believed that the chaos of such a childhood was reason enough to drink abusively as an adult (McPeek, 1943).

Early behavioral clinicians—and there were very few in the 1930s, 1940s, and 1950s—adopted the uncomplicated view that alcoholic behavior was the means the alcoholic had chosen for dealing with conditioned anxiety. This view was supported by two influential empirical studies by Conger (1951, 1956). Conger reported that animals subjected to an experimental stressor drank substantially more of a solution containing alcohol than when they were not stressed; the alcohol in the solution, presumably, dampened the stress experience. Unfortunately, Conger's "successful" effort to confirm what has come to be called the tension-reduction hypothesis of alcoholism led behaviorists to extrapolate prematurely from data on lower animals and to conclude that the theory also had important validity when applied to human alcoholics.

Many other beliefs about etiology, all unsupported by empirical research, held sway during the 1930s. Among the most interesting, from the vantage point that 50 years provides, was the widespread conviction that drinking distilled spirits was a necessary condition for alcoholism: many believed that beer and wine were not addictive.

ETIOLOGY—1985

By 1985 the existence of a genetically determined predisposition to alcoholism has been generally accepted. Operating independently of the environmental effect of living with alcoholic parents (an effect that has not yet been clearly linked to the development of alcoholism; Vaillant, 1983), a genetically based predisposition to alcoholism was not a central feature of the original disease model of alcoholism from the late 1930s, despite the support it gives that model. The most influential of the studies leading to acceptance of a genetic predisposition to alcoholism in some children of alcoholics was first reported by Goodwin and his colleagues (Goodwin, Schulsinger, Hermansen, Guze, & Winokur, 1973; Goodwin, Schulsinger, Moller, Hermansen, Winokur, & Guze, 1974) and later confirmed by Cloninger and his co-workers (Cloninger, Bohman, & Sigvardsson, 1981). Goodwin found that adopted-out Danish male biological offspring of alcoholics raised by nonalcoholics nonetheless are significantly more likely to develop alcoholism than the biological offspring of nonalcoholics, even though some of the latter were raised by alcoholics. Goodwin and his colleagues (Goodwin, Schulsinger, Knop, Mednick, & Guze, 1977) also reported that by contrast, the role of genetics in predisposing women to develop alcoholism does not appear to be strong.

Precisely how a predisposition to alcoholism is transmitted is now the object of intense research. Best guesses are that it is mediated by the central nervous system—so that the much-maligned disease model of alcoholism may yet be empirically vindicated. That is, if predisposition to alcoholism is found to involve a difference between prealcoholics and others in CNS functioning, either in rate or locus of ethanol metabolism (Li, 1983) or in rate or manner of tolerance development (Nathan, 1982)—the two have been foci of research in this context—then a central tenet of the disease model will be supported.

While learning processes also play an undoubted role in the etiology of alcoholism, the precise nature of that role remains uncertain. It is likely that there is an interaction among classical conditioning (in which alcohol consumption comes to be associated with a reduction in conditioned anxiety), operant conditioning (in which alcohol consumption is reinforced by peer approval, enhanced relaxation, increased social skill, etc.), and modeling (in which alcohol consumption and its antecedents and consequences are modeled after parents and peers), and that all together, mediated simultaneously by attitudes and expectations surrounding alcohol and alcoholism, determine alcohol use and abuse. It is also clear that the tension-reduction model, by itself, no longer provides an adequate understanding of the development of alcoholism (Marlatt, 1979; Marlatt & Rohsenow, 1980).

Numerous laboratory studies of the social learning mechanisms involved in the alcohol consumption of alcoholics and nonalcoholics have demonstrated that learning plays an important role (e.g., Bigelow, Cohen, Liebson, & Faillace, 1972; Mendelson & Mello, 1966; Nathan et al., 1970). Nonetheless, none of these studies has yet precisely delineated the relationship between learning and alcoholism, though many behavioral clinicians are sure one exists.

And though research by behavioral researchers during the past decade also strongly suggests that cognitive factors play an important mediating role in the development of alcoholism, its precise nature remains to be shown. Unforeseen 50 years ago, these data on the role of cognitions in alcoholism indicate that what heavy drinkers or alcoholics believe causes their drinking affects its nature and extent. And how they feel about the likelihood that alcoholism treatment will work for them is equally important to the success or failure of that treatment (Marlatt & Gordon, 1985; Moos & Billings, 1982).

In like fashion, while it seems clear that psychiatric disorder is related to alcoholism, the precise nature of this relationship is unknown. That is, while some alcoholics drink to excess to dampen anxiety, reduce feelings of depression, or blot out hallucinations and delusions, it is unclear whether those who suffer from anxiety disorder, dysthymic disorder, or schizophrenia, for example, are more inclined either genetically or reactively to develop alcoholism (e.g., Barry, 1980; Cloninger, Reich, & Wetzel, 1979; Krueger, 1980). 1980).

Although a connection between childhood antisocial behavior and alcoholism seems likely from Vaillant's longitudinal research (1983) and, more recently, Tarter's studies of neuropsychological dysfunction among those at risk for alcoholism (Tarter, Hegedus, Goldstein, Shelly, & Alterman, 1984), it is uncertain whether the connection is causal or simply correlative.

What is also clear—again, from Vaillant's uniquely powerful research design—is that alcoholism is *not* a consequence of inadequate child-rearing practices, emotional turmoil, psychological disorder, emotional deprivation or poorly or excessively gratified dependency needs in childhood. Despite the common conviction during the past 50 years and before that these are causes of alcohol-ism, Vaillant's data suggest otherwise.

Treatment

TREATMENT — 1935

In 1935 bizarre drugs and medicines were still used to treat alcohol-ism. One was Mrs. Moffat's Shoo Fly Powders for Drunkenness, an over-the-counter potion that was condemned in 1935 under the Federal Food, Drug, and Cosmetic Act after a panel of experts tes-tified that it contained enough antimony and potassium tartrate to be classified as a poison. While there were no reports of deaths from ingestion of the Shoo Fly Powders, it was thought entirely possible that deaths attributed to alcohol withdrawal or acute liver failure might instead have been caused by Shoo Fly Powder poisoning. One troubling aspect of the case, when the time came to ban their sale, was that for approximately 60 years the manufacturer had sold about 50,000 powders annually to persons prepared to testify that it was an effective treatment for drunkenness.

To this end it is also worth noting that for centuries ethanol itself was considered a valuable therapeutic agent for a variety of condi-tions serious enough to require hospitalization. A note in a popular journal in 1930, for example, observed that while per capita con-sumption of alcohol in hospitals had declined an average of 40% be-tween 1906 and 1922, the United States was still reporting a con-sumption level of 7 liters of alcohol per hospital patient per year, all for "therapeutic purposes." Per capita consumption of alcohol in the United States in 1981 was 2.8 gallons (National Institute on Alco-hol Abuse and Alcoholism [NIAAA], 1983); 7 liters constitutes more than half this total!

It seems likely that 50 years ago, much more alcohol detoxification took place in jails than in hospitals or clinics since public drunken-ness was a crime in most places until the 1970s, and since intoxicated persons were also jailed for other crimes committed while they were intoxicated. It is also certain that a substantial number of deaths associated with detoxification, especially from complications of de-lirium tremens, occurred in jails.

Inpatient alcoholism treatment and rehabilitation appear to have been much less available 50 years ago than now. Moreover, inpatient programs, when offered, were more often housed in state mental hospitals and prisons than in facilities devoted exclusively to alcoholism treatment. At the same time, influential advocates of dedicated treatment programs did exist. For example, the famous Johns Hopkins psychiatrist Adolf Meyer was quoted during that time as saying that "the most dependable means available [for alcoholism treatment] are asylums for drunkards with more or less efficient provisions for after care, insisting on total abstinence, during the period of physical and character reconstruction." Meyer's statement accords well with current thinking on treatment in most regards except for his view that the alcoholic's character must be reconstructed during treatment to bring his moral sense and character back up to normal levels.

Despite Meyer's convictions, however, there were only a few private hospitals for the treatment of alcoholism, and few private psychiatric hospitals had wards for alcoholics; there were even fewer public facilities specifically designed for treating alcoholism. Hence the alcoholic who both needed and wanted inpatient treatment but did not have the means to pay for it (there were few third-party reimbursers in the 1930s to pay for such treatment) had to seek it in inadequately funded state mental hospitals. Treatment in such places was typically uninformed and laden with moral imperatives; the stigma of alcoholism in the state hospitals was as profound as the stigma of tertiary neurosyphilis, still a source of many of their patients at that time.

In the 1930s, involvement by professionals, especially physicians, in alcoholism treatment was minimal. Doctors saw alcoholics when they were called upon to treat the long-term physical sequellae of alcoholism (which they recognized as such only a portion of the time). And when chronic alcoholics did suffer from one or another of the physical consequences of alcoholism, they were limited in their access to general hospitals, which actively resisted admitting known alcoholics, even when they were suffering from life-threatening conditions. That resistance, unfortunately, continues in muted form to this day.

A strongly judgmental, moralistic, condemnatory, infantilizing view of the alcoholic in treatment prevailed in the 1930s, as for centuries before and decades after. In 1935, for example, Professor Yandell Henderson of the Yale Center of Alcohol Studies was said to have observed that "a man of strong will can reform from chronic inebriety more easily than a dipsomaniac or morphinist," suggesting that strong will was required for recovery just as weak will had led to initial descent to alcohol addiction.

Before 1935 and the founding of Alcoholics Anonymous, there appears to have been little tradition of self-help for alcohol problems. And of course it was several years before the AA fellowship began to grow and groups proliferated nationwide. Alcoholics probably were reluctant to organize self-help groups because of the enormous stigma attached to alcoholism 50 years ago, a reason to admire the enormous courage of the founders of AA in being willing to identify themselves as alcoholics and to face the prejudice they knew they would experience.

There also appears to have been only uneven recognition, until very recently, of alcoholism as a chronic condition. The founding of Alcoholics Anonymous, with its emphasis on the lifelong burden of sobriety the recovering alcoholic must carry, and, much later, the cognitive social-learning theorists' emphasis on relapse as predictable and cognitively mediated contributed to this important recognition.

There also appears to have been little or no understanding 50 years ago that treatment programs designed for white, middle-aged, male alcoholics might not be equally helpful for women, non-Caucasians, the young, and the old. That understanding too has come only very recently.

TREATMENT — 1985

By 1985 a plethora of treatment approaches, personnel, facilities, and beliefs have developed. Self-help groups like AA, Al-Anon, and Alateen have become highly visible and very influential. Outpatient and inpatient treatment, halfway houses, night and day hospital programs all claim their adherents. Some alcoholism workers believe that drugs and hospital settings work best, while others advocate nonmedical detoxification and treatment. Some workers believe that professionals are most effective with alcoholics, while others believe just as strongly that paraprofessionals are best. Treatments that focus on the individual and his or her pathology, the family and its pathology, the stressors of the work site and the community all have been developed and have their supporters. Treatments based on behavioral, cognitive social-learning, psychoanalytic, family systems, rational emotive, multimodal, client-centered, and primal perspectives are offered. From a paucity of treatment programs and approaches in 1935, an overwhelming array of different programs and approaches have now developed.

Nowadays alcoholism treatment, irrespective of content or theoretical orientation, rarely focuses on moral reeducation. In like fashion, alcoholism workers seem much less convinced that their alcoholic patients are morally deficient. In fact considerable empirical data suggest that alcoholics do not differ along most dimensions, including moral sense, from nonalcoholics with comparable cultural and socioeconomic backgrounds (Cahalan, 1982; Vaillant, 1983).

There is greater understanding that alcoholism is chronic, remitting, and recurrent, which affects treatment programming in useful ways. This represents an important though unintentional collaboration of Alcoholics Anonymous (which has emphasized both chronicity and recoverability) and the behavioral social-learning perspective epitomized by Marlatt and Gordon (1985), who stress the phenomenology of the recovery period and the near inevitability of relapses.

Self-help groups are now centrally involved in alcoholism treatment, both because much more treatment of a variety of kinds is being undertaken and because many have become convinced that self-help is often the sole pathway out of alcoholism. The main self-help groups are Alcoholics Anonymous and allied groups; AA has become the treatment of choice for many alcoholics and is almost certainly the most widely known and best-respected treatment modality worldwide.

Professionals are also much more involved in alcoholism treatment nowadays, reflecting the lessening of the stigma attached to working with alcoholics, the increased scientific respectability accorded research on alcoholism, and the increased availability of third-party reimbursement for professional treatment.

Both because public drunkenness is no longer a crime in most places and in recognition of the obvious negative consequences of unattended alcohol withdrawal in jails, detoxification is now accorded more concern by trained workers, and so alcoholics are now more often detoxified in hospitals and nonmedical detoxification facilities rather than in jails. Thus, significantly fewer people die from the complications of withdrawal now than 50 years ago.

During the 1980s it has also become evident that rates of recovery from alcoholism vary with certain prognostic signs, mostly specific to the individual, including age, vocational status, marital status, level of motivation for change, prior drinking history, and prior treatment experience. By contrast, recovery rates seem to depend much less on factors specific to treatment, such as content, form, theoretical orientation, or intensity (Emrick, 1974, 1975; Nathan & Skinstad, in press). No consistent differences in outcome have been reported for one or another of the multitude of treatment programs, methods, and procedures developed during recent decades. The increased availability of empirical data on individual predictors of treatment outcome, in turn, has led to concerted efforts to match the best treatment to the individual (Moos & Billings, 1982).

These data on predictors of treatment outcome, mostly gathered during the 1970s and 1980s, have brought into serious question a belief that characterized the 1930s and all intervening decades until recently—that there is one most successful treatment method. For a time this treatment of choice was individual psychoanalysis; for a longer time it was intensive involvement in the fellowship of Alcoholics Anonymous; for a time behavioral approaches to treatment were considered most promising. Yet the plethora of current data on predictors and covariates of treatment outcome strongly indicate that there is no single approach that yields more positive results than any other, though many still believe there is (Armor, Polich, & Stambul, 1978; Polich, Armor, & Braiker, 1981; Vaillant, 1983).

Another belief about treatment still maintained by many in the absense of empirical support is that recovering alcoholics can understand and treat other alcoholics better than those who have not themselves experienced alcoholism. This persists, like the belief that one treatment method is superior, in the face of evidence that therapists' training, background, and identity (as recovering alcoholic or not) have no demonstrable effect on treatment outcome (Emrick, 1974, 1975; Nathan & Skinstad, in press; Armor et al., 1978; Polich et al., 1981).

Prevention

PREVENTION—1935

Two principal prevention approaches characterized the 1930s. Though Prohibition extended only through the early part of the 1930s, its numerous supporters continued to advocate prohibiting alcohol, to whatever extent was possible, after repeal of the Eighteenth Amendment. But there were also many who recognized that Prohibition, however desirable its goals, was simply unworkable in

our society. In its stead they proposed making the sale and distribution of alcoholic beverages as difficult as possible by imposing
stringent taxes that would markedly raise the price, enacting legal
restraints on sale to certain groups of people (e.g., those below a certain age), and restricting distribution to certain places and certain
hours. Despite strong support for them, there continues to be active
debate on whether such restrictions have much effect on the prevalence of alcoholism and alcohol-related injury or death (Nathan,
1983).

In the 1930s and before there also was advocacy for a different—
and distinctly unproven—control strategy: restricting the sale of
high-proof beverages, in the mistaken belief that distilled spirits are
largely or solely responsible for alcoholism. Thus:

> From the point of view of the prevention of drunkenness, the superior-
> ity of the more dilute beverages, such as the lighter beers and natural
> wines, is therefore mainly due to the fact that the bulk of the fluid
> makes it very difficult for the drinker to consume a very large dose of
> alcohol within a moderate period. (Testimony before United States
> Senate, 1935)

> If we could largely confine our drinking to beverages below 15 or 18
> percent of alcohol by volume, the peculiar American problem would
> largely disappear, alike in its individual, its social, and its political
> aspects. Since 3.2 beer was declared legally nonintoxicating in March,
> 1933, and prior to the reopening of the saloons after repeal of prohibi-
> tion in December of that year, light beer has proved to be an effective
> agency to replace and diminish to an appreciable degree the consump-
> tion of spirits. The drinking of beer by young men, particularly college
> students——those under as well as those over twenty-one—should
> be encouraged as a means of keeping them away from spirits. (Dr.
> Yandell Henderson, Yale University, 1934)

Restrictions on advertising alcoholic beverages were also proposed in 1935, in the belief that this would decrease alcoholism. Bill-
board advertising was targeted for legislative restriction in 1935, and
in 1939 proposals before the United States Congress would have
prohibited alcohol advertising on radio.

Another prevention effort during the 1930s (and practiced for centuries before and decades after) involved making an example of
alcoholics by judging them harshly and treating them punitively.
Fines for public drunkenness, for example, were widely imposed
before the 1970s, when public drunkenness was decriminalized,

though they varied enormously in amount. In 1939, for example, fines ranged from 50 cents an occasion in Delaware and $1 in New Jersey to $3,000 and two years in jail for a second offense in Florida. There is no evidence that fines for public drunkenness altered rates of alcoholism anywhere.

PREVENTION — 1985

Alcohol prevention strategies in the 1980s have concentrated on alcohol education programs for high-risk and special groups, including adolescents, women, the elderly, and minorities. These programs generally have two immediate aims: to educate people on the behavioral, psychological and psychiatric, and physiological effects of alcohol, the range and variability of both normal and abusive drinking in the United States, and alcohol's short- and longer-term effects on both social drinkers and abusive drinkers; and to make attitudes toward consumption, especially heavy consumption, more negative—or at least more wary. The ultimate goal is to reduce overall consumption levels and, especially, the prevalence of abusive drinking and alcoholism.

Other current prevention efforts harken back to the 1930s and before, such as attempts to lower the use of alcoholic beverages by raising the legal age for purchase and consumption, increasing taxes, demanding labels that warn of risks to health, and restricting advertising to decrease demand.

This decade has also seen strong legal and professional efforts to protect innocent members of society from the most damaging consequences of alcoholism. There has been an attack on drunk driving by more stringent law enforcement, random highway checks on blood alcohol level, and federal legislation to encourage all states to set 21 as the legal drinking age. Fetal alcohol syndrome (FAS) has been confronted by federal and state programs aimed at encouraging pregnant women and women of childbearing age to reduce or stop drinking, training physicians and nurses to identify women at risk for delivering FAS neonates, and alerting the general public to the hazards of drinking during pregnancy (Nathan, 1983; NIAAA, 1983, 1986).

The net result of current efforts to prevent alcoholism has been disappointing in the extreme. These efforts, which generally differ little in methods, goals, or achievements from those of 1935, have consistently yielded reports of increased public awareness of the hazards of heavy alcohol use and of desirable changes in attitudes toward drunkenness and alcoholism. But there are few documented instances of change in level or pattern of alcohol consumption by the groups to which alcohol education has been directed (Nathan, 1983).

By contrast, the net result of current efforts to diminish two specific consequences of alcohol abuse—drunken driving, especially by teenagers, and fetal alcohol syndrome—has been positive. Both have decreased, while arrests for drunken driving have increased in recent years (NIAAA, 1983, 1986).

Conclusions

1. Significant progress has been made during the past 50 years in identifying and understanding the effects of alcohol on human behavior. The dimensions of behavioral pathology induced by acute and chronic alcohol abuse have been much better delineated during these five decades. Behavioral scientists have played important roles in this successful search for understanding.

2. Significant progress has also been made in demonstrating the genetic predisposition to alcoholism that seems to characterize some of those with at least one alcoholic parent. However, the ultimate effects of a genetically based predisposition to alcoholism, the percentage of those with an alcoholic parent who carry this predisposition, the factors governing its expression, and the way it is transmitted remain uncertain. Behavioral scientists are deeply involved in studying these issues.

3. Progress in understanding other aspects of alcoholism's etiology, however, has been limited by the expense, complexity, and difficulty of longitudinal research, the best strategy for studying psychosocial, environmental, and learning-based factors in the natural history of the disorder, which are of special interest to behavioral scientists.

4. Relatively little progress has been made in developing effective treatment programs for alcoholics. In fact, it now seems unclear that treatment per se influences an alcoholic's decision to stop drinking. More important than form, locus, or intensity of treatment are age, sex, education, and, above all, motivation to change.

5. The progress made in treatment over the past 50 years has involved productive research strategies to reliably assess outcome and identify predictors of outcome. And the elimination of moral

reeducation approaches to treatment probably should be considered progress as well.

6. Little or nothing has been achieved in the prevention area, despite much costly rhetoric and many millions of dollars in federal and state funds. A complete rethinking of strategy and tactics is clearly called for in this area.

REFERENCES

Armor, D. J., Polich, J. M., & Stambul, H. B. (1978). *Alcoholism and treatment.* New York: Wiley.
Bacon, S. D. (1945). Excessive drinking and the institution of the family. In *Alcohol, science, and society* (pp. 223–238). New Haven: Yale Center of Alcohol Studies.
Barry, H., III. (1980). Psychiatric illness of alcoholics. In E. Gottheil, A. T. McClellan, & K. A. Durley (Eds.), *Substance abuse and psychiatric illness.* Elmsford, NY: Pergamon Press.
Berry, M. N., Fanning, D. C., Grivell, A. R., & Wallace, P. G. (1980). Ethanol oxidation by isolated hepatocytes from fed and starved rats and from rats exposed to ethanol, phenobarbitone or 3-amino-triazole. *Biochemical Pharmacology, 29,* 2161–2168.
Bigelow, G., Cohen, M., Liebson, I., & Faillace, L. (1972). Abstinence or moderation? Choice by alcoholics. *Behaviour Research & Therapy, 10,* 209–214.
Braiker, H. (1982.) The diagnosis and treatment of alcoholism in women. In *Special population issues,* Alcohol and Health Monograph 4. Washington, DC: National Institute on Alcohol Abuse and Alcoholism.
Cahalan, D. (1982). Epidemiology: Alcohol use in American society. In E. L. Gomberg, H. R. White, & J. A. Carpenter (Eds.), *Alcohol, science and society revisited* (pp. 96–118). Ann Arbor and New Brunswick, NJ: University of Michigan Press and Rutgers Center of Alcohol Studies.
Cahalan, D., & Room, R. (1974). *Problem drinkers among American men.* New Brunswick, NJ: Rutgers Center of Alcohol Studies.
Cloninger, C. R., Bohman, M., & Sigvardsson, S. (1981). Inheritance of alcohol abuse. *Archives of General Psychiatry, 38,* 861–868.
Cloninger, C. R., Reich, T., & Wetzel, R. (1979). Alcoholism and affective disorders: Familial associations and genetic models. In D. W. Goodwin (Ed.), *Alcoholism and affective disorders.* New York: Spectrum.
Conger, J. J. (1951). The effects of alcohol on conflict behavior in the albino rat. *Quarterly Journal of Studies on Alcohol, 12,* 1–29.
Conger, J. J. (1956). Alcoholism: Theory, problem and challenge. II. Rein-

22

NEBRASKA SYMPOSIUM ON MOTIVATION, 1986

forcement theory and the dynamics of alcoholism. *Quarterly Journal of Studies on Alcohol, 17*, 291–324.

Crowell, C. R., Hinson, R. E., & Siegel, S. (1981). The role of conditional drug responses in tolerance to the hypothermic effects of alcohol. *Psychopharmacology, 73*, 51–54.

Cutter, H. S. G., Schwaab, E. L., & Nathan, P. E. (1970). Effects of alcohol on its utility for alcoholics. *Quarterly Journal of Studies on Alcohol, 30*, 369–378.

Davies, D. L. (1962). Normal drinking by recovered alcohol addicts. *Quarterly Journal of Studies on Alcohol, 23*, 94–104.

Dollard, J. (1945). Drinking mores of the social classes. In *Alcohol, science, and society* (pp. 95–104). New Haven: Yale Center of Alcohol Studies.

Emrick, C. D. (1974). A review of psychologically oriented treatment of alcoholism. I. The use and interrelationships of outcome criteria and drinking behavior following treatment. *Quarterly Journal of Studies on Alcohol, 35*, 523–549.

Emrick, C. D. (1975). A review of psychologically oriented treatment of alcoholism. II. The relative effectiveness of different treatment approaches and the effectiveness of treatment versus no treatment. *Journal of Studies on Alcohol, 36*, 88–109.

Fleeson, W., & Gildea, E. F. (1942). A study of the personalities of 289 abnormal drinkers. *Quarterly Journal of Studies on Alcohol, 3*, 409–432.

Glueck, S., & Glueck, E. (1950). *Unravelling juvenile delinquency.* New York: Commonwealth Fund.

Goodwin, D. W. (1985). Genetic determinants of alcoholism. In J. H. Mendelson & N. K. Mello (Eds.), *The diagnosis and treatment of alcoholism* (pp. 65–87). New York: McGraw-Hill.

Goodwin, D. W., Schulsinger, F., Hermansen, L., Guze, S. B., & Winokur, G. (1973). Alcohol problems in adoptees raised apart from alcoholic biological parents. *Archives of General Psychiatry, 28*, 238–243.

Goodwin, D. W., Schulsinger, F., Knop, J., Mednick, S., & Guze, S. B. (1977). Alcoholism and depression in adopted-out daughters of alcoholics. *Archives of General Psychiatry, 34*, 751–755.

Goodwin, D. W., Schulsinger, F., Moller, N., Hermansen, L., Winokur, G., & Guze, S. B. (1974). Drinking problems in adopted and unadopted sons of alcoholics. *Archives of General Psychiatry, 31*, 164–169.

Heath, C. W. (1946). *What people are.* Cambridge: Harvard University Press.

Hooten, E. (1945). *Young man, you are normal.* New York: Putnam.

Jellinek, E. M. (1941). Classics of the alcohol literature. A document of the Reformation Period on inebriety: Sebastian Franck's "On the horrible vice of drunkenness," etc. *Quarterly Journal of Studies on Alcohol, 2*, 391–395.

Jellinek, E. M., & Jolliffe, N. (1940). Effects of alcohol on the individual: Review of the literature of 1939. *Quarterly Journal of Studies on Alcohol, 1*, 110–181.

Jellinek, E. M., & McFarland, R. A. (1940). Analysis of psychological experiments on the effects of alcohol. *Quarterly Journal of Studies on Alcohol, 1*, 272–371.

Krueger, D. W. (1980). Countertransference in the treatment of the alcoholic patient. In W. Fann, A. Pokorny, I. Karacan, & R. Williams (Eds.), *Phenomenology and treatment*. New York: Spectrum.

Lewis, N. D. C. (1940). Personality factors in alcoholic addiction. *Quarterly Journal of Studies on Alcohol, 1*, 21–44.

Lex, B. W. (1985). Alcohol problems in special populations. In J. H. Mendelson & N. K. Mello (Eds.), *The diagnosis and treatment of alcoholism* (pp. 89–188). New York: McGraw-Hill.

Li, T.-K. (1983). The absorption, distribution, and metabolism of ethanol and its effects on nutrition and hepatic function. In B. Tabakoff, P. B. Sutker, & C. L. Randall (Eds.), *Medical and social aspects of alcohol abuse* (pp. 47–77). New York: Plenum.

Lieber, C. S. (1980). Metabolism and metabolic effects of alcohol. *Seminars in Hematology, 17*, 85–99.

Marlatt, G. A. (1978). Craving for alcohol, loss of control, and relapse: A cognitive-behavioral analysis. In P. E. Nathan & G. A. Marlatt (Eds.), *Alcoholism: New directions in behavioral research and treatment*. New York: Plenum.

Marlatt, G. A. (1979). Alcohol use and problem drinking: A cognitive-behavioral analysis. In P. C. Kendall & S. D. Hollon (Eds.), *Cognitive-behavioral interventions: Theory, research, and procedures*. New York: Academic Press.

Marlatt, G. A., Demming, B., & Reid, J. B. (1973). Loss of control drinking in alcoholics: An experimental analogue. *Journal of Abnormal Psychology, 81*, 233–241.

Marlatt, G. A., & Gordon, J. R. (1985). *Relapse prevention*. New York: Guilford.

Marlatt, G. A., & Rohsenow, D. J. (1980). Cognitive processes in alcohol use: Expectancy and the balanced placebo design. In N. K. Mello (Ed.), *Advances in substance abuse* (Vol. 1). Greenwich, CT: JAI Press.

McPeek, F. W. (1943). Youth, alcohol and delinquency. *Quarterly Journal of Studies on Alcohol, 4*, 568–579.

Mendelson, J. H., & Mello, N. K. (1966). Experimental analysis of drinking behavior of chronic alcoholics. *Annals of the New York Academy of Sciences, 133*, 828–845.

Mirsky, I. A., Piker, P., Rosenbaum, M., & Lederer, H. (1941). "Adaptation" of the central nervous system to varying concentrations of alcohol in the blood. *Quarterly Journal of Studies on Alcohol, 2*, 35–45.

Moos, R. H., & Billings, A. G. (1982). Conceptualizing and measuring coping resources and processes. In L. Goldberger & S. Breznitz (Eds.), *Handbook of stress*. New York: Free Press.

Nathan, P. E. (1982). Blood alcohol level discrimination and diagnosis. In E. M. Pattison & E. Kaufman (Eds.), *Encyclopedic handbook of alcoholism* (pp. 64–71). New York: Gardner Press.

Nathan, P. E. (1983). Failures in prevention: Why we can't prevent the devastating effect of alcoholism and drug abuse on American productivity. *American Psychologist, 38*, 459–467.

Nathan, P. E., & Skinstad, A.-H. (in press). Outcomes of treatment for alcoholism: Current data. *Journal of Consulting and Clinical Psychology*.

Nathan, P. E., Titler, N. A., Lowenstein, L. M., Solomon, P., & Rossi, A. M. (1970). Behavioral analysis of chronic alcoholism. *Archives of General Psychiatry, 22*, 419–430.

National Institute on Alcohol Abuse and Alcoholism. (1983). *Fifth special report to the U.S. Congress on alcohol and health*. Washington, DC: Author.

National Institute on Alcohol Abuse and Alcoholism. (1986). *Sixth special report to the U.S. Congress on alcohol and health*. Washington, DC: Author.

Newman, H. W. (1941). Acquired tolerance to ethyl alcohol. *Quarterly Journal of Studies on Alcohol, 2*, 453–463.

Pattison, E. M., Sobell, M. B., & Sobell, L. C. (Eds.). (1977). *Emerging concepts of alcohol dependence*. New York: Springer.

Polich, J. M., Armor, D. J., & Braiker, H. B. (1981). *The course of alcoholism: Four years after treatment*. New York: Wiley.

Schilder, P. (1941). The psychogenesis of alcoholism. *Quarterly Journal of Studies on Alcohol, 2*, 277–292.

Shapiro, A. P., & Nathan, P. E. (1986). Human tolerance to alcohol: The role of Pavlovian conditioning processes. *Psychopharmacology, 88*, 90–95.

Siegel, S. (1975). Evidence from rats that morphine tolerance is a learned response. *Journal of Comparative and Physiological Psychology, 89*, 498–506.

Tabakoff, B., & Rothstein, J. D. (1983). Biology of tolerance and dependence. In B. Tabakoff, P. B. Sutker, & C. L. Randall (Eds.), *Medical and social aspects of alcohol abuse* (pp. 187–220). New York: Plenum.

Tarter, R. E., Hegedus, A., Goldstein, G., Shelly, C., & Alterman, A. (1984). Adolescent sons of alcoholics: Neuropsychological and personality characteristics. *Alcoholism: Clinical and Experimental Research, 8*, 216–222.

Tiffany, S. T., & Baker, T. B. (1981). Morphine tolerance in rats: Congruence with a Pavlovian paradigm. *Journal of Comparative and Physiological Psychology, 95*, 747–762.

Vaillant, G. E. (1983). *The natural history of alcoholism.* Cambridge: Harvard University Press.

Wiens, A. N., & Menustik, C. E. (1983). Treatment outcome and patient characteristics in an aversion therapy program for alcoholism. *American Psychologist, 38,* 1089–1096.

Wiens, A. N., Montague, J. R., Manaugh, T. S., & English, C. J. (1976). Pharmacological aversive counterconditioning to alcohol in a private hospital: One year follow-up. *Journal of Studies on Alcohol, 37,* 1320–1324.

Winokur, G., Reich, T., Rimmer, J., & Pitts, F. (1970). Alcoholism. III. Diagnosis and familial psychiatric illness in 259 alcoholic probands. *Archives of General Psychiatry, 23,* 104–111.

The Four Alcoholisms: A Developmental Account of the Etiologic Process

Robert A. Zucker[1, 2]

Michigan State University

Introduction

Some 33 years ago in the first Nebraska Symposium on Motivation, the organizers of this distinguished series noted that "the problems of motivation are significant for and relevant to practically every phase of contemporary psychology. Motivation provides a central theme around which a vast amount of experimental data from many divergent sources can be assembled and evaluated. It is also an area of great current theoretical interest and endeavor" (Psychology Department, University of Nebraska, 1953, p. iii). In considering the topic of the present symposium, alcohol and addictive behavior, one could just as well substitute the generic phrase "drug taking and drug abuse" for the term "motivation" in the statement above. Alternatively, one could substitute "alcohol," that drug of most prevalent national use and abuse, and the statement would continue to be appropriate. This is not simply a convenient position of 1986. In the first symposium Vincent Nowlis examined the modification of motivational systems in adults through the use of drugs. His interest in that topic in 1953 was no doubt stimulated both by scientific curiosity and by his own experience living in a drug-using society. He noted that "chemical agents modify relationships among situations, intervening variables, and responses . . . in brief spans of time" (Nowlis, 1953, p. 131).

This chapter starts at the same point—the ingestion of a chemical

1. I am especially indebted to Kristine Freeark for her advice and help in preparing this chapter.

2. Support for some of the work reported here comes from grants to me and to Robert B. Noll from the Michigan Department of Mental Health.

agent by a person in a social context for the purpose of bringing about a change. This is an interactive set of relationships, and if the agent is a good one Nowlis knew—as have countless persons for centuries past—that the effects of such an encounter will be significant and will involve pronounced release of affect and changes in social behavior whose power can be likened to that of psychotherapy. Such an experience we call *drug use;* a substance is voluntarily selected and ingested to bring about some change in process or state. My special interest here is not in the brief drug-taking event, but rather in the natural evolution of patterns of drug use that eventually lead to abusive involvement over significant portions of a lifetime. The drug of particular interest is alcohol, and most especially that outcome known as alcoholism. My intent is to review our own and other investigators' work describing the unfolding and evolution of serious alcohol problems during the life course. The special thesis I am proposing is that the evidence is now sufficient to support a conceptualization of four different kinds of alcoholism that have different sequelae and different histories and that in fact reflect different developmental processes.

To reach this conclusion several literatures need to be reviewed that lead in this direction. Also relevant are data from a still early-stage longitudinal study being conducted by our research group on the developmental characteristics of individuals and families with an alcoholic parent, using a high-risk design to track etiologic process. The first half of the chapter examines and discusses these sets of findings. In the second half I consider where these data fit into the large scheme of longitudinal studies on drinking and on phenomena other than alcohol problems that have a bearing on these issues. A review of this latter work reveals significant problems with many of the research designs and data currently available in the alcohol field. Grappling with those problems in the context of other developmental literatures suggests some different conceptions of the disease or disorder process, and some different perspectives emerge on the nature of the alcoholic course over developmental time. This constitutes the second half of the chapter.

Epidemiologic and Developmental Perspectives on Etiology

A brief review of the epidemiologic data sets the context for the etiologic problem. Tables 1 and 2 present recent population estimates of the prevalence of alcohol and other drug problems in urban areas. Rates are derived from the National Institute of Mental Health (NIMH) Epidemiologic Catchment Area study (Boyd, et al., 1984; Myers et al., 1984; Robins et al, 1984). The original data were weighted to reflect population rates of lifetime prevalence in three Environmental Catchment Area (ECA) sites, involving the metropolitan areas surrounding Baltimore, Maryland, St. Louis, Missouri, and New Haven, Connecticut. Data were generated using the NIMH Diagnostic Interview Schedule (DIS) (Robins, Helzer, Croughan, & Ratcliff, 1981), administered to a probability sample drawn from all usual residents in these three geographic areas. Interviews were completed between 1980 and 1982. The figures presented here are recomputations from data in the 1984 reports, averaged across the three geographic sites so as to provide a crude index of national urban prevalence rates for these problems. The data presented for both alcoholic and other drug symptomatology are a summation of rates of chronic problems (i.e., alcohol dependence or drug dependence) *and* of acute problems (i.e., alcohol abuse or drug abuse).

The figures in Table 1 reiterate facts long known to alcohol and drug researchers, namely that substance-use disorders over the life span are far more common among men than women, and that alcohol is the number one drug of abuse. The data also indicate that within these urban areas, approximately one out of seven persons can be expected to show an alcohol abuse/dependence problem during his or her lifetime (one out of six for any substance-related

Table 1

Lifetime Prevalence of Alcohol Abuse/Dependence and Drug Abuse/Dependence Averaged Across Three ECA Sites: Total and by Sex

Substance-Use Disorders	Total	Males	Females
Alcohol abuse/dependence	13.6 (0.7)	24.3 (1.4)	4.4 (0.5)
Drug abuse/dependence	5.6 (0.5)	7.0 (0.8)	4.4 (0.6)
Total substance-use disorder	16.7 (0.8)		

Note. Computed from Robins et al. (1984), Tables 1 and 3. ECA = Epidemiologic Catchment Area; numbers in parentheses are SEs.

disorder) and that the magnitude of the problem is elevated to a ratio of one in four when we consider lifetime prevalence of alcohol problems among men. This figure is substantially lower for women (approximately one in 25).

These data can also be set in the broader context of prevalence rates for any diagnosable psychiatric disorder. The ECA study reports a lifetime prevalence of 32.6% for any DSM-III diagnosis. The most common diagnostic category is substance abuse. As Table 1 also shows, given the 16.7% lifetime prevalence figure for substance-use disorders, one out of two of these diagnosable psychiatric difficulties is a drug problem, and a bit more than 40% of all psychiatric difficulties are alcohol connected. So the problem population is a massive one.

Table 2 shows data concerning age- and sex-related variations in six-month prevalence of the two subtypes of substance abuse/dependence. The age trends need to be viewed with some caution because they are cross sectional rather than longitudinal. Nonetheless, in terms of currently active disorder (i.e., six-month prevalence figures) for alcohol abuse/dependence, the trend is for the highest rates to occur before the mid-40s, followed by a dropoff in the older

Table 2

Lifetime and Six-Month Prevalence of Alcohol Abuse/Dependence and Drug Abuse/Dependence by Age, Averaged Across Three ECA Sites

	Age group							
	18–24		25–44		45–64		65+	
	Life-time	Six-Month	Life-time	Six-Month	Life-time	Six-Month	Life-time	Six-Month
Alcohol abuse/ dependence	13.6	6.8	17.7	7.0	12.1	3.9	6.5	1.7
Drug abuse/ dependence	13.5	6.3	8.2	2.5	0.6	0.1	0.1	0.0

Note. Computed from Robins et al. (1984), Table 6, and Myers et al. (1984), Table 4 (averaged data).

segments of the population. For women the dropoff occurs in the 20s, a pattern that is also true of drug-related disorder in both men and women. It is important to remember that these rates are not simply indicators of problems; they are in fact rates of diagnosable disorder—which implies severity of trouble, additivity of problems across several areas of functioning, and sustained presence of the difficulty over a period of time (a minimum of one month).

Although age, sex, and prevalence rates provide a context for etiologic process, a possibly more direct lead to etiology can be provided by evidence on co-occurrence of symptoms. If two clusters of problems repeatedly are displayed together, it is more likely that there is a common element in their background. Thereafter, if the

Table 3

Odds Ratio for Coexistence in the Past Month of Substance Abuse/Dependence Disorders With Other DSM-III Disorders

	Alcohol Abuse/ Dependence	Drug Abuse/ Dependence	Antisocial Personality	Manic Episode	Major Depressive Episode
Alcohol abuse/ dependence	—				
Drug abuse/ dependence	10.7***	—			
Antisocial personality	15.5***	24.2***	—		
Manic episode	14.5***	3.4	6.7*	—	
Major depressive episode	4.1***	4.2*	5.1**	—a	—

Note. Adopted from Boyd et al. (1984), Tables 2 and 5.

aThese episodes are both categorized as major affective disorders, but they cannot co-occur within the same time frame.

* $p < .05$.   ** $p < .01$.   *** $p < .001$.

investigator has an etiologic understanding of one of the symptom displays, a set of parallel etiologic hypotheses can be generated about the other. Table 3, adapted from data provided by Boyd et al. (1984), is a start at estimating this process, again using actual data weighted over the three ECA sites to reflect occurrence in the community populations from which the data were generated. In evaluating the magnitude of co-occurrence, the odds ratio was used as a statistic; it is the ratio of the product of the two co-occurrences (present A/present B × absent A/absent B) divided by the product of the two non–co-occurrences (present A/not present B × not present A/present B). The data show that in order of decreasing co-occurrence, alcohol-related diagnoses are most likely to be associated with antisocial personality, followed by manic episodes, drug abuse or dependence, and to a lesser but still significant degree by major depressive episodes. The order of strength of co-occurrence is slightly different for drug abuse/dependence; again, antisocial personality is the most frequently co-occurring diagnostic syndrome, followed by alcohol abuse/dependence, major depressive episode, and manic episode.

It is important to underscore the usefulness of these population-generated estimates. They provide a beginning map of the unbiased population display of these troubles. When treatment-based samples are used to generate the same data, one cannot disentangle the selectivity of who goes into treatment from the co-occurrence one observes. Of course, further levels of breakdown of the ECA data would be even more useful in tracing etiology. Thus, a breakdown of co-occurrence phenomena with age would provide even more direct clues to etiologic process, which might be obscured when later-stage disorder is merged with early-stage disorder. Nonetheless, these associational data provide some beginnings. Their relevance will become increasingly clear later in the chapter.

How early does alcoholism begin? An apparently simple answer is that it does not begin until sometime after the individual starts drinking alcoholic beverages. This has led a number of investigators to become interested in the first drinking experience, both as a marker and as a possibly important transition point in etiologic process. In fact, in the early 1950s Albert Ullman (1953) suggested that clear memory of the first drinking event was itself of diagnostic significance for later alcoholism because it indicated that this particular experience was prepotent for these drinkers. Thus a person who would later be a normal drinker would not find the experience particularly important, and the memory of it would be vague at best. In contrast, those who would later be alcoholics remembered the experience vividly and sometimes with a sense of specialness—frequently because it involved becoming intoxicated even at the first encounter.

Anecdotal reports in the literature give some sense of the difference in these two kinds of experience—both in type of encounter reported and in age when it occurred. One man in Ullman's (1953) sample, drawn from a House of Correction population, had his first drink at age 17 when he was working with a lumbering crew. He recalls "coming to town on a Saturday night with the men of the crew, and joining them in a tavern. There he had his first drink— whiskey. He did not like its taste, but drank it and more. Eventually he became deeply intoxicated, then sick, and had to be taken back to camp by some of the men. The humiliation of his drinking performance was deep, and he met it by trying to outdrink all others on succeeding Saturday nights" (Ullman, 1962, p. 261).

A male college student reports a very different experience:

Q. Do you remember the very first drink you ever had?
A. Yes.
Q. Can you tell me about it?
A. I was thirteen. I was on a trip out to California with some boys—about fourteen boys—and there was very little supervision. And we were staying in a hotel in San Francisco and some of the boys, including myself, asked a taxi driver to buy us a bottle of bourbon. It was just sort of a for kicks type thing. I think that was the first time you might say I really had a drink.

The words "you might say I really had a drink" caused some suspicion on the part of the interviewer, who probed further. Actually, this young man had had sips of wine in his home for as long as he could remember and really did not recall his first drink at all (Ullman, 1962, pp. 263–264).

These accounts lead in two quite different directions; one suggests a very early onset experience, the other suggests onset begins in adolescence. Table 4 presents a compendium of empirical work on onset and summarizes results from a variety of samples. Among the males, beginning drinking ages range from 12 to 18; female data from parallel samples and cohorts show slightly older beginnings ranging between 14 and 20. Although generational (cohort) differences appear to be as large as differences between alcoholic and nonalcoholic groups, it is noteworthy that none of the age means locate first drinking experiences before early adolescence. The data are therefore in close agreement with both earlier (Maddox & McCall, 1964) and more recent studies (e.g., Jessor & Jessor, 1977; Kandel, Kessler, & Margulies, 1978) of the process of initiation into alcohol use, which locate the phenomenon in adolescence. Given this congruence of results, one might conclude that the anecdotal accounts of earlier drinking experiences reflect rare and unimportant events that are largely irrelevant both to the phenomena of adolescence and to drinking and problem-drinking etiology. But aside from the anecdotal evidence, no sustained empirical investigations have explored this. It is just this issue of the possible relationship (or lack thereof) between early developmental phenomena and eventual alcoholic etiology that has been a major research commitment for me, my colleagues, and students since the late 1970s.

Earlier Work

To give a brief account of the background for the current work, an earlier project begun in New Jersey in the middle 1960s concerned the role of personality, family, and parent influences in predicting individual differences in alcohol consumption and abuse among adolescents. That project was a community-based field study interwoven with more epidemiologically oriented research being carried on at Rutgers at the time. In the process of selecting predictor variables for the study that would take account of group influences—at the level of community and family—as well as individual influences, it became clear that a within-discipline conceptual framework would be too simplistic and also would not do justice to the multiple contributors to what eventually becomes the act of taking alcohol. The first attempts to develop a more appropriate conceptual framework began then.

In analyzing and understanding the Rutgers Community Study data base, some issues had to be faced that I believe are uniformly present for any investigator doing applied behavioral research who still has hopes of connecting this work to more general theories of behavior. In this case, I refer to the fact that the alcohol-related variables—the specific dependent variables of interest—frequently were best predicted by independent variables that had to do with alcohol, (e.g., attitudes about drinking, earlier drinking experiences). In these circumstances the temptation is present to develop a good predictive model based on these "proximal measures," but

Table 4
*Reports of Age of First Drinking Experience
in Alcoholic and Nonalcoholic Samples*

Investigators	Sample	Sex	Reported Mean Age at First Drink
Glatt (1961)	192 middle-class English alcoholics (hospitalized)	M	17.6
Rosenberg (1969)	50 inpatient alcoholics under age 30	M	15.3
Park (1973)	806 Finnish Alcoholics	M	16.4
Trice & Wahl (1958)	133 inpatient alcoholics	M	17.6
Trice & Wahl (1958)	119 members of AA	M	17.6
Ullman (1953)	143 county correctional facility inmates	M	18.2
Hesselbrock et al. (1984)	89 inpatient alcoholics; with diagnosis of antisocial personality	M	12.1
Hesselbrock et al. (1984)	91 inpatient alcoholics without diagnosis of anti-social personality	M	15.6
Ullman (1957)	401 college students	M	ca. 16
Glatt (1961)	77 middle-class English alcoholics (hospitalized)	F	19.7
Hesselbrock et al. (1985)	47 normal adults (age 26)	M & F	13.9
Hesselbrock et al. (1984)	12 inpatient alcoholics with diagnosis of anti-social personality	F	14.2
Hesselbrock et al. (1984)	52 inpatient alcoholics without diagnosis of anti-social personality	F	16.3
Ullman (1957)	397 college students	F	ca. 16

one ends up with a set of findings that is generalizable to little else. I am happy to report that we fought off this urge and instead began to evolve a set of classifications of influencing structures that has been both empirically useful and conceptually fruitful in helping us develop some interesting hypotheses about the development of normal and abusive drinking behavior.

As I have already suggested, one set of classifications involves the distinction between *drinking-specific factors* (those related to the acquisition, regulation, and availability of alcohol itself) and *nondrinking-specific factors* (those relating to non-alcohol-specific influences that are necessary precursors to the drinking experience but are also common pathways to other outcomes). The model that was eventually developed, which took account of these sets of influences, was derived partly from delinquency theory and partly from a broader biopsychosocial frame of reference (cf. Engel, 1977). The core hypothesis was that problem use of alcohol in adolescence was one of a class of behaviors that could be subsumed under the antisocial label. Other parts of the model posited that these behaviors were regulated by biological mechanisms combined with personality and familial processes. Although no developmental research was carried out, the cross-sectional data that tested the socialization aspects of the model supported it (Zucker & Barron, 1973; Zucker & Devoe, 1974; Zucker & Fillmore, 1968).

That research led in a number of directions: (1) the data clearly indicated that problem drinking in adolescence was closely tied to earlier involvement in a variety of deviant activities, suggesting that a general theory of the acquisition of conduct problems, with some modification, might be applicable to the acquisition of alcohol problems. (2) Striking parallels were noted between the familial and personality findings observed for these adolescent problem drinkers and the cross-sectional and retrospective findings reported for alcoholics some 20 to 30 years older. This suggested that the early problem users might to some degree be drawn from the same mold as later alcoholic individuals. If so, and if these familial and individual difference patterns were present within a year or two after the start of alcohol use, might not potential risk factors be isolated before *any* alcohol involvement was present?

With these questions in mind, in the mid-1970s a decision was made to mount a high-risk, longitudinal study as a way of getting a hold on possible etiologic process by utilizing the experiments of nature. If one can track a high-risk sample with such a design, the yield of diagnoses at the end of the pipeline will be greater than for the comparable but lower-risk group. If, in addition, the investigator picks the right variables to track, then retrospective identification of truly precursive variables becomes possible.

Our study's particular focus is upon children of alcoholics, already well identified as a high-risk population. Approximately 14 million Americans either are alcohol dependent or suffer from problem drinking (U.S. Department of Health, Education, and Welfare, 1978). This represents about 1 of every 11 adults. In addition, it has been estimated that slightly fewer than 7 million children under the age of 18 are currently growing up in families with an alcoholic parent, and an additional 22 million have already done so and moved on into adulthood (Russell, Henderson, & Blume, 1985). Such families have been found to have significant difficulties with behavioral, occupational, and interpersonal functioning, and intense marital conflict, parental deviance, and inconsistent parenting have also frequently been noted. Divorce rates seven times higher than those for the general population are reported in these homes, provided drinking is still going on (Paolino & McCrady, 1977).

Children of alcoholics become alcoholic adults six to ten times more frequently than children with nonalcoholic parents (Cotton, 1979; Goodwin, 1979). In addition, a wide variety of clinical and empirical studies on children of alcoholics have noted hyperactivity (Cantwell, 1972; Morrison & Stewart, 1973; Tarter, Hegedus, & Gavaler, 1985), difficulty with interpersonal relationships (Cermak, 1984; Morehouse & Richards, 1982), antisocial characteristics (Berry, 1967; Herjanic, Herjanic, Penick, Tomelleri, & Armbruster, 1977; Jones, 1968; McCord & McCord, 1960; O'Gorman & Ross, 1984; Rydelius, 1981), impulsivity (Knop, Teasdale, Schulsinger, & Goodwin, 1985; Rydelius, 1983), and difficulties in intellectual development (Ervin, Little, Streissguth, & Beck, 1984; Gabrielli & Mednick, 1983). The data also strongly suggest that many of the children in these families display a constellation of adverse temperamental factors that make them particularly difficult to manage and more likely to be the victims of parental criticism (Garmezy, 1981; Patterson & Bank, in press). Other studies, concerning neurophysiological functioning in these children, suggest possible biological antecedents to alcoholism that are marked by differences in event-related brain potentials (Begleiter, Porjesz, Bihari, & Kissin, 1984), electroencephalographic patterns (Gabrielli et al., 1982; Pollock et al., 1984) and neuropsychological test findings (Knop, Goodwin, Teasdale, Mikkelsen, & Schulsinger, 1984; Tarter, Hegedus, Goldstein, Shelly, & Alterman, 1984).

Despite this considerable menu of biological, psychological, and social difficulties, a bit fewer than 50% of the children of alcoholic parents develop alcohol problems as adults, and an even smaller group of them become frankly alcoholic. Thus, having an alcoholic parent greatly increases risk, yet many children of alcoholic parents do not have alcohol problems during adulthood, nor do they all experience significant problems during childhood. Contrasts over time can therefore permit an examination of factors that produce risk and those that insulate against it.

These individual difference factors represent a potential wealth of etiologic leads. Some recent and imaginative attempts have been made to tie them together (e.g., Tarter, Alterman, & Edwards, 1985). The factors represent a conceptual as well as an empirical challenge in that they require sophisticated integrative models if they are to be useful in mapping out developmental processes. Conceptualizations based upon multiple regression models are not adequate to this task because they take no account of the fact that behavior ultimately takes place at the microlevel of specific and concrete transactions between self and environment (cf. Sameroff, 1975). Thus, summative conceptualizations that aggregate behaviors over many spheres of influence and over comparatively long spans of life process will obscure the nature and variations of the process being studied. What is needed instead is a fine-grained understanding of the specific developmentally linked paths to alcohol use and abuse that takes some account of the biopsychosocial nature of the process.

All these issues lead directly toward our current study and the model that underlies it. In dealing with the problem of what to investigate, we felt two questions needed to be addressed: First, what domains need to be adequately assessed, or controlled, in order to carefully chart the major sources of variance that contribute to later alcohol-related problem behavior and later insulation against such problems? Second, even with a fairly complete coverage of the domains, how is one to conceptually organize the way these potential influences relate to each other? Figure 1 reflects in schematic form an initial effort at answering both these questions.

The figure shows, both cross sectionally and longitudinally, that drinking behavior is acquired in an interactive process involving cultural/situational (Class I) influences, familial (Class II) influences, peer-based (Class III) influences, and intraindividual (including physiological) influences (Class IV) and indicates that such processes can be expected to interact with each other at any one de-

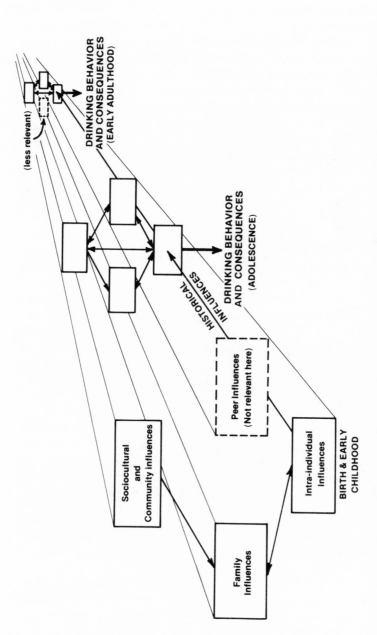

Figure 1. A heuristic model for changes in influencing structures affecting drinking behavior over developmental time. (Substantially as reported in Zucker, 1979. Figure reproduced with permission of the publisher. Copyright 1979 by Plenum Publishing Corporation.)

velopmental time point; but it also shows ebb and flow in salience at different developmental epochs. With this organizing structure as a guide, the predictive model was put into place.

Starting from the developmental period of the preschool years, we formulated the following hypothetical model:

Phase 1

(1) Temperament differences and individual differences in impulsivity (Class IV influences); along with (2) family socialization to aggression (Class II/Class IV interaction); along with (3) socialization to negative mood (Class II/Class IV interaction); and (4) early socialization to attitudes about alcohol, the development of cognitive structures about alcohol and other drugs, and earlier learning about alcohol use (Class II/Class IV interaction; Class I/Class II and Class I/Class IV interactions).

Phase 2

(1) All enhanced by parent modeling effects for aggression, negative mood, and alcohol use (Class II influences).

Phase 3

In middle childhood and the adolescent years will lead to: (1) great coping difficulties in school (Class IV effects); (2) an earlier move to a more deviant peer group (Class III/Class IV interaction); (3) possibly more peer relationship problems (Class III/IV interaction); (4) greater aggressiveness, alcohol consumption, and other drug use (Class IV effects).

Phase 4

In adulthood will lead to more deficient patterns of adult skills in: (1) management of aggression (i.e., greater antisocial behavior is anticipated [Class IV]; (2) achievement-oriented activities (more occupational difficulties are anticipated [Class IV/Class III and Class IV/Class I interaction effects]); (3) interpersonal behavior (more interpersonal difficulties, particularly in marriage, are anticipated [Class IV/Class III interactions]); (4) alcohol and drug use (more substance abuse is expected [Class IV influence]).

The Michigan State University Longitudinal Study[3]

With this work as conceptual background, the high-risk study was put into place. The developmental span of the research is from 3 to 21 years of age. A five-wave follow-through design is being used that starts out with target children between the ages of 3 and 6 years. Recontact is to be made at three-year intervals. The present report addresses only early-stage outcomes from the preschool to school onset (T_1) data collection.

The target children being followed are males in families where there is an alcoholic father.[4] As already noted, such families are highly likely to yield offspring who are alcohol dependent and alcohol abusing when they reach adulthood (Cotton, 1979; Deutsch, DiCicco, & Mills, 1982; Rydelius, 1981; Vaillant, 1983). At least 25% to 30% of these children can be expected to become alcohol dependent in adulthood, and an additional number will show less obvious drug abuse and/or alcohol problems. Although these families are not the only ones out of which alcoholism develops, they clearly are an important subset. Because there is a significant preponderance of males among alcoholics, this is the target group that should produce the highest yield of symptomatic individuals in later life. And on the grounds of continuity of process and existing cross-sectional data, one would also expect these male children to have other kinds of significant difficulty long before any adult symptomatic status is achieved.

The choice of families with an alcoholic father is a straightforward one, given the project's focus on childhood experiences and outcomes and the awareness that alcoholism is more common among men (i.e., fathers) than women. Nonetheless, our earlier experience in selecting a risk group was a difficult one. One research design that we had to discard called for using pregnant wives of alcoholics, initially in their third trimester, who would be followed through the pregnancy and longitudinally thereafter. It became clear that the three-month developmental window was not large enough to generate a sufficient subject yield, so this design was discarded. A second beginning involved locating high-risk children by way of

3. My primary collaborator in this work has been Robert B. Noll. I gratefully acknowledge his significant and multifaceted contributions to the research reported here.
4. Families are not excluded if the mother is also alcoholic, but they are not selected on the basis of maternal alcohol-use patterns.

their alcoholic fathers, who in turn would be identified through area alcoholism treatment facilities. After securing agreements from all the local area agencies to do preliminary screening of their client populations, here also we discovered something that seems obvious in retrospect but was not so beforehand: the natural history of alcoholic disorders, as it unfolds in families and in contact with agencies, is such that most alcoholics are already well past the childbearing years when they finally make treatment agency contact. Thus, to pursue our interest in documenting early family and individual markers of risk, we would need to seek other sources of a high-risk population.

All of these problems were eventually overcome, and the study of young male children of alcoholic fathers and suitable control families was begun in 1981. We solved the problem by using a population-based sample of male alcoholics who were apprehended as drunk drivers. Alcoholism is ensured by selecting drivers who, at the time of arrest, have blood alcohol levels (BAL) high enough to be presumptive evidence of tolerance. The BAL we selected is 0.15% (150 mg/100 ml) or higher, a level that requires a 175-pound man to have consumed approximately 9 ounces of 80-proof liquor in an hour, if drinking on an empty stomach, or about 11 ounces if drinking on a full stomach. Considering that alcohol is metabolized at a constant rate, any individual drinking for more than an hour must have drunk more than these amounts in order to maintain that BAL. This is a significant level of consumption. Analyses of alcohol-use patterns show that our selection criteria are adequate to ensure a diagnosis, according to the research diagnostic criteria (RDC) (Spitzer, Endicott, & Robins, 1975), of definite alcoholic in more than 80% of the cases; 100% of the cases make a "probable or definite" criterion. Other tallies also show that 73% of these men meet a criterion of positive family history for alcoholism, while only 10% of control fathers do, further demonstrating that this is an appropriate parent group. All males who have this BAL, who are currently married and living with their spouses, and who have sons between the ages of 3.0 and 6.0 are recruited for the study. Our recruitment success rate is over 95%.

To initially check that all fathers do in fact meet the diagnostic criteria necessary for study participation, screening items from the Short Michigan Alcohol Screening Test (SMAST); (Selzer, 1975) are included in the initial health history given to respondent families at the time project consent is obtained. This allows the interviewer to verify level of alcohol involvement before going beyond the first family contact. To date only 2% of those recruited have missed the admission criterion at this stage.

Last, the same health history also inquires about possible fetal alcohol syndrome (FAS) in the target child (or children, if there are both boys and girls of the appropriate age), because of the mother's drinking during pregnancy. Although the mother's alcohol dependence is itself no basis for either excluding or including the family in the research, a history of an alcohol intake of six drinks per day or more during the pregnancy (a conservative criterion according to Abel, 1981) is cause for excluding the family from the study. So also are presumptive FAS signs such as abnormal (less than 70) IQ and any of the gross physical anomalies reported for FAS (Abel, 1981; Clarren & Smith, 1978).

Currently one contrast (control) group is used in the study. This is a yoked control and allows findings from the alcoholic families to be contrasted with those from a socially comparable but non-alcohol-abusing population. To avoid spurious contrasts resulting from sociodemographic and community differences, following Garbarino and Sherman (1980) and the Palo Alto socioenvironmentalists (Moos, Finney, & Chan, 1981), we have opted to use community controls who reside in the same census tracts as the high-risk families but are asymptomatic for alcohol/drug problems. Child participants in this group are the individuals who are yoked with the high-risk target children. Matching is for age ($\pm$ 6 months), sex, and family sibling composition insofar as possible. Because this set of controls is yoked to the alcoholic group rather than simply group matched, we end up with a case-control design (Schlesselman, 1982). Community contrast families are recruited door to door by a recruiter trained in field survey techniques who follows a grid pattern in the neighborhood and makes inquiries of each family approached until a suitable matched control family is located.

Table 5 presents a brief summarization of the basic study design. More detailed accounts are provided in several papers by our group (Zucker, Baxter, Noll, Theado, & Weil, 1982; Zucker, Noll, et al., 1984).

At present 64 families have been recruited into the study. Selection/recruitment procedures have proved more than adequate. Of all alcoholic families potentially qualified as respondents, 93% have agreed to be approached by study staff. Of those so approached all have agreed to participate, as have 100% of the potential community control families. We also have had no dropouts so far, once the families are formally recruited into the study. The data reported here are early analyses of the T_1 assessment, based upon 20 families (10 alcoholic, 10 control).

According to best-estimate data, derived from two questionnaires and one interview source, 100% of the high-risk fathers make either a "probable or definite" alcoholic diagnosis, and 80% make the "definite" diagnosis criterion level, using the Feighner criteria (Feighner et al., 1972). Mean age of the male target children is 49 months for both high-risk and community comparison families. Parents are approximately 30 years of age, family social status is at the level of skilled and semi-skilled workers (Social Prestige scores of 28.52 for the alcoholic families, 31.65 for controls, based upon the Duncan TSE12 Socioeconomic Index; Featherman & Stevens, 1980), and target children are most often second children in both sets of families. There are no differences on these or any other family demographic characteristics.

Analyses of the child data set so far have focused primarily on developmental functioning of the children and the development of their conceptions of alcoholic beverages (Noll & Zucker, 1983). Figure 2 depicts the findings from the Yale Developmental Inventory assessment. It shows that the high-risk boys are four months less advanced in general development ($p < .05$), seven months less advanced in fine motor development ($p < .01$), four months less advanced in adaptive development (a composite measure of verbal and motor intellectual abilities involving reasoning, reflecting, and interpreting skills) ($p < .05$), four months less advanced in language development ($p < .05$), and five months less advanced in personal/social development (social maturity items, ability to dress self, engage in cooperative play, etc.) ($p < .05$). These differences cannot be accounted for by chronological differences in children's ages (there were none) or by heritable differences in endowment (the alcoholic parents were, in fact, slightly higher in IQ than controls).

In an effort to assess both knowledge of and conceptions about alcoholic beverages in these families, children participate in several tasks that assess their experiences of and cognitions about alcohol (cf. Noll, 1983). Since knowledge of alcoholic beverages is gleaned from experience explicitly through the family's activities and also by way of exposure to the media (most particularly television advertising), any attempt to assess the child's capacity to understand alcohol as a concept and to identify the beverage and its uses should allow for some separation of these two sources of effect. The Smell Recognition Task in fact eliminates the contribution of media influences. Children are asked to play a smelling game—to identify

Table 5

Basic Risk Study Design: Michigan State University Longitudinal Study

High-Risk Families	Comparison (Control) Families
Fathers arrested for driving while impaired (DWI) with blood alcohol levels of 0.15% or higher when apprehended	Fathers have no alcohol-related arrest history
Fathers meet research diagnostic criteria at least for "probable alcoholism" (virtually all meet "definite alcoholism" criterion)	Fathers have no alcohol-related diagnosis
Families are intact and have a male target child between the ages of 3.0 and 6.0	Same criteria as high-risk families: in addition, comparison families reside in same neighborhoods, are yoked to high-risk families for age of target child, and where possible have parallel sibling composition (number, sex, age)

Note. Initial data collection done on father, mother, and target child involves approximately 12 hours of family contact. During this contact time (partially at the university and partially at family's home) 20 hours of questionnaire, laboratory interaction data, developmental assessments, a physical exam, and extensive observer ratings are collected (in the blind) on all families. Follow-up with parallel data collection is at three-year intervals.

the contents of different jars (which contain popcorn, perfume, cigarettes, Play-Doh, beer, wine, whiskey, and apple juice). The first set of exposures is with no other cues; a second trial is done with an array of color photographs of these objects/beverages to facilitate identification.

The ability to correctly identify alcoholic beverages from smell, with or without picture cues, is one indicator of the extent to which the child has an accurate cognitive map—or set of cognitive structures—about alcohol. Another measure, the Appropriate Beverage Identification Task, assesses the extent to which the child already

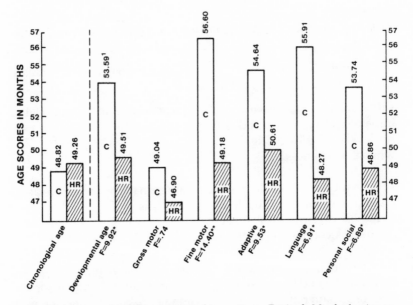

Figure 2. Scores on Yale Developmental Inventory—Revised. Matched-pair comparisons between high-risk (HR) and control (C) children. (Source: Noll & Zucker, 1983.) All mean ages are adjusted cell means. $*p < .05$, $**p < .01$. (All matched pairs ANCOVA, chronological age as covariate [N = 9 pairs].)

understands norms about alcohol use. In contrast to the Smell Recognition Task, responses to this instrument are potentially affected both by immediate family experiences and by exposure to media influence. Children are shown a number of drawings of festive and everyday situations in which beverages might be consumed (e.g., lunch, a Fourth of July picnic, an evening party for adults). Situations shown vary in the extent to which they involve adults only, adults and children, and children only; they also depict some male and some female characters. Along with the pictures, an array of photographs of different alcoholic and nonalcoholic beverages are shown. Children are asked what the person(s) in the drawings might like to drink, and they point out their choices from the photographic array. After the choices have been made, questioning establishes whether the child can also name (identify) all of the beverage photographs and group them into alcoholic and nonalcoholic categories. Last, children are directly queried about who uses these substances, whether they themselves intend to use them (or have) and when, as well as their like and dislike of the beverages if they have had any exposure. From these data one can infer, at quite young ages, the child's awareness of common social norms for alcohol use (that is, adults drink alcoholic beverages, children don't; men drink more than women; situational differences exist in beverage consumption patterns, such that it is socially appropriate to drink alcohol at an adult party but not at breakfast, etc.). One can also establish the extent to which the child is able to identify and categorize using the alcohol concept. Last, one can obtain information about personal experience and expectations concerning the child's own use and his or her attitudes about such use.

From this data set, even with the small sample, clear evidence was found for children's early knowledge of the social norms governing alcohol use. Across both high-risk and control boys, the data on the appropriate beverage task showed that alcoholic beverages were selected as the beverage of choice for adults but not for children ($p <$ .01), and more often for men than for women ($p < .001$). Trends were observed for risk status differences, in that boys from the alcoholic families tended to select alcoholic beverages more often for adults to drink than did control boys and for high-risk boys to identify alcoholic beverages by smell alone rather than needing picture cues for prompting, but these differences need replication. Last, the data on children's direct experience with alcoholic beverages at this young age gives some sense of the complexity of the processes involved in learning about and dealing with this drug. Among those who had correctly identified alcohol by smell (who we thus knew had had experience with these substances), two-thirds of the children reported that they disliked the substance, but the great majority (90%) also reported planning to use it when they grew up.

Given the tentative nature of some of these findings and the fact that they might be conceived of as special to this highly alcohol-exposed set of families, we decided to explore these phenomena more thoroughly with a normal population. For his master's research one of my students, Gregory Greenberg, performed these tasks and a number of others with nursery school children ranging in age from 2½ to 6 years old. The study examined whether differences in alcohol consumption that exist between parents of preschool children, as well as possible child developmental and cognitive (intellectual) ability differences, would predict individual differences in the child's awareness of norms regarding drinking and his or her ability to identify alcoholic beverages. The procedure was conducted in the child's preschool, by an examiner experienced in child assessment who was well trained both in these alcohol concept tasks and in the Peabody Picture Vocabulary Test—Revised

(Dunn & Dunn, 1981), the measure we used to assess cognitive ability differences among the subjects. Via questionnaire, parents also provided background demographic information as well as self-report consumption data on a variety of alcoholic and nonalcoholic beverages. Included in this beverage-consumption questionnaire were standard questions that have been used in the American Drinking Practices Survey (Cahalan, Cisin, & Crossley, 1969), which allowed us to code for quantity-frequency-variability (QFV) class, and also for "escape drinking" motivations.

Figure 3, from the first extensive report of the study (Greenberg, Zucker, & Noll, 1985), illustrates the developmental findings; differentiation in the understanding of norms about alcoholic beverage use becomes increasingly clearer with increasing child age. By age 6 the children make no mistake in assigning alcoholic beverages to adults and nonalcoholic beverages to children. But even *children as young as 30 months of age are already substantially able to understand the norm.* Other results showed that these preschoolers also know the sex norm (i.e., adult men drink more than adult women); that cognitive ability differences had little to do with ability to correctly identify alcoholic beverages; and that there was a low-order but significant correlation between ability to identify alcoholic beverages correctly and parents' consumption level. Parents' consumption level was also positively related to the child's likelihood for selecting alcoholic beverages as the beverage of choice for adults in adult situations where either alcoholic or nonalcoholic beverages might be consumed. So these results extend the generality of the risk study findings and indicate that both acquaintance with and cognitive structures about the use of alcohol develop early, and at least in part are tied to parental patterns of consumptions.

Turning back to the risk study itself, other parts of the etiologic theory call for differences to be found initially between parents in the two groups. We expect these differences to be related to the parents' own history of aggression and to a derivative of that—marital discontent and dislike. Both of these factors are seen as contributing to the child's socialization to heightened aggressive activity. Tables 6 and 7 summarize data from mothers and fathers in these families that is supportive of the theory. Both parents in the high-risk families report more childhood aggression in their own backgrounds and more antisocial and aggressive activity in adulthood (Table 6). In addition, using Benjamin's (1984) Structural Analysis of Social Behavior (SASB) model, INTREX Questionnaire data from the couples showed that parents in the alcoholic families reported their in-

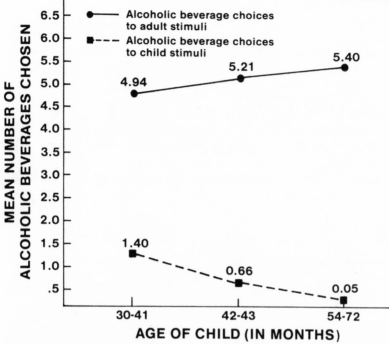

Figure 3. Mean number of alcoholic beverage drinking choices made by preschoolers as related to child's age and age of stimulus figure (N = 131). (Reported means are weighted scores based upon choices with 10 stimuli.)

terchanges to be significantly less friendly both for themselves and in how they perceived their spouses than was true of the community control parents (Table 7). These reports of greater dislike and anger are both supplemented and validated by external evidence of heightened marital conflict within the alcoholic families. At the moment 64 families have been recruited into the study. From their recruitment into the study until the end of the initial data collection phase, 8.5% of the alcoholic couples had either separated or divorced; none of the control couples had done so.

Let me briefly summarize these results.

1. The findings show that a group of 4-year-old children who are disproportionately likely to become alcoholic some 20 to 30 years later are already exposed to parental models who themselves have been more antisocial than controls as children and who continue that pattern into adulthood in their work life, in direct aggressive activity, and in continued trouble with the law. These results are in substantial agreement with a number of the earlier longitudinal studies done on older samples of those who later became alcoholics

Table 6
Antisocial Behavior in Alcoholic and Community Control Families: Parent Data

---

In childhood and adolescence
Alcoholic fathers and their wives both report more

Delinquent activity (e.g., truancy, joyriding, shoplifting)
Overt aggression (e.g., fighting in school, beating up people, killing animals)
School-related antisocial behavior (e.g., suspension from school, cursing at teachers)

In adulthood
Alcoholic fathers and their wives both report more

Job-related antisocial behavior (e.g., fired for absenteeism, three or more jobs in a year)
Trouble with the law (e.g., taking part in robberies, resisting arrest)

Note. All differences are significant at $p < .05$ or better, based on self-report questionnaire data from Zucker, Weil, Baxter, & Noll (1984).

(McCord, 1984; McCord & McCord, 1960; Robins, 1966; Vaillant, 1983).

2. The data also show greater dislike as part of the marital transactions in these families, shared by both parties in the relationship.

3. Other family climate results (Zucker, Weil, Baxter, & Noll, 1984) show that the alcoholic families are less likely to pursue moral/religious activities and interests that might moderate the dislike. In addition, the fathers see the family as allowing them their own independence to a disproportionately greater degree than is true of their wives or of either husbands or wives in the contrast families.

4. The developmental data on these children indicate that there are already substantial developmental deficits that may in part be accounted for by disturbances in family functioning. We continue to track this process.

5. The predictive model we are using specifies that the children themselves will become more aggressive and interpersonally more conflicted as they get older. The child data set we have assembled does not indicate that the parents see this as happening yet, although observer descriptions are beginning to suggest it is taking place.

Table 7
Perceptions of Interpersonal Relationships Between Spouses in Alcoholic and Community Control Families

---

Focus on self in interpersonal relationship

Wife as initiator: alcoholic wives perceive self as less affiliative than do controls; alcoholic husbands' response to what wives offer is less affiliative than for controls ($p < .05$)

Husband as initiator: alcoholic husbands perceive self as less affiliative than do controls; alcoholic wives' response to what husbands offer is less affiliative than for controls ($p < .001$)

Focus on other in interpersonal relationship

Wife as receiver of action: alcoholic wives perceive that what husbands offer is less affiliative than for controls; alcoholic husbands' perception of how wives respond is that it is less affiliative than for controls ($p < .05$)

Husband as receiver of action (and wife's perception of how he responds to her offers): no difference

---

Note. Data based on Structural Analysis of Social Behavior (SASB)–INTREX Questionnaires (Zucker et al., 1984).

6. Last, we have information about how eventual alcohol problems may begin to capture these children's lives. The alcohol concept data show that cognitive structures about alcohol have already begun to evolve, and social norms about alcohol use are already known at this age. How this knowledge might contribute to a later pattern of problem alcohol consumption, and how such a pattern might be enhanced by a behavioral style of greater aggression and greater interpersonal hostility, remains to be traced out in later years.

Confluences in the Longitudinal Evidence

The data presented so far support a continuity model of etiologic process for alcoholism. The predictions were theoretically derived, and the early data (both early in the developmental sense and early in our own study) tend to confirm such a process. Nonetheless, these findings still leave considerable gaps. The most obvious is that

52

NEBRASKA SYMPOSIUM ON MOTIVATION, 1986

we do not yet know which of the high-risk boys will eventually move into a pattern of chronic alcohol abuse.

There is, however, a way of getting a better hold on the mechanisms involved later in the process by examining completed longitudinal studies. These studies, although begun at later periods in development, share the advantage that they have already been carried forward into adulthood. The particular studies that meet these criteria are (a) the Oakland Growth Study (Jones, 1968, 1971); (b) the St. Louis Child Guidance Clinic Study (Robins, 1966; Robins et al., 1962); (c) the Columbia Follow-up Study (Berry 1967; Ricks & Berry, 1970); (d) the Cambridge-Somerville Youth Study (McCord & McCord, 1960, 1962); (e) the Vaillant Follow-up Study of Core City Residents (Vaillant, 1983; Vaillant & Milofsky, 1982); and (f) the Physique and Delinquency Study (Monnelly, Hartl, & Elderkin, 1983; Sheldon, 1949). The evidence from these studies presents a compelling case for continuity of process.

A recently completed review of these studies by myself and Edith Lisansky Gomberg (Zucker & Gomberg, 1986) articulates a number of areas of across-study agreement that are relevant to the present case. The following points recapitulate the discussion of the relevant areas of agreement from that paper:

1. *Childhood antisocial behavior is consistently related to later alcoholic outcome.* The five studies that examined this attribute (a–e)[5] all found more antisocial and aggressive activity among future alcoholics.

2. *More childhood difficulty in achievement-related activity is consistently found in those who later become alcoholics* (b, d–f). The studies documented poorer school performance (e), less productivity in high school (d), completing fewer years of schooling (e, f), and more school truancy (b) among boys who became alcoholics. It is premature to attribute all these difficulties to lack of achievement strivings in the prealcoholic group. Learning factors, including neurological deficits, have been posited as other possible underlying mechanisms for the behavioral differences. Whatever the mechanism, findings from other recent, not yet alcoholic but high-risk samples examined in studies by Hegedus, Alterman, and Tarter (1984) and by Knop, Teasdale, Schulsinger, and Goodwin (1985) are also consistent with deficits in this area. All together these studies clearly tie earlier achievement-related difficulties to heightened risk.

5. To facilitate frequent reference, these studies are referred to by the letters (a) through (f) that designate them above.

3. There is substantial agreement across studies that *males who later become alcoholics are more loosely tied to others interpersonally*. These findings vary from observations of being less dependent, less considerate, and less accepting of dependency (d), to a greater incidence of leaving home earlier (b, f), to the observation that these children are more indifferent to their mothers and are cool and indifferent to siblings (a). The interpersonal deficits one might infer from such data cannot be separated from the more general effects of antisocial character and parent-child conflict. Clearly some relationship among these three aspects of behavior would be expected, but the degree of independence of the variables and the extent of their separate etiologic contribution remains to be established.

4. *Heightened marital conflict is reported with consistently greater frequency in the prealcoholic homes* (a, b, d, e). The mechanism by which this conflict contributes to later alcoholism in the children still requires elaboration. Two of the most plausible explanations for this relationship are that conflict with parents leads to greater estrangement from the family, which moves the child more quickly into the heavier drinking peer culture, or alternatively, that conflict leads to other sequelae (e.g., antisocial behavior) that in turn become the direct pathway to alcoholism.

5. *Parent-child interaction in prealcoholic families is characterized by inadequate parenting and lack of contact with the parent(s)* (a–f). The behaviors involved have been variously described in the studies as including inadequate or lax supervision, an absence of parental demands, and parents' lack of interest or affection for the child, but the overarching characterization is one of inadequate contact (that is, not enough contact). Other ingredients relating to poor disciplinary practices may eventually be implicated, but they are not clearly substantiated by these data.

6. *Parents of prealcoholics are also more often inadequate role models for later normality* (a, b, d, e, f). They are more likely to be alcoholic, antisocial, or sexually deviant. These studies consistently relate parental alcoholism to the child's later alcoholism. Antisocial or sexually deviant behavior by parents has not been so frequently reported, but in half the studies these variables were simply not assessed. When they have been measured, the association is found (a, b). These studies of older families clearly jibe with our own observations.

Thus the jigsaw puzzle being assembled in separate sections of the developmental map seems ready to be joined together. (1) Early observations of poorer personal/social development can be linked to later childhood antisocial behavior and adult alcoholism. (2) Early developmental differences in cognitive functioning appear to presage later observed differences in achievement-oriented activity. (3) Interpersonal difficulties in these high-risk familes have not yet been well documented, but our clinical observations of early oppositionalism fit with the later observations of less dependency and less consideration among those who later become alcoholic persons. (4) Heightened marital conflict in the preschool years is substantiated by self-report data from both parents and by the higher rate of separation or divorce in the high-risk families than in the control families. (5) Evidence from diagnostic interview data and from a number of self-report questionnaire measures also establishes continuity of process as this relates to deviance in the parents of prealcoholics. These inadequacies and deviances are already capable of being identified when the children are preschoolers. (6) At the moment, with the data we have analyzed, we have only some inferential evidence and some ethnographic evidence suggesting that parent-child interaction patterns in the prealcoholic families are inadequate and lacking in contact. For one thing, the findings of early developmental deficits in a variety of areas, but most especially in language development, suggest such a process. For another, one ethnographic study from our project (Baxter-Hagaman, 1986) provides observational data showing that these patterns of (lack of) contact are in place in the high-risk families very early. Nonetheless, more robust evidence of this will have to wait for analysis of our parent-child interaction data, currently in process.

These significant correspondences provide a strong argument for continuity of developmental process in the etiology of alcoholism, stretching all the way from early childhood to adulthood. The early continuities are even more compelling when matched up with longitudinal studies of the evolution of problem behavior in boys from preschool to the middle childhood years (cf. Richman, Stevenson, & Graham, 1982) in other nonalcoholic developmental studies. The parallels are rather remarkable across a variety of domains.

Given the correspondences, the questions can very well be asked, Why has it taken so long to see them? And why has the argument been so fierce, that such continuity does not exist? (Vaillant, 1980, 1983). There are a number of reasons. Arguments for discontinuity have confused the issues and the data and in the process have provided fuel for controversy (Zucker & Gomberg, 1986). The most central problem is the field's willingness to continue using one "alcoholic" label for the disorder—with its implications of a unitary developmental process for alcoholism—even when many researchers and clinicians are aware that such a perspective is no longer adequate. A second, related problem is that issues of continuity and discontinuity of alcoholic etiologic processes will get confused if one attempts to superimpose a unitary explanatory model onto two or three or four separate sets of phenomena. Under these conditions one would be more likely to conclude that the process is discontinuous, especially if the samples one is examining are heterogenous for type of disorder. Any continuity of process would be seen at best as ill defined and at worst as nonexistent.

Given this state of confusion, the reader may well wonder how the data just presented appear so aptly to fit a model of process continuity. Our reply is that the continuity described is not artificial but in fact can be displayed because the sample from which it is generated is homogeneous and also is the most common, albeit restricted, population base out of which future alcoholics are produced. (More about this in the next section.) In these respects the model we have formulated (and the data that substantiate it) is adequate as one subtype but is inadequate as a general developmental model of alcoholic etiology. The remainder of the chapter first examines more systematically what has been left out of consideration both in our own data and in the longitudinal studies just reviewed and then proposes a general developmental model, with subtypes, that can better integrate the existing data as well as the discrepancies.

Issues Overlooked in Previous Etiologic Model Building

Previous longitudinal studies, including our own, have heavily tied etiology to the development of antisocial behavior. As already noted earlier in this chapter, one consistently strong association that has been replicated several times over is between earlier antisocial behavior and later alcoholic outcome. Although this finding is not in dispute, its limitations have not been equally well highlighted. This association is most frequently documented in high-risk samples, which have by necessity been preponderantly blue collar and have, by their nature, also been high yield for later alcoholism; but they simultaneously have been high yield for early (childhood) occurrence of antisocial behavior among their members (cf. Elliott & Huizinga, 1983; Robins, 1978). Thus *the alcoholism-antisocial behavior connection has not been tested as adequately longitudinally among middle-class groups,* and *the etiologic connections established are most relevant for blue-collar alcoholism.*

In the same vein, *there is, by now, substantial documentation that there are consistent social-class differences in rates of heavy consumption, in drinking-related problems, and in alcoholism.* Figure 4, based upon national survey data for men aged 21 to 59 and reproduced from Cahalan and Cisin's (1976) demographic summary of drinking practices in the United States, indicates a consistently higher rate of problem-drinking signs among males of lower social position *at all phases of the adult life span.* To underscore the relevance of this point, these differences are not just bound to the American population, but can be found as well in other careful population-based studies. The study of the Lundby cohort in Sweden (Ojesjo, Hagnell, & Lanke, 1983) is one such piece of work that duplicates the American findings.

By far the preponderance of longitudinal studies focus upon a male subject population; this is also true of the Michigan State study. Yet the evidence for sex differences, in the direction of greater consumption and greater prevalence of alcoholism among men (see Table 1, for example) is a steadfast epidemiologic fact. Thus *current theories of alcoholic etiology are heavily male based,* and the question whether lower prevalence rates for women reflect a more truncated, slower, albeit similar process to that found among men, or instead indicate a qualitatively different process and a different etiologic chain is still to be answered.

Related to the previous point, *there is significant evidence that negative-affect phenomena* (e.g., depression, low self-esteem) *play a much greater etiologic role in ontogenesis for female alcoholism than for male alcoholism* (e.g., Cadoret, 1981; Schuckit, Pitts, Reich, King, & Winokur, 1969; Wilsnack, Klassen, & Wilsnack, 1986). However, such evidence has not received as much weight as it should in pointing the field toward positing multiple alcoholisms and searching for multiple etiologic pathways. Additionally, although depressive symptoms have most often been noted in women alcoholics, other investigations, particularly of middle-class respondents (e.g., Kaplan & Pokorny, 1978; Williams, 1966), suggest that depression may play an etiologic role for male respondents' problem drinking as well, especially if the population happens to be one that is more internalizing in its coping style.

Despite the substantial evidence already reviewed for continuity of process in the development of alcoholism in male, blue-collar

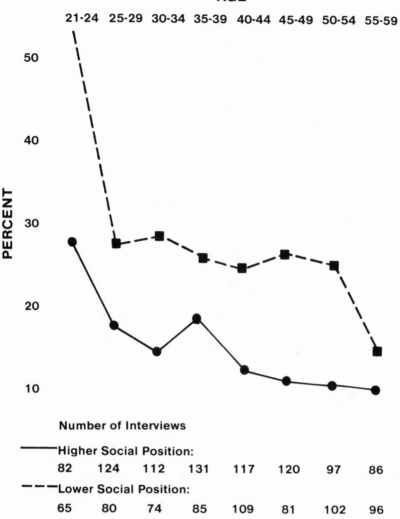

AGE

| 21-24 | 25-29 | 30-34 | 35-39 | 40-44 | 45-49 | 50-54 | 55-59 |

Number of Interviews

Higher Social Position:

| 82 | 124 | 112 | 131 | 117 | 120 | 97 | 86 |

Lower Social Position:

| 65 | 80 | 74 | 85 | 109 | 81 | 102 | 96 |

Figure 4. The relationship of high drinking-problems score (seven or more current problems) to age within two socioeconomic groups, for men aged 21–59. Combined U.S. National Surveys of 1967 and 1969; data from the Social Research Group, George Washington University and School of Public Health, University of California at Berkeley. (Source: Cahalan & Cisin, 1976, p. 98. Figure reproduced with permission of the authors and publisher. Copyright 1976 by Plenum Publishing Corporation.)

populations, *there also is evidence for considerable discontinuity in the development and evolution of drinking problems over time.* Studies examining the stability of drinking problems from adolescence to young adulthood (Jessor, 1985; Temple & Fillmore, 1986; Yamaguchi & Kandel, 1984), from young adulthood into middle adulthood (Fillmore, Bacon, & Hyman, 1979), and within adulthood itself (Cahalan, 1970; Goodwin, Crane, & Guze, 1971) all demonstrate a substantial migration of individuals from prior problem-drinking status into later non-problem-drinking status, and vice versa, among both men and women. In fact, stability over periods as long as 4 to 5 years appears to be the exception rather than the rule. In addition, such shifts in problem-drinking status appear to be keyed to the changes that occur over major developmental stages, or over major life transitions within stages (e.g., separation or divorce) (Cahalan, 1970; Wilsnack & Cheloha, 1985).

It is important to note that the studies demonstrating discontinuity over time have most often been population studies (thus involving a greater range of drinking adaptations), whereas the longitudinal studies that demonstrate continuity of process most often either have involved clinical samples or have followed individuals who have already repeatedly had the opportunity to observe (and model) heavy drinking by way of their exposure in high-risk environments. Thus, where continuity is present the initial intensity of the behavior is greater, or the opportunity to learn and overlearn the phenomenon is enhanced.

There are significant age changes in rates of alcohol problems and alcoholism across the life span. This conclusion has already been documented in Table 2 and Figure 4, but it needs underscoring. Recent research on patterns of women's drinking (Fillmore, 1984; Wilsnack, Wilsnack, & Klassen, 1984) indicates both that the age (developmental) patterns in the population may be shifting for women and also that *for both sexes, increases and decreases in problem rates can be keyed into developmental shifts in age-related roles* (cf. Blane, 1979; Wilsnack & Cheloha, 1985). This point has not yet infiltrated the etiologic literature or the theories.

To conclude this discussion, what is needed is an etiologic framework that covers long spans of developmental time and accounts for developmental discontinuity as well as continuity; one that is broad enough to account for these varied findings and systems of data, including those related to social class, age, sex, and the major life-span transitions that occur over the course of development; and one that can handle multiple factor influences in etiology, whether or not they lead to a final common pathway of outcome. The next section presents such a framework.

A Probabilistic Risk Framework for the Etiology of Clinical Disorder

PROBABILISTIC MODELS OF DISORDER / DISEASE

Given the evidence from diverse sources that heavily implicates causative influences as far apart as social structure and the central nervous system, one may very well ask whether a conceptual model that utilizes a disease framework is appropriate. *Webster's New World Dictionary*, 2nd college edition, defines disease as "a destructive process in an organ or organism, with a specific cause and characteristic symptoms." The notion of process typically implies the notion of *course*—of a specified sequence of events. Such a perspective also implies coherence across transitions and some ability to specify the nature of the latent coherence of mechanism.

As I have already noted, the evidence from medical/clinical, epidemiological, genetic, and longitudinal studies is of such weight for the operation of multiple processes in the development of severe and chronic alcohol problems (what we have come to call alcoholism) that the notion of one final common pathway of outcome is no longer workable. Given this state of affairs, it is my thesis that the most appropriate way to encompass multiple processes in a common etiologic model is to move to a probabilistic conceptual framework of both risk and clinical disorder. Within such a framework, with an appropriate set of predisposing etiologic factors operating within the model, one can conceive of risk as a relative summation or cumulation of relevant contributory influences operating by addition and interaction in some instances, by subtraction or dampening in others, and by maintenance (and stability) in still others. In order for this perspective to be accurate, it must be construed as a dynamic process that is anchored within developmental time and that operates in varying degrees throughout the life span of the individual. As the summations, subtractions, and interactions occur, risk ebbs and flows. What we call a clinical case is simply the event that occurs when relative risk becomes great enough that previously epiphenomenal symptomatic manifestations go over threshold. This may happen because symptoms are now displayed with greater intensity, frequency, or regularity than previously. Or they may move to a different display system (e.g., from covert to overt). In those circumstances "going critical" now involves a set of behavioral/physiological manifestations that become regarded as symptomatic. At that point, clinically one typically no longer speaks of "risk" but instead talks about "disease"; but in fact the additive, subtractive, and potentiating processes have been operating before as well as after the "disease threshold" event. This reformulation is more closely tied to the probabilistic nature of the event-cumulation interplay than is the common view of both etiology and disorder.

There are other implications of such a framework. One is that the notion of disease, as a progressive process, needs to be questioned for any set of symptomatic displays. If etiology is regarded as both additive and subtractive, then one also needs to look for evidence that shows degradation or diminution of symptoms over developmental time as well as for accretion. There is, for example, a good deal of evidence relating to severe symptomatic drinking behavior that is consistent with such a subtractive view, at least as far as some types of "alcoholism" are concerned (Cahalan, 1970; Fillmore et al., 1979; Goodwin et al., 1971; Roizen, Cahalan, & Shanks, 1978). That is, longitudinal follow-up on what one would commonly call disease at Time 1 shows the absence of such "process" at Time 2.

There is of course the alternative possibility that when the summative process reaches a certain level of accretion a different, irreversible process (e.g., Korsakoff's syndrome) takes place. The probabilistic framework would simply lead the investigator to specify more carefully what triggers such process shift (e.g., repetitions, metamorphosis, evolution of neuroanatomical structures), with particular regard both for the level of biopsychosocial system(s) involved and for the developmental stage(s) when such shifts are most likely to occur.

A PROBABILISTIC FRAMEWORK

Figure 5 is a graphic representation of such a probabilistic model. It illustrates by a grid the developmental flow of risk factors over the lifetime of the individual (the Y axis) and highlights the potential for both continuity and discontinuity of sustaining risk across life stages. The X axis illustrates the biopsychosocial set of structures that are potentially available as systems influencing risk or insulating against risk at each of the age stages. The particular structures I have chosen to emphasize here represent a somewhat expanded view of the biopsychosocial domain initially described in an earlier version of the model (Zucker, 1979; also Figure 1). Here the influencing domain is broadened to more explicitly represent biological systems as a separable level of influencing system.

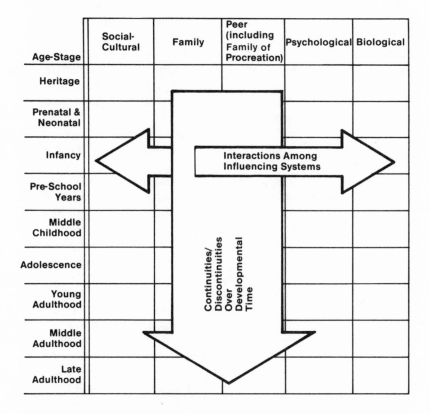

Figure 5. A biopsychosocial and developmental grid for identifying risk elements in psychopathology. (Relative risk at any age involves additive and subtractive elements in the grid that may at a particular age stage go over threshold to display as a clinical case.)

Cumulative continuity or unpatterned accretion? Some findings concerning the natural history of developmental continuity and change. With such a framework, one might conclude that a simple additive model, involving all cells and all life stages in the grid, is the most accurate representation of etiologic process. Such a conclusion would not do justice to the substantial evidence within the etiologic literature on alcoholism for *some* continuity of process, and it would also ignore the significant developmental literature in other areas that indicates the time flow—down the grid so to speak—is neither entirely fixed nor entirely haphazard.

Different elements of the grid may have more or less initial salience on the basis of systematic influences rather than random process. Thus an etiologic factor such as a genetic diathesis for initially higher activity level, or more aggressiveness, is more likely to continue to manifest itself through a number of life stages, though its impact might be moderated or potentiated by other interactive elements. A parallel social example, being born into a home with highly antisocial parents, is also likely to manifest itself over a number of developmental stages. Such interactive melding over developmental time has been termed *interactional continuity*, and it has been observed in a variety of content areas (Block, 1971; Caspi, 1986; Huesmann, Eron, Lefkowitz, & Walder, 1984; Loeber, 1985; Zucker & Gomberg, 1986).

In addition to such interactive enhancement of process, other factors play a role in sustaining regularity of behavior. Clearly one such element is practice, or rehearsal, which fine tunes a repertoire and also increases the probability that a particular behavior will emerge as an outcome of an action sequence. Such practice enhances across-stage continuity of behavior, especially when pretransitional activities share some elements with the posttransition activity. Under those conditions process coherence is most likely to take place (Alexander & Campbell, 1967; Elder, 1984). When such a process summates over time, along with fine tuning and evolution of repertoire, behavioral consistency is enhanced. In the personality domain, Caspi (1986) has termed this process *cumulative continuity*, but evidence for this snowballing effect may be found in other behavioral and psychopathological realms (Cahalan, 1970; Hans & Marcus, 1984; Loeber, 1986; Patterson, 1982). Given that such cumulation typically involves some evolution of the behavioral display, regularity is better understood as *coherence of process rather than as a strict repetition*. Evidence for such qualitative identity across time may be found in areas ranging from the development of curiosity, competence, and resilience in infancy and early childhood (Arend, Gove, & Sroufe, 1979) all the way to continuity in relational issues involving depression in adolescence and closeness in early adulthood (Kandel & Davies, 1986).

With this as background, one may conceive of the alcoholisms as a number of biopsychosocial processes that vary in duration and pattern—that are linked to important marker events likely to enhance cumulation of behavior along the developmental trajectory for some processes and, alternatively, lead to diminution of process for others. An adequate specification of etiology requires mapping the necessary cells in the developmental grid. Thus different etiologies imply different mosaics of risk elements, both within and across developmental periods. Once these mosaics are established, determining an individual's level of risk involves a simple comparison of the degree to which their own biopsychosocial history fits with the already established developmental risk mosaic.

The rest of this chapter is a beginning effort at charting such multiple etiologies. At the moment, I believe the evidence is sufficiently compelling to warrant the delineation of four types; (1) antisocial alcoholism, (2) developmentally cumulative alcoholism, (3) developmentally limited alcoholism, and (4) negative affect alcoholism. As an initial point of reference, Table 8 briefly summarizes the characteristics that distinguish them.

The Four Alcoholisms

Type 1, *antisocial alcoholism,* is the most frequently studied and the one we know most about. It is characterized by both the early presence of antisocial behavior and the early onset of alcohol problems. The NIMH ECA data shown in Table 3 indicate that it is probably the most common type, although the co-occurence of alcohol problems and a history of antisocial activity is not sufficient to establish it. Severity and persistence of antisocial activity into adulthood and an early (preadolescent) history of socialization to aggression are critical differentiating factors. It has previously been described as alcoholism with sociopathy, alcoholism with antisocial personality, and primary sociopathy with a secondary diagnosis of alcoholism (Lewis, Rice, & Helzer, 1983; Penick et al., 1984; Stabenau, 1984; Winokur, Rimmer, & Reich, 1971). It has been documented in women (Hesselbrock et al., 1984; Martin, Cloninger, & Guze, 1984),

Table 8
The Four Alcoholisms: Some Distinguishing Characteristics

Antisocial Alcoholism	Developmentally Cumulative Alcoholism
More frequently male	Seen in both males and females but more evident in males
More frequently lower class	Not social-class specific
Early onset, with history of overt antisocial activity as well as alcohol problems	A cumulative extension of adolescent problem drinking and delinquency
Parents more frequently alcoholic or antisocial	Parents more deviant and punitive than in developmentally limited alcoholism—parents less aggressive than in antisocial alcoholism
continued social/personal and legal difficulties in adulthood	Poorer career adaptation and marriage than in developmentally limited alcoholism
Apparent heavy genetically mediated diathesis	Genetic diathesis more environmentally mediated
Early treatment entry; poor prognosis	Later treatment entry

Developmentally Limited Alcoholism	Negative Affect Alcoholism
Seen in both males and females but more evident in males	More frequently female
Not social-class specific	More frequently middle class
An extension of adolescent problem drinking	Use of alcohol for "effect" drinking to cope with or enhance relationships
Associated with separation from family of origin; association with heavy drinking by peers	Family history of unipolar affective disorder
Drops out in middle 20s with successful assumption of adult career and family roles	Experience of unsatisfying social relationships with peers, in job and/or in marriage
	Genetic diathesis associated with mood regulation
Infrequent treatment entry	Later treatment entry

but it is far more common in men. It is also far more common in lower-class individuals, where its display is not complicated by sociocultural factors that may inhibit the direct expression of aggression. This is the subtype most often being tracked in high-risk studies that use offspring of alcoholic parents. This circumstance is an artifact of the way most of these studies, including our own, recruit their respondents—through clinics or social agencies that serve a primarily blue-collar clientele. There is substantial evidence from a variety of sources that the developmental experiences of this alcoholic type, from early childhood onward, are the most pathogenic (e.g., Robins, 1966; Rydelius, 1981).

Type 2, *developmentally cumulative alcoholism*, has also been called primary alcoholism (Schuckit et al., 1969) by psychiatric investigators whose basic data source has been anamnestic material related by the symptomatic individual or a close relative at or shortly after hospitalization. It has been called primary for a number of reasons: one is that the symptomatic behavior considered primary is established—typically by the respondent's own retrospective account—to have occurred before the onset of any other psychiatric condition. In contrast, alcoholism occurring after a depressive episode would be diagnosed as secondary alcoholism. Frequently the primary versus secondary distinction is also presumed to be evidence for cause, so that in the example just given depression might be considered the cause of alcoholism if it were primary but would be considered its result if the alcoholism were primary.

The term has also been used because the case has been put forth that the developmental course of alcoholism is heavily driven by cultural and genetic factors that jointly determine onset and course and are not influenced by earlier social or learning history (Mello, 1982; Vaillant, 1980; Vaillant & Milofsky, 1982). Thus the alcoholic process is construed as a primarily biologically driven event sequence, triggered by availability of and pressure to use alcohol. Thereafter its course is seen as a physiologically driven event series. In these respects the alcoholism, as a biological disease entity, is considered the primary causative influence.

It is important to note that both these positions about "disease course" are based upon a presumption that the etiologic literature has adequately assessed the possibility of earlier developmental influences upon alcoholic outcome and found consistent evidence for no prior developmental contribution. The problem with this stance is that in a large number of longitudinal studies that purportedly deal with this issue, data have not been available until adolescence or thereafter—and thus cannot speak to this issue. In addition, where early developmental data have been available, the evidence has indicated some continuity of process (Zucker & Gomberg, 1986).

In the term developmentally cumulative alcoholism the notion of developmental cumulation implies that risk is more closely tied to normal, culturally prescribed processes of drinking and problem drinking than in antisocial alcoholism but that the additive process has, over the life course, become sufficiently cumulative so that thereafter it has a different trajectory than if it were simply regulated by normative developmental trends in the culture. In this regard it is a more severe form of alcohol problem than Type 3, developmentally limited alcoholism, but it has more benign origins (and course) than Type 1. Its occurrence cuts across social class and sex. Mortality rates should be lower than for Type 1, and onset is later (cf. Penick et al., 1984; Schuckit et al., 1969). It differs from antisocial alcoholism in adulthood in that antisocial behavior is less. It is precisely the lack of obviously disordered behavioral characteristics in adulthood that make the earlier developmental pathways more obscure. Nonetheless, based on the lack of antisocial behavior and the lack of sex differences, one would anticipate a more benign set of family experiences in childhood than is true for Type 1 alcoholics. Recent work that examines this issue in fact strongly substantiates these hypotheses (Cadoret, Troughton, & Widmer, 1984).

What then drives it, and how is it cumulative? The most plausible hypothesis is a simple one that takes account of earlier origins and of cumulation across life stages. Parent-child interactions will have been harsher than for nonalcoholic individuals, and parents, as models, will have been more deviant. In addition, the individual will have been socialized to a great degree to regard alcohol consumption as a way of coping with stress. The one additional element is that the early, poorer socialization start should result in a greater likelihood of peer, career, and marital difficulty during later life stages. When the luck of the draw leads to such poorer across-transition outcomes, then a reactive adaptation of abusive drinking has a higher probability. Should such across-transition poor adaptations snowball over several stages of adulthood, then what has begun as a reactive alcoholic process (cf. Knight, 1937; Levine & Zigler, 1981) cumulates across time in an iterative process of increasing coping difficulty and increasing life trouble. The physiological sequelae of chronic alcohol dependence clearly also potentiate the coping failures and enhance the likelihood of cumulation.

Type 3, *developmentally limited alcoholism,* has been called *frequent heavy drinking* by Howard Blane (1979). The phenomenon has also been described in general form in two of the major longitudinal investigations of drinking and problem-drinking trajectories during young adulthood (Donovan, Jessor, & Jessor, 1983; Yamaguchi & Kandel, 1984). It refers to a pattern of drinking that involves high consumption levels, that peaks in early adulthood, that is responsible—on an event rather than a person basis—for the highest age rates of alcohol problems on the developmental continuum, that is somewhat more common in men than in women, that cuts across social classes, and that for the largest proportion of affected individuals drops off by the mid-20s.

Howard Blane describes it most clearly:

> Frequent heavy drinking refers to a pattern of drinking in which relatively large amounts of alcohol are consumed per occasion and occasions are spaced relatively frequently over time. A standard technical definition is drinking five or more drinks of any alcoholic beverage at least as often as once a week. (1979, p. 8)

> Frequent heavy drinking is not chronic in the sense of being continuous nor pervasive in the sense of affecting all spheres of the individual's life. Heavy drinking may occur several times a week, and the consequences of drinking may indeed affect a person's life, but intake is episodic and occurs within a more-or-less conventionally ordered lifestyle. More critically, perhaps, alcohol is not a guiding principle in the frequent heavy drinker's life. Drinking episodes are self-limiting and circumscribed events that occur independently of other significant life events. Important for the moment, they recede into the background of one's existence as other activities come to the fore. Further, the consequences to physical health of frequent heavy drinking stem from the acute consequence of alcohol intake, such as hangovers, blackouts, and gastritis. Except for fatal overdose, . . . these are all temporary and as far as is known not ultimately hazardous to health, unless they occur in the context of heavy, almost daily intake over many years. (1979, p. 9)

He continues: these drinkers

> are a group at risk for suffering acute physical effects of alcohol, behavioral concomitants of intoxication (incoordination and disinhibition, including belligerence, crying, "silliness," raucousness, impulsive behavior, poor judgment), and negative social and interpersonal

consequences (fights, impaired driving ability, fractured relationships with friends and relatives, destruction of property, job difficulties, arrests or other involvement with police). Some of the behaviors enumerated are identical to behaviors that contribute to a diagnosis of alcoholism, particularly those in the area of social and interpersonal consequences. Given this partial coincidence of acute and chronic behavioral signs, it becomes only too easy to confound them in attempting to distinguish alcoholics from frequent heavy drinkers who are not alcoholic. (1979, p. 10)

However,

In alcoholism, many problems and adverse consequences of drinking manifest for long periods of time are concentrated in a single individual; that is, the alcoholic shows many of the psychological, physical, and social concomitants of alcoholism. The young frequent heavy drinker, on the other hand, consistently shows one or a few adverse consequences, but typically a great many signs, each persisting over time, do not cluster in a single individual. (1979, p. 10)

Blane does not deal with what drives these individuals into this adaptation or with what leads to a decrease in the problems in the middle 20s. These issues have been more carefully explored in the Colorado and New York studies. Richard Jessor (1985) documents the developmental changes toward increased conventionality and intolerance for deviance that occur during this age stage. He notes that "development, at least in the mid- and later twenties, appears to be in the direction of greater personality, perceived environment, and behavioral conventionality. That direction may well follow from the assumption of new life roles in work and family and the occupancy of new social contexts other than that of school, both factors constituting conventionalizing influences" (p. 131). What is significant here is that a decrease in conventionality and an increase in tolerance for deviance and rebelliousness have already been documented as factors that presage problem drinking in adolescence. Conversely, the Colorado work notes that a reversal in these factors in the middle 20s appears to be connected to drawing these rates down. In the language of our developmental model, across-stage life demands presage the onset of a *developmental discontinuity* in abusive drinking behavior.

Type 4, *negative affect alcoholism*, is in some ways both the most and the least well documented of these etiologic types. Identified in the psychiatric literature as far back as 1966 (Pitts & Winokur, 1966), it has since been closely tied to alcoholic symptomatology in women (Cadoret, 1981; Schuckit et al., 1969; Wilsnack, Wilsnack, & Klassen, 1987; Winokur et al., 1971). Within this literature it has been termed *affective disorder alcoholism* as well as primary affective disorder (with secondary alcoholism), and it has been significantly linked to a family history of unipolar affective disorder and to higher suicidal risk among those afflicted.

The heavily inpatient nature of the samples studied so far has contributed to difficulties in understanding the unbiased population etiology of this type. For one thing, as I have already noted, psychiatric inpatients are more likely to be of lower social status and also to reflect a subset of the disorder that is at the extreme of the continuum. Anamnestic history taking in these settings is likely to be both inaccurate and developmentally incomplete given the typically heavy medical interests of the investigatory teams. Nonetheless, where there has been an attempt to explore the significance of such factors (e.g., Schuckit & Winokur, 1972), women with affective disorder were likely to have more benign social histories and on follow-up from hospitalization were found to make better and quicker recoveries.

Although the hospital studies are often difficult to interpret for these reasons, signs of negative affect—that is, anxiety and feelings of alienation, hostility, and criticality—have appeared as precursive elements especially in studies involving middle-class subjects and noninstitutionalized populations. It is noteworthy that in the follow-up to the College Drinking Study (Fillmore et al., 1979) a cluster of drinking for "feeling adjustment" during the college years (drinking to be less shy, to aid in forgetting disappointments) was discovered to be a significant predictor of later problem alcohol use among women in midlife. Such a cluster can be interpreted in motivational terms concerned with the relief of negative affect. In a set of studies of middle-class males, Williams (1966, 1968) found that higher initial levels of anxiety and depression and lower levels of self-esteem were associated with greater alcohol consumption and with more problem-drinking signs, again with a sample of college students. In still another longitudinal study of middle-class women—the Oakland Growth Study (Jones, 1971)—the data show that a depressive adaptation during the high-school years, marked by a family history of conflict and by having a "sour and disagreeable mother," is associated with problem drinking in adulthood.

These findings are incomplete and are frequently based on few respondents. What is impressive, however, is the degree to which negative affect phenomena appear to be implicated in the etiologic of alcoholism process when respondents are female or middle class. Although there is much to be done to fill in the etiologic chain— especially as it relates to early social history—a burgeoning developmental literature on parent behaviors and child-rearing practices in depressive homes suggests that a linkage may be discovered between the social deprivation occurring in such households and greater vulnerability to interpersonal stress and to problem use of alcohol in adulthood (Cytryn et al., 1984; Hirsch, Moos, & Reischl, 1985; Weissman, Paykel, & Klerman, 1972). This would be especially true when the depressive household has at least one adult family member who uses alcohol excessively and thus provides a role model for eventual emulation. Research is needed on these issues.

What has been presented here is a hypothesis—that alcoholism in the singular is no longer an appropriate conceptualization for several sets of phenomena that have different origins and different patterns of development. What these different patterns share is simply that when they present overtly as symptomatic displays, their phenotypic manifestations have the use of alcohol as a common element.

The evidence pieced together in the previous section to justify this schema is obviously incomplete. To truly specify the etiologies is to thoroughly describe the mosaic pattern within the etiologic grid for each type. Such a task is much too lengthy to pursue here, and some of the evidence does not yet exist. Clearly, the biological side of the grid deserves considerably more attention than space allows here. The way cumulations and discontinuities occur in later adulthood also has been only minimally addressed. Nonetheless, there are data sets currently available that begin to address differences among types. One such is Joan McCord's (1981) careful paper on alcoholism and criminality. Based on follow-up data from the Cambridge-Somerville Youth Study, the data set has the special advantage that it was an initially community based sample rather than a clinical sample, and it was homogeneous for social class and gender.

Thus the unknown selectivity and restrictiveness of clinical sampling is avoided and the confounding effects of gender mixture and differences in social class, with their associated differences in hardship and differential access to the opportunity structure, are controlled. Table 9 presents my reanalysis of these data, to highlight differences between antisocial and developmentally cumulative alcoholism (Table 9).

The results between the groups perfectly fit the hypothesized structure of differences in childhood and adult functioning. Antisocial alcoholics are more externalizing as children and have a less benign childhood environment. In adulthood they have more relational difficulties, expressed both in jobs and in married life (Table 9). And though far fewer differences exist between developmentally cumulative alcoholism and no alcoholism, other of McCord's findings also are consistent with the hypothesized structure, of a more troubled early environment and adolescence (greater aggressiveness) among the alcoholic but not antisocial group.

Table 9
Characteristics That Distinguish Developmentally
Cumulative Alcoholism From Antisocial Alcoholism
in Men with Lower Social Status (%)

Characteristics	Developmentally Cumulative Alcoholism ($N=30$)	Antisocial Alcoholism ($N=40$)	pa
Childhood characteristics			
Shyness	30	10	< .02
Resentment of authority	10	35	< .02
Childhood environment			
Parental affection	67	40	< .10
Supervision after school	63	38	< .10
High parental expectations	30	10	< .02
Self-confident mother	41	11	< .02
Aggressive parent	7	43	< .02
Adult characteristics			
Married	53	31	< .10
White-collar worker	37	18	< .02

Source: Data reanalyzed from McCord (1981). Figures reproduced with permission of the author and publisher. Copyright 1981 by Alcohol Research Documentation.

Note. Developmentally cumulative alcoholism is what McCord calls noncriminal alcoholism; antisocial alcoholism is what McCord calls criminal alcoholism.

aBased on Fisher exact tests (two-tailed).

The reader will note the lack of previous reference to that pioneering typologist E. M. Jellinek, who took great pains to delineate the multiple kinds of alcoholisms in his classic work *The Disease Concept of Alcoholism* (1960). A considerably more extensive review of the multiple alcoholism hypothesis that is planned will take careful account of Jellinek's work. But for the moment I simply note that Jellinek's main focus was drinking-specific behavior and its unfolding, not the interplay of drinking- and non-drinking-specific factors in their developmental context. In those regards, his developmental perspective reflected a narrower conception of the risk grid and a less well articulated conception of the interplay of life stages and drinking events than is true of the present exposition.

Even without considering Jellinek, the broad hypothesis being advanced here is not a new one (Barbor & Lauerman, 1986). But neither has it been the primary hypothesis of the field. The assembled data and the theoretical rationale presented now make the case that it is time to regard it as such. To borrow from a neighboring field, schizophrenia research, the challenge now is to study and understand and seek to prevent and treat the group of alcoholisms, because there is no single one.

The evidence presented also has argued the case that these different alcoholisms are best regarded as problems that display in a matrix, one that is limited or encouraged by the major parameters of the culture and the individual's biological apparatus. Within these limits, the process of becoming alcoholic or not, or changing from that adaptation after having entered it, is conceived to be a summative result of events that cumulate or subtract across life stages. The work of effectively charting these events and understanding how best to proceed in treatment must therefore be set in a life-grid perspective and be able to differentiate among the phenotypic displays of "alcoholism" that in fact reflect different courses. This perspective has major implications for the assessment of alcoholic functioning when the individual presents at the start of the intervention process. It also has equally major implications for the evaluation of prognosis and for the design of treatment plans. It requires that treatment personnel look more closely at history as well as at the current stimulus events that produced the existing symptoms. A good treatment plan must take account of the alcoholic trouble in a life context in order to appropriately understand what trajectory the intervention is attempting to change.

The limitations of space require that this chapter only present a sample of the evidence and begin tracing out implications rather than describing them in exhaustive detail.[6] It remains for another publication to complete that work. Nonetheless, the material discussed here represents a necessary first step in that process.

REFERENCES

Abel, E. L. (1981). Behavioral teratology of alcohol. *Psychological Bulletin, 90,* 564–581.

Alexander, C. N., & Campbell, E. Q. (1967). Peer influences on adolescent drinking. *Quarterly Journal of Studies on Alcohol, 28,* 444–453.

Arend, R., Gove, F. L., & Sroufe, L. A. (1979). Continuity of individual adaptation from infancy to kindergarten: A predictive study of ego-resiliency and curiosity in preschoolers. *Child Development, 50,* 950–959.

Barbor, T. F., & Lauerman, R. J. (1986). Classification and forms of inebriety: Historical antecedents of alcoholic typologies. In M. Galanter (Ed.), *Recent developments in alcoholism* (Vol. 4, pp. 113–144). New York: Plenum.

Baxter-Hagaman, J. A. (1986). *Young alcoholic families and the transmission of risk: Environmental and family interaction differences from the MSU Longitudinal Study.* East Lansing, MI: Unpublished doctoral dissertation, Department of Psychology, Michigan State University.

Begleiter, H., Porjesz, B., Bihari, B., & Kissin, B. (1984). Event-related brain potentials in boys at risk for alcoholism. *Science, 225,* 1493–1496.

Benjamin, L. S. (1984). Principles of prediction using structural analysis of social behavior. In R. A. Zucker, J. Aronoff, & A. I. Rabin (Eds.), *Personality and the prediction of behavior* (pp. 121–174). Orlando, FL: Academic Press.

Berry, J. C. (1967). *Antecedents of schizophrenia, impulsive character and alcoholism in males.* Unpublished Ph.D. dissertation, Teachers College, Columbia University.

Blane, H. T. (1979). Middle-aged alcoholics and young drinkers. In H. T. Blane & M. E. Chafetz (Eds.), *Youth, alcohol and social policy.* New York: Plenum.

Block, J. (1971). *Lives through time.* Berkeley, CA: Bancroft Books.

Boyd, J. H., Burke, J. D., Jr., Gruenberg, E., Holzer, C. E., III, Rae, D. S., George, L. K., Karno, M., Stoltzman, R., McEvoy, L., & Nestadt, G. (1984). Exclusion criteria of DSM-III: A study of co-occurrence of hierarchy-free syndromes. *Archives of General Psychiatry, 41,* 983–989.

---

6. Also missing here is any discussion of the ways alcoholic drug involvement, at different life stages, interfaces with other types of drug use and abuse. Charting such processes is also exceptionally important but is beyond the scope of this chapter.

Cadoret, R. J. (1981). Depression and alcoholism. In R. E. Meyer et al. (Eds.), *Evaluation of the alcoholic: Implications for research, theory and treatment* (pp. 59–66). National Institute on Alcohol Abuse and Alcoholism, Research Monograph No. 5. (DHHS Publication No. [ADM] 81-1033). Rockville, MD: U.S. Department of Health and Human Services.

Cadoret, R. J., Troughton, E., & Widmer, R. (1984). Clinical differences between antisocial and primary alcoholics. *Comprehensive Psychiatry, 25,* 1–8.

Cahalan, D. (1970). *Problem drinkers.* San Francisco: Jossey-Bass.

Cahalan, D., & Cisin, I. H. (1976). Drinking behavior and drinking problems in the United States. In B. Kissin & Begleiter (Eds.), *The biology of alcoholism: Vol. 4. Social aspects of alcoholism.* New York: Plenum.

Cahalan, D., Cisin, I., & Crossley, H. (1969). *American drinking practices: A national study of drinking behavior and attitudes.* New Brunswick, NJ: Publications Division, Rutgers Center of Alcohol Studies.

Cantwell, D. P. (1972). Psychiatric illness in the families of hyperactive children. *Archives of General Psychiatry, 70,* 414–417.

Caspi, A. (1986). *Moving against and moving away: Life course continuities in explosive and withdrawn behaviors.* Unpublished doctoral dissertation, Department of Human Development and Family Studies, Cornell University.

Cermak, T. L. (1984). Children of alcoholics and the case for a new diagnostic category of codependency. *Alcohol Health and Research World,* pp. 38–42.

Clarren, S. K., & Smith, D. W. (1978). The fetal alcohol syndrome. *New England Journal of Medicine, 298,* 1063–1067.

Cotton, N. (1979). The familial incidence of alcoholism: A review. *Journal of Studies on Alcohol, 49,* 89–116.

Cytryn, L., McKnew, D., Zahn-Waxler, C, Radke-Yarrow, M., Gaensbauer, T., Harmon, R., & Lamour, M. (1984). A developmental view of affective disturbances in the children of affectively ill parents. *American Journal of Psychiatry, 141,* 219–222.

Deutsch, C., DiCicco, L., & Mills, D. J. (1982). Services for children of alcoholic parents. In National Institute on Alcohol Abuse & Alcoholism (Ed.), *Prevention, intervention and treatment: Concerns and models.* Alcohol and Health Monographs No. 3. Washington DC: Author.

Donovan, J. E., & Jessor, R. (1985). Structure of problem behavior in adolescence and young adulthood. *Journal of Consulting and Clinical Psychology, 53* (6), 890–904.

Donovan J. E., Jessor, R., & Jessor, L. (1983). Problem drinking in adolescence and young adulthood: A followup study. *Journal of Studies on Alcohol, 44,* 109–137.

Dunn, L. M., & Dunn, L. M. (1981). *Peabody Picture Vocabulary Test—Revised.* Circle Pines, MN: American Guidance Service.

Elder, G. H., Jr., (Ed.). (1984). *Life course dynamics: From 1968 to 1980.* Ithaca, NY: Cornell University Press.

Elliott, D. S., & Huizinga, D. (1983). Social class and delinquent behavior in a national youth panel: 1976–1980. *Criminology, 21* (2), 149–177.

Engel, G. L. (1977). The need for a new medical model: A challenge to biomedicine. *Science, 196,* 129–136.

Ervin, C. S., Little, R. S., Streissguth, A. P., & Beck, D. E. (1984). Alcoholic fathering and its relation to child's intellectual functioning: A pilot investigation. *Alcoholism: Clinical and Experimental Research, 8,* 362–365.

Featherman, D. L., & Stevens, G. (1980). *A revised socioeconomic index of occupational status.* Center for Demography and Ecology Working Paper No. 79–148. Madison: University of Wisconsin.

Feighner, J. P., Robins, E., Guze, S., Woodruff, R. A., Winokur, G., & Munoz, R. (1972). Diagnostic criterion for use in psychiatric research. *Archives of General Psychiatry, 26,* 57–63.

Fillmore, K. M. (1984). When angels fall . . . : Women's drinking as a cultural preoccupation and as a reality. In S. Wilsnack & L. Beckman (Eds.), *Alcohol problems in women* (pp. 7–36). New York: Guilford.

Fillmore, K. M., Bacon, S. D., & Hyman, M. (1979). *The 27 year longitudinal panel study of drinking by students in college, 1949–1976.* Final report to the National Institute on Alcohol Abuse and Alcoholism under Contract No. (ADM) 281-76-0015. Berkeley: Social Research Group, University of California.

Gabrielli, W. F., & Mednick, S. A. (1983). Intellectual performance in children of alcoholics. *Journal of Nervous and Mental Disease, 171,* 444–447.

Gabrielli, W. F., Mednick, S. A., Volavka, J., Pollack, V. E., Schulsinger, F., & Itil, N. (1982). Electroencephalograms in children of alcoholic fathers. *Psychophysiology, 19,* 404–407.

Garbarino, J. R., & Sherman, D. (1980). High-risk neighborhoods and high-risk families: The human ecology of child maltreatment. *Child Development, 51,* 188–198.

Garmezy, N. (1981). Children under stress: Perspectives on antecedents and correlates of vulnerability and resistance to psychopathology. In A. I. Rabin, J. Aronoff, A. M. Barclay, & R. A. Zucker (Eds.), *Longitudinal research in alcoholism.* Boston: Kluwer-Nijoff.

Glatt, M. M. (1961). Drinking habits of English (middle-class) alcoholics. *Acta Psychiatrica Scandiavica, 37,* 88–113.

Goodwin, D. (1979). Alcoholism and heredity. *Archives of General Psychiatry, 36,* 57–61.

Goodwin, D. W, Crane, J. B., & Guze, S. B. (1971). Felons who drink: An eight-year follow-up. *Quarterly Journal of Studies on Alcohol, 32,* 136–147.

Greenberg, G. S., Zucker, R. A., & Noll, R. B. (1985, August). The development of cognitive structures about alcoholic beverages among preschoolers. Paper presented at the American Psychological Association meetings, Los Angeles, CA.

Hans, S., & Marcus, J. (1984, October). A process model for the development of schizophrenia. Paper presented at the meetings of the Society for Life History Research in Psychopathology, Baltimore, MD.

Hegedus, A. M., Alterman, A. I., & Tarter, R. E. (1984). Learning achievement in sons of alcoholics. *Alcoholism: Clinical and Experimental Research, 8,* 330–333.

Herjanic, B. M., Herjanic, M., Penick, E. C., Tomelleri, C., & Armbruster, R. B. S. (1977). Children of alcoholics. In F. A. Sexias (Ed.), *Currents in alcoholism* (Vol. 2, pp. 445–455). New York: Grune and Stratton.

Hesselbrock, M. N., Hesselbrock, V. M., Babor, T. F., Stabenau, J. R., Meyer, R. E., & Weidenman, M. (1984). Antisocial behavior, psychopathology, and problem drinking in the natural history of alcoholism. In D. W. Goodwin, K. T. VanDusen, & S. A. Mednick (Eds.), *Longitudinal research in alcoholism,* (pp. 197–214). Boston: Kluwer-Nijhoff.

Hesselbrock, V. M., Stabenau, J. R., & Hesselbrock, M. N. (1985). Minimal brain dysfunction and neuropsychological test performance in offspring of alcoholics. In M. Galanter (Ed.), *Recent developments in alcoholism* (Vol. 3, pp. 65–82). New York: Plenum.

Hirsch, B. J., Moos, R. H., & Reischl, T. M. (1985). Psychosocial adjustment of adolescent children of a depressed, arthritic, or normal parent. *Journal of Abnormal Psychology, 94,* 154–164.

Huesmann, L. R., Eron, L. D., Lefkowitz, M. M., & Walder, L. O. (1984). Stability of aggression over time and generations. *Developmental Psychology, 20,* 1120—1134.

Jellinek, E. M. (1960). *The disease concept of alcoholism.* New Haven: Hillhouse Press.

Jessor, R. (1985). Adolescent problem drinking: Psychosocial aspects and developmental outcomes. In L. H. Towle (Ed.), *Proceedings: NIAAA-WHO Collaborating Center designation meeting & alcohol research seminar.* DHHS Publication No. (ADM) 85-2370. Washington, DC: U.S. Government Printing Office.

Jessor, R., & Jessor, S. L. (1977). *Problem behavior and psychosocial development: A longitudinal study of youth.* New York: Academic.

Jones, M. C. (1968). Personality correlates and antecedents of drinking patterns in adult males. *Journal of Consulting and Clinical Psychology, 32,* 2–12.

Jones, M. C. (1971).Personality antecedents and correlates of drinking patterns in women. *Journal of Consulting and Clinical Psychology, 36,* 61–69.

78

Kandel, D. B., & Davies, M. (1986). Adult sequelae of adolescent depressive symptoms. *Archives of General Psychiatry, 43,* 255–262.

Kandel, D. B., Kessler, R. C., & Margulies, R. Z. (1978). Antecedents of adolescent initiation into stages of drug use: A development analysis. In D. B. Kandel (Ed.), *Longitudinal research on drug use: Empirical findings and methodological issues* (pp. 73–99). Washington, DC: Hemisphere.

Kaplan, H. B., & Pokorny, A. D. (1978). Alcohol use and self-enhancement among adolescents: A conditional relationship. In F. Seixas (Ed.), *Currents in alcoholism: Vol. 4. Psychiatric, psychological, social and epidemiological studies* (pp. 51–75). New York: Grune and Stratton.

Knight, R. P. (1937). The psychodynamics of chronic alcoholics. *Journal of Nervous and Mental Disease, 86,* 538–543.

Knop, J., Goodwin, D. W., Teasdale, T. W., Mikkelsen, U., & Schulsinger, F. (1984). A Danish prospective study of young males at high risk for alcoholism. In D. W. Goodwin, K. T. Van Dusen, & S. A. Mednick (Eds.), *Longitudinal research in alcoholism.* Boston: Kluwer-Nijhoff.

Knop, J., Teasdale, J. W., Schulsinger, F., & Goodwin, D. W. (1985). A prospective study of young men at high risk for alcoholism: School behavior and achievement. *Journal of Studies on Alcohol, 46,* 273–278.

Levine, J., & Zigler, E. (1981). The developmental approach to alcoholism: A further investigation. *Addictive Behaviors, 6,* 93–98.

Lewis, C. E., Rice, J., & Helzer, J. E. (1983). Diagnostic interactions: Alcoholism and antisocial personality. *Journal of Nervous and Mental Disease, 171* (2), 105–113.

Loeber, R. (1985). Patterns and development of antisocial child behavior. In G. J. Whitehurst (Ed.), *Annals of child development* (Vol. 2, pp. 77–116). Greenwich, CT: JAI Press.

Loeber, R. (1986). The natural histories of juvenile conduct problems, substance use, and delinquency: Evidence for developmental progressions. Unpublished paper, University of Pittsburgh, Western Psychiatric Institute and Clinic.

Maddox, G. L., & McCall, B. C. (1964). *Drinking among teenagers.* New Brunswick, NJ: Rutgers Center of Alcohol Studies.

Martin, R. L., Cloninger, C. R., & Guze, S. B. (1984). The longitudinal course of alcoholism among women criminals: A six-year follow-up. In D. W. Goodwin, K. T. VanDusen, & S. A. Mednick (Eds.), *Longitudinal research in alcoholism* (pp. 39–52). Boston: Kluwer-Nijhoff.

McCord, J. (1981). Alcoholism and criminality: Confounding and differentiating factors. *Journal of Studies on Alcohol, 42* (9), 739–748.

McCord, W., & McCord, J. (1960). *Origins of alcoholism.* Stanford: Stanford University Press.

McCord, W., & McCord, J. (1962). A longitudinal study of the personality of alcoholics. In D. J. Pittman and C. R. Snyder (Eds.), *Society, culture, and drinking patterns*. New York: John Wiley.

McCord, J. (1984). Drunken drivers in longitudinal perspective. *Journal of Studies on Alcohol, 45,* 316–320.

Mello, N. (1982). An examination of some etiological theories of alcoholism. *Academic Psychology Bulletin, 4,* 467–474.

Monnelly, E. P., Hartl, E. M., & Elderkin, R. (1983). Constitutional factors predictive of alcoholism in a follow-up of delinquent boys. *Journal of Studies on Alcohol, 44,* 530–537.

Moos, R. H., Finney, J. W., & Chan, D. A. (1981). The process of recovery from alcoholism: Comparing alcoholic patients and matched community controls. *Journal of Studies on Alcohol, 42,* 383–402.

Morehouse, E. R., & Richards, T. (1982). An examination of dysfunctional latency age children of alcoholic parents and problems in intervention. *Journal of Children in Contemporary Society, 15,* 21–33.

Morrison, J. R., & Stewart, M. A. (1973). The psychiatric status of the legal families of adopted hyperactive children. *Archives of General Psychiatry, 28,* 888–891.

Myers, J. K., Weissman, M. M., Tischler, G. L., Holzer, C. E., III, Leaf, P. J., Orvaschel, H., Anthony, J. C., Boyd, J. H., Burke, J. D., Jr., Kramer, M., & Stoltzman, R. (1984). Six-month prevalence of psychiatric disorders in three communities: 1980–1982. *Archives of General Psychiatry, 41,* 959–967.

Noll, R. B. (1983). *Young male offspring of alcoholic fathers: Early developmental differences from the MSU Vulnerability Study.* Unpublished doctoral dissertation, Department of Psychology, Michigan State University, East Lansing.

Noll, R. B., & Zucker, R. A. (1983, August). *Developmental findings from an alcoholic vulnerability study.* Paper presented at the annual meeting of the American Psychological Association, Anaheim, CA.

Nowlis, V. (1953). The development and modification of motivational systems in personality. In Psychology Department, University of Nebraska (Ed.), *Current theory and research in motivation* (pp. 114–138). Lincoln: University of Nebraska Press.

O'Gorman, P. O., & Ross, R. A. (1984). Children of alcoholics in the juvenile justice system. *Alcoholic Health and Research World,* 43–45.

Ojesjo, L., Hagnell, O., & Lanke, J. (1983). Class variations in the incidence of alcoholism in the Lundby Study, Sweden. *Social Psychiatry, 18,* 123–128.

Paolino, T. J., Jr., & McCrady, B. S. (1977). *The alcoholic marriage: Alternative perspectives.* New York: Grune and Stratton.

Park, P. (1973). Developmental ordering of experiences in alcoholism.

Quarterly Journal of Studies on Alcohol, 34, 473–488.

Patterson, G. R. (1982). *Coercive family process.* Eugene, OR: Castalia.

Patterson, G. R., & Bank, L. (in press). Bootstrapping your way in the nomological thicket. *Behavioral Assessment.*

Penick, E. C., Powell, B. J., Othmer, E., Bingham, S. F., Rice, A. S., & Liese, B. S. (1984). Subtyping alcoholics by coexisting psychiatry syndromes: Course, family history, outcome. In D. W. Goodwin, K. T. VanDusen, & S. A. Mednick (Eds.), *Longitudinal research in alcoholism* (pp. 167–196). Boston: Kluwer-Nijhoff.

Pitts, F. N., & Winokur, G. (1966). Affective disorder. VII: Alcoholism and affective disorder. *Journal of Psychiatric Research, 4,* 37–50.

Pollock, V. E., Volavka, J., Mednick, S. A., Goodwin, D., Knop, J., & Schulsinger, F. (1984). A prospective study of alcoholism: Electroencephalographic findings. In D. W. Goodwin, K. T. VanDusen, & S. A. Mednick (Eds.), *Longitudinal research in alcoholism* (pp. 125–145). Boston: Kluwer-Nijhoff.

Psychology Department, University of Nebraska. (1953). *Current theory and research in motivation.* Lincoln: University of Nebraska Press.

Richman, N., Stevenson, J., & Graham, P. J. (1982). *Preschool to school: A behavioral study.* London: Academic.

Ricks, D., & Berry, J. C. (1970). Family and symptom patterns that precede schizophrenia. In M. Roff & D. F. Ricks (Eds.), *Life history research in psychopathology.* Minneapolis: University of Minnesota Press.

Robins, L. N. (1966). *Deviant children grown up.* Baltimore: Williams and Wilkins.

Robins, L. N. (1978). Sturdy childhood predictors of adult antisocial behavior: Replications from longitudinal studies. *Psychological Medicine, 8,* 611–622.

Robins, L. N., Bates, W. N., & O'Neal, P. (1962). Adult drinking patterns of former problem children. In D. Pittman & C. R. Snyder (Eds.), *Society, culture, and drinking patterns.* New York: John Wiley.

Robins, L. N., Helzer, J. H., Croughan, J., & Ratcliff, K. S. (1981). The NIMH diagnostic interview schedule: Its history, characteristics, and validity. *Archives of General Psychiatry, 38,* 381–389.

Robins, L. N., Helzer, J. E., Weissman, M. M., Orvaschel, H., Gruenberg, E., Burke, J. D., Jr., & Reiger, D. A. (1984). Lifetime prevalence of specific psychiatric disorders in three sites. *Archives of General Psychiatry, 41,* 949–958.

Roizen, R., Cahalan, D., & Shanks, P. (1978). "Spontaneous remission" among untreated problem drinkers. In D. B. Kandel (Ed.), *Longitudinal research on drug use: Empirical findings and methodological issues* (pp. 197–221). New York: John Wiley.

Rosenberg, C. M. (1969). Young alcoholics. *British Journal of Psychiatry, 115,* 181–188.

Russell, M., Henderson, C., & Blume, S. B. (1985). *Children of alcoholics: A review of the literature.* New York: Children of Alcoholics Foundation.

Rydelius, P. A. (1981). Children of alcoholic fathers: Their social adjustment and their health status over 20 years. *Acta Paediatrica Scandinavica, 286,* 1–83.

Rydelius, P. A. (1983). Alcohol-abusing teenage boys. *Acta Psychiatrica Scandinavia, 68,* 381–385.

Sameroff, A. (1975). Transactional models in early social relations. *Human Development, 18,* 65–79.

Schlesselman, H. (1982). *Case control studies.* New York: Oxford University Press.

Schuckit, M. A., Pitts, F. N., Reich, T., King, L. J., & Winokur, G. (1969). Alcoholism. I: Two types of alcoholism in women. *Archives of General Psychiatry, 20,* 301–306.

Schuckit, M. A., & Winokur, G. (1972). A short term follow up of women alcoholics. Diseases of the Nervous System, 33, 672–678.

Selzer, M. (1975). A self-administered Short Michigan Alcoholism Screening Test (SMAST). *Journal of Studies on Alcohol, 36,* 117–126.

Sheldon, W. H. (1949). *Varieties of delinquent youth: An introduction to constitutional psychiatry.* New York: Harper and Row.

Spitzer, R., Endicott, J., & Robins, E. (1975). Clinical criteria for psychiatric diagnosis and DSM-III. *American Journal of Psychiatry, 132,* 1187–1192.

Stabenau, J. R. (1984). Implications of family history of alcoholism, antisocial personality, and sex differences in alcohol dependence. *American Journal of Psychiatry, 141* (10), 1178–1183.

Tarter, R. E., Alterman, A. I., & Edwards, K. L. (1985). The vulnerability to alcoholism in men: A behavior-genetic perspective. *Journal of Studies on Alcohol, 46,* 329–356.

Tarter, R. E., Hegedus, M. P. A., & Gavaler, B. S. (1985). Hyperactivity in sons of alcoholics. *Journal of Studies on Alcohol, 46,* 259–261.

Tarter, R. E., Hegedus, A. M., Goldstein, G., Shelly, C., & Alterman, A. I. (1984). Adolescent sons of alcoholics: Neuropsychological and personality characteristics. *Alcoholism: Clinical and Experimental Research, 8,* 216–222.

Temple, M. T., & Fillmore, K. M. (1986). The variability of drinking patterns and problems among young men, age 16–31: A longitudinal study. *International Journal of the Addictions, 20* (11–12), 1595–1620.

Trice, H. M., & Wahl, J. R. (1958). A rank order analysis of the symptoms of alcoholism. *Quarterly Journal of Studies on Alcohol, 19,* 636–648.

Ullman, A. D. (1953). The first drinking experience of addictive and of "normal" drinkers. *Quarterly Journal of Studies on Alcohol, 14*, 181–191.

Ullman, A. D. (1957). Sex differences in the first drinking experience. *Quarterly Journal of Studies on Alcohol, 18*, 229–239.

Ullman, A. D. (1962). First drinking experience as related to age and sex. In D. J. Pittman & C. R. Snyder (Eds.), *Society, culture, and drinking patterns* (pp. 259–269). New York: John Wiley.

U.S. Department of Health, Education, and Welfare. (1978). *Third special report to the U.S. Congress on alcohol and health.* Washington, DC: Author.

Vaillant, G. E. (1980). Natural history of male psychological health. VIII: Antecedents of alcoholism and "orality." *American Journal of Psychiatry, 137*, 181–186.

Vaillant, G. E. (1983). *The natural history of alcoholism.* Cambridge: Harvard University Press.

Vaillant, G. E., & Milofsky, E. S. (1982). The etiology of alcoholism: A prospective viewpoint. *American Psychologist, 37*, 494–503.

Weissman, M. M., Paykel, E. S., & Klerman, G. L. (1972). The depressed woman as a mother. *Social Psychiatry, 7*, 98–108.

Williams, A. F. (1966). Social drinking, anxiety, and depression. *Journal of Personality and Social Psychology, 3*, 689.

Williams, A. F. (1968). Psychological needs and social drinking among college students. *Quarterly Journal of Studies on Alcohol, 29*, 355.

Wilsnack, R. W., & Cheloha, R. (1985, August). *Women's roles and problem drinking across the lifespan.* Paper presented at the Annual Meeting of the Society for the Study of Social Problems, Washington, DC.

Wilsnack, R. W., Klassen, A. D., & Wilsnack, S. C. (1986). Retrospective analysis of lifetime changes in women's drinking behavior. *Advances in Alcohol and Substance Abuse, 5* (3), 9–28.

Wilsnack, R. W., Wilsnack, S. C., & Klassen, A. D. (1984). Women's drinking and drinking problems: Patterns from a 1981 national survey. *American Journal of Public Health, 74*, 1231–1238.

Wilsnack, S. C., Wilsnack, R. W., & Klassen, A. D. (1987). Antecedents and consequences of drinking and drinking problems in women: Patterns from a U.S. National Survey. In P. C. Rivers (Ed.), *Alcohol and addictive behavior.* Nebraska Symposium on Motivation, Vol. 34. Lincoln: University of Nebraska Press.

Winokur, G., Rimmer, J., & Reich, T. (1971). Alcoholism IV: Is there more than one type of alcoholism? *British Journal of Psychiatry, 118*, 525–531.

Yamaguchi, K., & Kandel, D. B. (1984). Patterns of drug use from adolescence to adulthood. III: Predictors of progression. *American Journal of Public Health, 74*, 673–681.

Zucker, R. A. (1979). Developmental aspects of drinking through the young adult years. In H. T. Blane & M. E. Chafetz (Eds.), *Youth, alcohol and social policy* (pp. 91–146). New York: Plenum.

Zucker, R. A., & Barron, F. H. (1973). Parental behaviors associated with problem drinking and antisocial behavior among adolescent males. In M. E. Chafetz (Ed.), *Research on alcoholism: Vol. 1. Clinical problems and special populations* (pp. 276–296). Washington, DC: Department of Health, Education, and Welfare. DHEW Publication (NIH) 74–675.

Zucker, R. A., Baxter, J. A., Noll, R. B., Theado, D. T., & Weil, C. M. (1982, August). *An alcoholic risk study: Design and early health related findings.* Paper presented at the American Psychological Association Meetings, Washington, DC.

Zucker, R. A., & Devoe, C. I. (1974). Life history characteristics associated with problem drinking and antisocial behavior in adolescent girls: A comparison with male findings. In R. D. Wirt, G. Winokur, & M. Roff (Eds.), *Life history research in psychopathology* (Vol. 4, pp. 109–135). Minneapolis: University of Minnesota Press.

Zucker, R. A., & Fillmore, K. M. (1968, September). *Motivational factors and problem drinking among adolescents.* Paper presented at the 28th International Congress on Alcohol and Alcoholism, Washington, DC.

Zucker, R. A., & Gomberg, E. S. L. (1986). Etiology of alcoholism reconsidered: The case for a biopsychosocial proces. *American Psychologist, 41,* 783–793.

Zucker, R. A., Noll, R. B., Draznin, T. H., Baxter, J. A., Weil, C. M., Theado, D. P., Greenberg, G. S., Charlot, C., & Reider, E. (1984, April). *The ecology of alcoholic families: Conceptual framework for the Michigan State University longitudinal study.* Paper presented at the National Council on Alcoholism, National Alcoholism Forum Meetings, Detroit, MI.

Zucker, R. A., Weil, C. W., Baxter, J. A., & Noll, R. B. (1984, October). *Differences in interpersonal and individual psychopathology in young families at high risk for the development of alcoholism.* Paper presented at the Society of Life History Research in Psychopathology Meetings, Johns Hopkins University, Baltimore, MD.

Antecedents and Consequences of Drinking and Drinking Problems in Women: Patterns from a U.S. National Survey[1]

Richard W. Wilsnack, Sharon C. Wilsnack, and Albert D. Klassen

University of North Dakota

*U*ntil recently, nearly all research on alcohol use and abuse either focused exclusively on men or made no distinction between men's and women's drinking. In the English-language research literature published between 1929 and 1970, Sandmaier (1980) found only 28 studies of alcoholic women. Researchers may have neglected the study of alcohol problems in women partly because fewer women alcoholics than men alcoholics were hospitalized in most clinical research settings (e.g., VA or state hospitals), and thus women were less accessible as research subjects. Furthermore, evidence suggesting higher rates of alcoholism in men than in women, and the potential effects of drinking problems on male employment and crime, may have led earlier generations of researchers to view men's drinking as more socially significant and more in need of study. That most alcohol researchers were male may also have contributed to the relative lack of interest in special characteristics or needs of female problem drinkers and alcoholics (Vannicelli, 1984).

During the past decade, both research on and public awareness of alcohol problems in women have increased dramatically. One major reason for increased attention is that the women's movement of the 1960s and 1970s made the public more aware of a broad range of issues related to women. Women's drinking has gained attention

1. The research reported here was supported by Research Grant No. R01 AA04610 from the National Institute on Alcohol Abuse and Alcoholism. We are grateful to the staff of the National Opinion Research Center, which carried out the survey fieldwork, and to Brett Schur for invaluable computer programming assistance.

also because of widespread publicity since 1973 about the fetal alcohol syndrome (Jones, Smith, Ulleland, & Streissguth, 1973; Landesman-Dwyer, 1982). In addition, the changing social roles of women have led some researchers and laypeople to voice concerns that increased vulnerability to traditionally masculine problems—including alcoholism—might be a "price" of women's liberation (Fillmore, 1984; Wilsnack, 1976). Responding to public concern about the "women's alcohol problem," a 1979 federal initiative on women and alcohol from the U.S. Department of Health, Education, and Welfare and two national research conferences on women and alcohol (National Institute on Alcohol Abuse and Alcoholism [NIAAA], 1980, 1986) have helped to stimulate further interest in women's issues among alcohol researchers.

Although studies of men still greatly outnumber studies of women, publications and funded research on women and alcohol have increased markedly. For example, by 1982 the *Journal of Studies on Alcohol* was abstracting in one year nearly twice as many studies on women's drinking and alcoholism as had been published in the four decades up to 1970; and this increase was aside from research on the fetal alcohol syndrome or research on other aspects of alcohol consumption that took gender differences into account. Research funded by the National Institute on Alcohol Abuse and Alcoholism included only three studies of women drinkers or alcoholics in NIAAA's first five years (1971–1976) but 26 such studies in the next 10 years. The new publications and research projects focusing on women's drinking have examined potential antecedents of alcohol problems in women (e.g., childhood experience, affective disorders, stressful life events, sexual and reproductive dysfunction, and sex-role conflicts); have compared women with men in terms of their family histories, symptomatology, and course of alcohol problems; and have evaluated women's experiences with alcoholism treatment, including inducements and barriers to obtaining treatment as well as treatment outcomes (for overviews of this research, see Kalant, 1980; NIAAA, 1986; Wilsnack & Beckman, 1984).

Some Limitations of Available Research

Despite the increase in the quantity of research on women and alcohol, the research effort as a whole has had some fundamental limitations that seriously constrain inferences about the etiology and consequences of alcohol problems in women. Three limitations of recent research strategies deserve special attention here.

One limitation is the gap between clinical studies of alcoholic women and general population surveys of women's drinking and problem drinking. Clinical research, typically conducted by psychologists and psychiatrists, is generally based on small, nonrepresentative samples of women in treatment for alcoholism. Although such samples make it hard to generalize findings, clinical studies do permit detailed measurement of personality traits, socialization experiences, and adult life events. In contrast, general population surveys, more often carried out by sociologists and epidemiologists, may gather data from large, representative samples of drinkers, but the surveys generally obtain less detailed data, narrower in scope, than clinical studies, and the survey samples often include only small numbers of severe problem drinkers or alcoholics. The clinical research has yielded data and hypotheses about how women's alcohol problems may be influenced by variables such as family history, life stress, social support, self-concept and self-esteem, depression, and sexual and reproductive disorders (see Gomberg & Lisansky, 1984; Wilsnack & Beckman, 1984). Methodological concerns (such as difficulties of measurement) and sociological perspectives have led most general population surveys to focus on drinking behavior and its most proximal antecedents or correlates (e.g., drinking contexts or beliefs about drinking), with little attention to the more distal psychosocial variables studied in clinical research. The gap between clinical and survey research has made it difficult to determine the similarities and differences between alcoholic women in treatment and problem-drinking women not in treatment and to determine what the personality characteristics and experiences studied by clinicians could explain about problem drinking among women in the general population.

A related limitation of recent research strategies is the tendency to investigate only one type of variable at a time (e.g., personality variables or environmental variables), with few attempts to study how different kinds of influences on women's drinking interact. Research on personality attributes has related women's drinking and problem drinking to self-concept and self-esteem (e.g., Beckman, 1978b; Carroll, Malloy, Roscioli, Pindjak, & Clifford, 1982; McLachlan, Walderman, Birchmore, & Marsden, 1979), depression (e.g., Bander, Rabinowitz, Turner, & Grunberg, 1983; O'Sullivan, 1984; Schuckit, 1986), sex-role attributes and sex-role conflicts (e.g.,

Anderson, 1984; Beckman, 1978a; Wilsnack, 1976), socialization experiences and feelings about parents (e.g., Gomberg, 1980; Wright, 1983), and sexual experience and sexual satisfaction (e.g., Beckman, 1979; Klassen & Wilsnack, 1986; Peterson, Hartsock, & Lawson, 1984). Research on environmental conditions has investigated how women's drinking and problem drinking are affected by stressful life events and social support (e.g., Cooke & Allan, 1984; Holubowycz, 1983; Morrissey & Schuckit, 1978), by role-related demands and opportunities (Chetwynd & Pearson, 1983; Johnson, 1982; Liban & Smart, 1980; Volicer, Cahill, & Smith, 1981), and by drinking contexts and the drinking behavior of significant others (e.g., Ahern et al., 1984; Clark, 1981; Dahlgren, 1979; Dull, 1983; Harford, 1978, 1984). Unfortunately, most studies of personality factors fail to measure environmental influences as well, while most studies of environmental influences omit personality attributes. The result is an accumulation of fragmented, unintegrated findings based typically on bivariate relationships. More complex multivariate models of drinking behavior have most often been models of adolescent drinking (e.g., Biddle, Bank, & Marlin, 1980; Jessor & Jessor, 1977; Zucker, 1979) or models that give little attention to gender differences or distinctive characteristics of women's drinking (e.g., Aneshensel & Huba, 1983; Greeley, McCready, & Theisen, 1980; Jessor, Graves, Hanson, & Jessor, 1968).

A third limitation of most research on women's drinking has been the failure to obtain time-ordered data. Many characteristics of alcoholic women in clinical studies, such as depression, low self-esteem, and sexual and reproductive problems, could be antecedents, consequences, or both, of heavy drinking. It is difficult to unravel the time-ordered relationships of such variables on the basis of one-time studies of women who have been alcoholic for a number of years. Similarly, most studies of women's drinking in the general population have been cross-sectional surveys of samples questioned only once. To date there have been no longitudinal studies of representative national samples of female drinkers. The limited longitudinal research on adult drinking behavior has focused primarily on men (Cahalan & Room, 1974; Fillmore & Midanik, 1984; Vaillant, 1983) or has studied limited samples of both men and women, such as Mary Cover Jones's (1981) analysis of drinking practices of subjects in the Oakland (California) Growth Study, and Fillmore, Bacon, and Hyman's (1979) 27-year followup of a 1949–1950 sample of college students (Straus & Bacon, 1953). Many important questions about the etiology and consequences of alcohol problems in women cannot be answered in the absence of better time-ordered data.

1981 National Survey of Women's Drinking

In the fall of 1981, our research group at the University of North Dakota, with the assistance of the National Opinion Research Center, University of Chicago, conducted the first national survey of drinking and drinking problems specifically among women. The survey was designed to overcome some of the limitations of earlier research. The survey questionnaire allowed us to measure three major sets of hypothetical antecedents of drinking (personality characteristics, perceived characteristics of the social environment, and life-historical events) as well as a large number of variables directly pertaining to drinking behavior and drinking problems. The sampling plan systematically oversampled heavier-drinking women, yielding a larger subsample of such women than any previous survey. Although the survey focused on women, it also included a representative national sample of men for comparative analyses. The survey questionnaire was designed to include drinking behaviors and drinking problems that might be particularly relevant to women, and the wording, sequence, and format of questions were devised to maximize the validity of women's self-reports. To ascertain the time sequence of certain variables in relation to drinking, we asked respondents to indicate ages when significant life experiences occurred as well as ages of major changes in their drinking behavior. The sections that follow describe the methodology of the 1981 survey in more detail, summarize findings from analyses of bivariate relationships in the 1981 data, and report initial multivariate analyses of relationships among women's drinking, its antecedents, and its consequences.

Methods

SAMPLE DESIGN

Previous national surveys of drinking behavior in the general population included only very small numbers of heavier-drinking and problem-drinking women, because of the relatively low rates of heavy drinking and problem drinking among women. To overcome this limitation, the 1981 survey initially screened a large number of women and oversampled those with heavier-drinking patterns.

National surveys in the 1970s found that approximately 20% of American women reported having four or more drinks per week (Clark & Midanik, 1982; Johnson, Armor, Polich, & Stambul, 1977). Roughly the same proportion of women reported one or more problem consequences of drinking or symptoms of alcohol dependence in two national surveys (Cahalan, 1970; Clark & Midanik, 1982). We reasoned that the 20% of women who regularly consumed the most alcohol ($\geq$ 4 drinks per week) would include most of the women who drank enough to be at risk for drinking-related problems. Accordingly, the sample was designed to include approximately 500 women who consumed at least four drinks per week (moderate to heavy drinkers), women whose drinking would make them the most "eligible" for drinking-related problems.

The sample was also designed to include approximately 500 lighter-drinking and abstaining women from the remaining 80% of women in the general population. However, whenever screening procedures revealed that a woman was a *former* problem drinker, she was also included in the survey. Finally, since it seemed important to determine whether findings obtained for women would differ from those obtained for men, the sample design included a separate subsample of 500 men. Weighting procedures in data analyses enabled us to adjust for effects of sample stratification and variations in response rates.

Sampling and interviewing were carried out by the National Opinion Research Center (NORC). From its Master National Probability Sample Frame, NORC selected 4,032 households to be screened for potential respondents. The households were situated in 101 primary sampling units in the 48 contiguous states. The sampling procedures excluded persons who were under age 21 or who lived in institutions. Ultimately, interviews were completed with 500 moderate-to-heavy-drinking women, 39 former problem drinkers, 378 light-drinking or abstaining women, and 396 men. Among individuals identified as eligible for interviews, the completion rate was 89% for moderate-to-heavy-drinking women and former problem drinkers, 83% for light-drinking and abstaining women, and 66% for men. A major factor lowering the completion rate for men was that employment or job seeking made them less available for interviews.

DATA COLLECTION

Data were collected by 120 NORC interviewers. All but 4 interviewers were women, and none had a history of alcohol-related problems or moral objections to the use of alcohol. The interviewers administered three instruments. A *household enumeration,* completed by any responsible person in the household, asked for the name, sex, and age of each adult (over 21) member of the household. A *screening interview* was administered to every adult woman located through the household enumeration. This five-minute interview included questions on drinking behavior embedded in a series of questions about social and recreational activities, health, and use of other substances such as coffee and tobacco. Using detailed quantitative criteria, interviewers classified each woman as a moderate to heavy drinker (four or more drinks per week), former problem drinker, light drinker, or infrequent drinker/abstainer. The main *survey questionnaire,* described below, was administered to all moderate-to-heavy-drinking women and former problem drinkers and to those men and lighter-drinking and abstaining women who had been randomly predesignated for interviews. Interviews averaged between 90 and 120 minutes. Care was taken to ensure privacy. Interviews took place between September and December 1981, so as to be completed before the onset of holiday drinking.

MEASURES

Survey questionnaire. The interview questionnaire included questions about current alcohol consumption, lifetime history of alcohol use (with ages of major increases or decreases in consumption levels), drinking contexts, problem consequences of drinking, symptoms of alcohol dependence, and attitudes and beliefs about drinking. Questions about drinking-related problems included a number of problems that may be particularly relevant to women: for example, impairment of household role performance, problems in relationships with children, and accidents in the home. In addition, the questionnaire measured demographic characteristics (e.g., education, household income, and marital and employment status) and a large number of variables that have been suggested as possible antecedents or consequences of women's drinking and drinking-related problems. These variables included measures of (1) socialization and personality characteristics (e.g., perceived parental characteristics including parental warmth, strictness/permissiveness, and drinking behavior; religious background; and the respondent's perceived traits, values, and attitudes toward sex roles); (2) the perceived social environment (e.g., drinking behavior of significant others, gender-differentiated drinking norms, social support, and characteristics of the respondent's primary interpersonal relationship); and (3) life experiences that might be associated with problem drinking (e.g., stressful life events, depression and anxiety, sexual experience and sexual dysfunction, obstetrical and gynecological disorders, use of other drugs, and antisocial behavior). The questionnaire was pretested with 100 randomly selected respondents in Phoenix, Philadelphia, and Pensacola in the spring of 1981.

Throughout the questionnaire, the wording and sequence of questions were designed to maximize the validity of self-reports. For example, drinking questions in the screening interview included a wide range of response categories and implied that frequent or heavy drinking was acceptable and normal (e.g., one early question asked, "In a typical week, would you say that you usually have at least one drink such as beer, wine, liquor, or mixed drinks every day?"). Questions on potentially sensitive topics were asked toward the end of the interview, after rapport with the interviewer was well established. Questions about sexual experience and about antisocial behavior were presented in self-administered handouts, which respondents then placed in sealed "privacy envelopes" without having to reveal their responses to the interviewer. Efforts to minimize distress about answering sensitive questions succeeded well enough that only 4 of the 1,317 respondents refused to complete the interview once it had begun.

Drinking levels. The questionnaire responses enabled us to estimate levels of alcohol consumption in three ways. The first measure (30-day quantity-frequency [Q-F] index) conformed as closely as possible to the method of measurement used in previous time-trend analyses of national survey data (Clark & Midanik, 1982; Johnson et al., 1977). Respondents indicated how often they had drunk each of three beverages—wine, beer, and liquor—in the 30 days preceding the survey and how many drinks of that beverage they usually had on a day when they drank it. Consistent with Johnson et al. (1977) and Clark and Midanik (1982), a glass of wine was assumed to contain 4 ounces of 15% ethanol, a drink of beer was assumed to contain 12 ounces of 4% ethanol, and a drink of liquor or a mixed drink was assumed to contain 1 ounce of 45% ethanol. Information about drinking quantity, frequency, and ethanol content for all three beverages was combined to estimate an individual's average consumption of ounces of ethanol per day during the 30 days preceding the survey.

Respondents consuming 1 ounce of ethanol or more per day on the 30-day Q-F index were categorized as heavier drinkers. Respondents consuming 0.22 to 0.99 ounces of ethanol per day were labeled moderate drinkers. Respondents who sometimes drank alcoholic beverages but whose average consumption of ethanol was less than 0.22 ounces per day were labeled lighter drinkers. Respondents who never drank alcoholic beverages, or who had not done so for at least a year, were categorized as abstainers. These drinking levels are clearly arbitrary. However, because the available data from previous surveys were organized in terms of these four drinking levels, the 30-day Q-F index has been used for all time-trend analyses of women's alcohol consumption over the past decade and all comparisons with previous survey findings.

Our second measure of drinking levels was based on revised estimates of daily ethanol consumption, using detailed information not available in some earlier surveys. This information included distinctions between use of regular wine (12% ethanol) and fortified wine (18% ethanol); self-reports of how many ounces of beer or liquor were usually contained in a drink; and an updated estimate that the average ethanol content in liquor in 1981 had declined to 41% (personal communication from G. Marshall, Distilled Spirits Council of the United States, Inc., 1982). Such revisions caused only a slight reduction in assigned drinking levels, lowering 2% of the women and 1% of the men from the moderate drinking level to the lighter drinking level, with almost no effect on the heavier drinking category.

The revised estimate of daily ethanol consumption in the preceding 30 days was used in a third measure, the total consumption index, that included occasions when respondents engaged in unusually heavy drinking. This measure, adapted from Polich and Orvis (1979), modified estimates of daily consumption by taking into account days when the respondent reportedly had six or more drinks. Ethanol consumption on these days was conservatively estimated to be 3 ounces. The modification was important because occasions of unusually heavy drinking might have more serious consequences than more routine drinking behavior would, and because respondents might not consider or report such occasions of heavy drinking as part of their typical or "usual" patterns of drinking in the preceding 30 days. Since the total consumption index estimates average daily ethanol consumption from both the respondent's typical drinking behavior (in the preceding 30 days) and self-reported episodes of unusually heavy drinking in the past 12 months, we use it as our primary measure of alcohol consumption levels over a 12-month period.

In developing drinking measures for the 1981 survey, we considered using an index of blood alcohol content (BAC) similar to that used by Johnson et al. (1977). Drinking levels based on BAC can take into account the fact that women on the average weigh less and have less body fluid than men. However, Johnson's estimates also assumed that respondents' daily alcohol intake was consumed entirely in one or two hours. Since we had no data on how rapidly women or men drank, and since there is evidence (both from Johnson et al. and from the 1981 survey) that gulping drinks or having several drinks in quick succession is considerably less common among women than among men, we decided against using a BAC index in the analyses presented here.

Drinking consequences. Measures of drinking consequences have not become standardized across surveys to the extent that measures of alcohol consumption have. The 1981 questionnaire incorporated items used in past surveys plus new items that might have special relevance for women, so the resulting sets of questions did not exactly parallel earlier indexes of adverse drinking consequences.

Following the lead of previous survey research, questions about drinking-related problems asked about driving while intoxicated, increased belligerence, damage to job chances, and spouse's or partner's complaints about drinking and threats to leave the drinker. In an attempt to sample more adequately women's problems resulting from drinking, the questionnaire also asked about drinking-related accidents in the home, interference with housework, and problems in relations with children. The number of different consequences experienced in the year preceding the survey is used here as an index of the extent of problem consequences of drinking.

Questions about symptoms of alcohol dependence were based on five indicators from past surveys: drinking-related memory lapses (blackouts), rapid drinking, drinking in the morning, inability to stop drinking before becoming intoxicated, and inability to reduce alcohol consumption over time. The number of different symptoms occurring in the preceding year is used here as an index of alcohol dependence.

DATA ANALYSIS

Bivariate and multivariate analyses of the 1981 data have used a variety of parametric and nonparametric procedures, ranging from contingency tables, *t*-tests, and nonparametric measures of association to product-moment correlations, multiple regression analyses, and path analyses. All of these analyses have been based on weighted data and based on a general conceptual model of hypothesized influences on drinking behavior and adverse drinking consequences.

Weighting procedures enabled us to estimate distributions and relationships of variables in the general population, by compensating for unequal probabilities of respondent inclusion in the survey. Specifically, weighting compensated for variations in inclusion based on sample stratification by drinking level and by sex; probabilities of household selection; missing dwelling units at sampled household addresses; nonresponse rates for screening interviews in segments of primary sampling units; and nonresponse rates for the survey questionnaire in segments of primary sampling units. The statistical significance of findings reported here is based conservatively on weighted *N*s equal to actual numbers of survey respondents.

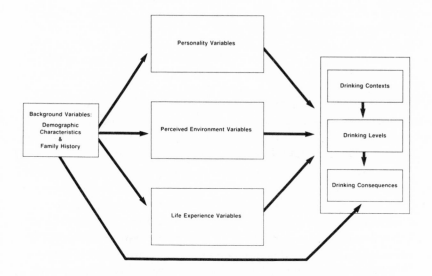

Figure 1. Conceptual model of influences on women's drinking behavior and drinking consequences.

Analyses of bivariate and multivariate relationships have been guided by the conceptual model presented in Figure 1. The initial influences on women's drinking behavior and drinking consequences are assumed to be the individual's demographic and family background, including such variables as the respondent's age, education, religious orientation, and recalled patterns of parental behavior (including drinking). These background variables are assumed to affect three major sets of influences on drinking behavior: personality characteristics (including beliefs, attitudes, and values); perceived environment variables (including social interaction, social support, and social norms); and life experiences (including stressful events, affective disorders, sexual functioning, obstetrical and gynecological disorders, and antisocial behavior). Background, personality, social environment, and life experiences presumably can all affect the contexts of drinking behavior, levels of alcohol consumption, and drinking consequences. Among the drinking variables, drinking contexts are assumed to influence consumption levels, which in turn should affect drinking consequences. We have used this conceptual model to help us decide which relationships among variables it is most important to measure and test, and which variables should be treated as independent and dependent in any particular analysis.

RESULTS OF TIME-TREND AND BIVARIATE ANALYSES

The first stage of analyzing data from the 1981 survey involved analyses of distributions, time trends, and bivariate relationships. The main effort was to describe current patterns of women's drinking behavior and drinking consequences and to determine how the drinking behavior and consequences were related to possible antecedents. The results of these analyses are summarized here, without the detailed tabular data that have already been reported elsewhere.

DISTRIBUTIONS AND TIME TRENDS OF WOMEN'S DRINKING

One of the first important tasks was to compare distributions of women's drinking behavior and drinking consequences in 1981 with the patterns reported in previous national surveys (R. Wilsnack, Wilsnack, & Klassen, 1984; S. Wilsnack, Wilsnack, & Klassen, 1986). We found that, contrary to widespread media publicity, there were no dramatic increases in drinking or heavy drinking among women between 1971 and 1981. Frequent media reports of a recent "epidemic" of alcoholism in women may reflect a delayed reaction to earlier changes in women's drinking behavior (i.e., between World War II and the early 1970s); greater visibility of women's alcohol problems, perhaps because the traditional social stigma for women with drinking problems has been reduced enough to allow increased numbers of such women to enter treatment; and social discomfort about women's liberation from traditional sex roles, attributing to this liberation increased risks of stress-related disorders such as ulcers, coronary heart disease, and alcoholism (see also Fillmore, 1984).

Although women in general did not markedly increase their alcohol consumption during the decade preceding the survey, some subgroups of women showed more limited changes in drinking. For example, in 1981 a higher percentage of women aged 35–64 were drinkers than in all but one of the eight previous surveys conducted during the 1970s. There were significant upward linear trends ($p <$ .05) in the percentages of women aged 35–49 and 50–64 who were drinkers. The percentage of women aged 35–49 who were *heavier* drinkers (1 or more ounces of ethanol per day) rose in 1981 (to 9% as compared with a nine-year average of 5% for previous surveys), a significant increase over the distribution of percentages in earlier surveys ($p <$ .05). If these patterns persist, they would support claims of a modest recent increase in alcohol consumption among middle-aged women.

DEMOGRAPHIC CORRELATES OF WOMEN'S DRINKING
AND DRINKING PROBLEMS

Results of the 1981 survey indicated that certain subgroups of women have greater risks of becoming heavy drinkers and/or developing drinking problems (R. Wilsnack et al., 1984; S. Wilsnack, Wilsnack, & Klassen, 1986). These include young women aged 21–34, never-married and divorced or separated women, unemployed women seeking work, and women cohabiting with quasi-marital partners. In addition, women drinkers with *part-time* paying jobs outside the home had higher rates of alcohol dependence symptoms than women drinkers who were housewives or who were working full-time for pay. The risks for women drinkers who are employed part-time or are living with quasi-marital partners had not been identified in earlier surveys. It may be that women who are unmarried, unemployed or working part-time, separated or divorced, or living with quasi-marital partners are in statuses that may seem impermanent, insecure, and/or relatively unconstrained by traditional role expectations. Such women may drink more heavily in response to stresses related to the impermanence or insecurity of their positions, or because their drinking is less subject to monitoring and feedback from others, or for both reasons. Heavy drinking, of course, may also increase the likelihood that women will find themselves in impermanent statuses—for example, divorced or separated.

DEPRESSION AND DRINKING

The interview questionnaire included an extensive set of questions adapted from the depressive disorder section of the National Institute of Mental Health (NIMH) Diagnostic Interview Schedule (NIMH, 1979, 1981; Robins, 1980, 1981). The questions identified both current and past episodes of clinically diagnosable depressive disorders and obtained information on the number, severity, and age at occurrence of such episodes and on the presence or absence of precipitating events.

Depressive symptoms and depressive episodes were more closely related to chronic or modal drinking (30-day Q-F index) than to episodes of exceptionally heavy drinking. Among heavier-drinking women who reported consuming an average of 1 ounce or more of ethanol per day in the 30 days preceding the 1981 survey, 61% reported having had at least one period of depressed mood lasting two weeks or more, compared with 38% of long-term abstainers (gamma for five drinking levels = .23). Among the heavier drinkers, 19% had had at least three depressive episodes (depressed mood plus three or more criterion symptoms such as sleep and appetite disturbances, fatigue, or loss of sexual interest), compared with 3% of long-term abstainers (gamma = .39). Suicidal behavior was associated with more extreme levels of drinking. A past suicide attempt was reported by 0.2% of long-term abstainers, 5% of women averaging 1 to 2 ounces of ethanol per day, 10% of women averaging 2 or more ounces of ethanol per day, and 24% of women who reported having six or more drinks in a day at least three days a week (gamma for eight consumption levels = .51).

OBSTETRICAL AND GYNECOLOGICAL DISORDERS

Findings from the 1981 survey (S. Wilsnack, Klassen, & Wilsnack, 1984) were generally consistent with findings from other studies that have linked heavy drinking with a variety of obstetrical and gynecological problems (e.g., Little & Ervin, 1984; Russell, 1982; Sokol, Miller, & Reed, 1980). The percentages of women in the 1981 survey who had experienced dysmenorrhea, heavy menstrual flow, and premenstrual discomfort increased with drinking level among drinkers, and women who reported consuming six or more drinks a day at least once a week were more likely to have experienced these problems than all other women (80% vs. 59%; $p < .001$, gamma = .47). Gynecological surgery other than hysterectomy was somewhat more common among women who had consumed 1½ ounces of ethanol or more during the 30 days preceding the survey (15% vs. 11%; $p < .10$, gamma = .23 in comparison with all other women). Lifetime experiences of pregnancy complications were more common (p's ranging from $< .05$ to $< .001$) among women with very high levels of current alcohol consumption: miscarriage or stillbirth and prematurity were more common among women drinking six or more drinks per day at least three times a week, and infertility and babies with birth defects were more common among women drinking six or more drinks per day at least five times a week.

SEXUAL EXPERIENCE AND SEXUAL DYSFUNCTION

Our analyses of relationships between women's drinking and sexual experience have focused on perceived effects of drinking on sexual feelings and sexual behavior, relationships between drinking and nontraditional sexual behavior, and relationships between drinking and lifetime history of sexual dysfunction (Klassen & Wilsnack, 1986). With regard to *perceived effects* of drinking on sexuality, a majority of women drinkers reported that drinking reduced their sexual inhibitions and helped them feel closer to and more open with others. These effects were reported most often by women at higher levels of drinking, suggesting that positive expectations about the effects of drinking on intimacy and sexuality may be motives for heavier drinking among some women.

In response to questions about *sexual experience*, moderate and heavier drinkers were considerably more likely than abstainers and lighter drinkers to acknowledge several types of nontraditional sexual behavior, including premarital intercourse, masturbation to orgasm, and homosexual feelings (all p's $<.001$). These associations may reflect a disinhibiting effect of alcohol on sexual feelings and behavior, and/or the effects of a generalized moral value system that regulates both drinking and sexual activity. Despite the overall positive relationship between drinking and more permissive sexual behavior, there was some evidence of a subgroup of more extreme heavy drinkers whose sexual attitudes and behavior were relatively conservative. It may be that while many women engage in both drinking and sexual activity as part of a liberal value system or nontraditional life-style, other women—perhaps those with sexual conflicts or inhibitions—may drink in part as a form of self-medication for sexual difficulties.

This last interpretation is consistent with the data on drinking and *sexual dysfunction*. On an index combining lifetime lack of sexual interest, low frequency of orgasm, and vaginismus, moderate drinkers were significantly lower than lighter and heavier drinkers combined ($p<.02$). This curvilinear relationship between sexual dysfunction and summary drinking levels (lighter, moderate, and heavier) suggests that moderate alcohol consumption may facilitate women's sexual functioning. An alternative interpretation is that inhibition suppresses both drinking and sexual functioning at lower levels of consumption, whereas at higher levels of consumption drinking is a cause and/or a consequence of sexual dysfunction.

TEMPORARY ABSTENTION: A NEGLECTED PHENOMENON IN WOMEN'S DRINKING

An unexpected finding of the 1981 survey was the relatively high rates of sexual and reproductive dysfunction (Klassen & Wilsnack, 1986; S. Wilsnack et al., 1984) and drinking-related problems and alcohol dependence symptoms (R. Wilsnack et al., 1984) reported by women who had drunk alcohol in the past 12 months but not in the past 30 days (9% of the total female sample). Among these temporary abstainers, women who had previously drunk at more than minimal levels (more than one drink per month) exceeded all other women in rates of sexual dysfunction, including lack of sexual interest, primary anorgasmia, low frequency of orgasm, vaginismus, partner wanting sex more often than respondent, and partner taking too long to climax (all p's $<.05$; gammas ranged from .33 to .54). Temporary abstainers who previously drank only infrequently exceeded other women in rates of reproductive problems, including menstrual disorders, hysterectomies, and premature deliveries (p's<.001; gammas ranged from .46 to .61). In addition, temporary abstainers in general were more likely to report past problem consequences of drinking and past symptoms of alcohol dependence than women who were currently light drinkers. Temporary abstention may be one way women respond to problems that they perceive as caused or worsened by drinking. The number of women thus motivated to abstain may be sizable: of female respondents in the 1981 survey who reported drinking more than one drink a month, 20% had wondered at some time whether they might be developing a drinking problem.

DRINKING AND SOCIAL ROLES: AGE DIFFERENCES

Relationships between drinking and marital, work, and child-rearing roles among women in the 1981 survey (Wilsnack & Cheloha, 1985) suggest that risks of adverse drinking patterns are increased not by having *too many* roles (as proposed, e.g., by Johnson, 1982) but by having *too few* roles. Furthermore, the role deprivation associated with problem drinking is different for women at different ages.

Young women drinkers (*aged 21–34*) were most likely to report alcohol dependence symptoms, drinking-related problems, and repeated episodes of drunkenness or extreme alcohol consumption if they *lacked* stable marital and work roles. Women drinkers *aged 35–49* had the highest risks of adverse drinking patterns if they had *lost* important family roles (i.e., if they were divorced or separated, or if they no longer had children living at home). These middle-aged women were more likely to report drinking problems and dependence symptoms the longer they had been divorced and the more recently their children had left home.

Women drinkers *aged 50–64* were most likely to report adverse drinking patterns if they were married with no children at home and had no paid employment. These women may be trapped or stranded in social positions with insufficient role opportunities or responsibilities. Finally, women drinkers *aged 65 and older* were very unlikely to report any adverse drinking patterns. The few who did were women who said that they liked to get help from others in making decisions but who lacked role partners to confide in and seek advice from. These analyses suggest that risks of problem drinking may change over women's lives and may affect different women at different life stages, depending in part on experiences of role deprivation. Strategies for treating and preventing women's drinking problems may therefore need to be tailored to deal with different role problems at different stages of women's lives.

GENDER-ROLE ORIENTATION AND WOMEN'S DRINKING

The 1981 survey measured three distinct aspects of gender-role orientation: traditionally gender-typed personality traits; traditionally gender-typed personal values; and the traditionality of social roles actually performed. A general hypothesis, based on previous theory and research (e.g., Beckman, 1978a; Scida & Vannicelli, 1979; Wilsnack, 1973, 1976) was that discrepancies among these three aspects of gender-role orientation would be associated with higher rates of heavy drinking and drinking-related problems.

Analyses of relationships in the 1981 data between the three aspects of gender-role orientation and women's drinking and drinking problems have found little support for the discrepancy hypothesis, although there is some evidence in the data that gender-role discrepancies may be linked to drinking in middle-aged and older women rather than in younger women (S. Wilsnack, Klassen, & Wright, 1986). The most consistent finding was that *nontraditionality* in all three aspects of gender-role orientation (traits, values, and social roles) was strongly and positively related to women's heavy drinking and drinking problems. An additional finding was that women who scored as "androgynous" on the measure of personality traits (that is, who were high on both traditionally masculine and traditionally feminine traits) showed the lowest levels of drinking and the lowest rates of drinking-related problems. The positive relationships between gender-role nontraditionality and women's drinking may reflect (1) increased drinking opportunities and more permissive drinking norms associated with nontraditional lifestyles for women and/or (2) the use of alcohol to reduce tension or stress created by society's expectations of more traditional gender-typed behavior. Psychological androgyny (the ability to flexibly combine traditional masculine and traditional feminine characteristics) may enable women to maintain a psychological balance or integration that protects against the excessive use of alcohol.

DRINKING BY SIGNIFICANT OTHERS

Women's drinking levels and adverse drinking consequences were strongly associated with the perceived drinking levels of their husbands or partners and strongly associated with perceived frequent drinking by close associates (closest brother or sister, closest male friend, and closest female friend) (R. Wilsnack et al., 1984). Men's drinking and its adverse consequences were also strongly associated with the number of significant others perceived to be frequent drinkers (S. Wilsnack, Wilsnack, & Klassen, 1986). These patterns are consistent with the hypothesis that substance use is encouraged by differential association with supportive companions (e.g., Akers, Krohn, Lanza-Kaduce, & Radosevich, 1979). However, men drinkers drank less if they lacked contacts with neighbors and friends living nearby, whereas women drinkers were unaffected by this kind of social isolation (Streifel, 1986).

We expected to find that women were more influenced by a spouse's drinking than men were (Dahlgren, 1979; Haer, 1955; Hall, Hesselbrock, & Stabenau, 1983; Suffet & Brotman, 1976). However, the association between current drinking and spouse's perceived drinking level was stronger for men than for women (Streifel, 1986). Analyzing the relative influences of husbands and wives on drinking behavior over time in marital "drinking partnerships" may require longitudinal data, such as our current five-year followup to the 1981 survey is intended to provide. One clue to differences in influences of spouse's drinking may be that women more readily identify their spouses as "problem drinkers," a negative perception that may discourage imitation. Of the women surveyed, 5% identified their spouses as problem drinkers, while less than 0.5% of men reported having a problem-drinking spouse, contrary to the survey evidence of self-reported problem drinking by wives. Women who viewed their husbands or partners as problem drinkers drank less and reported fewer alcohol dependence symptoms than women who viewed their spouses merely as frequent drinkers.

FEMALE/MALE COMPARISONS

Other comparisons between the female and male samples showed some expected differences (S. Wilsnack, Wilsnack, & Klassen, 1986). In general, men were more likely to drink and more likely to drink heavily than women were. And in general, drinking men were more likely to report drinking problems and alcohol dependence symptoms than drinking women were, although there has been an upward trend in reporting of alcohol dependence symptoms by both men and women drinkers over the past decade.

In a few instances, however, drinking behavior and its consequences were unexpectedly similar among men and women. A decline in drinking and heavy drinking among men aged 35–49 over the decade 1971–1981 made the men's drinking levels in 1981 roughly the same as those of women in the same age group. Men were as likely as women (12% vs. 9%) to report temporary abstention (drinking in the past 12 months but not in the past 30 days), and both men and women who were temporary abstainers reported more drinking problems and dependence symptoms than light drinkers of the same sex did. At consumption levels of 2 ounces of ethanol or more per day, the high probabilities of experiencing drinking-related problems and dependence symptoms were *not* significantly different for men and women, although the problems women were most likely to report specifically involved relationships with children and fights with spouses or people outside the family.

Among both women and men, young adults (aged 21–34) were the most likely to report drinking problems, alcohol dependence symptoms, and episodes of heavy drinking and intoxication; 70% of drinking men aged 21–34 reported four or more occasions of having six or more drinks in a day during the preceding 12 months. Unlike women, however, men over 65 (39 respondents) had higher probabilities of reporting heavy drinking, drinking problems, and dependence symptoms than men aged 50–64. These over-65 patterns may be related to the increased probability of heavy drinking among retired or disabled men (but not women) and to evidence of heavy consumption, drinking problems, and dependence symptoms among a clear majority of the small number of men (20 respondents) employed only part time.

RETROSPECTIVE DATA AND LIFETIME DRINKING HISTORIES

An important asset of the 1981 survey was the collection of retrospective data on the timing of major life experiences, including a lifetime drinking history. Other studies have demonstrated the feasibility of obtaining retrospective drinking data that are sufficiently reliable and valid for time-ordered analyses of aggregated data (Bernadt, 1983; Midanik, 1982; Polich, 1981; Skinner, 1984).

However, the 1981 survey was one of the first attempts to collect lifetime drinking histories and other retrospective data from a large general population sample in such a way that it is possible to analyze both antecedents and consequences of drinking changes (see R. Wilsnack, Klassen, & Wilsnack, 1986).

Using a procedure adapted from Robins (1980, 1981), each woman (and man) who reported having more than one drink a month in the preceding year, or who reported ever having wanted to reduce or stop drinking, was asked at what age she began drinking and at what ages (if ever) her drinking patterns changed, in terms of specified categories of quantity and frequency. Women could report up to six stages of their drinking histories. Of the women asked to provide drinking histories, 94% provided complete information about drinking, and 99.6% of these provided their ages at the onset of each stage they reported. An indication of the importance of obtaining drinking histories, and the ability of women to recall drinking changes, is that 42% reported that at different times they had both increased and decreased their alcohol consumption; 23% reported increases in drinking levels over time, with no reductions; and 10% reported steadily decreasing drinking. Only 25% of the women claimed they had stayed at one level of quantity-frequency since they began drinking.

More than 90% of the respondents indicated that their current drinking levels were the same as the levels reported at the last stage of their drinking histories. For these women, the consumption level in ounces of ethanol per day estimated from the last stage of the drinking history (nine possible levels in ounces/day) correlated .63 with a continuous-variable measure of current drinking calculated from the more detailed 30-day quantity-frequency data obtained elsewhere in the questionnaire.

Among the women providing drinking histories, the median age for starting to drink was 18, and 87% had begun drinking by age 21; even among drinkers aged 65 and over, 72% said they had begun drinking before age 25. Although the youthful onset of women's drinking has apparently been typical for many decades, early experience (before age 25) with drinking *problems* and alcohol dependence symptoms was much more likely to be reported by young women drinkers (under age 35) than by women in any of the older age groups. This discontinuity suggests that there have been important recent changes in *how* women drink (though not in amount), or changes in how their drinking and its effects are perceived by themselves and others.

Other temporal analyses related ages of reported changes in drinking behavior to the ages of onset of depressive episodes and obstetrical-gynecological disorders. The drinking histories indicated that experience with depressive episodes was more closely related to any *lifetime* experience with high levels of alcohol consumption (≥ 24 drinks/week) than to *current* drinking at that level. In other words, heavy drinking associated with depression might be overlooked by inquiring only about women's current drinking. The onset of heavy drinking (at both a 7 drinks/week level and a 24 drinks/week level) typically occurred *after* the first depressive episode, according to women reporting both. Similarly, the onset of drinking at least seven drinks per week occurred predominantly *after* initial experiences with reproductive problems, according to women reporting both. These findings call into question any simple ideas that women's depression and reproductive problems are solely consequences of heavy drinking. The findings suggest that depression and reproductive problems may also be antecedents of heavy drinking or may relate to drinking in an interactive, mutually reinforcing "vicious cycle." In general, the findings demonstrate the benefits of obtaining retrospective data in cross-sectional surveys, as a record of variation in behavior over time (such as alcohol consumption) and as a basis for analyzing causal relationships (in more than one direction).

Multivariate Approaches: Path Analysis

Nearly all of the research summarized thus far, carried out by ourselves and others, has relied on bivariate and cross-sectional analyses. A better understanding of women's drinking behavior requires multivariate analyses, in which many different influences on women's drinking can be arranged in a time sequence, showing how these influences affect one another and how they affect drinking behavior indirectly as well as directly. Unfortunately, time-ordered multivariate analyses of drinking behavior are rare (see, e.g., Aneshensel & Huba, 1983; Biddle, Bank, & Marlin, 1980; Greeley, McCready, & Theisen, 1980), and none pertain specifically to women. We are now able to present initial results of time-ordered analyses incorporating very large sets of variables that directly or indirectly affect women's drinking behavior and its consequences. These initial results describe relationships relevant to many earlier bivariate hypotheses about women's drinking and provide the foundations for developing multivariate theoretical models of women's drinking.

The simplest statistical procedure for analyzing and describing complex time-ordered relationships among many variables is path analysis. Path analysis and related techniques are amply explained in recent texts on multivariate analysis (e.g., Cohen & Cohen, 1983; Pedhazur, 1982). Briefly, path analysis is based on arranging all the variables to be analyzed in a time sequence, so that each variable is assumed to have its effects before, after, or at the same time as specific other variables. Path analysis then uses the standardized coefficients from a series of multiple regression equations to show how much each variable affects each of the subsequent variables. The results of a path analysis can be summarized in a path diagram, with arrows showing how each variable is connected to other variables, and with numerical values (path coefficients) that show how strong the connection is between any two variables. If, for example, a path coefficient has a value of 0.5, this indicates that if the independent variable changed one standard deviation, the dependent variable would change 0.5 standard deviation.

Like any other statistical technique, path analysis requires some simplifying assumptions. One major set of assumptions is that relationships between nonsimultaneous variables are one-directional and that it is known which variables come earlier and which variables come later in the time sequence. Other necessary assumptions are that all the influences on a particular variable (such as influences on the level of alcohol consumption) have linear effects, and that these effects can simply be added together. We shall reexamine these assumptions after describing the initial results of our analyses.

As explained earlier, our research on women's drinking has been guided by a conceptual model in which women's demographic characteristics and family history influence their personality characteristics, perceived environmental conditions, and lifetime experiences, which in turn influence drinking contexts, drinking behavior, and drinking consequences. What was unusual about our use of path analyses was that our conceptual model and the research literature led us to begin with an exceptionally large set of 100 variables that we thought might influence women's drinking behavior. In our judgment, these variables had to be arranged in a time-ordered sequence of at least ten stages. We assigned variables to different stages by estimating how long the variables had influenced behavior, how recently they had reached their present values, and how immediately and specifically they were likely to influence drinking behavior. The variables in the ten stages are summarized below and are displayed in Table 1 in the Appendix.

STAGES OF VARIABLES

The variables in the first stage, origins and upbringing, included the respondent's age; whether the respondent was the youngest child in her family; the size of the community in which she grew up; her parents' characteristics (their drinking, their religiosity, how loving they were toward her, and how strict they were); her mother's employment; and any loss of or separation from her biological parents in childhood.

The second stage, early adult experiences, included the respondent's level of education; her religious affiliation; and her nontraditional sexual experience (including masturbation and premarital coitus). The third state, lifetime experiences, included experiences of depression, mania, anxiety, and their severity; experiences with a variety of obstetrical and gynecological problems; the number of children the respondent had had; experiences with divorce, drug use, and participation in antisocial behavior; and whether the respondent had ever had a spouse with a drinking problem. The fourth stage, recent experiences, included an index of the number of major adverse stressful life events experienced in the preceding three years, and information on whether the respondent's last or only child had left home within the preceding three years.

After the four stages measuring experiences came the stages measuring current characteristics of the respondent, starting with the broadest, stablest, most fundamental personal characteristics and progressing to attributes that were more changeable and situational and more specifically related to drinking behavior. The fifth stage, current personality characteristics, included the respondent's description of herself in terms of traditionally feminine and traditionally masculine behavior traits and values; her perceived similarity to her parents; her current anxiety and dissatisfaction with herself; and her orientation toward homosexual activity.

The sixth stage, current roles and role relationships, included measures of the extent and the traditionality of employment; having or not having a spouse, a romantic partner, and/or someone else to confide in; the frequency of contact with friends, neighbors, and kin; the number of children under age 18 living with the respondent; the respondent's current health and drug use; household income and the portion of it provided by the respondent; the employment status of the responder.t's spouse or living partner; and the spouse or partner's education relative to the respondent's.

The seventh stage, consequences of role performance, included measures of the respondent's number of regular household role responsibilities; the perceived difficulty of her role responsibilities, and her level of satisfaction with current paid employment; sexual dysfunctions and dissatisfactions; how satisfied her spouse or living partner seemed with the respondent; and how much trust, conflict, and decision making were part of the respondent's closest personal relationship, at present and in comparison with the past.

The eighth stage, current attitudes and moral judgments, included the respondent's optimism or pessimism about reaching personal goals; her attitudes about men's and women's performing traditional and nontraditional roles; and an index of traditional morality, based on the respondent's religiosity and her attitudes toward men's and women's drinking and toward sexual relations between unmarried partners.

The ninth stage, drinking contexts, included indicators of the availability of alcoholic beverages in the respondent's home; pressure to drink from a spouse or living partner; the frequency of nonsocial drinking at home, such as when doing chores; perceived social norms about men's and women's drinking; and an index of exposure to other people's drinking, based on the drinking patterns of significant others (spouse, closest sibling, and closest male and female friends) and on the frequency of being in places where other people were drinking.

The tenth stage, perceived effects of drinking, included a variety of desirable and undesirable effects that a respondent might believe resulted from her drinking. We had asked respondents whether drinking made them feel more self-assured, relaxed, cheered up, emotionally closer to other people, better able to enjoy sex, less bothered by physical pains and discomforts, or better able to express anger and unhappiness. We had also asked respondents whether drinking made them feel depressed or physically uncomfortable and whether they felt that drinking set a bad example or added too many calories to their diet.

The 100 variables in the ten stages were used to predict four characteristics of drinking behavior. The first characteristic was whether a woman drank at all or had abstained completely from alcohol during the preceding 12 months. The second characteristic was the level of alcohol consumption by women drinkers in the preceding 12 months, measured as the average number of ounces of ethanol (absolute alcohol) consumed per day. The level of consumption was estimated by combining data on the quantity and frequency of drinking in the preceding 30 days and data on the number of occasions when a respondent had six or more drinks in a day during the preceding 12 months. The third characteristic, problem consequences of drinking, was measured as the number of different behavior problems resulting from drinking that a woman drinker experienced in the preceding 12 months, based on a list of nine potential problems (see p. 94). The fourth characteristic, symptoms of alcohol dependence, was measured as the number of different symptoms of alcohol dependence that a woman drinker experienced during the preceding 12 months, based on a list of five potential symptoms (see p. 94).

To predict whether women were abstainers or drinkers, we did not use the measures of perceived effects of drinking or the measure of private drinking at home, because these measures would not have been meaningful for many of the abstainers. To predict the numbers of problem consequences of drinking and symptoms of alcohol dependence, we added an eleventh stage to our set of variables, consisting of two measures of alcohol consumption: average daily intake of ethanol during the preceding 30 days, and the number of occasions in the preceding 12 months when the respondent had consumed six or more drinks in a day. We expected that the amount of alcohol a woman drank would have the most direct and immediate impact on problem consequences and alcohol dependence and might be an important way that other variables increased the risks of behavior problems or dependence symptoms.

WINNOWING OUT VARIABLES

A path analysis of over 100 variables in ten or eleven stages would be extraordinarily difficult to interpret or to present in a diagram. It was imperative to try to reduce the number of variables in the analyses without damaging the ability to explain variation in drinking behavior. Drawing on ideas from Alwin and Hauser (1975) and Klassen (1980), we developed a procedure for gradually winnowing inessential variables out of the analysis, using results from repeated hierarchical regression analyses.

Initially, all the variables were introduced in the proper time sequence in hierarchical regression analyses for seven drinking variables, including both 30-day and 12-month abstention versus drinking, 30-day ethanol intake, occasions of extremely heavy drinking and of becoming drunk during the preceding 12 months, and the 12-month totals of different drinking-related problems and alcohol dependence symptoms. The effects of each independent variable on drinking behavior were evaluated by five criteria, based on standardized regression coefficients and F values for unstandardized coefficients at each stage of hierarchical regressions, and on the total indirect effect of the independent variable on the dependent measure of drinking behavior. The initial criterion levels were set low (e.g., standardized coefficients or total indirect effects of at least .09, or F values of at least 2.0). Variables were eliminated from the initial regression analyses only if they did not satisfy *any* of the five criteria for *any* of the seven drinking variables.

We then restricted our attention to the four measures of drinking behavior examined here. For each of the four drinking measures we repeated hierarchical regression analyses, gradually raising the criteria for retaining variables until all the independent variables entering an equation had, at some stage of the hierarchical analysis, standardized coefficients of at least .11 *or* unstandardized coefficients with F values of at least 2.9. We decided to stop the winnowing process at that point because each additional variable removed from one of the equations would have reduced the explained variance of the dependent drinking measure by 0.3% or more.

The winnowing process yielded a set of 22 variables that could explain 50% of the variance in women's drinking versus abstention; 18 variables that could explain 42% of the variance in alcohol consumption levels of women drinkers; 29 variables that could explain 44% of the variance in the number of different problem consequences experienced by women drinkers; and 13 variables that could explain 32% of the variance in the number of different alcohol dependence symptoms experienced by women drinkers. The direct and total indirect effects of independent variables on the four measures of drinking behavior are summarized in Tables 2 through 5 in the Appendix.[2]

2. The correlation matrix for all variables used in the path analyses is too extensive to reproduce here but is available on request from the authors.

PATH ANALYSES AND EXCERPTED DIAGRAMS

For each measure of drinking behavior, path analyses then required calculating a series of multiple regression equations showing how much each variable was affected by all the variables in preceding stages. The standardized regression coefficients from these equations could then be used in a path diagram to describe how a set of variables influenced one another and ultimately affected drinking behavior. We followed the convention of using standardized regression coefficients as path coefficients because they make it easier to compare how strongly different variables are connected within the same diagram or path model. The direct effect of one variable on a later variable is indicated by a path coefficient. The indirect effect of one variable on a later variable by one particular route through intermediate variables can be calculated by multiplying the path coefficients. Tables 6 through 9 in the Appendix summarize data from the path analyses for each of the four measures of drinking behavior. In each table, the figures above the diagonal show the path coefficients for direct paths between particular variables. The figures below the diagonal show the t values for the unstandardized coefficients on which the path coefficients are based, to indicate the statistical significance of effects.

The reduced sets of variables and their connections summarized in Tables 6 through 9 are still too numerous and complex to be displayed or comprehended easily in path diagrams. However, it is possible to present diagrams of *excerpts* from the complete path analyses. The diagrams presented in the following pages show only those variables that are connected to drinking behavior, directly or indirectly, by the strongest statistically significant paths. All paths shown are based on regression coefficients with F values of 3.9 or more, significant at the $p < .05$ level for the degrees of freedom in all analyses ($df = 1,300+$). The excerpted diagrams for drinking versus abstention and for problem consequences of drinking show variables connected to drinking behavior by paths with path coefficients of .11 or more. The excerpted diagram for levels of drinking shows variables linked to drinking levels by paths of .10 or more. For symptoms of alcohol dependence, the smaller number of explanatory variables allowed us to show all the statistically significant paths ($p < .05$) connecting variables to dependence symptoms.

Readers should bear in mind that paths weaker than those specified above were omitted from the diagrams. Variables connected to drinking behavior *only* by such weaker paths were also omitted from the diagrams. Measures of unexplained variance, and correlations between variables in the same stage, which are often shown in path diagrams, had to be omitted because they would overcrowd the diagrams and tables presented here. Finally, it is important to remember that the process of winnowing out inessential variables eliminated those variables that did not have any substantial effects specifically on the measures of drinking behavior. Therefore, the tables and diagrams presented here do not provide complete maps of all the potential influences on women's drinking behavior that were measured in our analyses. Instead, we have summarized and diagramed those specific influences on drinking behavior that were so strong they should not be ignored.

RESULTS

DRINKING VERSUS ABSTENTION

Figure 2 shows the set of variables that best predicts whether women abstained from alcohol during the preceding 12 months or drank any alcohol during that time. Some of the patterns in the diagram are unsurprising enough to enhance the credibility of the path-analytic approach. The $-.19$ path from traditional morality to any drinking shows that women who espoused traditional morality—that is religiously active women who disapproved of drinking and nonmarital sex—were more likely than other women to be abstainers. The arrows pointing to traditional morality indicate that women were more likely to be morally conservative in this way if they were older, if they considered themselves to be fundamentalist Protestants, if they had never had nontraditional sexual experience (such as masturbation and premarital intercourse), and if they recalled having been strictly controlled by their parents (including a nondrinking mother) when they were growing up.

However, drinking or abstaining was not simply a moral decision. The paths in the lower-right-hand corner of the diagram show that women's drinking was strongly associated with the regular availability of alcoholic beverages at home. Whereas traditional morality and fundamentalist Protestantism discouraged such supplies, a home supply of alcoholic beverages was encouraged by a high-status life-style in which a well-educated woman was married to an even better-educated spouse in a high-income household. Ag-

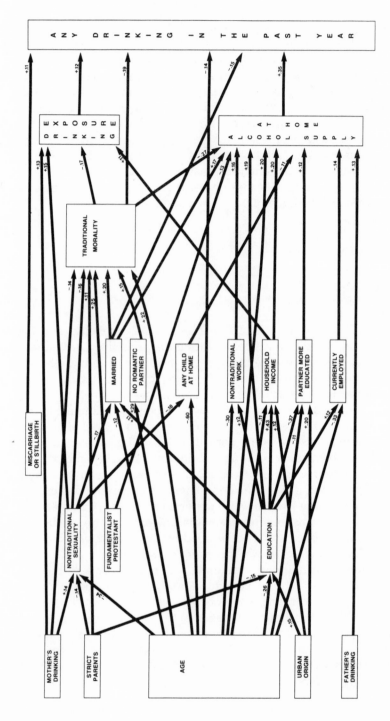

Figure 2. Influences on whether women drank or abstained in the preceding 12 months.

ing and marriage were associated with traditional moral standards that discouraged drinking, but aging and marriage otherwise made women more likely to have a supply of alcoholic beverages at home, perhaps because of related responsibilities for hospitality. (The effects of aging and marriage illustrate how path analysis can reveal conflicting indirect effects of the same variables on drinking behavior.) Women were also more likely to keep alcoholic beverages on hand at home either if they did not work for pay at all or if they worked full-time in jobs typically held by men. A parsimonious interpretation might be that these two employment characteristics indicate women who are more likely than others to have discretionary income to spend on alcohol, either being affluent enough not to need paid employment or earning relatively generous income from traditionally male occupations.

Paths in the upper-right-hand corner of the diagram show that women were also more likely to drink if they were exposed to other people's drinking. Traditional morality made such exposure less likely; higher household income made such exposure more likely. A woman was also more likely to spend time with drinkers if her mother had been a drinker and if the woman herself had had experience with nontraditional sexuality. These patterns, and the links of nontraditional sexual experience with parents who were not strict and a mother who was a drinker, suggest that a woman's current exposure to drinking is likely to be increased by the long-term development of a relatively liberated or nontraditional life-style (see also Klassen & Wilsnack, 1986).

Independent of the effects of traditional morality, exposure to drinking, and availability of alcoholic beverages at home, women were more likely to drink if they were unmarried or if they had experienced a miscarriage or stillbirth, patterns consistent with earlier findings connecting women's drinking to a lack or loss of family roles (Wilsnack & Cheloha, 1985). Apart from all these other influences, younger women were more likely to be drinkers, a pattern that might be a result of historical changes in social norms, age-specific drinking norms, or changes in the effects of alcohol as women age.

LEVEL OF ALCOHOL CONSUMPTION

Figure 3 shows the variables that most strongly influence the levels of alcohol consumption among women drinkers. Perhaps the most

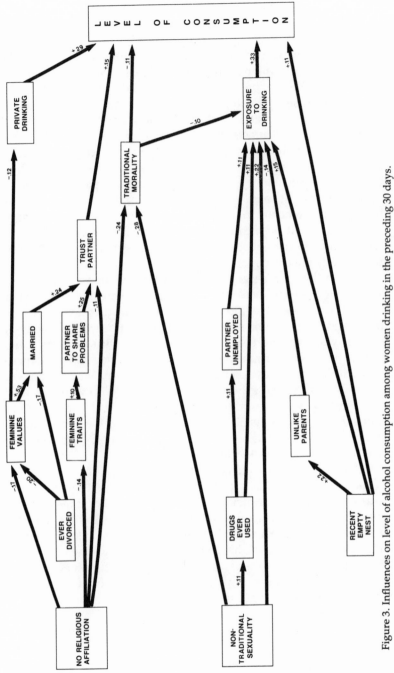

Figure 3. Influences on level of alcohol consumption among women drinking in the preceding 30 days.

unexpected finding is indicated by the cluster of variables at the upper center of the diagram. The paths from these variables indicate that a woman drinker was likely to drink more if she had a trusting marital relationship in which she could talk with her spouse about her feelings and problems. The implication is that women's drinking is more likely to be a social activity in a good, supportive marriage than a response to being socially isolated or alienated. However, if a woman, regardless of the quality of her social relationships, did much of her drinking privately at home rather than in public or at parties, her level of consumption was likely to be higher than other women's, perhaps because of the absence of social restraints.

Further evidence that women's drinking is strongly influenced by social contexts is that women drank more, the more they were exposed to other people's drinking. Among women drinkers, as among all women (see Figure 2), exposure to drinking was greater for those women who had histories of nontraditional life-styles, indicated among drinkers by experiences with use of other drugs and nontraditional sexual activity. Women were also more likely to find themselves in drinking situations if established roles in their families had been reduced or disrupted—for example, by a spouse's involuntary unemployment or the recent departure of the last child from the household. In general, reduced family roles may give women more opportunities to be with other people in drinking situations, and a spouse's unemployment in particular may increase a woman's exposure to her spouse's drinking.

There is an old idea that individuals who drink in spite of personal moral standards that discourage drinking are more likely to become heavy or problem drinkers (Mizruchi & Perrucci, 1962; Skolnick, 1958), either because of the conflict and tension they experience from violating their own rules or because only people who feel compelled to drink will override their own moral inhibitions. The idea that morally conflicted drinking is especially hazardous is not supported by our data (see also Larsen & Abu-Laban, 1968; Schlegel & Sanborn, 1979). Among women drinkers, traditional moral standards that included disapproval of drinking tended to restrict or reduce the amount of alcohol consumed. For women with conservative moral values, drinking was *not* simply an all-or-nothing, abstinence-or-drunkenness choice.

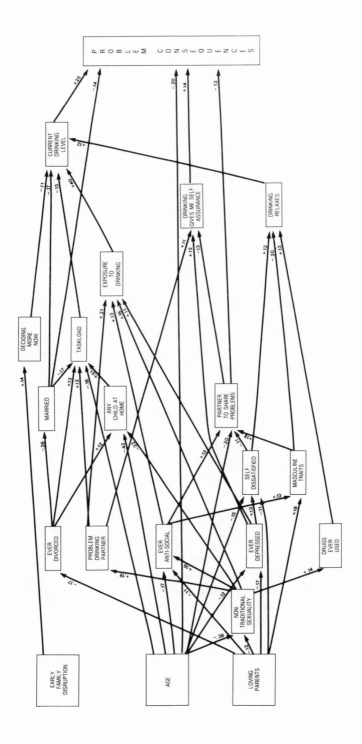

Figure 4. Influences on problem consequences of drinking among women drinking in the preceding 30 days.

PROBLEM CONSEQUENCES OF DRINKING

Figure 4 shows how a relatively large set of variables affects whether women experience social and behavioral problems as consequences of drinking. The strongest paths at the far right of the diagram indicate that the women most likely to get in trouble because of drinking include not only the heaviest drinkers but also the youngest drinkers. Perhaps young women are the most likely to misbehave as they become intoxicated, or perhaps other people react particularly negatively to young women who have been drinking.

When one looks back to see what influences women to become consistently heavy drinkers, some paths at the top of the diagram cast doubts on a recent well-publicized hypothesis about women's problem drinking. The hypothesis is that as women try to combine family responsibilities and paid employment, the conflicts and overloads from too many role demands, plus the availability of more money to buy alcoholic beverages, lead more of them to become problem drinkers (Fortino, 1979; Johnson, 1982; Sandmaier, 1980; Working wives, 1978). The negative path from "taskload" to "current drinking level" means that women drinkers with multiple responsibilities for housekeeping, child rearing, *and* earning income drank *less* than women drinkers with fewer tasks to perform, and the women with heavier taskloads thereby indirectly protected themselves against adverse consequences of drinking. Furthermore, women who reported that they had greater responsibilities for making family decisions presently than in the past ("deciding more now") also tended to restrict or curtail their drinking.

Figure 4 also shows that women's drinking problems result not simply from how much they drink but also from *why* they drink. Women experienced more problems because of their drinking if they expected drinking to make them feel more self-assured. If women also believed that drinking helped them relax, they were likely to drink more heavily and thereby increase the risks of problem consequences. Furthermore, the women most likely to believe that drinking made them feel relaxed and self-assured were women whose experiences and feelings about themselves had been relatively unpleasant. A woman was more likely to say that drinking gave her self-assurance if she had ever been severely depressed, if she had ever had a partner with a drinking problem, and if she could not talk with her current partner about her feelings and problems. A woman was more likely to say that drinking relaxed her if she was dissatisfied with herself and if she felt that she was unconfident, indecisive, and unable to stand up well under pressure (in other words, that she lacked socially desirable traditionally masculine traits).

SYMPTOMS OF ALCOHOL DEPENDENCE

Problem consequences of drinking seem to be partially warded off by women's social roles and responsibilities. In contrast, in Figure 5 roles and responsibilities do not seem to offer women drinkers protection from becoming dependent on alcohol, as indicated by the absence of social role variables from the influences on symptoms of alcohol dependence. Instead, dependence on alcohol appears to result more simply from the personal troubles of women drinkers.

At the bottom of the diagram, a history of depression directly increased the risks that women drinkers would develop symptoms of alcohol dependence. Past experiences with depression and with antisocial behavior also made women drinkers more likely to associate at present with other drinkers, indirectly increasing women's risks of becoming alcohol dependent by influencing them to drink more heavily. Finally, a history of problems with anxiety made women drinkers more likely to view drinking as a way to cheer themselves up, which in turn made them more likely to develop alcohol dependence. The best protection against the risks from personal problems was the experience of love, acceptance, and praise from one's parents when growing up. Women drinkers who recalled such loving treatment from their parents were less likely to report past depression, anxiety, or antisocial behavior and less likely to perceive drinking as a way to cheer themselves up.

Although psychological problems contribute to a woman's dependence on alcohol, it is important to recognize that women's risks of alcohol dependence are powerfully affected by *how* they drink, independent of *why* they drink. At the upper right of Figure 5, the most powerful influence on symptoms of alcohol dependence was how much alcohol a woman regularly consumed, and chronically heavy drinking was facilitated mainly by drinking privately at home and by frequent exposure to other people's drinking. Alcohol dependence was less influenced by a history of using other substances and was not additionally influenced at all by occasions of unusually heavy consumption (six or more drinks in a day).

It is important also not to overlook that *young* women drinkers had the greatest risks of becoming alcohol dependent and were

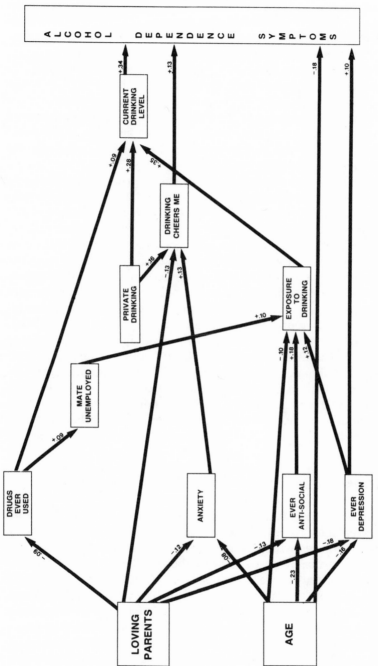

Figure 5. Influences on alcohol dependence symptoms among women drinking in the preceding 30 days.

most likely to have experienced the depression and anxiety that intensified reliance on alcohol. One possible interpretation of the age effect might be that as women drinkers age, they are likely to "mature out" of habits of instrumental drinking and are likely to mature out of or work through the psychological or social problems that earlier might have caused them to drink, so that these problems seem less serious or more forgettable in retrospect. A more somber possible interpretation might be that demands and conditions of women's lives today are creating motives and opportunities for alcohol dependence in young women that earlier generations did not have to deal with.

Figure 5 shows that relatively few variables had strong effects on symptoms of alcohol dependence, and all the variables in the path analysis could explain only a relatively small percentage of the variance of symptoms (32%). Those who favor biological explanations of alcohol dependence might argue that the results of the path analysis were limited because the analysis did not include biological or genetic data. However, neither mother's nor father's drinking, as recalled by respondents, had any significant impact on dependence symptoms, while parental love and praise had several strong indirect effects reducing the likelihood of symptomatic drinking. Given the recent evidence for some genetically related vulnerability to alcohol addiction (Bohman, Sigvardsson, & Cloninger, 1981; Deitrich & Spuhler, 1984; Goodwin, 1979), the most reasonable conclusion is that an adequate explanation of alcohol dependence in women will have to combine variables indicating the nature of the individual with variables indicating how the individual has been nurtured.

MODIFYING THE PATH ANALYSES

Some of the results and interpretations presented here may be revised in the process of reexamining and modifying some of the assumptions on which the path analyses were based. One assumption that probably needs to be modified is that all the connections between variables are one-directional. At least some of the relationships between variables are likely to be reciprocal or interdependent, that is, two-directional. In Figure 2, for instance, a woman's moral viewpoint about alcohol may be influenced by her recent drinking experience and exposure to drinking, as well as being an influence upon these. And regular drinking habits may encourage a woman to keep a supply of alcoholic beverages at home, but an available supply in turn encourages drinking.

Such reciprocal relationships are likely to be so nearly simultaneous that they cannot be resolved simply by longitudinal data collection. The large numbers of variables in the models would probably permit the use of two-stage least squares (Berry, 1984; Heise, 1975) to separate the components of some two-directional relationships in the later stages of the path analyses, but it seems preferable to take advantage of the greater flexibility and sensitivity of nonrecursive analyses based on maximum likelihood estimates (Bentler, 1980; Hanushek & Jackson, 1977; Pedhazur, 1982; Turkington, 1985) or asymptotically distribution-free estimates (Huba & Harlow, 1983). Unfortunately, we did not have the capability to apply these latter techniques to the large number of variables in our initial analyses. Furthermore, constructing nonrecursive models requires careful consideration of the theoretical bases for predicting reciprocal relationships; some hypothetical two-way relationships might involve negative feedback that results in an apparent lack of simple connections between the variables. Given the complexity of the tasks involved in nonrecursive analyses, we decided to carry out simpler one-directional path analyses first, arranging variables in what we judged to be the most likely or most important sequences.

Another assumption that will have to be modified in subsequent analyses is that all the influences on women's drinking behavior are linear and additive. Although the prediction of nonlinear or interactive influences will depend on prior theoretical developments or exploratory analyses, it is already clear that aging interacts in complex ways with other variables influencing women's drinking. Women's problem drinking is affected by the lack or loss of different combinations of roles at different ages (Wilsnack & Cheloha, 1985), and preliminary analyses suggest that problem drinking may also be particularly associated with employment problems among women aged 21–34 and with a spouse's involuntary unemployment among women aged 50–64. Unfortunately, path analysis and path diagrams are not suitable for evaluating or displaying complex interaction effects of independent variables. The interactions of role- and family-related variables with age will necessitate separate path analyses of drinking behavior for separate age groups of women. These age-group analyses must be based on fewer variables than were presented here, because the smaller numbers of respondents in each age group will restrict the degrees of freedom for multivariate analysis.

Readers familiar with path analysis may wonder why we relaxed the assumption that path variables are interval-scale variables by incorporating ordinal variables (e.g., frequency of drinking privately at home) and dichotomous variables (e.g., recent departure of the last child from home) into the analyses, and in particular by path analyzing a dichotomous dependent variable (drinking or abstention during the preceding 12 months). There are three reasons for our pragmatic approach. First, it is not likely that the ordinal or dichotomous measures of some independent variables distorted the relative size of the coefficients in each path analysis (Boyle, 1970), although it may be possible in the future to further refine the estimates of effects of ordinal and nominal variables if there are good theoretical reasons for doing so (Glisson & Mok, 1983; Winship & Mare, 1983). Second, for analyzing the dichotomy of drinking or abstention, there were no discrete-variable techniques known to us (e.g., based on logit models) that would produce an equivalent of a path analysis (see Winship & Mare, 1983). Third, applying ordinary least-squares linear regression methods to drinking versus abstention was not likely to produce serious distortions of coefficients because the percentages in the two categories (39% abstaining for the preceding 12 months, 61% drinking) were well within the limits within which linear and logit analyses of a dichotomous variable would produce similar results (Cleary & Angel, 1984; Knoke, 1975).

One other modification of the path analyses should be considered. The path analyses presented here in Tables 6 through 9 describe *all* the possible time-ordered connections between variables in each path model. Such just-identified models cannot be tested for accuracy and do not provide tests of any hypotheses underlying a model. Furthermore, although variables were selected for the analyses on the basis of hypothesized bivariate relationships with drinking behavior, there are no available theoretical frameworks complex enough to predict all the major paths in any one of the diagrams here. A desirable future objective will be to use the descriptive findings here and in other research on women's drinking, to generate sets of hypotheses for overidentified path models, predicting that only *some* of the possible time-ordered connections among variables exist. There are well-established statistical methods (Pedhazur, 1982) that could then be used to test how well the overidentified hypothetical models fit data from the 1981 survey, our current five-year followup to the 1981 survey, and other multivariate sets of data on women's drinking in the general population.

CONCLUSIONS

The complexity of the path analyses and the lack of any simple or unified explanation for such complexity lead to one basic conclusion: women's use and abuse of alcohol does not have any single, simple cause. To state that conclusion another way, changing any one cause or condition will *not* greatly affect most women's drinking behavior. The basic conclusion has some important specific implications. There are at least four important ways that explanations of women's drinking behavior cannot be simplified, as indicated not only by the variables included in the diagrams, but also by variables excluded from them.

First, the drinking behavior of women in the general population is not simply part of a syndrome of using many different drugs at the same time. The numbers of other substances (legal or illegal) that women reported using at the time of the 1981 survey did not help to explain their levels of alcohol consumption or adverse drinking consequences, and so current drug use was eliminated from the path analyses and diagrams. Multiple drug use may be important in the behavior of some problem-drinking women in treatment, but apparently many women in the general population drink heavily or with adverse consequences independent of any concurrent use of other drugs (cf. Celentano & McQueen, 1984; Robins & Smith, 1980). However, the number of different drugs that women had ever used in the past *was* associated, directly and indirectly, with higher levels of current drinking and greater numbers of adverse drinking consequences. It seems that current heavy and problem drinking was typically not a supplement, but very possibly a substitute, to the use of other psychoactive drugs in the past. Women who drank heavily, symptomatically, or in ways that caused them social problems were more likely to show signs of a lifetime pattern of using chemical assistance, perhaps as a strategy for feeling better or having a good time. Therefore, people trying to help women with alcohol problems may need to be sensitive not just to a woman's concurrent drug use, but also to her longer-term tendencies toward self-medication.

A second lack of simplicity is that women's drinking behavior is not simply a response to objective levels of stress in their lives. An index of the number of major stressful life events experienced by women in the three years preceding the 1981 survey had no relationships with any of the four measures of drinking behavior (see also Cooke & Allan, 1984). The index of stressful life events was therefore eliminated from the path analyses. However, specific experiences that could be distressing (miscarriage, divorce, spouse's problem drinking, spouse's current unemployment, and the recent departure of the last child from home) *were* associated with increased drinking levels, problems, and symptoms. These particular events may increase women's use of alcohol in part because they seem uncontrollable and involuntary (Holubowycz, 1983) or because these events are likely to produce *chronic* unhappiness, disorganization, or stressful impositions on women's daily lives (cf. Eckenrode, 1984; Pearlin, Lieberman, Menaghan, & Mullan, 1981; Verbrugge, 1981).

A third lack of simplicity is that women's drinking behavior is not simply a result of using alcohol to improve sexual relationships or experiences or a consequence of participating in nontraditional sexual activity. Measures of perceived effects of drinking on sexuality did not help to explain any of the four measures of drinking in multiple regression analyses, and so the perceived effects on sexuality were eliminated from the path analyses. Furthermore, a history of nontraditional sexual experience had no major direct effects on women's drinking behavior. Earlier research, largely based on bivariate analyses, has found that heavier-drinking women are more likely to perceive desirable sexual effects of drinking (Beckman, 1979; Klassen & Wilsnack, 1986), and that sexual dysfunction is associated with women's problem drinking (see Wilsnack, 1984). However, when the effects of other variables are taken into account, nontraditional sexual experience and expected sexual effects of drinking do not have any major direct effects by themselves on how women in the general population drink.

On the other hand, the diagrams here show numerous *indirect* ways nontraditional sexual experience increases the probability that women will drink, drink heavily, and have problems because of drinking. These indirect connections suggest that nontraditional sexual experience influences drinking behavior as part of a nontraditional life history or life-style that may include greater freedom from conservative moral constraints, use of other drugs, association with drinkers, and fewer traditional family roles. Such a nontraditional life-style could leave women less protected, by social or psychological restraints, against risks of problem drinking and could provide women with increased opportunities to drink heavily. The differences in drinking behavior between women with the most conservative and most nontraditional life-styles may also show the effects of variation in the general moral value system of society that affects women's lives (see Klassen, 1982; Klassen & Wilsnack, 1986).

The fourth and most important way explanations of women's drinking behavior cannot be simplified is that different drinking behaviors have different causes. Individual variables may influence more than one kind of drinking behavior, but different drinking behaviors result from very different *combinations* of causes. What leads women to drink rather than to abstain is not the same as what determines how much women will drink; and influences on how much women drink are not the same set of influences that cause women to have problems with their drinking or to become dependent on alcohol. Decisions to drink or to abstain are most strongly affected by personal moral standards and the availability of alcohol at home. Among women who drink, levels of alcohol consumption are influenced most by association with other drinkers, by nonsocial drinking at home, and by the quality of married life. Problems resulting from drinking, and symptoms of alcohol dependence, are affected not merely by levels of alcohol consumption but also by what women expect drinking to do for them. Drinking-related problems are affected also by the drinker's family roles and role relationships, whereas alcohol dependence is influenced more by the drinker's upbringing and personal troubles. One implication is that to help women who are in trouble because of their drinking, it is essential to learn more than just what led them to start drinking or to increase their alcohol consumption.

Even if we could be certain what leads women to become problem drinkers or alcohol dependent, we would still not be able to say *when* women will become problem drinkers or alcohol dependent, *how long* it will take for problems or dependence to develop, or *how long* the problems or dependence will persist. The effects of aging, the uncertain transitions from drinking to problems or dependence, and the conjectures of arranging influences on drinking in only one time sequence, all indicate the need for better information on how women's drinking behavior and its influences change over time. Some of this information can be recalled by women drinkers, but much of it must be gathered and validated over an extended time period. To obtain some of the needed information, we are in the process of compiling and analyzing data from five-year follow-up interviews with women drinkers from our original survey sample. We hope that the results of the follow-up interviews will enable us to draw better maps of how time sequences and time lags of multiple variables affect drinking behavior at different stages of women's lives. Better maps are essential, because any attempt to deal with all of women's drinking problems in terms of a single set or a single sequence of causes is no longer good enough.

APPENDIX

Table 1
Variables for Path Analysis of Women's Drinking Behavior

I. ORIGINS AND UPBRINGING

1. *Age of respondent*
2. *Youngest child?* (at least one older sibling, none younger) (yes/no)
3. *Community size when growing up* (for the typical community lived in before age 16; 6 levels)
4. *Father's drinking* (when the respondent was growing up; 4 levels)
5. *Mother's drinking* (when the respondent was growing up; 4 levels)
6. *Parents' religiosity* (during the respondent's childhood; 3 levels)
7. *Mother ever employed?* (full time or part time, when the respondent was growing up) (yes/no)
8. *Parental love* (index of being accepting, praising, and loving toward the respondent when the respondent was growing up; 2 questions, 9 levels)
9. *Parental strictness* (index of being strict or controlling toward the respondent, about sexual and nonsexual matters, when the respondent was growing up; 4 questions, 17 levels)
10. *Loss of or separation from either biological parent before age 6?* (yes/no)
11. *Loss of or separation from either biological parent between ages 6 and 16?* (yes/no)

II. EARLY ADULT EXPERIENCES

12. *Level of education* (7 levels)
13. *Religious affiliation?* (yes/no)
14. *Fundamentalist Protestant?* (yes/no)
15. *Nontraditional sexual experience* (index based on ever having had premarital coitus and/or a self-induced sexual climax; 2 questions, 3 levels)

III. LIFETIME EXPERIENCES

16. *Ever experienced severe depression?* (index based on ever having had periods of two weeks or more of feeling depressed with multiple

Table 1 *(continued)*

symptoms of depression, ever having thought about committing suicide, and/or ever having attempted suicide; 4 levels)
17. *Ever experienced mania?* (one week or more of happiness or excitement extreme enough to provoke negative social reactions) (yes/no)
18. *Anxiety level* (degree to which anxiety has interfered with the respondent's everyday life; 5 levels)
19. *Ever had a premature baby?* (yes/no)
20. *Ever had an abortion?* (yes/no)
21. *Ever had a miscarriage or stillbirth?* (yes/no)
22. *Ever had a baby with a birth defect?* (yes/no)
23. *Ever had a hysterectomy?* (yes/no)
24. *Ever had gynecological surgery other than a hysterectomy or tubal ligation?* (yes/no)
25. *Ever had breast surgery other than a biopsy?* (yes/no)
26. *Ever been unable to become pregnant after trying for at least one year?* (yes/no)
27. *Ever experienced menstrual difficulties?* (index based on 3 symptoms; 4 levels)
28. *Ever experienced menstrual irregularity?* (index based on 2 symptoms; 3 levels)
29. *Total number of children* (that the respondent had ever had)
30. *Ever experienced a divorce or separation?* (from a spouse or quasi-marital partner) (yes/no)
31. *Lifetime use of drugs other than alcohol and tobacco* (how many of 9 drugs ever used)
32. *Lifetime experience of antisocial behavior* (how many of 5 types of antisocial behavior the respondent had ever participated in)
33. *Ever had a husband or living partner who had a drinking problem?* (yes/no)

IV. RECENT EXPERIENCES
34. *Recent stressful life events* (total number of major stressful events experienced in the preceding three years, from a list of 18 such events)
35. *Recent empty nest?* (last or only child left home for good in the preceding 3 years) (yes/no)

V. CURRENT PERSONALITY CHARACTERISTICS
36. *Traditionally feminine traits* (index based on 2 questions from Spence & Helmreich, 1978; 9 levels)
37. *Traditionally masculine traits* (index based on 4 questions from Spence & Helmreich, 1978; 17 levels)

Table 1 (continued)

38. Traditionally feminine values (index based on 2 goals or ideals derived from Jessor & Jessor, 1977; 11 levels)
39. Traditionally masculine values (index based on 5 goals or ideals derived from Jessor & Jessor, 1977; 26 levels)
40. Own characteristics resemble father's? (yes/no)
41. Own chracteristics resemble mother's? (yes/no)
42. Own characteristics resemble both parents' in some ways? (yes/no)
43. Currently a nervous or anxious person? (yes/no)
44. Dissatisfaction with your own personality traits (4 levels)
45. Importance of having people that you like want to be with you (6 levels)
46. Importance of getting help from others in making hard decisions (6 levels)
47. Would it be possible to enjoy sex with another woman? (yes/no)

VI. CURRENT ROLES AND ROLE RELATIONSHIPS
48. Currently working for pay? (yes/no)
49. Working full time for pay? (vs. part time or not at all)
50. Unemployed and looking for work? (yes/no)
51. Nontraditionality of employment (index based on the amount of time the respondent is currently working for pay, and the percentage of the respondent's occupational category who are men; higher scores indicate employment that is more nontraditional for women)
52. Married? (yes/no)
53. Divorced or separated? (from a spouse or quasi-marital partner) (yes/no)
54. Any current romantic relationship? (includes spouse or quasi-marital partner) (yes/no)
55. How easy is it to talk about feelings and problems with your spouse or living partner? (5 levels)
56. How many people (besides your spouse or living partner) can you discuss personal problems with?
57. Frequency of contact with neighbors, friends, and relatives (11 levels)
58. Any children at home aged 18 or younger? (yes/no)
59. Total number of children at home aged 18 or younger
60. General health in the preceding year (4 levels)
61. Total number of drugs currently used regularly, other than alcohol and tobacco (several times a week or more, from a list of 9 types of drugs)
62. Total household income for the preceding year (before taxes; 17 levels)
63. Portion of household income provided by the respondent (5 levels)
64. Spouse or living partner currently unemployed and looking for work? (yes/no)
65. Difference of spouse or living partner's education from the respondent's own

Table 1 (*continued*)

education (13 levels; higher scores indicate that the spouse or living partner is the more educated)
66. *Absolute difference of spouse or living partner's education from the respondent's own education* (7 levels)

VII. CONSEQUENCES OF ROLE PERFORMANCE
67. *Number of major role responsibilities* ("taskload" from a list including child care, taking care of major repairs, housekeeping, and earning income outside the home; 5 levels)
68. *Difficulty in handling all your responsibilities?* (3 levels)
69. *Desire to work at your current paying job?* (for reasons other than income; 4 levels)
70. *Does your sexual partner want sex more often than you do?* (yes/no)
71. *Does your sexual partner reach a sexual climax too soon?* (yes/no)
72. *Does your sexual partner take too long to reach a sexual climax?* (yes/no)
73. *In how many ways would your spouse or living partner want you to be different?* (4 levels)
74. *Degree of trust in spouse or living partner* (index based on 2 questions; 7 levels)
75. *Degree of conflict with spouse or living partner* (index based on 2 questions; 7 levels)
76. *Ability to influence spouse or living partner* (index based on 2 questions; 7 levels)
77. *Change in trust of spouse or living partner, over time* (3 levels)
78. *Change in amount of time spent with spouse or living partner, over time* (3 levels)
79. *Change in amount of conflict with spouse or living partner, over time* (3 levels)
80. *Change in how often the respondent has been making important decisions affecting her life with her spouse or living partner, over time* (3 levels)

VIII. CURRENT ATTITUDES AND MORAL JUDGMENTS
81. *Subjective probability of attaining important personal goals* (7 levels)
82. *Attitude toward traditional male/female role differences* (index based on agreement or disagreement with 5 questions about traditional gender differences in role performed, derived from Spence & Helmreich, 1978; 16 levels, with high scores indicating disapproval of traditional role differences)
83. *Traditional morality* (index based on level of religiosity, approval or disapproval of men's and women's drinking, and approval or disapproval of sexual relations between unmarried partners; 10 levels)

Table 1 (continued)

IX. DRINKING CONTEXTS

84. *Availability of alcoholic beverages at home* (4 levels)
85. *Frequency of recent pressure to drink from a spouse or living partner* (in the preceding 12 months; 3 levels)
86. *Any drinking at home in the preceding 30 days, while doing work or other things?* (separate from drinking at home while relaxing with family or friends) (yes/no)
87. *Perceived social attitudes toward men's and women's drinking* (index based on perceived approval or disapproval of 4 behavior patterns; 27 levels, with high scores indicating perceived social disapproval)
88. *Perceived difference in social attitudes toward men's and women's drinking* (difference between perceived social approval or disapproval of 2 types of men's behavior and 2 parallel types of women's behavior; 37 levels, with high scores indicating greater perceived social disapproval of women's drinking than of men's)
89. *Exposure to other people's drinking* (index based on the frequency of being in settings where other people were drinking, during the preceding 30 days, and the number of significant others—spouse, closest sibling, and closest male and female friends—who are perceived as frequent or problem drinkers; 9 levels)

X. PERCEIVED EFFECTS OF DRINKING (how consistently drinking is perceived to produce each of the following effects in the respondent, based on 3 levels of response to each question)

90. *Greater self-assurance* (index based on 2 questions)
91. *Greater relaxation* (index based on 2 questions)
92. *Cheering up*
93. *Greater closeness to and openness with other people* (index based on 2 questions)
94. *Greater ability to enjoy sexual activity* (index based on 2 questions)
95. *Relief from physical pain or discomfort*
96. *Easier expression of feelings when angry or upset*
97. *Increased depression*
98. *Physical discomfort*
99. *Behavior that is morally or socially undesirable* (index based on 3 questions)
100. *Consumption of too many calories*

Table 2
Effects of Independent Variables on Women's Drinking versus Abstention in the Preceding 12 Months

Variables by Stages	Direct Effect	Indirect Effect	Total Effect	Extraneous Effect	Total Statistical Association
Origins and upbringing					
Age	−.14	−.03	−.17	−.11	−.28
Childhood community size	.01	.11	.12	.08	.20
Father's drinking	.06	.11	.17	.12	.29
Mother's drinking	.03	.12	.15	.17	.32
Parental strictness	−.09	−.09	−.18	−.09	−.27
Early adult experiences					
Level of education	.04	.07	.10	.13	.23
Fundamentalist Protestant	−.04	−.12	−.16	−.09	−.26
Nontraditional sexual experience	−.07	.14	.07	.18	.25
Lifetime experiences					
Had miscarriage or stillbirth	.11	.00	.11	−.05	.06
Current roles and role relationships					
Currently working for pay	−.10	.01	−.09	.24	.15
Doing nontraditional work	.07	.03	.10	.05	.15
Married	−.15	−.04	−.19	.15	−.04
No romantic relationship	−.10	−.05	−.15	.04	−.10
Any children at home	−.08	−.02	−.10	.17	.07
Household income	.05	.10	.15	.08	.23
Spouse/partner unemployed	−.09	.03	−.06	.00	−.06
Spouse/partner more educated	.11	.02	.13	.00	.13
Consequences of role performance					
Role responsibilities	.07	.05	.12	.05	.17
Partner climaxes too soon	.06	.02	.09	.01	.10
Current attitudes and moral judgments					
Traditional morality	−.19	−.12	−.31	−.18	−.49

(*continued*)

Table 2 (continued)

Variables by Stages	Direct Effect	Indirect Effect	Total Effect	Extraneous Effect	Total Statistical Association
Drinking contexts					
Alcohol available at home	.35	.00	.35	.21	.56
Exposure to drinking	.12	.00	.12	.30	.42

Note. Effects are calculated in terms of standardized values, based on a weighted N of 917 women. Total statistical association is the correlation (Pearson r) between each independent variable and the dependent variable. Extraneous effects include effects of antecedent variables and all other effects unexplained by variables and paths in the model.

Table 3
Effects of Independent Variables on Level of Alcohol Consumption Among Women Drinking in the Preceding 30 Days

Variables by Stages	Direct Effect	Indirect Effect	Total Effect	Extraneous Effect	Total Statistical Association
Early adult experiences					
No religious affiliation	.04	.06	.10	.01	.11
Nontraditional sexual experience	−.09	.16	.07	.02	.09
Lifetime experiences					
Ever divorced	.05	.07	.11	.04	.15
Drugs ever used	.08	.10	.18	.03	.21
Recent experiences					
Recent empty nest	.11	.06	.17	.01	.18
Current personality characteristics					
Traditionally feminine traits	−.09	−.03	−.12	.00	−.12
Traditionally feminine values	−.05	−.07	−.12	−.03	−.15
Unlike parents	−.02	−.06	−.08	.04	−.04

Table 3 *(continued)*

Variables by Stages	Direct Effect	Indirect Effect	Total Effect	Extraneous Effect	Total Statistical Association
Curent roles and role relationships					
Married	−.08	.02	−.06	−.07	−.12
Talk about problems with					
partner	−.09	.01	−.09	−.03	−.11
Spouse/partner unemployed	.05	.06	.11	.03	.14
Consequences of role performance					
Degree of spouse/partner trust	.15	−.02	.13	−.10	.02
Current attitudes and moral judgments					
Disapproval of traditional					
male/female role differences	−.09	−.04	−.13	.14	.01
Traditional morality	−.11	−.08	−.19	−.05	−.25
Drinking contexts					
Private drinking at home	.29	.01	.30	.12	.42
Exposure to drinking	.33	.01	.34	.11	.44
Perceived effects of drinking					
Greater relaxation	.08	.00	.08	.13	.22
Easier to express angry feelings	.08	.00	.08	.12	.20

Note. Effects are calculated in terms of standardized values, based on a weighted N of 624 current women drinkers. Total statistical association is the correlation (Pearson r) between each independent variable and the dependent variable. Extraneous effects include effects of antecedent variables and all other effects unexplained by variables and paths in the model.

136

NEBRASKA SYMPOSIUM ON MOTIVATION, 1986

Table 4

Effects of Independent Variables on Problem Consequences of Drinking Among Women Drinking in the Preceding 30 Days

Variables by Stages	Direct Effect	Indirect Effect	Total Effect	Extraneous Effect	Total Statistical Association
Origins and upbringing					
Age	−.20	−.04	−.23	−.00	−.24
Parental love	.01	−.13	−.12	−.01	−.13
Separation from parent before age 6	.07	.02	.09	.01	.10
Early adult experiences					
Nontraditional sexual experience	.01	.13	.14	.09	.23
Lifetime experiences					
Ever depressed	.08	.04	.12	.14	.26
Ever divorced	.05	.01	.06	.13	.20
Drugs ever used	.10	.07	.17	.09	.26
Antisocial behavior	.10	.01	.11	.15	.27
Had problem-drinking partner	.04	.05	.09	.11	.19
Current personality characteristics					
Traditionally feminine traits	−.03	−.07	−.10	−.02	−.13
Traditionally masculine traits	−.06	−.03	−.09	−.02	−.11
Characteristics resemble father's	.05	.01	.05	.02	.08
Dissatisfied with own traits	.08	.03	.11	.07	.18
Current roles and role relationships					
Married	−.14	−.01	−.15	.01	−.14
No romantic relationship	−.08	−.02	−.11	.07	−.04
Talk about problems with partner	−.13	−.05	−.18	−.01	−.19
Any children at home	−.13	−.07	−.20	.19	−.01
Number of children at home	.10	.02	.11	−.07	.05
General health	.06	.03	.09	−.07	.02
Spouse/partner unemployed	.07	.05	.11	.06	.18
Consequences of role performance					
Role responsibilities	−.05	−.04	−.10	.14	.04

Table 4 *(continued)*

Variables by Stages	Direct Effect	Indirect Effect	Total Effect	Extraneous Effect	Total Statistical Association
Make more family					
decisions now	−.09	−.02	−.11	.06	−.05
Drinking contexts					
Perceived social disapproval					
of men's and women's					
drinking	−.09	.04	−.05	−.09	−.14
Exposure to drinking	.05	.13	.18	.15	.33
Perceived effects of drinking					
Greater self-assurance	.14	.00	.15	.15	.30
Greater relaxation	−.07	.04	−.03	.16	.13
Physical discomfort	−.05	−.03	−.08	.05	−.02
Drinking patterns					
Heavy drinking occasions	.08	.00	.08	.22	.31
Current drinking level	.25	.00	.25	.21	.46

Note. Effects are calculated in terms of standardized values, based on a weighted *N* of 624 current women drinkers. Total statistical association is the correlation (Pearson *r*) between each independent variable and the dependent variable. Extraneous effects include effects of antecedent variables and all other effects unexplained by variables and paths in the model.

NEBRASKA SYMPOSIUM ON MOTIVATION, 1986

Table 5

Effects of Independent Variables on Alcohol Dependence Symptoms Among Women Drinking in the Preceding 30 Days

Variables by Stages	Direct Effect	Indirect Effect	Total Effect	Total Extraneous Effect	Total Statistical Association
Origins and upbringing					
Age	−.18	−.02	−.20	.00	−.20
Parental love	.02	−.11	−.09	−.01	−.10
Lifetime experiences					
Ever depressed	.10	.02	.12	.13	.26
Anxiety level	.07	.03	.10	.09	.19
Ever divorced	.08	.02	.09	.09	.18
Drugs ever used	.09	.07	.15	.08	.24
Antisocial behavior	.06	.02	.08	.12	.20
Current roles and role relationships					
Any children at home	−.09	−.04	−.13	.12	−.01
Spouse/partner unemployed	.08	.05	.12	.06	.18
Drinking contexts					
Private drinking at home	.02	.12	.13	.08	.22
Exposure to drinking	.00	.11	.12	.14	.26
Perceived effects of drinking					
Cheering up	.13	.01	.14	.03	.17
Drinking patterns					
Current drinking level	.34	.00	.34	.10	.45

Note. Effects are calculated in terms of standardized values, based on a weighted *N* of 624 women drinkers. Total statistical association is the correlation (Pearson *r*) between each independent variable and the dependent variable. Extraneous effects include effects of antecedent variables and all other effects unexplained by variables and paths in the model.

Table 6

Path Analysis of Influences on Women's Drinking Versus Abstention During the Preceding 12 Months: Standardized Path Coefficients (Above Diagonal) and Their t Values (Below Diagonal)

Variables	A1	A2	A3	A4	A5	A6
A1 Age						−.26
A2 Childhood community size						.15
A3 Father's drinking						−.06
A4 Mother's drinking						.01
A5 Parental strictness						−.15
A6 Level of education	−7.79	4.36	−1.63	<1	−4.52	
A7 Fundamentalist Protestant	1.20	−2.91	−1.69	−2.31	1.20	
A8 Nontraditional sexual experience	−9.43	<1	<1	3.66	−4.00	
A9 Had miscarriage or stillbirth	2.05	−1.29	1.26	1.18	2.33	−1.63
A10 Currently working for pay	−8.28	<1	1.22	1.15	−1.91	3.16
A11 Doing nontraditional work	−7.42	<1	<1	<1	−1.59	3.20
A12 Married	−2.90	<1	<1	<1	<1	2.60
A13 No romantic relationship	6.85	<1	−1.45	<1	−1.41	−1.47
A14 Any children at home	−16.50	<1	1.86	1.59	1.87	<1
A15 Household income	−2.83	3.36	1.26	1.37	<1	11.89
A16 Spouse/partner unemployed	<1	<1	<1	1.47	<1	<1
A17 Spouse/partner more educated	−2.33	4.76	<1	<1	<1	−8.22
A18 Role responsibilities	<1	<1	<1	<1	<1	−1.33
A19 Partner climaxes too soon	1.16	<1	1.20	<1	<1	<1
A20 Traditional morality	4.32	−2.36	−2.36	−3.50	2.96	<1
A21 Alcohol supply at home	3.71	1.09	3.23	2.23	−1.13	3.94
A22 Exposure to drinking	<1	<1	1.22	2.92	<1	1.40
DV Any drinking past 12 months	−2.88	<1	1.66	<1	−2.58	<1

Note. Path coefficients and their *t* values are calculated for a weighted *N* of 917 women, equal to the actual number of women respondents interviewed. Variables are listed here in order of entry into the analysis; path coefficients are not calculated for pairs of variables entered simultaneously. On the basis of degrees of freedom (reduced by multivariate procedures), path coefficients are significant at the $p \leq .05$ level (two-tailed) if $t = \pm 1.97$, and at the $p \leq .01$ level (two-tailed) if $t = \pm 2.59$. However, significance tests should not be strictly interpreted for paths to dichotomous variables (such as married/not married) because of heteroskedasticity (see Goldberger, 1964).

(*continued*)

Table 6 (continued)

Variables		A7	A8	A9	A10	A11	A12
A1	Age	.04	−.34	.09	−.33	−.30	−.12
A2	Childhood community size	−.10	−.02	−.05	.00	.01	−.01
A3	Father's drinking	−.06	.00	.05	.05	.02	.02
A4	Mother's drinking	−.09	.14	.05	.05	−.01	−.01
A5	Parental strictness	.04	−.14	.09	−.07	−.06	.03
A6	Level of education			−.07	.12	.12	.11
A7	Fundamentalist Protestant			.01	.03	−.01	.05
A8	Nontraditional sexual experience			.00	−.05	−.06	−.17
A9	Had miscarriage or stillbirth	<1	<1		.00	−.03	.03
A10	Currently working for pay	<1	−1.34	<1			
A11	Doing nontraditional work	<1	−1.58	<1			
A12	Married	1.39	−3.95	<1			
A13	No romantic relationship	<1	2.05	<1			
A14	Any children at home	<1	−5.14	1.07			
A15	Household income	1.34	−1.44	<1			
A16	Spouse/partner unemployed	−1.27	−2.11	<1			
A17	Spouse/partner more educated	<1	1.20	<1			
A18	Role responsibilities	<1	<1	<1	8.45	<1	−3.15
A19	Partner climaxes too soon	<1	2.31	−1.71	<1	<1	−1.36
A20	Traditional morality	7.03	−4.03	<1	−1.21	1.48	3.23
A21	Alcohol supply at home	−3.31	<1	1.49	−2.19	2.77	2.62
A22	Exposure to drinking	−1.20	3.25	<1	−1.21	<1	<1
DV	Any drinking past 12 months	−1.09	−1.70	3.41	−1.71	1.30	−2.55

Table 6 (*continued*)

A13	A14	A15	A16	A17	A18	A19	A20	A21	A22	DV
.29	−.60	−.11	−.03	−.11	.02	.07	.22	.20	−.01	−.14
−.01	.01	.12	.01	.20	.00	.04	−.09	.04	−.02	.01
−.06	.06	.05	−.04	.03	.03	.06	−.09	.13	.05	.06
−.02	.06	.05	.06	.00	.00	−.01	−.14	.09	.13	.03
−.06	.06	.02	.01	−.02	−.02	−.03	.11	−.04	−.04	−.09
−.06	−.02	.43	−.04	−.37	−.06	.01	.03	.19	.07	.04
−.02	.03	.05	−.05	.04	.02	.02	.25	−.13	−.05	−.04
.08	−.18	−.05	−.09	.06	.03	.12	−.16	.04	.15	−.07
−.02	.03	.03	−.01	−.02	.00	−.08	.02	.05	.02	.11
					.45	−.06	−.08	−.14	−.09	−.10
					.03	−.02	.08	.16	.00	.07
					−.18	−.10	.20	.17	−.05	−.15
					−.07	−.09	.15	.08	−.12	−.10
					.50	.00	.09	−.11	−.10	−.08
					−.02	−.12	−.09	.20	.11	.05
					.02	.03	−.03	.01	.07	−.09
					−.07	−.01	.06	.12	.04	.11
−1.36	12.33	<1	<1	−1.93			−.01	.10	.10	.07
−1.18	<1	−1.82	<1	<1			−.05	.05	.05	.06
2.53	1.78	−1.75	<1	1.44	<1	−1.36		−.27	−.17	−.19
1.33	−2.10	3.72	<1	2.85	2.03	1.27	−5.91			.35
−1.85	−1.72	1.98	1.65	<1	1.71	1.17	−3.36			.12
−1.81	−1.70	1.04	−2.80	2.89	1.58	1.92	−4.45	8.48	3.21	

Table 7
Path Analysis of Influences on Level of Alcohol Consumption Among Women Drinking in the Preceding 30 Days: Standardized Path Coefficients (Above Diagonal) and Their t Values (Below Diagonal)

Variables	B1	B2	B3	B4	B5
B1 No religious affiliation			.07	.03	−.01
B2 Nontraditional sexual experience			.07	.11	−.02
B3 Ever divorced	1.69	1.58			.02
B4 Drugs ever used	<1	2.60			.05
B5 Recent empty nest	<1	<1	<1	1.04	
B6 Traditionally feminine traits	−3.05	<1	<1	<1	<1
B7 Traditionally feminine values	−3.93	−2.15	−4.75	<1	1.93
B8 Unlike parents	<1	<1	<1	<1	5.13
B9 Married	1.19	<1	−4.48	<1	<1
B10 Talk about problems with partner	−1.76	1.55	<1	−1.62	1.02
B11 Spouse/partner unemployed	<1	<1	1.82	2.48	<1
B12 Degree of spouse/partner trust	−2.35	<1	<1	<1	<1
B13 Disapproval of traditional male/female role differences	1.74	6.87	2.23	1.11	<1
B14 Traditional morality	−5.55	−6.44	−1.79	−1.72	−2.00
B15 Private drinking at home	<1	1.11	<1	1.59	1.45
B16 Exposure to drinking	1.04	4.62	<1	2.36	3.37
B17 Greater relaxation	−2.41	1.60	<1	2.88	<1
B18 Easier to express angry feelings	−2.85	3.42	1.33	<1	<1
DV Level of alcohol consumption	<1	−1.98	1.05	1.93	2.58

Note. Path coefficients and their t values are calculated for a weighted N of 624 women, equal to the actual number of women interviewed who were current drinkers. Variables are listed here in order of entry into the analysis; path coefficients are not calculated for pairs of variables entered simultaneously. On the basis of degrees of freedom (reduced by multivariate procedures), path coefficients are significant at the $p \leq .05$ level (two-tailed) if $t = \pm 1.97$, and at the $p \leq .01$ level (two-tailed) if $t = \pm 2.59$. However, significance tests should not be strictly interpreted for paths to dichotomous variables (such as married/not married) because of heteroskedasticity (see Goldberger, 1964).

Table 7 *(continued)*

B6	B7	B8	B9	B10	B11	B12	B13	B14
−.14	−.17	.02	.04	−.09	−.01	−.11	.08	−.24
.00	−.09	−.01	−.02	.07	−.03	.04	.31	−.28
−.02	−.20	−.03	−.17	−.02	.08	−.03	.10	−.08
.04	.04	−.03	−.02	−.08	.11	.00	.05	−.07
.00	.08	.22	−.01	.05	−.03	.02	−.03	−.09
			−.03	.10	−.06	.10	−.01	.08
			.53	.07	.01	.00	−.06	.09
			−.06	.08	−.02	.02	.05	.06
<1	14.04	−1.54				.24	−.09	.03
2.18	1.50	1.78				.25	−.06	−.02
−1.32	<1	<1				−.04	−.02	−.04
2.16	<1	<1	4.32	5.44	<1		.08	.03
<1	−1.11	1.06	−1.62	−1.32	<1	1.76		
1.93	1.75	1.40	<1	<1	<1	<1		
<1	−2.08	1.00	−1.41	−1.70	<1	<1	−1.32	−1.34
<1	<1	−3.17	<1	<1	2.45	<1	<1	−1.99
<1	<1	<1	<1	<1	<1	<1	−1.77	−2.60
<1	<1	<1	<1	<1	1.35	<1	−2.32	−2.84
−2.21	<1	<1	−1.60	−2.15	1.17	3.38	−1.82	−2.21

(continued)

Table 7 (*continued*)

	Variables	B15	B16	B17	B18	DV
B1	No religious affiliation	−.01	.05	−.13	−.16	.04
B2	Nontraditional sexual experience	.06	.22	.09	.20	−.09
B3	Ever divorced	.01	.03	−.02	.07	.05
B4	Drugs ever used	.08	.11	.15	.00	.08
B5	Recent empty nest	.07	.15	.00	−.05	.11
B6	Traditionally feminine traits	−.02	−.02	.04	.02	−.09
B7	Traditionally feminine values	−.12	.04	−.01	.03	−.05
B8	Unlike parents	.05	−.14	−.01	−.01	−.02
B9	Married	−.08	.05	.03	−.02	−.08
B10	Talk about problems with partner	−.08	−.02	.00	−.01	−.09
B11	Spouse/partner unemployed	.04	.11	.02	.07	.05
B12	Degree of spouse/partner trust	.03	−.04	.01	−.04	.15
B13	Disapproval of traditional male/female role differences	−.07	−.00	−.10	−.13	−.09
B14	Traditional morality	−.07	−.10	−.16	−.17	−.11
B15	Private drinking at home			.12	.05	.29
B16	Exposure to drinking			.03	.07	.33
B17	Greater relaxation	2.24	<1			.08
B18	Easier to express angry feelings	<1	1.29			.08
DV	Level of alcohol consumption	6.61	7.22	1.86	1.80	

Table 8

Path Analysis of Influences on Problem Consequences of Drinking Among Women Drinking in the Preceding 30 Days: Standardized Path Coefficients (Above Diagonal) and Their t Values (Below Diagonal)

Variables		C1	C2	C3	C4
C1	Age				−.38
C2	Parental love				−.12
C3	Separation from parent before age 6				.04
C4	Nontraditional sexual experience	−9.42	−2.98	−1.11	
C5	Ever depressed	−2.56	−3.85	−1.45	2.14
C6	Ever divorced	−1.89	−3.94	1.35	<1
C7	Drugs ever used	1.61	−1.70	<1	2.92
C8	Antisocial behavior	−3.78	−2.59	<1	3.52
C9	Had problem-drinking partner	1.45	−2.32	1.49	4.01
C10	Traditionally feminine traits	−1.54	3.63	−2.01	<1
C11	Traditionally masculine traits	−1.13	4.14	<1	<1
C12	Characteristics resemble father's	1.41	2.68	<1	1.46
C13	Dissatisfied with own traits	−3.06	−2.52	1.57	−1.89
C14	Married	<1	<1	<1	−1.22
C15	No romantic relationship	2.61	−1.56	<1	<1
C16	Talk about problems with partner	−3.90	1.41	<1	<1
C17	Any children at home	−9.25	1.15	<1	−5.01
C18	Number of children at home	−7.33	1.01	<1	−3.86
C19	General health	−1.42	<1	−1.18	4.57
C20	Spouse/partner unemployed	−1.08	<1	<1	−1.14
C21	Role responsibilities	−3.75	−2.41	<1	−2.26
C22	Make more family decisions now	−1.73	1.12	2.87	−1.22
C23	Perceived social disapproval of men's and women's drinking	3.67	1.12	<1	<1
C24	Exposure to drinking	<1	1.46	<1	3.03
C25	Greater self-assurance	<1	<1	1.37	<1
C26	Greater relaxation	<1	<1	1.92	1.46
C27	Physical discomfort	−2.44	<1	<1	1.41
C28	Heavy drinking episodes	−1.41	<1	1.43	−1.27
C29	Current drinking level	<1	<1	<1	−1.54
DV	Drinking problem consequences	−3.54	<1	1.57	<1

Note. Path coefficients and their t values are calculated for a weighted N of 624 women, equal to the actual number of women interviewed who were current drinkers. Variables are listed here in order of entry into the analysis; path coefficients are not calculated for pairs of variables entered simultaneously. On the basis of degrees of freedom (reduced by multivariate procedures), path coefficients are significant at the $p \leq .05$ level (two-tailed) if $t = \pm 1.97$, and at the $p \leq .01$ level (two-tailed) if $t = \pm 2.59$. However, significance tests should not be strictly interpreted for paths to dichotomous variables (such as married/not married) because of heteroskedasticity (see Goldberger, 1964). *(continued)*

Table 8 (*continued*)

	Variables	C5	C6	C7	C8
C1	Age	−.12	−.09	.08	−.17
C2	Parental love	−.17	−.17	−.07	−.11
C3	Separation from parent before age 6	−.06	.06	.01	.02
C4	Nontraditional sexual experience	.10	.02	.14	.16
C5	Ever depressed				
C6	Ever divorced				
C7	Drugs ever used				
C8	Antisocial behavior				
C9	Had problem-drinking partner				
C10	Traditionally feminine traits	<1	<1	1.16	−1.41
C11	Traditionally masculine traits	<1	2.14	−1.38	2.82
C12	Characteristics resemble father's	1.10	<1	<1	<1
C13	Dissatisfied with own traits	2.69	−1.91	2.17	−1.99
C14	Married	<1	−5.53	<1	<1
C15	No romantic relationship	−1.01	3.27	<1	−1.79
C16	Talk about problems with partner	<1	−1.08	<1	−2.71
C17	Any children at home	<1	2.87	<1	2.07
C18	Number of children at home	1.73	1.79	<1	2.50
C19	General health	−3.16	−1.53	−2.99	−1.67
C20	Spouse/partner unemployed	1.34	1.20	2.20	<1
C21	Role responsibilities	<1	3.08	−1.37	<1
C22	Make more family decisions now	<1	−1.64	<1	<1
C23	Perceived social disapproval of men's and women's drinking	<1	1.26	<1	1.64
C24	Exposure to drinking	2.17	<1	1.69	2.57
C25	Greater self-assurance	2.16	<1	<1	<1
C26	Greater relaxation	1.39	<1	2.41	<1
C27	Physical discomfort	1.76	<1	<1	1.13
C28	Heavy drinking episodes	1.26	<1	1.40	<1
C29	Current drinking level	<1	1.13	1.75	<1
DV	Drinking problem consequences	1.73	1.12	2.19	2.06

Table 8 (*continued*)

Var	C9	C10	C11	C12	C13	C14	C15	C16	C17
C1	.07	−.07	−.05	.07	−.15	.04	.13	−.20	−.42
C2	−.10	.16	.18	.12	−.11	.04	−.07	.07	.05
C3	.06	−.09	.02	−.01	.07	−.03	−.04	.03	.00
C4	.19	−.03	−.04	.07	−.09	−.06	−.01	.01	−.22
C5		.04	.00	.05	.13	.02	−.05	.05	.04
C6		−.02	.10	.02	−.09	−.26	.15	−.05	.12
C7		.05	−.06	.03	.10	−.01	−.01	−.01	.02
C8		−.07	.13	.03	−.09	.03	−.09	−.13	.09
C9		.07	−.05	.02	−.06	−.03	−.02	−.07	−.01
C10	1.47					.01	.01	.04	.07
C11	−1.04					−.04	.06	.18	−.04
C12	<1					.00	.02	.04	−.05
C13	−1.32					.01	−.01	−.11	−.02
C14	<1	<1	<1	<1	<1				
C15	<1	<1	1.24	<1	<1				
C16	−1.46	<1	3.81	<1	−2.34				
C17	<1	1.72	<1	−1.17	<1				
C18	<1	1.07	<1	<1	−1.30				
C19	<1	1.26	3.50	<1	3.23				
C20	<1	−1.54	<1	<1	<1				
C21	3.08	1.44	1.88	2.62	−1.20	−3.19	<1	−2.25	7.33
C22	2.03	<1	<1	<1	1.06	−1.21	<1	<1	<1
C23	−2.10	<1	<1	<1	<1	<1	<1	<1	<1
C24	4.47	−1.03	<1	<1	<1	<1	<1	<1	−1.44
C25	2.02	<1	−1.08	<1	1.91	<1	−1.19	−2.41	<1
C26	−1.25	1.53	−3.55	<1	2.38	<1	<1	<1	<1
C27	<1	<1	−1.44	<1	<1	−1.28	−1.57	<1	<1
C28	<1	−1.46	<1	<1	−1.34	−1.94	<1	−1.16	<1
C29	<1	−1.77	<1	1.25	<1	−2.56	−1.16	−1.83	<1
DV	<1	<1	−1.23	1.10	1.67	−2.21	−1.47	−2.77	−1.63

(*continued*)

Table 8 (*continued*)

Variables		C18	C19	C20	C21
C1	Age	−.34	−.07	−.05	−.18
C2	Parental love	.04	.00	.02	−.10
C3	Separation from parent before age 6	.02	−.05	−.04	.03
C4	Nontraditional sexual experience	−.18	.21	−.06	−.10
C5	Ever depressed	.08	−.14	.07	.02
C6	Ever divorced	.08	−.07	.06	.13
C7	Drugs ever used	−.01	−.13	.10	−.06
C8	Antisocial behavior	.11	−.08	−.02	.01
C9	Had problem-drinking partner	.00	−.02	.03	.12
C10	Traditionally feminine traits	.05	.05	−.07	.06
C11	Traditionally masculine traits	.01	.16	.00	.08
C12	Characteristics resemble father's	−.03	−.03	−.01	.10
C13	Dissatisfied with own traits	−.06	.14	−.01	−.05
C14	Married				−.17
C15	No romantic relationship				−.04
C16	Talk about problems with partner				−.09
C17	Any children at home				.51
C18	Number of children at home				−.09
C19	General health				.10
C20	Spouse/partner unemployed				−.05
C21	Role responsibilities	−1.32	2.45	−1.26	
C22	Make more family decisions now	<1	<1	<1	
C23	Perceived social disapproval of men's and women's drinking	<1	−1.10	<1	2.19
C24	Exposure to drinking	1.01	1.07	2.04	<1
C25	Greater self-assurance	1.03	<1	<1	<1
C26	Greater relaxation	1.56	<1	<1	<1
C27	Physical discomfort	<1	<1	<1	−1.40
C28	Heavy drinking episodes	<1	<1	1.27	−1.28
C29	Current drinking level	<1	1.59	1.41	−2.13
DV	Drinking problem consequences	1.31	1.37	1.56	<1

Table 8 (*continued*)

Var	C22	C23	C24	C25	C26	C27	C28	C29	DV
C1	−.10	.22	−.06	−.06	.03	−.15	−.09	−.05	−.20
C2	.06	.06	.07	.00	.01	.03	−.01	−.03	.01
C3	.14	.03	.01	.07	.10	−.02	.07	.01	.07
C4	−.07	−.02	.16	.05	.09	.08	−.08	−.08	.01
C5	.04	−.04	.11	.12	.08	.09	.07	.05	.08
C6	−.09	.07	−.01	.03	−.01	.01	−.01	.06	.05
C7	−.01	−.03	.08	.04	.13	−.04	.08	.09	.10
C8	.01	.09	.13	−.01	.00	.06	−.03	.02	.10
C9	.10	−.11	.21	.11	−.07	.01	−.04	.01	.04
C10	.01	.03	−.05	−.02	.08	.04	−.08	−.08	−.03
C11	−.02	.01	−.04	−.06	−.20	−.07	−.02	−.03	−.06
C12	−.05	.04	.01	.02	−.04	.03	.03	.06	.05
C13	.05	−.02	−.02	.11	.13	.01	−.07	.00	.08
C14	−.08	.02	.05	.02	−.02	−.09	−.14	−.17	−.14
C15	−.02	.06	−.04	−.08	−.02	−.10	.02	−.07	−.08
C16	.04	.02	−.03	−.13	.05	.00	−.06	−.09	−.13
C17	.01	−.03	−.12	−.10	−.08	.06	.08	.07	−.13
C18	−.01	−.04	.08	.09	.14	−.03	−.01	−.07	.10
C19	−.04	−.06	.05	−.01	.02	−.02	.00	.08	.06
C20	.03	−.04	.09	.04	.03	−.01	.07	.07	.07
C21		.13	.00	−.03	.03	−.08	−.08	−.13	−.05
C22		−.02	.06	−.01	.03	−.06	−.10	−.11	−.09
C23	<1			.02	−.04	.00	.13	.08	−.09
C24	1.39			.03	.05	−.18	.19	.40	.05
C25	<1	<1	<1				.08	−.01	.14
C26	<1	<1	<1				.10	.12	−.07
C27	−1.26	<1	−3.41				−.10	−.09	−.05
C28	−1.88	2.50	3.42	1.37	1.87	−1.89			.08
C29	−2.35	1.73	7.70	<1	2.36	−1.96			.25
DV	−2.00	−1.97	<1	3.18	−1.53	−1.12	1.73	4.72	

Table 9

Path Analysis of Influences on Alcohol Dependence Symptoms Among Women Drinking in the Preceding 30 Days: Standardized Path Coefficients (Above Diagonal) and Their t Values (Below Diagonal)

Variables	D1	D2	D3	D4	D5	D6	D7	D8	D9	D10	D11	D12	D13	DV
D1 Age		-.16	-.08	-.10	.02	-.23	-.34	-.03	-.02	-.10	.03	.02	.02	-.18
D2 Parental love	-3.89		-.18	-.12	-.18	-.09	-.13	.07	.02	-.01	.04	-.13	-.04	.02
D3 Ever depressed	-2.02	-4.38						.03	.05	.06	.12	-.05	.01	.10
D4 Anxiety level	-2.42	-2.93						-.01	.04	.02	.03	.13	.00	.07
D5 Ever divorced	<1	-4.38						.12	.07	.05	.02	-.07	.07	.08
D6 Drugs ever used	-5.80	-2.24						.00	.09	.05	.08	.06	.09	.09
D7 Antisocial behavior	-8.54	-3.24						.05	-.02	.06	.18	-.05	.00	.06
D8 Any children at home	<1	1.76	<1	<1	2.99	<1	1.29			-.07	-.08	.00	-.05	-.08
D9 Spouse/partner unemployed	<1	<1	1.15	<1	1.51	2.04	<1			.03	.10	.07	.06	.08
D10 Private drinking at home	-2.36	<1	1.35	<1	1.21	1.19	1.43	-1.55	<1			.16	.28	.02
D11 Exposure to drinking	<1	<1	2.81	<1	<1	1.96	4.30	-1.79	2.39			.28	.35	.00
D12 Cheering up	<1	-2.59	-1.00	2.58	-1.33	1.07	<1	<1	1.65	3.27	7.97		.04	.13
D13 Current drinking level	<1	<1	<1	<1	1.51	2.09	<1	-1.21	1.54	6.60	7.97	<1		.34
DV Alcohol dependence symptoms	-4.02	<1	2.23	1.60	1.73	1.92	1.37	-1.96	1.80	<1	<1	2.96	7.02	

Note. Path coefficients and their t values are calculated for a weighted N of 624 women, equal to the actual number of women interviewed who were current drinkers. Variables are listed here in order of entry into the analysis; path coefficients are not calculated for pairs of variables entered simultaneously. On the basis of degrees of freedom (reduced by multivariate procedures), path coefficients are significant at the $p \le .05$ level (two-tailed) if $t = \pm 1.97$, and at the $p \le .01$ level (two-tailed) if $t = \pm 2.59$. However, significance tests should not be strictly interpreted for paths to dichotomous variables (such as married/not married) because of heteroskedasticity (see Goldberger, 1964).

REFERENCES

Ahern, F. M., Johnson, R. C., Ross, H. L., Aher, E. H., Harris, J. H., McClearn, G. E., & Wilson, J. R. (1984). Spouse resemblance for alcohol-related behaviors. *Behavior Genetics, 14*, 595.

Akers, R. L., Krohn, M. D., Lanza-Kaduce, L., & Radosevich, M. (1979). Social learning and deviant behavior: A specific test of a general theory. *American Sociological Review, 44*, 635–655.

Alwin, D. F., & Hauser, R. M. (1975). The decomposition of effects in path analysis. *American Sociological Review, 40*, 37–47.

Anderson, S. C. (1984). Alcoholic women: Sex-role identification and perceptions of parental personality characteristics. *Sex Roles, 11*, 277–287.

Aneshensel, C. S., & Huba, G. J. (1983). Depression, alcohol use, and smoking over one year: A four-wave longitudinal causal model. *Journal of Abnormal Psychology, 92*, 134–150.

Bander, K. W., Rabinowitz, E., Turner, S., & Grunberg, H. (1983). Patterns of depression in women alcoholics. *Alcoholism: Clinical and Experimental Research, 7*, 105.

Beckman, L. J. (1978a). Sex-role conflict in alcoholic women: Myth or reality. *Journal of Abnormal Psychology, 87*, 408–417.

Beckman, L. J. (1978b). The self-esteem of alcoholic women. *Journal of Studies on Alcohol, 39*, 491–498.

Beckman, L. J. (1979). Reported effects of alcohol on the sexual feelings and behavior of women alcoholics and nonalcoholics. *Journal of Studies on Alcohol, 40*, 272–282.

Bentler, P. B. (1980). Multivariate analysis with latent variables: Causal modeling. *Annual Review of Psychology, 31*, 419–456.

Bernadt, M. W. (1983). Drinking histories: Are they accurate? *Neuropharmacology, 22*, 571–572.

Berry, W. D. (1984). *Nonrecursive causal models.* Quantitative Applications in the Social Sciences No. 37. Beverly Hills: Sage.

Biddle, B. J., Bank, B. J., & Marlin, M. M. (1980). Social determinants of adolescent drinking: What they think, what they do and what I think and do. *Journal of Studies on Alcohol, 41*, 215–241.

Bohman, M., Sigvardsson, S., & Cloninger, C. R. (1981). Maternal inheritance of alcohol abuse: Cross-fostering analysis of adopted women. *Archives of General Psychiatry, 38*, 965–969.

Boyle, R. P. (1970). Path analysis and ordinal data. *American Journal of Sociology, 75*, 461–480.

Cahalan, D. (1970). *Problem drinkers: A national survey.* San Francisco: Jossey-Bass.

Cahalan, D., & Room, R. (1974). *Problem drinking among American men.* New Brunswick, N. J.: Rutgers Center of Alcohol Studies.

Carroll, J. F. X., Malloy, T. E., Roscioli, D. L., Pindjak, G. M., & Clifford, J. S. (1982). Similarities and differences in self-concepts of women alcoholics and drug addicts. *Journal of Studies on Alcohol, 43,* 725–738.

Celentano, D. D., & McQueen, D. V. (1984). Multiple substance abuse among women with alcohol-related problems. In S. C. Wilsnack & L. J. Beckman (Eds.), *Alcohol problems in women: Antecedents, consequences, and intervention* (pp. 97–116). New York: Guilford.

Chetwynd, S. J., & Pearson, V. (1983). Reported drinking practices amongst women working in the home. *Community Health Studies, 7,* 278–284.

Clark, W. B. (1981). Public drinking contexts: Bars and taverns. In T. C. Harford & L. S. Gaines (Eds.), *Social drinking contexts* (pp. 8–33). Research Monograph No. 7 of the National Institute on Alcohol Abuse and Alcoholism (U.S. Department of Health and Human Services Publication No. ADM-81-1097). Washington, DC: U.S. Government Printing Office.

Clark, W. B., & Midanik, L. (1982). Alcohol use and alcohol problems among U.S. adults: Results of the 1979 national survey. In *Alcohol consumption and related problems* (pp. 3–52). Alcohol and Health Monograph No. 1 (U.S. Department of Health and Human Services Publication No. ADM-82-1190). Washington, DC: U.S. Government Printing Office.

Cleary, P. D., & Angel, R. (1984). The analysis of relationships involving dichotomous dependent variables. *Journal of Health and Social Behavior, 25* 334–348.

Cohen, J., & Cohen, P. (1983). *Applied multiple regression/correlation analysis for the behavioral sciences* (2nd ed.). Hillsdale, NJ: Lawrence Erlbaum Associates.

Cooke, D. J., & Allan, C. A. (1984). Stressful life events and alcohol abuse in women: A general population study. *British Journal of Addiction, 79,* 425–430.

Dahlgren, L. (1979). Female alcoholics: IV. Marital situation and husbands. *Acta Psychiatrica Scandinavica, 59,* 59–69.

Deitrich, R. A., & Spuhler, K. (1984). Genetics of alcoholism and alcohol actions. In R. G. Smart et al. (Eds.), *Research advances in alcohol and drug problems* (Vol. 8, pp. 47–98). New York: Plenum.

Dull, R. T. (1983). Friends' use and adult drug and drinking behavior: A further test of differential association theory. *Journal of Criminal Law and Criminology, 74,* 1608–1619.

Eckenrode, J. (1984). Impact of chronic and acute stressors on daily reports of mood. *Journal of Personality and Social Psychology, 46,* 907–918.

Fillmore, K. M. (1984). "When angels fall": Women's drinking as cultural preoccupation and as reality. In S. C. Wilsnack & L. J. Beckman (Eds.), *Alcohol problems in women: Antecedents, consequences, and intervention* (pp. 7–36). New York: Guilford.

Fillmore, K. M., Bacon, S. D., & Hyman, M. (1979). *The 27 year longitudinal panel study of drinking by students in college, 1949–1976.* Final Report to the National Institute on Alcohol Abuse and Alcoholism (Contract No. ADM-281-76-0015). Berkeley: University of California at Berkeley, School of Public Health, Social Research Group.

Fillmore, K. M., & Midanik, L. (1984). Chronicity of drinking problems among men: A longitudinal study. *Journal of Studies on Alcohol, 45,* 228–236.

Fortino, D. (1979). Do working women drink too much? *Harper's Bazaar, 112* (4), 70.

Glisson, C. A., & Mok, H. M.-K. (1983). Incorporating nominal variables in path analysis: A cross-cultural example with human service organizations. *Journal of Applied Behavioral Science, 19,* 95–102.

Goldberger, A. S. (1964). *Econometric theory.* New York: John Wiley.

Gomberg, E. S. (1980). Risk factors related to alcohol problems among women: Proneness and vulnerability. In *Alcoholism and alcohol abuse among women: Research issues* (pp. 83–105). Research Monograph No. 1 of the National Institute on Alcohol Abuse and Alcoholism (U.S. Department of Health, Education, and Welfare Publication No. ADM-80-835). Washington, DC: U.S. Government Printing Office.

Gomberg, E. S. L., & Lisansky, J. M. (1984). Antecedents of alcohol problems in women. In S. C. Wilsnack & L. J. Beckman (Eds.), *Alcohol problems in women: Antecedents, consequences, and intervention* (pp. 233–259). New York: Guilford.

Goodwin, D. W. (1979). Alcoholism and heredity. *Archives of General Psychiatry, 36,* 57–61.

Greeley, A. M., McCready, W. C., & Theisen, G. (1980). *Ethnic drinking subcultures.* New York: Praeger.

Haer, J. L. (1955). Drinking patterns and the influence of friends and family. *Quarterly Journal of Studies on Alcohol, 16,* 178–182.

Hall, R. L., Hesselbrock, V. M., & Stabenau, J. R. (1983). Familial distribution of alcohol use: Assortative mating of alcoholic probands. *Behavior Genetics, 13,* 373–382.

Hanushek, E. A., & Jackson, J. E. (1977). *Statistical methods for social scientists.* New York: Academic.

Harford, T. C. (1978). Contextual drinking patterns among men and women. In F. Seixas (Ed.), *Currents in alcoholism* (Vol. 4, pp. 287–296). New York: Grune and Stratton.

154

Harford, T. C. (1984). Situational factors in drinking: A developmental perspective on drinking contexts. In P. M. Miller & T. D. Nirenberg (Eds.), *Prevention of alcohol abuse* (pp. 119–159). New York: Plenum.

Heise, D. R. (1975). *Causal analysis.* New York: John Wiley.

Holubowycz, O. T. (1983). The roles of life events and support networks in the aetiology of female alcohol dependence. *Australian Alcohol/Drug Review, 2,* 40–44.

Huba, G. J., & Harlow, L. L. (1983). Comparison of maximum likelihood, generalized least squares, ordinary least squares, and asymptotically distribution free parameter estimates in drug abuse latent variable causal models. *Journal of Drug Education, 13,* 387–404.

Jessor, R., Graves, T., Hanson, R. C., & Jessor, S. L. (1968). *Society, personality, and deviant behavior: A study of a tri-ethnic community.* New York: Holt, Rinehart and Winston.

Jessor, R., & Jessor, S. L. (1977). *Problem behavior and psychosocial development: A longitudinal study of youth.* New York: Academic.

Johnson, P. B. (1982). Sex differences, women's roles and alcohol use: Preliminary national data. *Journal of Social Issues, 38* (2), 93–116.

Johnson, P. B., Armor, D. J., Polich, S., & Stambul, H. (1977). *U.S. adult drinking practices: Time trends, social correlates and sex roles.* Working Note prepared for the National Institute on Alcohol Abuse and Alcoholism. Santa Monica, CA: Rand Corporation.

Jones, K. L., Smith, D. W., Ulleland, C. N., & Streissguth, A. P. (1973). Pattern of malformation in offspring of chronic alcoholic mothers. *Lancet, 1,* 1267–1271.

Jones, M. C. (1981). Midlife drinking patterns: Correlates and antecedents. In D. Eichorn et al. (Eds.), *Present and past in middle life.* New York: Academic.

Kalant, O. J. (Ed.) (1980). *Research advances in alcohol and drug problems: Vol. 5. Alcohol and drug problems in women.* New York: Plenum.

Klassen, A. D. (1980). Path analysis. Appendix to A. D. Klassen, C. J. Williams, & E. E. Levitt, *Sex and morality in the 20th Century United States.* Unpublished manuscript, Institute for Sex Research, Indiana University.

Klassen, A. D. (1982). *The undersocialized conception of woman.* Paper presented at the annual meeting of the Midwest Sociological Society, Des Moines, Iowa, April 1982.

Klassen, A. D., & Wilsnack, S. C. (1986). Sexual experience and drinking among women in a U.S. national survey. *Archives of Sexual Behavior, 15,* 363–392.

Knoke, D. (1975). A comparison of log-linear and regression models for systems of dichotomous variables. *Sociological Methods and Research, 3,* 416–434.

Landesman-Dwyer, S. (1982). Maternal drinking and pregnancy outcome. *Applied Research in Mental Retardation, 3*, 241–263.

Larsen, D. E., & Abu-Laban, B. (1968). Norm qualities and deviant behavior. *Social Problems, 15*, 441–450.

Liban, C., & Smart, R. G. (1980). Generational and other differences between males and females in problem drinking and its treatment. *Drug and Alcohol Dependence, 5*, 207–221.

Little, R. E., & Ervin, C. H. (1984). Alcohol use and reproduction. In S. C. Wilsnack & L. J. Beckman (Eds.), *Alcohol problems in women: Antecedents, consequences, and intervention* (pp. 155–188). New York: Guilford.

McLachlan, J. F. C., Walderman, R. L., Birchmore, D. F., & Marsden, L. R. (1979). Self-evaluation, role satisfaction, and anxiety in the woman alcoholic. *International Journal of the Addictions, 14*, 809–832.

Midanik, L. (1982). The validity of self-reported alcohol consumption and alcohol problems: A literature review. *British Journal of Addiction, 77*, 357–382.

Mizruchi, E. H., & Perrucci, R. (1962). Norm qualities and differential effects on deviant behavior: An exploratory analysis. *American Sociological Review, 27*, 391–399.

Morrissey, E. R., & Schuckit, M. A. (1978). Stressful life events and alcohol problems among women seen at a detoxication center. *Journal of Studies on Alcohol, 39*, 1559–1576.

National Institute of Mental Health. (1979, 1981). The NIMH Diagnostic Interview Schedule (DIS): Version I, 2-14-79. Version III, 2-5-81. Rockville, MD: Author.

National Institute on Alcohol Abuse and Alcoholism. (1980). *Alcoholism and alcohol abuse among women: Research issues.* NIAAA Research Monograph No. 1. (U.S. Department of Health, Education, and Welfare Publication No. ADM-80-835). Washington, DC: U.S. Government Printing Office.

National Institute on Alcohol Abuse and Alcoholism. (1986). *Women and alcohol: Health-related issues.* NIAAA Research Monograph No. 16. (U.S. Department of Health and Human Services Publication No. ADM-86-1139). Washington, DC: U.S. Government Printing Office.

O'Sullivan, K. (1984). Depression and its treatment in alcoholics: A review. *Canadian Journal of Psychiatry, 29*, 379–384.

Pearlin, L. I., Lieberman, M. A., Menaghan, E. G., & Mullan, J. T. (1981). The stress process. *Journal of Health and Social Behavior, 22*, 337–356.

Pedhazur, E. J. (1982). *Multiple regression in behavioral research* (2nd ed.) New York: Holt, Rinehart and Winston.

Peterson, J. S., Hartsock, N., & Lawson, G. (1984). Sexual dissatisfaction of female alcoholics. *Psychological Reports, 55*, 744–746.

Polich, J. M. (1981). Epidemiology of alcohol abuse in military and civilian populations. *American Journal of Public Health, 71,* 1125–1132.

Polich, J. M., & Orvis, B. R. (1979). *Alcohol problems: Patterns and prevalence and the U.S. Air Force.* Santa Monica, CA: Rand Corporation.

Robins, L. N. (1980, 1981). Washington University Followup Interview. Interview questionnaire for community survey of alcohol use and psychiatric disorders. Washington University School of Medicine, October 1980 and February 1981.

Robins, L. N., & Smith, E. M. (1980). Longitudinal studies of alcohol and drug problems: Sex differences. In O. J. Kalant (Ed.), *Research advances in alcohol and drug problems: Vol. 5. Alcohol and drug problems in women* (pp. 203–232). New York: Plenum.

Russell, M. (1982). Screening for alcohol-related problems in obstetric and gynecologic patients. In E. L. Abel (Ed.), *Fetal alcohol syndrome: Vol. 2. Human studies* (pp. 1–19). Boca Raton, FL: CRC Press.

Sandmaier, M. (1980). *The invisible alcoholics: Women and alcohol abuse in America.* New York: McGraw-Hill.

Schlegel, R. P., & Sanborn, M. D. (1979). Religious affiliation and adolescent drinking. *Journal of Studies on Alcohol, 40,* 693–703.

Schuckit, M. A. (1986). Genetic and clinical implications of alcoholism and affective disorder. *American Journal of Psychiatry, 143,* 140–147.

Scida, J., & Vannicelli, M. (1979). Sex-role conflict and women's drinking. *Journal of Studies on Alcohol, 40,* 28–44.

Skinner, H. A. (1984). Assessing alcohol use by patients in treatment. In R. G. Smart et al. (Eds.), *Research advances in alcohol and drug problems* (Vol. 8, pp. 183–207). New York: Plenum.

Skolnick, J. H. (1958). Religious affiliation and drinking behavior. *Quarterly Journal of Studies on Alcohol, 19,* 452–470.

Sokol, R. J., Miller, S. I., & Reed, G. (1980). Alcohol abuse during pregnancy: An epidemiologic study. *Alcoholism: Clinical and Experimental Research, 4,* 135–145.

Spence, J. T., & Helmreich, R. (1978). *Masculinity and femininity: Their psychological dimensions, correlates, and antecedents.* Austin: University of Texas Press.

Straus, R., & Bacon, S. D. (1953). *Drinking in college.* New Haven: Yale University Press.

Streifel, C. M. (1986). *The relevance of drinking companions to women's drinking behavior.* Master's thesis, Department of Sociology, University of North Dakota.

Suffet, F., & Brotman, R. (1976). Female drug use: Some observations. *International Journal of the Addictions, 11,* 19–33.

Turkington, D. A. (1985). A note on two-stage least squares, three stage least squares, and maximum likelihood estimation in an expectations model. *International Economic Review, 26,* 507–510.

Vaillant, G. E. (1983). *The natural history of alcoholism: Causes, patterns, and paths to recovery.* Cambridge: Harvard University Press.

Vannicelli, M. (1984). Treatment outcome of alcoholic women: The state of the art in relation to sex bias and expectancy effects. In S. C. Wilsnack & L. J. Beckman (Eds.), *Alcohol problems in women: Antecedents, consequences, and intervention* (pp. 369–412). New York: Guilford.

Verbrugge, L. M. (1983). *Pressures, satisfactions, and their link to physical health of young women.* Paper presented at the annual meeting of the American Psychological Association, Anaheim, CA, August 1983.

Volicer, B. J., Cahill, M. H., & Smith, J. L. (1981). Sex differences in correlates of problem drinking among employed males and females. *Drug and Alcohol Dependence, 8,* 175–187.

Wilsnack, R. W., & Cheloha, R. (1985). *Women's roles and problem drinking across the lifespan.* Paper presented at the annual meeting of the Society for the Study of Social Problems, Washington, DC, August 1985.

Wilsnack, R. W., Klassen, A. D., & Wilsnack, S. C. (1986). Retrospective analysis of lifetime changes in women's drinking behavior. *Advances in Alcohol and Substance Abuse, 5* (3), 9–28.

Wilsnack, R. W., Wilsnack, S. C., & Klassen, A. D. (1984). Women's drinking and drinking problems: Patterns from a 1981 national survey. *American Journal of Public Health, 74,* 1231–1238.

Wilsnack, S. C. (1973). Sex-role identity in female alcoholism. *Journal of Abnormal Psychology, 82,* 253–261.

Wilsnack, S. C. (1976). The impact of sex roles on women's alcohol use and abuse. In M. Greenblatt & M. A. Schuckit (Eds.), *Alcoholism problems in women and children* (pp. 37–63). New York: Grune and Stratton.

Wilsnack, S. C. (1984). Drinking, sexuality, and sexual dysfunction in women. In S. C. Wilsnack and L. J. Beckman (Eds.), *Alcohol problems in women: Antecedents, consequences, and intervention* (pp. 189–227). New York: Guilford.

Wilsnack, S. C., & Beckman, L. J. (Eds.) (1984). *Alcohol problems in women: Antecedents, consequences, and intervention.* New York: Guilford.

Wilsnack, S. C., Klassen, A. D., & Wilsnack, R. W. (1984). Drinking and reproductive dysfunction among women in a 1981 national survey. *Alcoholism: Clinical and Experimental Research, 8,* 451–458.

Wilsnack, S. C., Klassen, A. D., & Wright, S. I. (1986). Gender-role orientations and drinking among women in a U.S. national survey. In *Proceedings of the 34th International Congress on Alcoholism and Drug Dependence* (pp. 242–255). Calgary, Alberta: International Council on Alcohol and Addictions.

Wilsnack, S. C., Wilsnack, R. W, & Klassen, A. D. (1986). Epidemiological research on women's drinking, 1978–1984. In *Women and alcohol: Health-related issues* (pp. 1–68). Research Monograph No. 16 of the National Institute on Alcohol Abuse and Alcoholism (U.S. Department of Health and Human Services Publication No. ADM-86-1139). Washington, DC: U.S. Government Printing Office.

Winship, C., & Mare, R. D. (1983). Structural equations and path analysis for discrete data. *American Journal of Sociology, 89,* 54–110.

Working wives: Driven to drink? (1978). *Science News, 114,* 197.

Wright, L. S. (1983). Correlates of reported drinking problems among male and female college students. *Journal of Alcohol and Drug Education, 28* (3), 47–57.

Zucker, R. A. (1979). Developmental aspects of drinking through the young adult years. In H. T. Blane & M. E. Chafetz (Eds.), *Youth, alcohol, and social policy* (pp. 91–146). New York: Plenum.

Alcoholism: A Family Interaction Perspective

Theodore Jacob
University of Arizona

Theoretical and Methodological Developments

INTRODUCTION

*H*istorically, alcoholism has been defined as an individual problem, and as a result interpersonal factors in general and family factors in particular have received only parenthetical attention until quite recent times. Several reasons can be noted for this relative neglect of family influences in studies of alcoholism.

First, biased sampling has contributed to the stereotype of the alcoholic as a loner with few social ties. Early studies were generally based on hospitalized and arrested abusers, leading to the impression that alcoholics were a homogeneous group of "undersocialized, poorly integrated individuals comprised of homeless derelicts, chronic offenders and the mentally ill" (Bailey, 1961). Second, when alcoholism was reconceptualized as a medical rather than a moral problem, it remained within an individual context; alcoholism came to be considered a disease with a specific etiology, "set of symptoms, a typical course and predictable prognosis" (Steinglass, 1976a). Finally, social service agencies have been reluctant to deal with families when alcoholism has been involved; regardless of presenting problems, alcohol was considered so confounding that it precluded any family treatment and could be effectively dealt with only in an intensive individual modality. Such a view is supported by Steinglass's (1976a) review, which indicated that studies of family treatment with alcoholics were limited to a few clinical reports as recently as the mid-1970s and that there were virtually no reports of conjoint family treatment for alcoholism in leading professional journals on family issues.

In light of the foregoing considerations, it is not surprising that the earliest research from a "family perspective" focused on individual family members—most importantly the spouse and second-arily the children. After a brief review of these two literatures, I will discuss the newest area of study—investigations of relationships and interactions among family members when one of them is an alcoholic.

THE ALCOHOLIC'S SPOUSE

The vast majority of studies concerned with alcoholism and marital relationships have focused on the alcoholic's spouse rather than the relationship per se, have emphasized personality traits and charac-teristics rather than patterns of relating, and have been more con-cerned with wives of male alcoholics than with husbands of female alcoholics (Edwards, Harvey, & Whitehead, 1973; Jacob & Seilham-er, 1982; Nace, 1982; Royce, 1981).

Investigations of the alcoholic's wife during the past 40 years have been directed toward testing two major propositions. The earliest formulations about spouses of alcoholics were based on subjective impressions of psychodynamically oriented clinicians who depicted wives as psychologically disturbed. From this perspective, women with certain types of personalities were seen to marry alcoholics or potential alcoholics in order to satisfy unconscious needs of their own—in brief, the need to dominate a weak, dependent male. The literature supporting this hypothesis cites evidence that the wife of the alcoholic exhibits psychosocial problems, psychological decom-pensation such as depression, anxiety, or phobias, somatic dis-orders, or attempts to sabotage improvement when her husband shows signs of controlling his excessive drinking.

In contrast to the disturbed wife position, the "stressed wife" view suggested that the wife manifests neurotic traits and psychosocial disturbances as a consequence of living with an alco-holic. From this position, any uncooperative or dominant behavior that the wife exhibits is explained as a necessary coping mechanism developed to maintain family functioning and stability. Thus the wife tends to minimize changes in her husband's drinking patterns on the basis of experiences, viewing a period of abstinence as merely a temporary dry spell rather than an actual step toward recovery. That the alcoholic's wife may disparage improvement in her hus-band's behavior is not a result of her pathological needs but only a realistic recognition of his undependability.

Detailed evaluations of these two positions have been presented by various reviewers during the past decade, most of whom have emphasized major methodological and conceptual limitations that have characterized much of this literature (Edwards et al., 1973; Jacob & Seilhamer, 1982; Nace, 1982; Royce, 1981). Specifically, most reports in this literature have involved small, biased samples, most often limited to wives' reports obtained within clinical settings. Non-help-seeking wives are largely unrepresented—a subgroup of women who are generally believed to exhibit higher levels of functioning, self-esteem, and assertiveness than treatment-seeking spouses (Gorman & Rooney, 1979; Hurwitz & Daya, 1977). In addition, subjects have usually been assessed at times of acute stress such as the hospital admission of the alcoholic spouse or involvement with police or the courts. Furthermore, control groups have been absent or inappropriate, and there has been little recognition and control of major confounding influences such as poverty, unemployment, critical life events, and family violence. Finally, studies have been overwhelmingly cross sectional and based primarily on interviews or questionnaires of unsubstantiated reliability and validity.

In addition to such methodological problems, this literature has a history of restricted conceptual development. Ensuing initially from a psychodynamic framework, research efforts were primarily individually oriented, examining how alcoholics' spouses differed from normals and how they contributed to their spouses' drinking within the context of a deviant personality structure. As environmental perspectives became established, the wife was reconceptualized as responding to stressors initiated by her spouse's alcoholism. Research strategies derived from this framework were also limited, however, dealing mostly with a quasi quantification of stressors and correlating them with spouse functioning and drinking outcome. Subsequently, investigations of coping styles led to the identification of typical response patterns but failed to clarify their relation to spouse characteristics or situational variables. Thus the wife of the alcoholic was either villain or victim, with little attention given to the possibility of her dual role as "contributor-responder."

Recognizing the need to examine the alcoholic's spouse within a broader conceptual framework, Moos's work of the past decade has provided a welcome and necessary alternative to the one-sided approaches of the past (Finney, Moos, Cronkite, & Gamble, 1983). In essence, Moos has recommended integrating the "disturbed personality," "stress," and "coping" perspectives into a model that predicts spouse functioning from five sets of variables: (1) background characteristics (ethnic group, education, initial functioning); (2) level of functioning of the alcoholic partner and not simply drinking status per se; (3) life-changing events; (4) coping responses; and (5) family environment (Moos, Finney, & Gamble, 1982). From such a multifactorial perspective, it seems clear that further advances in understanding the nonalcoholic spouse's role in the alcoholic family will require the inclusion of several levels of influence and the acknowledgment and adequate measurement of bidirectional effects—that is, the alcoholic's impact on spouse functioning and the spouse's role in influencing the course of abusive drinking.

THE ALCOHOLIC'S CHILDREN

The literature on the children of alcoholics can be categorized into three areas of interest: health issues, alcohol-related issues, and psychosocial difficulties (e.g., Deutsch, DiCicco, & Mills, 1982; O'Gorman, 1981). Health-related issues have included fetal alcohol syndrome (FAS; Graham-Clay, 1983; Holzman, 1982; Rosett & Weiner, 1982; Warner & Rosett, 1975), child abuse and neglect related to alcoholism (el-Guebaly & Offord, 1979; Hindeman, 1977; Orme & Rimmer, 1981; Wilson, 1982), and links between alcoholism and hyperactivity (Alterman, Petrarulo, Tarter, & McGowan, 1982; Goodwin, Schulsinger, Hermansen, Guze, & Winokur, 1975; Morrison & Stewart, 1973; Tarter, McBride, Buonpane, & Schneider, 1977). The second area of interest, alcohol-related issues, includes, most importantly, the increased risk for alcoholism among children of alcoholics (Cotton, 1979; Goodwin, 1971). Interestingly but unfortunately, studies of family genetic (Cloninger, Bohman, & Sigvardsson, 1981; Kaij, 1960) and family environmental influences (Goodwin, Schulsinger, Hermansen, Guze, & Winokur, 1973; Wolin, Bennett, & Noonan, 1979) on the etiology of alcoholism have developed quite independent of one another, with few attempts to grapple with the joint effects most certainly involved. The final research direction has focused on the psychosocial and psychiatric disturbance exhibited by alcoholics' offspring during latency, adolescence, and early adulthood.

Although methodological difficulties and deficiencies have been evident in all of these subliteratures, the literature concerned with the alcoholic parent's impact on children's psychosocial and psychiatric functioning has been most open to criticism and qualification (Jacob, Favorini, Meisel, & Anderson, 1978; Jacob & Leonard, 1986; Wilson, 1982). This area comprises a relatively small set of empirical studies that generally have not included psychiatric control groups, so that specificity of effects cannot be determined. Furthermore, most studies have involved small samples of convenience, most often obtained within clinical treatment contexts and assessed almost exclusively with self-report procedures too often characterized by questionable psychometric properties. Furthermore, alcoholism diagnoses have been determined by a variety of procedures (making cross-study comparisons difficult), and drinking-related variables have infrequently been considered or controlled (e.g., severity and duration of alcoholism). In light of these problems, our confidence about the relation between parental alcoholism and the psychosocial functioning of offspring is far from complete.

Finally, until recently there has been no theoretically driven work in this area that has guided studies of offspring at "high risk" or aided interpretation of findings. A relatively recent exception is the work of Moore (1982). In developing a conceptual framework for studying the effects of parental alcoholism on children, Moore (1982) proposed that outcome depends upon the chronicity and severity of disruption of three primary factors: the quality of the affective relationship between parent and child, the consistency of parental supervision, and the level of direct parental socialization. According to this model, there are also secondary factors that mediate child adjustment by disrupting these primary factors, such as marital conflict, family crisis, social isolation, unemployment, and alcoholism. Thus child outcome would vary with the impact of these secondary factors upon the parental role. The importance of this framework is twofold. First, it suggests that alcoholism does not necessarily, in itself, produce impaired offspring, but does so only to the extent that it adversely affects marital and parental functions. Second, it directs attention to intrafamilial variables and processes that are, in effect, the interactional mechanisms that mediate child outcome (adaptive or impaired).

THE ALCOHOLIC'S FAMILY INTERACTIONS

Rationale. As we have seen, most of the literature relevant to family influences on alcoholism has been individually oriented. Investigators have endeavored to describe personality patterns and traits of spouses that may predate the partner's alcoholism or result from extended periods of family life involving an alcoholic partner and patterns of maladaptation manifested by children raised within a family including an alcoholic parent. In the first case, the role of the spouse in the etiology and maintenance of the partner's alcoholism has been a central issue, yet the data most important in exploring such relationships have been absent—the actual *patterns* of interaction between spouse and partner that potentiate or maintain the abusive drinking. Similarly, reports of the psychosocial and psychiatric status of alcoholics' children indicate that they often exhibit a variety of interpersonal and cognitive difficulties as preadolescents and adolescents and that they are at high risk for alcoholism and general psychiatric disturbances as adults. Again, the relevant literature implies that such outcomes result from disturbed patterns of marital and parent-child interaction associated with a family structure including an alcoholic parent. Close examination of this literature, however, reveals few efforts to describe actual *patterns of interaction* that may mediate adverse child outcomes or to document the temporal relationships between these processes and various child outcomes.

What seems to be missing from much of the literature, then, is an effort to describe actual patterns of interchange between the alcoholic and members of his or her family that are related to the etiology, course, and perpetuation of alcoholism. From my vantage point, there are two major contributions an interactional approach can make in efforts to elucidate the complex association between alcoholism and familial factors.

First, empirically based *descriptions* of family interactions involving an alcoholic are the *necessary building blocks* for theoretical, treatment, and prevention efforts to be forged in the years ahead. As noted previously, there are very few data of this sort in the literature, and for the most part clinical theory and practice have been based upon descriptions generated from self-reports and spouse reports obtained within clinical contexts, involving measures of unknown reliability and validity. We do not know to what extent these "pictures" of alcoholic-family relationships correspond to observed patterns of interchange, though there is reason to believe that reports of complex relationship events are vulnerable to significant distortion and bias (Wiggins, 1973). To develop theory and practice based upon what members actually do to one another over time and how such interchanges are in turn related to the development or perpetuation of such complex outcomes as "abusive drinking," one must obtain comprehensive descriptions of interactions involving alcoholics and their families.

Second, the description of alcoholics' interactions with their families should provide insights that can be transformed into programs of treatment and prevention. In particular, the field of marital and family therapy has undergone a vast expansion during the past decade, involving a variety of approaches applied to a wide range of disordered behavior. Of particular importance, family therapy has strongly emphasized repetitive and maladaptive patterns of interchange that can be corrected in order to allow the family to experience different, and one hopes more adaptive, modes of relating that do not support maladaptive behavior. Regarding treatment for alcoholism, there seems to be increasing interest in applying and testing the limits of family therapy approaches to abusive drinking either as the major therapeutic intervention or as adjuncts to other, concurrently instituted treatment modalities (McCrady, 1985; McCrady, Dean, Dubreuil, & Swanson, 1985; O'Farrell, Cutter, & Floyd, 1985). To the extent that interaction research can help clarify the nature of affective interchanges associated with the presence versus the absence of alcohol, problem-solving styles and their effectiveness, dominance patterns and their variations, and parent-child socialization practices involving the alcoholic parent, nonalcoholic parent, and child, it is increasingly likely that treatment (as well as prevention) programs will be founded on greater substance and less supposition than currently seems to be the case.

Historical influences. Although only recently applied to family studies of alcoholism, "family interaction" research has been evolving in the more general literature on family factors and psychopathology during the past 25 years—an approach that is best viewed as an assemblage of several models, the most influential being general systems theory, communication theory, and social learning theory.

The earliest influence on this model can be traced back to the 1950s, when the field was introduced to several "family theories" of schizophrenia, including the work of Bateson, Jackson, Haley, and Weakland; Bowen; Wynne; and Lidz (for reviews of this literature, see Mishler & Waxler, 1965; Olson, 1972; and Schuham, 1972). Based on an integration of systems and communication theories, these seminal writings had a major impact on psychiatric theory, research, and practice over much of the next two decades. Buttressing these forces were the contributions of family sociology—in particular, the contributions of Parsons and Bales (1955) and their analysis of instrumental and social-emotional role functions in ad hoc as well as nuclear family groups. Equally important, the flourishing small-group tradition (Waxler & Mishler, 1970) explored communication networks and power relationships in various types of organizations, providing a rich set of concepts and innovative laboratory procedures for studying group process and outcome. Finally the continued influence of behavioral psychology has been evident since the early 1960s, emphasizing as it has the specification of antecedent-consequent relationships, the careful definition and measurement of behavioral targets, and the analysis of Behavior × Situation relationships.

Alternatively referred to as family interaction, family systems, or behavioral family system research, this perspective is currently characterized by an attempt to identify patterns and processes that are associated with and serve to foster current, ongoing psychiatric disturbance and that predate and predict the development of psychiatric disorders in "high-risk" offspring. Notwithstanding the importance of interaction per se, it is also acknowledged that the family interaction perspective must be integrated with developmental, genetic, and personality literatures based on the assumption of an intimate and critical interplay between these influences on the development of behavior (Jacob, in press).

Regarding family studies of alcoholism, the major implication of this model is that we need to describe and understand *family processes* characterizing families with an alcoholic member and then relate these processes to family and individual outcomes. Stated in terms of significant questions to be addressed:

What aspects of family relationships serve to weaken family structure and stability, to promote or maintain abusive drinking patterns, and to render offspring more vulnerable to psychosocial and alcohol-related difficulties as youths and adults?

Conversely, what patterns of family interaction protect members and relationships from the devastating psychosocial effects that can be associated with abusive drinking?

Are any of these features—exacerbating or protective—unique to families of alcoholics, or are they shared with families characterized by different types of psychopathology?

To what degree do biological/hereditary versus family-environmental influences contribute separately and interdependently to these outcomes, and how might the environmental and "under the skin" variables be integrated into more illuminating research designs?

Finally, what methodologies are best suited for addressing these various levels of inquiry, and can a combination of methods clarify our understanding of family-psychopathology relationships?

Interaction studies involving alcoholics. Application of this interaction framework to studies of alcoholic families has only begun to take form during the past fifteen years. Among the earliest and most influential studies is the work of Gorad and his colleagues (Gorad, 1971; Gorad, McCourt, & Cobb,1971). Based on a communication-systems framework emanating from the work of Haley, Bateson, and Jackson (Bateson, Jackson, Haley, & Weakland, 1956), Gorad hypothesized that the alcoholic's style of interaction would be characterized by responsibility avoidance—an expectation that was supported in a study comparing alcoholic and nondistressed couples involved in a game simulation strategy. Subsequent studies using similar laboratory game procedures provided only partial support for these findings (Cobb & McCourt, 1979; Kennedy, 1976), although the various methodological differences and deficiencies that characterize this set of investigations limit the validity of cross-study comparisons. (See review by Jacob & Seilhamer, in press.) At the same time, these inconsistencies do suggest that group differences may be subtle and not readily evident in examining only the outcomes of interactions; the interaction process must also be considered.

The early process studies also had significant methodological problems and, as such, were of more value for the innovative paradigms and hypotheses they offered than for their substantive findings (Becker & Miller, 1976; Hersen, Miller, & Eisler, 1973). By far the most programmatic work in this literature has been conducted by Steinglass and his associates during the past decade (Steinglass, Tislenko, & Reiss, 1985).

Steinglass conceptualizes problems (stress, tension, etc.) as arising from three sources: individual psychopathology as it influences the adjustment of other family members; interactional conflicts that cannot be adequately explained by reference to disturbances in individual members; and dislocations and stress emanating from the immediate social environment and its effect on family stability. Problems in any of these areas can escalate until significant stress is experienced and substantial disruption to the family itself becomes likely. At this point alcohol ingestion, intoxication, and associated interactions may function as a solution to the "problem." If they are effective in reducing tension and perhaps temporarily solving a problem, short-term family stability may be achieved, and as a result the change from sober to intoxicated interactional states can serve to stabilize an unstable system.

> In some families, equilibrium might be thought of as being restored by increasing interactional distance (the drinker goes off to drink in the basement), or diminishing physical contact (no sex with someone who is drunk), or reducing tension in the family (familiar patterns of behavior are less tension provoking than unique patterns); whereas in other families alcohol might be associated with closer interactional distance (making contact by fighting after the alcoholic spouse has been drinking), disinhibition (alcohol permits ritualized sexual behavior), or maintaining distance from the social environment (fights with neighbors when drunk). (Steinglass, 1981b, p. 300)

The major implication of this model is that variation in drinking patterns can play a central role in adaptive and disruptive marital states and ultimately in the maintenance of heavy drinking—an assumption of major significance in theoretical developments linking interpersonal variables to dysfunctional behavior and of great potential importance to the development of family-oriented treatment and prevention programs.

Unfortunately, Steinglass's own efforts to assess this hypothesis directly have been limited to clinical observations of interactions during periods of sobriety and intoxication. Given the importance that Steinglass and others have ascribed to alcohol's role in stabilizing family structures, it is unfortunate that so little empirical effort has been directed toward this issue. Thus far only three studies have reported on experimental drinking procedures with alcoholic families.

Billings, Kessler, Gomberg, and Weiner (1979) compared the marital interactions of alcoholic couples with those of distressed (but nonalcoholic) couples and nondistressed (nonalcoholic) couples. Analyses of laboratory discussions, generated from standardized role-play procedures, indicated that both alcoholic and distressed couples differed from nondistressed couples in a number of ways (more hostile and coercion /attack statements and fewer friendly and cognitive acts). On the other hand, no differences were noted between alcoholic and distressed couples, nor were there any Group X Drinking Condition interactions. Notwithstanding the noteworthy design strategies used in this study, however, the experimental drinking procedure turned out to be an extremely weak manipulation—half the couples chose not to drink at all, and those who did drink consumed very little alcohol. Given these limitations, the absence of a drinking condition effect has very little meaning.

In a second study involving an experimental drinking procedure, Jacob, Ritchey, Cvitkovic, and Blane (1981) examined the interactions of alcoholic and normal control couples engaged in a structured problem-solving task. Although there were separate observations of mother-child and father-child interactions, the marital data are of most importance to the present discussion. During the drinking session, the alcoholics consumed sufficient alcohol to generate mean postsession blood alcohol concentrations (BACs) of 0.08%, whereas their wives, as well as both spouses in the control group, drank only a small amount (mean postsession BAC = 0.01%). Overall, the alcoholic couples were found to express more negative and less positive affect than control couples. In addition, the nondistressed husbands were found to contribute more of the problem solving than their wives, whereas the alcoholic husbands and their wives exhibited similar rates of problem solving. Most important, however, the alcoholic couples, but not the normal controls, expressed significantly more negative affect and disagreement when drinking than when not drinking. Although it is of considerable interest to the evolving literature on the acute effects of alcohol on family behavior, several important design limitations characterized this preliminary effort—small samples of alcoholic and control couples; the absence of a nonalcoholic, distressed comparison group; and the considerable diagnostic heterogeneity of both the alcoholics and their spouses.

A final study by Frankenstein, Hay, and Nathan (1985), involving alcoholic couples only, reported that couples exhibited greater positivity and problem solving in the drinking than in the nondrinking session—findings that appear to support Steinglass's notions regarding the reinforcing or adaptive effects alcohol might exert in alcoholic families. That Frankenstein obtained findings opposite to those reported by Jacob is probably best understood in light of several design features that differentiated these two studies. First, Frankenstein assessed alcoholic couples only, and it is uncertain whether other couples would have exhibited similar increases in positivity and problem solving in moving from the no drink to drink condition. Second, Jacob et al. (1981) served alcohol ad lib to both spouses during the marital discussions, whereas Frankenstein administered alcohol in a fixed-dose format to the alcoholics only and before actual discussion. Third, subject motivation and orientation differed across the two studies, one involving treatment seekers and the other involving participants in a research project. Finally, it is possible that Frankenstein's sample included subgroups that varied significantly in the positivity-enhancing effects that alcohol exerted on their interactions. (Of the eight alcoholics that Frankenstein assessed, two were female, six had completed at least college, one was a student, and one was retired.) Further discussion of these differences and their implications for cross-study comparisons can be found in Frankenstein et al. (1985) and Jacob and Seilhamer (in press).

Notwithstanding the promising research strategies and exciting interactional hypotheses that have been introduced in the developing interaction literature, it is obvious that the empirical data base is numerically and qualitatively limited. In an attempt to strengthen and extend this literature, my own research efforts have involved a more rigorous and programmatic examination of alcoholic-family interaction than has been accomplished during the past decade. As will be described below, key limitations reflected in the existing literature are addressed directly and systematically in the current investigation: the selection of a diagnostically homogeneous group of alcoholics with no additional psychiatric disorder or alcohol-abusing spouses; the inclusion of normal as well as psychiatric control groups, the latter comprising clinically depressed males (without evidence of alcohol abuse) rather than a heterogeneous group of maritally distressed couples; the introduction of an experimental drinking procedure in which couples consume significant amounts of alcohol ad lib; the application of a theoretically relevant, empirically based coding system to the videotaped laboratory interactions; and the assessment of relatively large subject samples so that statistical power can be maximized, family typologies can be explored, and follow-up of index cases and their offspring can be conducted.

Project Description

OVERVIEW

The broad objective of this research program is to develop an empirically based understanding of family interactions that characterize families with an alcoholic member, that serve to reinforce and perpetuate cycles of abusive drinking, and that predate and predict the development of abusive drinking as well as other psychiatric disturbance in "high risk" offspring. To this end, efforts of the past eight years have involved systematic evaluations of intact families with an alcoholic father and of two carefully selected control groups—families with a depressed (nonalcoholic) father and families with a nonalcoholic, nondisturbed father. For each family, extensive observation data are obtained within two contexts: (a) the controlled laboratory setting in which the major interest is the impact of alcohol ingestion (drink/no drink) and family subsystem (marital, parent-child and parent-parent-child) on the process and structure of family interactions, and (b) the natural home setting, in which attention is on the quantity, quality, and organization of interaction among different family subsystems. Supplementing and extending this observational data base, various report data are obtained from family members and others—information that will add to our understanding of drinking patterns, psychiatric status, marital relationship of parents, and the psychological, social, and academic functioning of the children. Key issues addressed in this research are the impact of alcoholism on the process and structure of family life; the role of family processes in maintaining alcohol abuse; the way varying patterns of family interaction potentiate or inhibit the development of alcoholism in children of alcoholics; and how observed patterns vary in relation to nature of dysfunction (alcoholism versus depression).

The project has now accumulated a relatively large data base, and major analyses have been done. Given this foundation, two new research efforts have recently been undertaken: the collection of family interaction data involving female alcoholics and female depressives and a follow-up assessment of all previously studied families aimed at charting the course of alcoholism and identifying family variables associated with differential outcomes for offspring.

SUBJECTS AND SUBJECT RECRUITMENT

Families from each of the three groups are recruited via newspaper advertisements and are paid for their involvement in the project—a procedure that has the advantage of rapidly identifying a significant number of potential research subjects from which final samples can be drawn, equating experimental and control groups as to "volunteer" status and general population characteristics, and circumventing difficulties and potential conflicts often associated with recruiting experimental subjects from clinical (treatment) settings; for example, the necessity for involving the alcoholic and his family in the research program before he begins therapy. All participating families must satisfy the following selection criteria: (a) the parents are currently living together, and the family contains at least one child between 10 and 18 years of age living at home; (b) no spouse of an index case reflects a current major psychiatric or alcohol-abuse disturbance; (c) no child exhibits a current major psychiatric or cognitive disturbance; (d) no family member is currently in psychiatric treatment; and (e) neither parent has any significant medical problem or is taking prescribed or nonprescribed medication that could cause adverse side effects when alcohol is consumed.

Subject screening procedures include telephone and in-person interviews as well as the collection of various report materials assessing psychopathology and drinking status; for example, the Beck Depression Inventory (BDI; Beck, Ward, Mendelson, Mock, & Erbaugh, 1961), Michigan Alcoholism Screening Test (MAST; Selzer, 1971), Impairment Index (II; Jessor, Graves, Hansen, & Jessor, 1968), and Quantity-Frequency Index (QFI; Ruggels, Armor, Polich, Mothershead, & Stephen, 1975). The Schedule for Affective Disorder and Schizophrenia (SADS) is administered to each spouse so that Research Diagonostic Criteria (RDC) can be determined (Spitzer & Endicott, 1977). To be accepted into the alcoholic group, the father must satisfy RDC for alcoholism as well as endorse disturbance in at least three of four domains specified by Feighner, Robins, Guze, Woodruff, Winokur, and Munoz (1972): medical problems, social problems, control problems, and prior identification of alcohol-related problems. Of particular importance, alcoholic subjects are excluded if they achieve an RDC of Major Depressive Disorder. In contrast, depressed subjects must satisfy RDC for Major Depressive Disorder and must not satisfy criteria for Alcoholism. Normal controls are included only if they achieve no RDC for current status.

The selection of depressed subjects and their families to represent one comparison group was based upon several considerations. First, selection of this relatively circumscribed and delimited group of psychiatric control families will allow for more precise and meaningful interpretation of interaction differences that do or do not emerge during the study. Second, depression research of the past ten years has focused increasingly on behavioral and family interaction models (Beck, 1971; Costello, 1972; Coyne, 1976; Coyne, Kahn, & Gotlib, in press; Ferster, 1973; Hinchliffe, Hooper, Roberts, & Vaughan, 1977; Lewinsohn, 1974; Lewinsohn & Schaffer, 1971; Libet, Lewinsohn, & Javorek, 1973; McLean, Ogston, & Grauer, 1973; Rehm, 1977), and we hope that present findings will provide additional and important data regarding interpersonal aspects of depression. Finally, greater attention has been directed to the relation between alcoholism and depression (Goodwin, 1979), and we hope the present study can further clarify the theoretical and treatment overlaps between these two disorders.

DATA COLLECTION PROCEDURES

Report procedures. Although the main thrust of this chapter will involve the laboratory observations, various other types of data collection also pertain to the study's overall goals. Self-report materials include structured interviews as well as questionnaires completed by all family members about one another and by teachers regarding the children. Supplementing the observational data, these data allow for a more comprehensive description of subjects and more systematic comparison with other clinical and research samples.

Drinking measures. Alcohol use and abuse information is collected using several self-report questionnaires in order to obtain a detailed picture of early drinking experiences, current attitudes toward alcohol, and consumption preferences as to frequency, type of liquor, and location of drinking. In addition to these retrospective reports, daily drinking data are obtained from each spouse during a 21-day period after the laboratory procedures. Finally, information on children's use of and opinions regarding alcohol are obtained through the Drinking Attitudes/Practices Questionnaire (Blane, 1979). We anticipate that a full description of the alcohol practices and attitudes of both adults and children will enrich and elaborate interpretations of the laboratory and home observation data as well as other report material.

Teacher ratings. For all offspring 6 years of age and older, teacher ratings of the children's social and academic behavior are collected by means of the Myklebust Pupil Rating Scale (Myklebust & Bosher, 1969) and the Conners Teacher Rating Form (Connors, 1969). Given the increased incidence of adolescent antisocial behavior among individuals who subsequently develop alcoholism (Jones, 1968; McCord & McCord, 1962; Robins, Bates, & O'Neal, 1962), as well as the hypothesized relationship between hyperactivity and alcoholism (Cantwell, 1972; Tarter, Hegedus, Goldstein, Shelly, & Alterman, 1983; Tarter et al., 1977), teacher rating data will allow for the assessment of these various interrelationships with a carefully described, narrowly defined sample of alcoholic subjects.

Family history. Family history interviews are conducted using the Family History Research Diagnostic Criteria (Andreasen, Endicott, Spitzer, & Winokur, 1977) and applied to all first-degree relatives in order to assess the extended family for psychiatric disorders. Both the index case and his spouse are interviewed so that the psychiatric status of the relatives of both parents can be determined and subsequently related to the development of psychiatric disturbance and alcohol abuse in offspring.

Additional measures. Each of the three family members who come to the laboratory sessions is assessed for reading and general intellectual ability with the Quick Test (Ammons & Ammons, 1962). Measures of marital functioning and satisfaction are collected from the parents through the Marital Adjustment Test (Locke & Wallace, 1959), the Family Assessment Measure (FAM; Skinner, Steinhauer, & Santa-Barbara, 1983), and the Dyadic Adjustment Scale (Spanir, 1976). Each parent also completes a Child Behavior Checklist (Achenbach, 1978; Achenbach & Edelbrock, 1979) on each child older than 6 years. In turn, each school-age child reports his or her perspective on the family's social functioning and the child's personal satisfaction using the Moos Family Environment Scale (Moos, 1974) and the Piers-Harris Self-Esteem Inventory (Piers & Harris, 1969).

Home observation procedures. After the final laboratory observation session, arrangements are made to monitor families in their homes for a period of 20 days. This monitoring includes not only daily reports of drinking and stressful events, but direct observation of family interaction collected by audiotape recorders placed in the home. To assess the impact of the observation/recording procedure on family behavior—that is, reactivity effects—family members first activate the recording apparatus at dinnertime; this week is referred to as the "fixed" recording condition. During a second week the family is told that we want to obtain a random sample of family life, and three recorders are placed in the home, each inside a small container. The family is told that each machine is activated automatically and randomly throughout the day. Actually only the apparatus in the dining area is functional, and it operates for the same one-hour period each day—during the family's dinner. This week of recording is referred to as the "random" recording condition. In essence, then, the fixed and random conditions both collect dinnertime interactions, but under two different levels of observational salience that let us consider the family's reaction to being recorded in their home.

Laboratory observation procedures. All families participate in three laboratory meetings, the first aimed at acclimating them to the experimental setting in order to minimize observer effects. Toward this end, both parents and their participating child (only the oldest child between 10 and 18 years of age accompanies the parents to the laboratory meeting) spend several hours together in the videotaping studio talking with our staff, completing questionnaires, and engaging in discussions among themselves during this first meeting.

During the second and third meetings, four combinations drawn from the three family members are separately engaged in videotaped discussions: mother-father, mother-child, father-child and mother-father-child. Discussion topics are based upon items from a Revealed Difference Questionnaire (RDQ; Jacob, 1974; Strodbeck, 1951) and the Areas of Change Questionnaire (ACQ; Weiss, 1980) to maximize personal relevance and investment. The second and third laboratory sessions are parallel in terms of the four combinations of family members discussing RDQ items and ACQ topics. Total time for each combination across both tasks ranges from 20 to 30 minutes. The only difference between the second and third sessions is the availability of alcoholic beverages to the parents in one of these meetings.

Experimental drinking. Most experimental drinking studies in the literature have assessed alcohol's impact on perceptual-motor functions and affective states. In contrast, few studies have attempted empirically based assessments of alcohol's effects on interpersonal patterns in general and marital or family interaction in particular.

Most relevant to the current effort, Steinglass's observations of in-toxicated and sober states have suggested that a couple's behavior during periods of drinking can have "adaptive" consequences for the alcoholic family that in turn may actually reinforce drinking. According to Steinglass (Steinglass & Robertson, 1983), these "adaptive" consequences all serve a common purpose—to tempo-rarily restore equilibrium in family life. In addition to Steinglass's study of differences between intoxicated and sober states, Wise-man's (1981) intensive interviews with alcoholics' wives suggest that sober states are "nonnormal" periods for alcoholics, that they are often associated with great tension and hypersensitivity, and most important, that the wife's reaction to the alcoholic when he is not intoxicated can be critical to future drinking states and rela-tionships. That is, "a wife will often use this time to complain, either verbally or by her actions how he has made her suffer during his drinking and drunken episodes [a reaction that] may well make sobriety as a continuous state not all that appealing to a man who would rather be drinking anyway."

In brief, both Steinglass and Wiseman suggest that variation in drinking patterns can play a central role in adaptive and disruptive marital states and ultimately in the maintenance of heavy drink-ing—an assumption of major significance in theoretical develop-ments linking interpersonal variables to dysfunctional behavior and of great potential importance to the development of family-oriented treatment and prevention programs. Notwithstanding these im-plications, it must be acknowledged that this model has received most of its support from theoretical and clinical or anecdotal reports of interaction between alcoholic and spouse (Jacob & Seilhamer, in press). Clearly, considerable empirical data are needed to provide stronger evidence for the validity of this model.

During the experimental drinking session, alcoholic beverages and salty snacks are placed on a small table within a few feet of where family members are seated. In addition, alcoholic beverages are made available to each parent when he or she is completing brief questionnaires before the start of family discussions as well as when that parent is not involved in a problem-solving discussion taking place in the experimental room. Alcoholics drank an average of 3.4 ounces of alcohol (mean postsession BAC = 0.086%), whereas the alcoholics' wives and both spouses in the depression and normal control groups consumed only small amounts of alcohol (mean postsession BAC = 0.015%). To control for order effects, half the families in each of the three experimental groups are randomly assigned to receive alcohol in the second meeting and only soft drinks in the third meeting, while the remaining subjects in each group receive alcohol in the third meeting and only soft drinks in the second. All families are required to accept taxi rides to and from the laboratory on the evening alcohol is consumed.

DATA REDUCTION AND ANALYSIS PROCEDURES

Although various types of report data are collected, collated, reduced, and analyzed, the materials of major interest to me are the laboratory and home interactions. The primary focus of data reduction for these materials involves coding the recordings into a sequence of behavioral units (codes) that preserve the affect, content, and context of the family discussions. A separate coding system is used for the laboratory data (videotapes of problem-solving interactions) versus the home data (audiotapes of natural dinnertime conversations) in order to most accurately capture the interaction in each setting.

The laboratory data are coded with a modification of Weiss's Marital Interaction Coding System (MICS; Hops, Wills, Patterson, & Weiss, 1972; Weiss, 1979). Like the original MICS, the abbreviated system is intended to objectively record both verbal and nonverbal behaviors of family members in a problem-solving situation. This abbreviated system consists of 16 unique behavior codes and several combination codes. The interactions are coded by a group of highly trained coders who do not know the nature of the project or the division of the families into diagnostic groups. Interobserver reliability indexes were calculated randomly on approximately 20% of the interactions. Using a point-by-point percentage agreement measure, reliability estimates were maintained at better than 70%.

Based on factor analyses that are described more fully in Jacob and Krahn (in press), the most frequently occurring codes were classified into several summary groupings. Codes grouped as *Positive* all reflect a positive evaluation by the speaker about the statements or actions of the other person. These codes include Agree, Approve, Assent, and Agree/Assent. Codes grouped as *Negative* reflect a negative evaluation by the speaker and include the codes of Criticize, Disagree, Put Down, and Negative Response. *Problem-Solving* behaviors all pertain to efforts at discussing and resolving the problems identified. Codes include Problem Description, Question, Command, Solution, and Problem Description/Question. *Humor-*

ous/Laugh behaviors include Humor, Smile-Laugh, and Talk, the last referring to conversation not related to the problem discussion. To date, aggregate analyses based on these four categories have been conducted on the laboratory interactions of the marital dyads.

As can be seen, these codes and the associated groupings can be organized around two primary dimensions: Personal Evaluation and Problem Resolution. These domains overlap with two seemingly universal (Foa & Foa, 1974; Triandis, 1978) dimensions of interpersonal behavior concerned with affect expression and solidarity on the one hand and skill performance and problem solving on the other. A third organizing dimension, referred to as System Organization, is focused on system properties related to interactional structure and patterning. Following Gottman's (1979) influential work in this area, assessment of System Organization involves sequential analysis procedures that address the interrelated concepts of reciprocity, rigidity, and predictability. Sequential analyses of laboratory interaction data are currently under way.

Laboratory Interactions of Alcoholics and Their Spouses

Although a considerable range of results is emerging from this project, the focus here will be on the marital interaction data obtained from the laboratory discussions.

FINDINGS AND INTERPRETATIONS

Before initiating the current project, we undertook a small sample pilot study in which eight alcoholics and eight normal controls were conducted through a simplified version of the previously described laboratory observation procedures, the most important feature being the experimental drinking manipulation. In several important respects, interactions of alcoholic couples from the pilot study (Jacob et al., 1981) and the current project (Jacob & Krahn, in press) were very similar; most important, alcoholic couples not only were more negative and less constructive in general, but became increasingly so during the drinking session. Most striking, the differences between alcoholic and comparison groups in terms of affective state could be accounted for almost entirely by the marked increase in negative communication that occurred during the drinking session.

On the one hand, one could say these findings are reasonable and expectable in light of the large clinical literature on alcoholism that has often and vividly described alcohol's deleterious impact on family life, in which conflict, dissatisfaction, and dissension are the norm (Black, 1979; Cork, 1969; Fox, 1962; Hecht, 1973). Given the great disturbance and disruption that are often brought on during heavy drinking and intoxication, the presence of alcohol and the drinking (even within the relatively restricted and "safe" confines of the interaction laboratory) could be providing powerful discriminative stimuli for both spouses, in effect communicating the expectancy that the subsequent interchanges will be aversive and punishing. Because of this expectancy (or "setting event"), the interaction comes to manifest lower rates of positive exchange and higher rates of negative exchange. (A variation on this theme suggests a conditioned emotional response associated with the stimulus of "drinking"—a response that at least for the nonalcoholic spouse, but probably for both spouses, is experienced as strongly negative.)

But there may be other ways to interpret present findings. Present results, for example, appear consistent with a considerable literature—both empirical and theoretical—concerned with people's expectations about alcohol's effects and their attributions about drunken behavior associated with periods of drinking (Brown, Goldman, Inn, & Anderson, 1980). Based upon cross-cultural studies of how different societies use and respond to alcohol as well as increasing awareness of the power of social labeling (Coleman, & Strauss, 1979; McAndrew & Edgerton, 1969), several investigators have proposed that alcohol influences behavior not necessarily through pharmacological action, but rather through the meaning people ascribe to intoxication. Specifically, it has been argued that many societies suspend their implicit social rules for a person who is intoxicated. As a result of this "time out" (McAndrew & Edgerton, 1969), an intoxicated individual can behave in a socially inappropriate way without fear of the normal social sanctions that would attend such behavior if it occurred while the person was not drinking. Thus, one is able to behave in a deviant fashion without being labeled "deviant" by attributing the behavior to the alcohol rather than to oneself.

The increased negativity evidenced by the alcoholic under drinking conditions, then, could be explained by this "deviance disavowal" process. That is, it could be argued that the alcoholic, knowing that his inappropriate behavior will be attributed to the alcohol, feels free to vent negative feelings that are aroused in the interaction itself or before the interaction. He can therefore become disagreeable, unpleasant, or aggressive and at the same time deny responsibility for his actions.

But, one might ask, does this "deviance disavowal" explanation have any special relevance to the alcoholic and the type of relationships he establishes with his family? Gorad addressed this very issue, proposing a most provocative theory that in effect integrates a "deviance disavowal" framework with a systems-communication model in order to give further meaning to the alcoholic's mode of relating. Specifically, Gorad suggested that alcoholics exhibit a "responsibility avoiding" communication style that is exaggerated during periods of drinking and intoxication.

Gorad (1971) begins by reminding us that communication is a multilevel process that includes two important components: the command aspect, which represents an overt, definable message, and a qualifying component that tells us how the command aspect is to be interpreted. The latter, often referred to as a metacommunication, can be transmitted through various verbal, nonverbal, metaphorical, or contextual cues. In the case of the alcoholic, the key qualification made about his behavior is that "I am not responsible for what I say or do; I am under the control of the alcohol." The significance of such a communication, of course, is that the person can exert great control over relationships in that he can do things for which he cannot be held responsible—he acts but avoids responsibility for his actions. The core aspect of this theory—that the alcoholic can attribute his deviant behavior to the alcohol and therefore avoid responsibility—has also been discussed in the social labeling literature, and it has been referred to as "deviance disavowal" or "timeout" by McAndrew (Coleman & Strauss, 1979; McAndrew & Edgerton, 1969).

Regarding present findings, one might conjecture that in essence the alcoholic attributes his nastiness to the alcohol. To the extent that this occurs (and his significant others accept this attribution), periods of drinking would allow him to vent negative affect toward the relationship in general and the spouse in particular that it would be more difficult to express if he were going to be held accountable for his behavior; as such, the context of drinking enables the alcoholic to express strongly held feelings that otherwise could be given only partial expression.

Other data collected in the pilot study (Jacob et al., 1981) lend indirect support to the responsibility-avoidance hypothesis. Specifically, we categorized all messages into two types: personally relevant and not personally relevant. The former included statements conveying feelings or attitudes about the spouse or about the marital relationship and most often used the words "I," "we," and "you." Most strikingly, alcoholics communicated the fewest personally relevant statements—that is, normal husbands made a higher proportion of personally relevant statements than alcoholic husbands and wives of alcoholics made a higher proportion than their alcoholic husbands, whereas normal husbands and their wives expressed similar rates of personally relevant statements.

Such findings suggest that the flow of communication is more unidirectional and less reciprocal in alcoholic couples than in normal couples—that is, alcoholics make fewer self-disclosing statements than their wives, so that alcoholics come to know more about their wives than their wives know about them—a status that from a communication perspective suggests that the alcoholic is in the more powerful, influential position (he who controls the flow of information controls the relationship) and that his low level of self-disclosure is consistent with a responsibility-avoiding style of communication.

LIMITATIONS AND QUALIFICATIONS

Although the present findings are certainly interesting and are consistent with clinical and theoretical expectations, several critical variables and analyses have not yet been examined. Thus it would be prudent to state that interaction hypotheses regarding alcohol's impact on family systems have yet to be thoroughly tested with this material.

1. In assessing these laboratory data, it is important to keep in mind that one cannot assume these patterns will generalize to interactions that might occur in more natural settings. For example, in the laboratory families are required (constrained) to discuss personally relevant, emotionally charged problems that occur in their day-to-day relationships. Conflictual issues are presented with the understanding that discussion is to occur. Within the privacy and freedom of the family's own home, however, members obviously have many more options for dealing with potentially disturbing situations. Most important, members can avoid discussing such issues by leaving the field, actually or functionally. The point is simply that our laboratory findings should be viewed as what occurs *when alcoholic families discuss interpersonal difficulties*. Whether discus-

sions of this nature occur in the natural environment cannot be determined without reference to other types of observations and reports.

2. Up to this point all the analyses conducted have been based upon differences in the rates of certain classes of behaviors across groups: drinking conditions, sex of participating child, and so forth. Without going beyond such assessments, one cannot really talk about patterns of interactions—only about *inferred* patterns of interaction. For example, knowing that both alcoholics and their spouses exhibit relatively high rates of negative behaviors (in contrast with various comparison groups) does not really tell us whether the couples exhibit any patterning or sequencing in their ongoing dialogues, whether behaviors affect the partners' subsequent expressions, or whether patterns of interaction change over time. To move beyond an assessment of rates (How much behavior occurred?) to an analysis of interaction (Did the behavior make a difference in how the partner behaved?) requires different types of analysis—in particular the application of sequential analyses and bivariate time-series analyses to the coded materials. Such assessments are now under way.

3. Admittedly, laboratory assessment of the acute effects of alcohol cannot usually measure impact over a range of drinking levels unless extended inpatient protocols are used. As a result, time-limited assessment of alcohol's effects cannot usually involve truly intoxicated subjects over long periods—data that were the basis of Steinglass's clinical and theoretical developments linking alcohol effects to stabilizing family systems. At the same time, it would be of considerable importance to perform more systematic and parametric studies of dose/response relationships in assessing marital and family interaction and to further manipulate expectancy and pharmacological influences on observed behavior.

Alcohol exerts clearly different effects on behavior as a function of the dose consumed. Of particular relevance is the observation that many of these effects, including effects on interpersonal behavior, may be biphasic. That is, at relatively low doses alcohol may have a positive effect on interpersonal interactions, whereas at moderate to very high doses the effect may be increasingly negative. It is of interest in this regard that Taylor and Gammon (1975) have reported such an effect of alcohol on aggressive behavior—decreases in aggresson at low doses and increases at high doses.

In the present study, subjects were allowed ad lib access to alcohol with the expectation that they would drink an amount typical for them. In the absence of a fixed dose, alcoholics drank more and achieved a higher blood alcohol concentration on drink night than did social drinkers or depressed men. Thus the social impairment of alcoholics and enhanced functioning of social drinkers while drinking could be attributed either to the differential influence of alcohol on alcoholics and social drinkers, or to the biphasic impact of low and high doses of alcohol, or to both.

An additional limitation might be noted. Although alcoholics drank more than the other two groups, it is not at all certain that they drank their typical amounts, and the "relatively" low blood alcohol concentrations ($m = 0.07\%$) suggest that they drank less than usual. At higher levels, one might anticipate an even greater deterioration of social interaction. Further research on these issues would clearly be relevant.

4. Finally, typologies seem increasingly critical in this area of research. Without question, there is great within-subject variance on many of the observation measures as well as report procedures used during this investigation, and it seems essential to identify subgroups that are associated with different family patterns and that exhibit different styles of interchange during periods of drinking. Several lines of research to this end are currently under way. In collaboration with Harvey Skinner, for example, we are beginning to examine family typologies by applying cluster analysis to the interaction data. Given the identification of a relatively small number of family types, we are planning to conduct a number of generalizability assessments to determine the relation between the various family types (as identified from the laboratory interaction data) and other data sets, including the home interactions, child-status measures, and drinking characteristics of the index cases.

Second, and most relevant to this chapter, a related line of research, concerned with the alcoholic's impact on family relationships, has highlighted the importance of drinking style and location for understanding alcoholic-family relationships. A major aim of this second investigation—as with the core study—is to examine the presence, degree, and nature of alcohol's impact on family relationships, with a particular interest in testing the hypothesis that drinking, at least in some alcoholic families, serves some adaptive functions and hence becomes tied to and reinforced by family processes. In particular, this work has suggested that drinking style and location may be critical variables for partitioning heterogeneous groups, and if undertaken it may significantly clarify the alcohol consumption/family stability relationship.

184
NEBRASKA SYMPOSIUM ON MOTIVATION, 1986

Drinking Style and Drinking Location: Impact on Marital Stability

Several years ago we began examining relationships among drinking, personality/psychopathology, and marital satisfaction measures (Jacob, Dunn, Leonard, & Davis, 1985) in an attempt to replicate a previous report by Steinglass (1981b). In the process we ran a series of correlations involving the alcoholics' Quantity-Frequency (QF) scores (the amount of absolute alcohol consumed during the previous month) and the spouses' scores on the MMPI, Beck Depression Inventory (Beck et al., 1961), Locke-Wallace Marital Adjustment Test (Locke & Wallace, 1959), and Dyadic Adjustment Scale (Spanier, 1976). In brief, findings from these assessments indicate that alcoholic husbands who had consumed large amounts of alcohol in the past month had wives who scored relatively low on various MMPI scales, scored relatively low on the Beck Depression Inventory, and reported relatively greater marital satisfaction on the Locke-Wallace Marital Adjustment Test and on the Dyadic Adjustment Scale. *Most important*, categorizing subjects into steady versus binge drinkers based on the Marlatt Drinking Profile (Marlatt, 1976) and then analyzing each group separately yielded a striking outcome: most correlations between QF scores and the symptom and marital satisfaction measures were not significant for the binge drinkers but were highly significant and consistent for the steady drinkers (Jacob, Dunn, & Leonard, 1983).

Although we considered various explanations of this outcome, our interest in the interactional aspects of the family led to the following hypothesis: marital/family relationships are more satisfying during high than during low consumption periods, which in turn serves to maintain or perpetuate drinking to the extent that the alcoholic's behavior is more predictable when he is consuming alcohol at a steady rate than when he is drinking episodically; stress in family life is minimized during periods of high alcohol consumption; and the family has adapted to and incorporated high-rate drinking into family life.

Despite the provocative nature of our preliminary findings and associated hypotheses, several important limitations were evident.

First, the reported findings were based upon a relatively small sample of families ($n = 27$) in which various selective factors could have produced an atypical group of married alcoholics. To assess the generalizability of the reported findings across various sociodemographic, treatment, and drinking parameters, a large ($n = 140$)

heterogeneous sample of alcoholics is currently being studied. Through a series of statistical analyses, it should be possible to determine the extent to which the consumption/family stability relationship is influenced by variations in such factors as family structure, duration of problem drinking, drinking pattern (binge versus steady), drinking setting (in home versus out of home), and current treatment status (seeking versus not seeking treatment).

Second, the sets of measures on which primary analyses were conducted were cross sectional and retrospective. Consequently we could say only that alcoholics who drank relatively large quantities of alcohol had wives who reported relatively few psychiatric symptoms and high marital satisfaction. To conclude that the variables in question are related over time, one would have to assess drinking, psychiatric symptoms, and marital satisfaction on a day-to-day basis and examine the actual covariation among these variables. As a first attempt at such an assessment, Nancy Jo Dunn's doctoral dissertation involved a small group of married alcoholics conducted through a three-month longitudinal data collection (Dunn, 1984).

THE LONGITUDINAL STUDY

Dunn's study was restricted to steady drinkers, since only this group exhibited a significant association between alcohol consumption and marital stability in the original study. Because drinking location (in-home versus out-of-home) was correlated with the binge/steady categorization, our original findings could have resulted from differences on either or both dimensions. To assess this issue more systematically, half of the selected subjects were in-home ($n = 4$) drinkers and half were out-of-home ($n = 4$) drinkers.

Procedurally, the eight couples were asked to provide daily records of alcohol consumption, psychiatric symptoms, and marital satisfaction ratings over a 90-day period. Each couple was paid a total of $350 in increasing monthly amounts—$50 the first month, $100 the second month, and $200 the third month for participating in the study. All subjects successfully completed the entire 90-day data collection.

Data analyses involved specification of the univariate Auto Regressive Integrated Moving Average (ARIMA) model for each of the variables in the study; that is, daily alcohol consumption, marital satisfaction ratings, and psychiatric symptom scores. Next, bivariate ARIMA models were developed to specify the relationship between each pair of variables for each couple, especially the husband's alcohol consumption and the wife's satisfaction ratings and daily symptom scores.

Univariate ARIMA models. Of particular interest, eight of the univariate models involved modeling the 90-day daily drinking behavior of our alcoholic subjects. Inspection of three time series yielded several interesting findings. Most of the *in-home drinkers* consumed alcohol at a fairly consistent and predictable level, the only exception being Husband 4, a "mixed" location drinker, whose pattern appeared more similar to that of husbands in the out-of-home group. In contrast, the *out-of-home* drinkers exhibited much greater variability in their consumption patterns—an impression that was supported statistically by seasonal (that is, seven-day fluctuations) ARIMA models in three of the four out-of-home drinkers.

Bivariate ARIMA models. The essence of the bivariate time-series procedure is to determine how well one can predict variation of a dependent variable from knowledge of the independent variable at various lags *and* beyond what is predictable from knowledge of the dependent variable alone at various lags. In addition, the bivariate procedure allows one to identify "causor" variables, which in essence indicate the direction of effect between two variables. This methodology yielded several exciting findings that differentiated the two groups.

In the *out-of-home group*, the most striking finding was a negative relation between alcohol consumption and the wives' marital satisfaction ratings at various lags for all four couples. Of particular importance, three of the four out-of-home drinkers had weekly seasonal drinking patterns, and all of these wives had a *five*-day lagged, negative relationship with the alcohol consumption; that is, five days after their husbands' drinking, wives' marital satisfaction (W-MS) decreased.

For illustrative purposes, this relationship can be examined more closely with Couple B's (out-of-home) bivariate model:

Saturday ▸ Thursday   ▸ Saturday ▸ Thursday
H drinks ▾ W-MS decreases ▸ H drinks ▸ W-MS decreases

Since the husband clearly drinks most heavily on Saturday, the model predicts that the wife's marital satisfaction will decrease on Thursday. If one were to predict the next sequence in this chain of events it would be that the husband would drink on Saturday, and it is certainly likely that after 18 years of marriage the wife would predict the same thing. Thus it may well be that the interpretation of this bivariate relationship is twofold: within a historical context, the wife's marital satisfaction does indeed decline five days later, but the decline in her marital satisfaction ratings reflects her *anticipation* of the husband's drinking in *two* days. It should be noted that this is *not* to say that the wife's marital dissatisfaction *causes* the husbands alcohol consumption (there is no support for that direction of effect) but rather that her marital dissatisfaction reflects anticipation. As has been recently noted in the behavioral/marital literature (Weiss & Weider, 1982), cognitive variables are extremely important in any marital relationship. The bivariate ARIMA models in this study certainly support the importance of further research in this area.

In the *in-home group*, two of four couples replicated the original cross-sectional findings quite clearly. For one couple, alcohol consumption was negatively associated with symptoms and positively associated with marital satisfaction ratings one and two days after alcohol consumption. Another couple reproduced the consumption/stability relationship in regard to a positive relationship between husband's drinking and wife's marital satisfaction ratings. Our third couple exhibited no relationship on any of the assessed variables, a finding that perhaps represents a statistical expression of total disengagement in the marriage. (Consistent with this view, this was the only couple who had experienced a marital separation, and the wife noted, "His drinking makes me wish I never went back after our separation last year.") Finally, the last couple produced a positive relation between husband's alcohol consumption and spouse's symptom ratings—a finding opposite in direction to that obtained with the original cross-sectional findings and more in line with the patterns exhibited by the out-of-home drinkers. It is of interest that this husband, though categorized as an in-home drinker based upon his Marlatt Drinking Profile data, was very different from the other three in-home drinkers when his 90-day data were examined. That is, Husband 4 drank only 56% of the time in the home, whereas Husbands 1, 2, and 3 consumed 77%, 94%, and 99% of their alcohol in the home. In actuality, then, Husband 4 represented a "mixed location" drinker, and the positive relation between his consumption and symptoms is more consistent with the four out-of-home drinkers than with the three in-home drinkers.

In examining apparent discrepancies between our originally reported cross-sectional findings and the current longitudinal results,

188

several factors must be considered, including differences in subjects studied, attention to synchronous versus lead/lag relationships, and global retrospective versus relatively specific and current reports. Most important to the present discussion, however, no distinction was ever made between in-home and out-of-home steady drinkers in the original study—a distinction that present results certainly support.

As noted, we are currently recruiting a large, heterogeneous sample of married alcoholics in an attempt to replicate and extend our earlier findings relating drinking style and location to marital stability. (In addition to replicating the original cross-sectional findings on this new sample of 140 married alcoholics, we are conducting 32 of these couples through the 90-day longitudinal procedure previously described—8 steady in-home drinkers, 8 steady out-of-home drinkers, 8 episodic in-home drinkers, and 8 episodic out-of-home drinkers.) In this effort, subjects are not excluded if other psychiatric disorders occur along with alcoholism or if the spouse manifests any current psychiatric disorders. Given this "open" selection strategy, we expect the sample to reflect considerable variability regarding husbands' psychiatric status and the psychiatric and alcohol-abuse status of the spouses. Preliminary analyses of relevant test data support this expectation. For example, 48% of the alcoholics exhibit a current psychiatric disorder in addition to alcoholism, the most common (additional) diagnoses being Major Depression, Antisocial Personality, and Drug Abuse. Spouses, on the other hand, reflect a range of psychiatric disorders, 46% of the sample achieving either current or lifetime RDC other than for alcoholism. Of particular interest, 17% of the wives have lifetime RDC for alcoholism, and 22% have a MAST score greater than 5, the suggested cut-off for predicting an alcoholism diagnosis in male samples (Favazza & Pires, 1974). Similarly, a number of wives (11%) consume two or more ounces of absolute alcohol per day, which translates roughly into a daily alcohol consumption rate of four "drinks." Such variations in psychiatric and drinking status should allow for the formation and analysis of interesting subgroups that may reflect patterns of interaction quite different from modal types; in particular, couples in which both spouses are alcohol abusers and couples in which there is significant psychopathology in husband or wife or both in addition to alcohol abuse.

Analyses of a subset ($n = 58$) of these subjects conducted last year appeared to support our original findings. Specifically, correlations between husbands' drinking and wives' marital satisfaction were generally positive for the total sample. When binge and steady groups were analyzed separately, group differences again mirrored those found previously—correlations were positive in both groups but stronger with steady than with binge drinkers. Finally, analyses of subgroups based upon primary drinking location (in home, out of home) crossed with drinking pattern (binge, steady) suggested that it was the steady, in-home group that exhibited the strongest correlations between husbands' QF scores and wives' BDI, LW, and DAS scores, whereas the steady out-of-home group as well as the two binge groups revealed noticeably weaker associations among these variables.

At this point in our efforts we have not yet analyzed the entire sample on the cross-sectional measures or the 32 couples conducted through the longitudinal data collection—analyses that should provide a more definitive understanding of factors that influence the strength and direction of association between consumption parameters (amount and pattern) and family status parameters (psychiatric and marital functioning). Such analyses will be done during the coming year with the expectation of clarifying those dimensions and mechanisms that may mediate the strength of the alcohol consumption/family stability relationship.

Differences in Laboratory Interactions as Related to Variations in Drinking Style and Location

To summarize, both the correlational and the time-series analyses clearly indicate the importance of defining more homogeneous subgroups within the larger sample of alcoholics. Two consequences of this subgrouping are most important: the family's response to the alcoholic's drinking is quite different depending upon the subgroups assessed, and one's conclusions regarding the alcohol consumption/family stability relationship become increasingly refined (and complex) as additional methods are brought to bear on this issue.

Notwithstanding the need to qualify conclusions because of small samples and the preliminary nature of our analyses, an increasingly clear picture seems to be emerging.

First, the family's response to the episodic drinker (the binge as well as the heavy weekend drinker) is clearly different from its response to the steady in-home drinker. For these drinkers alcohol consumption does not seem to have any adaptive or positive consequences for the family, with the possible exception of a "deviance disavowal" mechanism that may be operating to allow the expression of deviant behavior with fewer sanctions. For these individuals drinking most often takes place out of the home, and the variability in type and quantity of beverage consumed is significant.

At the other end of the continuum, the steady in-home drinkers (SI) appear to experience the least disruption in their lives as a result of the drinking, and at least in some cases they actually seem to experience benefits associated with drinking. That is, it is the SI group that most clearly shows the strong, significant correlations between amount consumed and marital satisfaction ratings of the wife, and at least for two of the three clearly defined SI drinkers conducted through the time-series analysis there was substantial support for the drinking/family stability relationship—that is, drinking increased marital satisfaction.

Given these differences in drinking style and impact that we have gleaned frm the cross-sectional and longitudinal data, a final question must be asked: If we reanalyze our laboratory data taking into account the dimensions of drinking style (binge, steady) and setting (in home, out of home), do we find correspondence in outcome across these different methods? Based on the original cross-sectional study, the preliminary replication and refinement of these relationships, and the intriguing time-series analyses, we would expect that our direct observations of alcoholic families in the interaction laboratory would yield subgroup differences that are very different than would be obtained without these subgroupings and that are consistent with the patterns we are beginning to discern from the cross-sectional and longitudinal data sets.

The analyses to be discussed involve the previously described sample of alcoholic couples now differentiated into binge (B) drinkers ($n = 17$) and steady (S) drinkers ($n = 32$). For each of three dependent variables (negativity, problem solving, and positivity), a three-way ANOVA was conducted involving alcoholism subgroup (binge/steady), drinking condition (drink/no drink), and member (husband/wife). In addition, the sample was differentiated into three more homogeneous subgroups (binge out of home, BO, $n = 11$; steady out of home, SO, $n = 17$; and steady in home, SI, $n = 15$) and then subjected to similar ANOVAs to further clarify the relative importance of the drinking style and location variables.

Negativity. For the two-group (binge/steady) analysis, a significant Group × Member interaction was obtained, indicating that the binge drinkers exhibited substantially higher rates of negativity than steady drinkers, whereas wives in both groups were very similar and had negativity scores that fell midway between those of the binge and steady husbands, $F(1, 47) = 6.42$, $p = .02$. The three-group analysis (BO, SO, SI) yielded a similar pattern—binge drinkers exhibited the highest rate of negativity—although a clearly significant effect was not obtained, $F(2, 40) = 2.30$, $p = .11$. Finally, the Group × Drinking Condition × Member interaction, although not significant, suggested that the binge drinker becomes more negative and his wife less negative in moving from the no drink to the drink condition.

Problem solving. With the two-group analysis, a Group × Drinking Condition interaction indicated that couples in the steady group become *more* problem focused and instrumental in the drinking session, whereas couples in the binge group become *less* task focused and less instrumental in the presence of the alcohol, $F(1, 47) = 3.74$, $p = .06$. When groups were further differentiated into BO, SI, and SO drinkers, a significant Group × Drinking Condition × Member interaction emerged, indicating that the reduced task focus is accounted for almost entirely by the binge drinker's spouse, who greatly decreases her task-directed activity in moving from the no drink to drink condition, $F(2, 40) = 3.36$, $p = .05$.

Positivity. For the three-group analysis, a Group × Drinking Condition interaction indicated that the SI drinkers became more positive during the drinking than the no drinking session, whereas both the BO and the SO drinkers showed little change in positivity across conditions, $F(2, 40) = 2.76$, $p = .08$. Interestingly, the Group × Drinking Condition interaction with only binge and steady groups was not significant, indicating the unique importance of the SI subgroup in differentiating positivity scores across drinking conditions.

Constructive communication. As a way of integrating these several measures into an overall communication index, we developed a composite score based upon the sum of positivity and problem solving and called it constructive communication (CC). Next we formed a difference score whereby CC in the no drink condition was subtracted from CC in the drink condition and then subjected these scores to a one-way ANOVA. As seen in Figure 1, the SI group was clearly differentiated from the SO and BO groups, indicating that communication in the SI group became more positive and problem

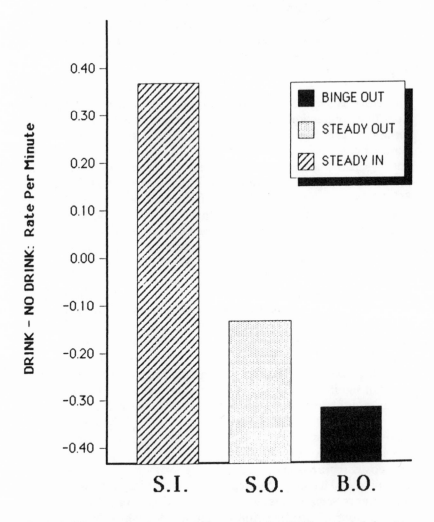

Figure 1. Change in rate of constructive communication (CC) from alcohol-absent to alcohol-present condition. Couples in the steady in-home group exhibit a notable increase in CC across conditions, whereas couples in the other two groups exhibit a decrease in CC from alcohol-absent to alcohol-present condition.

focused in the drink than in the no drink condition, F (2, 40) = 4.01, p = .03.

Now let me try to summarize the interaction findings. For the binge group, communications are generally negative and aversive. The locus of the negativity seems to reside in or be expressed by the binge drinker rather than his wife, and we see interactions becoming increasingly negative in the drinking session. Simultaneously, these couples show a decrease in problem-solving efforts during the drinking session, with the suggestion that the wife exhibits the more substantial reduction in task focus. One implication that might be read into these data is that negativity (especially the husband's) during the drinking session leads to an increase in off-task talk (especially by the wife); that is, his increasing anger and criticism result in her "backing off" from direct attempts to deal with areas of conflict—a sequence that suggests a coercive control mechanism at the center of this mode of relating—that is, his aversiveness/nastiness is reduced if she withdraws from attempts to change behavior. (This mechanism is not the same as the deviance disavowal explanation of aggressive behavior, but it seems consistent with it; that is, there are fewer negative sanctions if the person is seen to be drinking or under the influence of alcohol. In the present context the wife "backs off" from the arguments or does not counterattack because of the futility of dealing with her husband when he is drinking—meaning, when he is under the control of alcohol.) On the other hand, we could entertain the hypothesis that there is a negativity-accelerating process underlying the obtained findings in which cycles of negative reciprocity are strong and long lasting. Obviously other analytic procedures will be needed to determine which of these processes is operating.

For the SI group, communication is less negative than for the B group in general. (In fact, the rate of negativity for SI husbands *equals* that for the depressed and normal control husbands.) Although SI drinkers exhibit some increase in negativity in going from the no drink to the drink condition, it is moderate in comparison with the negativity change we see in the binge group. Problem solving actually improves a bit, and positivity increases quite clearly as a function of the drink condition. At this point we can certainly entertain the hypothesis that alcohol facilitates more problem-focused behavior, which is experienced as—or is in the context of—a positive mood. At the same time, we recognize that several important questions remain to be answered in subsequent efforts: Are there other changes in SI subjects' interactions that support what seems to be alcohol's social facilitating effect for these couples? For example, are there differences in the wife's contingent responses to her husband during the drink versus the no drink session? That is, beyond the husband's increase in positive communications and problem-solving efforts, does the wife respond to these changes contingently and sequentially? Again, other analytic procedures will be needed if we are to address these questions meaningfully.

Future Directions

Present findings, though provocative, are still preliminary and must be interpreted cautiously. In the months ahead, we will address many important questions in order to gain further understanding of relationships involving alcoholism subgroups and patterns of marital and family interaction.

First, we must determine if our laboratory findings hold up under closer scrunity. In particular, we have been analyzing data from relatively small samples, so that reliability and stability are of considerable concern. Analyses planned during the next year will capitalize on increasingly larger samples that have been collected during the past several years.

Second, all analyses conducted thus far have been based upon simple rate measures and have not directly examined patterns of mutual or reciprocal influence. A major analytic effort of the next year, therefore, will apply sequential analysis procedures to our laboratory data in an effort to identify and document changes in contingencies occurring between members. In this regard we hope to examine direction of effect via sequential analysis in a fashion analogous to use of the time-series methods with our previously described longitudinal data. Of particular importance to hypotheses raised in regard to steady in-home drinkers (SI), we will want to assess differences in wives' contingent responses to husbands during the drink versus the no drink sessions. That is, beyond overall increases in positivity and problem solving that are seen in the drink sessions, is there any evidence that the wife responds to these changes contingently and sequentially? Furthermore, we hope to examine the direction of influence involved in the increased negativity/decreased problem-solving relationship we find with binge drinkers and their spouses. Cycles of negative reciprocity—vis-à-vis the work of Gottman—will also be examined with a special interest in contrasting such patterns across the various subgroups we have studied thus far.

Third, the drinking style and location variables must be more precisely defined and more fully understood. As previously noted, our definitions of binge and steady drinking were based on a relatively simple questionnaire, and further work will certainly need to clarify the specific meanings and referents of these terms. Even among steady drinkers, there is great variability in pattern and amount, as seen in the further differentiation of the SI and SO groups, which were quite different in consistency of drinking as well as drinking cycles (heavy weekend drinking superimposed on a generally daily consumption pattern). Our binge drinkers represented a wide range of "styles," from several binges in a year separated by relatively long periods of abstinence to many periods of heavy, out-of-control drinking separated by several days to several weeks.

Fourth, the need to examine the unique nature of our sample and associated findings is certainly of major importance and is in fact being pursued at present in several ways. First, another sample of 50 male alcoholics is being recruited and conducted through the same procedures, as are groups of female alcoholics and female depressives. Together with the home observations on the core samples and the new samples, we will attempt to corroborate and elaborate on our preliminary interaction findings. Second, an independent sample of married alcoholics—a sample larger ($n = 140$) and more heterogeneous than that seen in the core study—has been collected during the past three years. Analyses of these data should allow for important replications and extensions of many of the key cross-sectional and longitudinal findings reported thus far.

Finally, the theoretical and empirical links between variations in drinking style and location and psychopathological syndromes certainly deserve further attention. Binge drinkers are clearly more disturbed and disruptive than steady drinkers, as is seen in scores from various personality, psychopathology, and marital adjustment measures. In particular, binge drinkers exhibit higher MMPI scores than do steady drinkers, and their profiles are characterized by a 4-9-8 pattern versus the 4-2 pattern seen among steady drinkers. In addition, and consistent with the MMPI differences, binge drinkers report significant social impairment associated with their drinking, including increased frequency of missing work, missed meals, fights, reckless driving, and physical abuse of spouse. Furthermore, binge drinkers report lower levels of marital satisfaction than steady drinkers and are married to women with higher symptom scores than steady drinkers. In essence, then, it appears that binge drinkers are involved in more sociopathic behavior, show more disturbed relationships in domains other than the marriage, and engage in a pattern of drinking that is unpredictable, at times chaotic, and certainly not incorporated into in-home family life.

At the other end of the continuum are the steady in-home (SI) drinkers. Compared with the binge drinkers, the SI drinkers seem to be least affected by their alcohol abuse and least impaired generally, as reflected in lower MMPI scores (the mean MMPI profile for this group is within the nonclinical range), relatively high marital satisfaction scores, and relatively low levels of social impairment related to drinking. The third group—steady out-of-home drinkers (SO)—seems to fall somewhere between the binge and SI groups in terms of associated background profile, although the relatively small samples we are analyzing make strong statements about group differences unwarranted.

In my survey of the literature on alcoholism typologies, various classifications appear relevant to the drinking style variable we have been examining. Jellinek (1960), for example, distinguished delta and gamma alcoholics, the former described as chronic alcoholics who drink more or less continuously and the latter as individuals who engage in episodic binges. Similarly, DSM = III (American Psychiatric Association, 1980) distinguishes alcohol abuse in terms of patterns or styles of drinking, referring to continuous drinking patterns on the one hand and episodic patterns on the other.

More relevant to psychopathological concomitants of different alcoholism types, Cloninger's adoption studies have identified two subgroups having quite different family genetic and environmental influences (Cloninger, Bohman, & Sigvardsson, 1981). The *male-limited* type is characterized by high heritability, early onset, and extensive treatment for both alcohol abuse and criminality in the biological parents—a profile that suggests an association between this type of alcoholism and an underlying personality disorder such as antisocial personality. In contrast, *milieu-limited* alcoholism is characterized by recurrent alcohol abuse without criminality in biological parents, later onset of problems, and occurrence in both men and women, and it has a better prognosis than the *male-limited* type.

Another typology relevant to the present discussion emerged from the application of cluster-analytic procedures to alcohol-use measures as well as demographic and personality variables. In this effort Morey, Skinner, and Blashfield (1984) have identified three alcoholism subgroups: Type A, or early-stage problem drinkers; Type B drinkers, characterized as "affiliative" drinkers with moderate alcohol dependence; and Type C or schizoid drinkers, exhibiting severe alcohol dependence. Comparisons among these subgroups indicate that Type B drinkers are more socially oriented and tend to drink daily, whereas Type C drinkers are more socially isolated, tend to drink in binges, report the most severe symptoms of alcoholism, and show higher levels of aggression, interpersonal disturbance, and marital disruption (Roberts & Morey, 1985). Many other typologies also map onto the dimension of drinking pattern and associated psychopathology, including the work of Schuckit (1985), Hesselbrock, Hesselbrock, and Stabenau (1985) and Sher and Levenson (1982). (See Babor and Lauerman's [1986] comprehensive review of alcoholism typologies for further references.)

In overview, then, it appears that many investigators have identified a fairly distinct subgroup of alcoholics characterized by an impulsive-aggressive-antisocial behavior cluster that often includes an episodic drinking style and significant interpersonal disturbance in various relationship domains—a subtype that is clearly relevant to our descriptions of binge drinkers.

For the steady drinkers (especially, the steady in-home group), the personality and psychopathology concomitants are less clear, though the literature suggests that these drinkers not only may be less severely dependent on alcohol and less severely disturbed, but perhaps may exhibit characteristics more aligned with an internalized personality style and reflective of underlying dysthmia, depression, and/or anxiety. If so, it is possible that this group includes an overrepresentation of anxious/inhibited men who are unassertive and passive, who have deficits in social skills (in particular, in expressing personal views and positive feelings), and who overcome these deficits by use of alcohol and are subsequently reinforced by the family's response to their change in behavior.[1]

1. At least some subgroups of alcoholics have been described as exhibiting social skills deficits in general and assertiveness difficulties in particular—a contention that has received some support in the empirical literature. Sugerman, Reilly, and Albahary (1965), for example, reported that "essential" alcoholics (those characterized by an inadequate personality and social immaturity) showed significant defects in interpersonal competence—a finding subsequently corroborated by Levine and Zigler (1973). For at least this type of alcoholic, the context of drinking would be hypothesized to enhance or be conducive to the expression of affect-ladden behavior by reducing anxiety and rigidity—a hypothesis that finds support in the work of Miller and Eisler (1977), who reported a negative correlation between negative assertion skills and alcohol consumption.

Although such a characterization is attractive and possibly accurate, it must be acknowledged at this point in our inquiry that the SI group is difficult to pigeonhole into a familiar, individually based personality type. That is, the group that exhibits the most theoretically and clinically interesting family process—interactions that appear to support or maintain abusive drinking—does not easily lend itself to reductionism. By and large, these men seem to be functioning (interpersonally, cognitively, occupationally) close to that large, nondescript gray area thought of as "generally within the normal range"—except when it comes to their too-often abusive drinking and drinking-related impairments. They hold regular jobs, do not beat their wives or children any more than their neighbors do, and may not exhibit any more peculiarities in personality than your average Cornhusker booster. Yet they reside within family structures that benefit or derive something from relationship events correlated with their high rate of drinking. Although subsequent analyses and data collections will continue to examine other individual-level variables for more compelling explanations, it may be that the answer lies not in individual characteristics but in interactions that prove to be more than the sum of their parts.

REFERENCES

Achenbach, T. (1978). The child behavior profile: I. Boys age 6–11. *Journal of Consulting and Clinical Psychology, 46,* 478–488.

Achenbach, T., & Edelbrock, C. (1979). The child behavior profile: II. Boys age 12–16 and girls age 6–11 and 12–16. *Journal of Consulting and Clinical Psychology, 47,* 223–233.

Alterman, A. I., Petrarulo, E., Tarter, R., & McGowan, J. R. (1982). Hyperactivity and alcoholism: Familial and behavioral correlates. *Addictive Behaviors, 7,* 412–421.

American Psychiatric Association. (1980). *Diagnostic and statistical manual of mental disorders* (3rd ed.). Washington, DC: Author.

Ammons, R. B., & Ammons, C. H. (1962). The Quick Test (QT): Provisional manual. *Psychological Reports,* Monograph Supplement I–VIII.

Andreasen, N., Endicott, J., Spitzer, R., & Winokur, G. (1977). The family history method using diagnostic criteria. *Archives of General Psychiatry, 34,* 1229–1235.

Babor, T. F., & Lauerman, F. J. (1986). Classification and forms of inebriety:

Historical antecedents of alcoholic typologies. In M. Gallanter (Ed.), *Research advances in alcoholism* (Vol. 4). New York: Plenum.

Bailey, M. (1961). Alcoholism and marriage: A review of research and professional literature. *Quarterly Journal of Studies on Alcohol, 22,* 81–97.

Bateson, G., Jackson, D. D., Haley, J., & Weakland, J. (1956). Toward a theory of schizophrenia. *Behavioral Science, 1,* 251–264.

Beck, A. (1971). Cognition, affect and psychopathology. *Archives of General Psychiatry, 24,* 495–500.

Beck, A., Ward, C., Mendelson, M., Mock, J., & Erbaugh, J. (1961). An inventory for measuring depression. *Archives of General Psychiatry, 4,* 53–63.

Becker, J. V., & Miller, P. M. (1976). Verbal and nonverbal marital interaction patterns of alcoholics and nonalcoholics. *Journal of Studies on Alcohol, 37,* 1616–1624.

Billings, A., Kessler, M., Gomberg, C., & Weiner, S. (1979). Marital conflict resolution of alcoholic and nonalcoholic couples during sobriety and experimental drinking. *Journal of Studies on Alcohol, 3,* 183–195.

Black, C. (1979). Children of alcoholics. *Alcohol Health and Research World, 4* (1), 23–27.

Blane, H. (1979). *Drinking Practices/Attitudes Questionnaire for Youth.* Unpublished manuscript, University of Pittsburgh.

Brown, S. A., Goldman, M. S., Inn, A., & Anderson, L. R. (1980). Expectations of reference from alcohol: Their domain and relation to drinking pattern. *Journal of Consulting and Clinical Psychology, 48,* 419–426.

Cantwell, D. (1972). Psychiatric illness in families of hyperactive children. *Archives of General Psychiatry, 27,* 414–417.

Cloninger, C. R., Bohman, M., & Sigvardsson, S. (1981). Inheritance of alcohol abuse: Cross fostering analysis of adopted men. *Archives of General Psychiatry, 38,* 861–868.

Cobb, J. C., & McCourt, W. F. (1979, September). *Problem solving by alcoholics and their families: A laboratory study.* Paper presented at the American Psychological Association meeting, New York.

Coleman, D. H., & Strauss, M. A. (1979). *Alcohol abuse and family violence.* Paper presented at the annual American Sociological Association meeting.

Connors, K. (1969). A teacher's rating scale for use in drug studies with children. *American Journal of Psychiatry, 126* (6), 884–888.

Cork, M. (1969). *The forgotten children.* Toronto: Paperjacks, in association with Addiction Research Foundation.

Costello, C. (1972). Depression: Loss of reinforcers or loss of reinforcers' effectiveness. *Behavior Therapy, 3,* 240–249.

200

NEBRASKA SYMPOSIUM ON MOTIVATION, 1986

Cotton, N. S. (1979). The familial incidence of alcoholism. *Journal of Studies on Alcohol, 40* (1), 89–116.

Coyne, J. (1976). Toward an interactional description of depression. *Psychiatry, 39,* 28–40.

Coyne, J. C., Kahn, J., & Gotlib, I. H. (in press). Depression. In T. Jacob (Ed.), *Family interaction and psychopathology: Theories, methods and findings.* New York: Plenum.

Deutsch, C., DiCicco, L., & Mills, D. J. (1982). *Services for children of alcoholic parents. Prevention, intervention and treatment: Concerns and models.* Alcohol and Health Monograph No. 3, DHHS Publication No. (ADM) 82-1192. Rockville, MD: NIAAA.

Dunn, N. J. (1984). *Patterns of alcohol abuse and marital stability.* Unpublished doctoral dissertation, University of Pittsburgh.

Edwards, P., Harvey, C., & Whitehead, P. C. (1973). Wives of alcoholics: A critical review and analysis. *Quarterly Journal of Studies on Alcohol, 34,* 112–132.

Favazza, A., & Pires, J. (1974). The Michigan Alcoholism Screening Test: Application in a general military hospital. *Quarterly Journal of Studies on Alcohol, 35,* 925–929.

Feighner, J., Robins, E., Guze, S., Woodruff, R., Winokur, G., & Munoz, R. (1972). Diagnostic criteria for use in psychiatric research. *Archives of General Psychiatry, 26,* 57–63.

Ferster, C. (1973). A functional analysis of depression. *American Psychologist, 28,* 857–870.

Finney, W. J., Moos, R. H., Cronkite, R. C., & Gamble, W. (1983). A conceptual model of the functioning of married persons with impaired partners: Spouses of alcoholic patients. *Journal of Marriage and the Family, 45,* 23–34.

Foa, V., & Foa, E. (1974). *Societal structures of the mind.* Springfield, IL: Charles C. Thomas.

Fox, R. (1962). Children in the alcoholic family. In W. Bier (Ed.), *Problems in addiction: Alcohol and drug addiction* (pp. 71–96). New York: Fordham University Press.

Frankenstein, W., Hay, W. M., & Nathan, P. E. (1985). Effects of intoxication on alcoholics' marital communication and problem solving. *Journal of Studies on Alcohol, 46,* 1–6.

Goodwin, D. (1971). Is alcoholism hereditary? A review and critique. *Archives of General Psychiatry, 25,* 545–549.

Goodwin, D. (1979). Genetics of alcoholism. In R. Pickens & L. Heston (Eds.), *Psychiatric factors in drug abuse.* New York: Grune and Stratton.

Goodwin, D. W., Schulsinger, F., Hermansen, L., Guze, S. B., & Winokur, G. (1973). Alcohol problems in adoptees raised apart from alcoholic biological parents. *Archives of General Psychiatry, 28,* 238–243.

Goodwin, D. W., Schulsinger, F., Hemansen, L., Guze, S. B., & Winokur, G. (1975). Alcoholism and the hyperactive child syndrome. *Journal of Nervous and Mental Disease, 160*, 349–353.

Gorad, S. (1971). Communicational styles and interaction of alcoholics and their wives. *Family Process, 10* (4), 475–489.

Gorad, S., McCourt, W., & Cobb, J. (1971). A communications approach to alcoholism. *Quarterly Journal of Studies on Alcohol, 32*, 651–668.

Gorman, J., & Rooney, J. (1979). The influence of Al-Anon on the coping behavior of wives of alcoholics. *Journal of Studies on Alcohol, 40*, 1030–1038.

Gottman, J. (1979). *Marital interaction: Experimental investigations.* New York: Academic Press.

Graham-Clay, S. (1983). Fetal alcohol syndrome: A review of the current human research. *Canada's Mental Health, 31* (2), 2–5.

el-Guebaly, N., & Offord, D. R. (1979). On being the offspring of an alcoholic: An update. *Alcoholism: Clinical and Experimental Research, 3* (2), 148–157.

Hecht, M. (1973). Children of alcoholics are children at risk. *American Journal of Nursing, 73* (10), 1764–1767.

Hersen, M., Miller, P., & Eisler, R. (1973). Interaction between alcoholics and their wives: A descriptive analysis of verbal and nonverbal behavior. *Quarterly Journal of Studies on Alcohol, 34*, 516–520.

Hesselbrock, V. M., Hesselbrock, M. N., & Stabenau, J. R. (1985). Alcoholism in men patients subtyped by family history and antisocial personality. *Journal of Studies on Alcohol, 46*, 59–64.

Hinchliffe, M., Hooper, D., Roberts, F., & Vaughan, P. (1977). The melancholy marriage: An inquiry into the interaction of depression: II. Expressiveness. *British Journal of Medical Psychology, 50*, 125–142.

Hindeman, M. (1977). Child abuse and neglect: The alcohol connection. *Alcohol and Research World, 1* (3), 2–6.

Holzman, I. R. (1982). Fetal alcohol syndrome (FAS)—a review. *Journal of Children in Contemporary Society, 15*, 13–19.

Hops, H., Wills, T., Patterson, G., & Weiss, R. (1972). *Marital Interaction Coding System.* Unpublished manuscript, University of Oregon Research Institute.

Hurwitz, J. I., & Daya, D. K. (1977). Non-help-seeking wives of employed alcoholics: A multilevel interpersonal profile. *Journal of Studies on Alcohol, 38*, 1730–1739.

Jacob, T. (1974). Patterns of family dominance and conflict as a function of child age and social class. *Developmental Psychology, 10*, 1–12.

Jacob, T. (Ed.). (In press). *Family interaction and psychopathology: Theories, methods, and findings.* New York: Plenum.

Jacob, T., Dunn, N. J., & Leonard, K. (1983). Patterns of alcohol abuse and family stability. *Alcoholism: Clinical and Experimental Research, 7*, 382–385.

Jacob, T., Dunn, N. J., Leonard, K., & Davis, P. (1985). Alcohol-related impairments in male alcoholics and the psychiatric symptoms of their spouses: An attempt to replicate. *American Journal of Drug and Alcohol Abuse, 11*, 55–67.

Jacob, T., Favorini, A., Meisel, S., & Anderson, C. (1978). The spouse, children, and family interactions of the alcoholic: Substantive findings and methodological issues. *Journal of Studies on Alcohol, 39*, 1231–1251.

Jacob, T., & Krahn, G. (in press). The classification of behavioral observation codes in studies of family interaction. *Journal of Marriage and the Family.*

Jacob, T., & Leonard, K. (1986). Psychosocial functioning in children of alcoholic fathers, depressed fathers, and control fathers. *Journal of Studies on Alcohol, 47*, 373–380.

Jacob, T., Ritchey, D., Cvitkovic, J., & Blane, H. (1981). Communication styles of alcoholic and nonalcoholic families when drinking and not drinking. *Journal of Studies on Alcohol, 42*, 466–482.

Jacob, T., & Seilhamer, R. A. (1982). The impact on spouses and how they cope. In J. Orford & J. Harwin (Eds.), *Alcohol and the family.* London: Croom Helm.

Jacob, T., & Seilhamer, R. A. (in press). Alcoholism and family interaction. In T. Jacob (Ed.), *Family interaction and psychopathology: Theories, methods and findings.* New York: Plenum.

Jellinek, E. M. (1960). *The disease concept of alcoholism.* New Haven: Hillhouse Press.

Jessor, R., Graves, T., Hanson, R., & Jessor, S. (1968). *Society, personality and deviant behavior.* New York: Holt.

Jones, M. C. (1968). Personality correlates and antecedents of drinking patterns in adult males. *Journal of Consulting and Clinical Psychology, 32*, 2–12.

Kaij, L. (1960). *Alcoholism in twins.* Stockholm: Almqvist and Wiksell.

Kennedy, D. L. (1976). Behavior of alcoholics and spouses in a simulation game situation. *Journal of Nervous and Mental Disease, 162*, 23–34.

Levine, J., & Zigler, E. (1973). The essential-reactive distinction in alcoholism: A developmental approach. *Journal of Abnormal Psychology, 81*, 242–249.

Lewinsohn, P. (1974). A behavioral approach to depression. In R. Friedman & M. Katz (Eds.), *The psychology of depression: Contemporary theory and research.* New York: John Wiley.

Lewinsohn, P., & Schaffer, M. (1971). The use of home observation as an integral part of the treatment of depression. *Journal of Consulting and Clinical Psychology, 37*, 87–94.

Libet, J., Lewinsohn, P., & Javorek, F. (1973). *The construct of social skill: An empirical study of several behavioral measures and their temporal stability, internal structure, validity and situational generalizability.* Unpublished manuscript, University of Oregon.

Locke, H., & Wallace, K. (1959). Short marital adjustment and prediction tests: Their reliability and validity. *Marriage and Family Living, 21,* 251–255.

Marlatt, G. (1976). The drinking profiles: A questionnaire for the behavioral assessment of alcoholism. In E. Mash & L. Terdal (Eds.), *Behavior therapy assessment: Diagnosis design and evaluation.* New York: Springer.

McAndrew, C, & Edgerton, B. (1969). *Drunken comportment: Social explanation.* Chicago: Aldine.

McCord, W., & McCord, J. (1962). A longitudinal study of the personality of alcoholics. In D. J. Pittman & C. R. Snyder (Eds.), *Society, culture, and drinking patterns* (pp. 413–430). New York: John Wiley.

McCrady, B. S. (1985). Alcoholism. In D. H. Barlow (Ed.), *Behavioral treatment of adult disorders.* New York: Guilford Press.

McCrady, B. S., Dean, L., Dubreuil, E., & Swanson, S. (1985). The problem drinkers project: A programmatic application of social learning based treatment. In G. A. Marlatt & J. Gordon (Eds.), *Relapse prevention.* New York: Guilford Press.

McLean, P., Ogston, K., & Grauer, L. (1973). A behavioral approach to the treatment of depression. *Journal of Behavior Therapy and Experimental Psychiatry, 4,* 323–330.

Miller, P. M., & Eisler, R. M. (1977). Assertive behavior of alcoholics: A descriptive analysis. *Behavior Therapy, 8,* 146–149.

Mishler, E. G., & Waxler, N. E. (1965). Family interaction processes and schizophrenia: A review of current theories. *Merrill-Palmer Quarterly of Behavior and Development, 11,* 269–315.

Moore, D. R. (1982). *Alcohol and family interaction: Child adjustment issues.* Unpublished manuscript.

Moos, R. (1974). *Family Environment Scale preliminary manual.* Palo Alto, CA: Consulting Psychologists Press.

Moos, R., Finney, J., & Gamble, W. (1982). The process of recovery from alcoholism: II. Comparing spouses of alcoholic patients and matched community controls. *Journal of Studies on Alcohol, 43,* 888–909.

Morey, L. C., Skinner, H. A., & Blashfield, R. K. (1984). A typology of alcohol abusers: Correlates and implications. *Journal of Abnormal Psychology, 93,* 408–417.

Morrison, J. R., & Stewart, M. A. (1973). The psychiatric status of the legal families of adopted hyperactive children. *Archives of General Psychiatry, 23,* 888–891.

204

NEBRASKA SYMPOSIUM ON MOTIVATION, 1986

Myklebust, H., & Bosher, B. (1969). The Pupil Rating Scale. In *Minimal brain damage in children* (pp. 294–302). Washington, DC: Department of Health, Education, and Welfare.

Nace, E. P. (1982). Therapeutic approaches to the alcoholic marriage. *Marital Therapy, 5,* 543–564.

O'Farrell, T. J., Cutter, H. S., & Floyd, F. J. (1985). Evaluating behavioral marital therapy for male alcoholics: Effects on marital adjustment and communication from before to after treatment. *Behavior Therapy, 16,* 147–169.

O'Gorman, P. (1981). Prevention issues involving children of alcoholics. In U.S. Department of Health and Human Services, *Services for children of alcoholics* (pp. 81–100). NIAAA Research Monograph 4. Washington, DC: Government Printing Office (Publication No. ADM 81-1007).

Olson, D. (1972). Empirically unbinding the double bind: Review of research and conceptual reformulations. *Family Process, 11,* 69–94.

Orme, T. C., & Rimmer, J. (1981). Alcoholism and child abuse: A review. *Journal of Studies on Alcohol, 42* (3), 273–287.

Parsons, T., & Bales, R. E. (1955). *Family, socialization and interaction process.* New York: Free Press.

Piers, E., & Harris, D. (1969). *The Piers-Harris Children's Self-Concept Scale.* Nashville, TN: Western Psychological Services.

Rehm, L. (1977). A self-control model of depression. *Behavior Therapy, 8,* 787–804.

Roberts, W. R., & Morey, L. C. (1985). Convergent validation of a typology of alcohol abusers. *Bulletin of the Society of Psychologists in Addictive Behaviors, 4,* 226–233.

Robins, L., Bates, W. M., & O'Neal, P. (1962). Adult drinking patterns of former problem children. In D. J. Pittman & C. R. Snyder (Eds.), *Society, culture and drinking patterns.* New York: John Wiley.

Rosett, H. L., & Weiner, L. (1982). Effects of alcohol on the fetus. In E. M. Pattison & E. Kaufman (Eds.), *Encyclopedic handbook of alcoholism.* New York: Gardner Press.

Royce, J. E. (1981). *Alcohol problems and alcoholism: A comprehensive survey.* New York: Free Press.

Ruggels, W., Armor, D., Polich, J., Mothershead, A., & Stephen, M. (1975). *A follow-up study of clients at selected alcoholism treatment centers funded by NIAAA.* Menlo Park, CA: Stanford Research Institute.

Schuckit, M. A. (1985). Studies of populations at risk for alcoholism. *Psychiatric Developments, 3,* 31–63.

Schuham, A. I. (1972). Activity, talking time, and spontaneous agreement in disturbed and normal family interaction. *Journal of Abnormal Psychology, 79* (1), 68–75.

Selzer, M. (1971). The Michigan Alcoholism Screening Test: The quest for a new diagnostic instrument. *American Journal of Psychiatry, 127,* 1653–1658.

Sher, K. J., & Levenson, R. W. (1982). Risk for alcoholism and individual differences in the stress-response-dampening effect of alcohol. *Journal of Abnormal Psychology, 91,* 350–367.

Skinner, H. A., Steinhauer, P. D., & Santa-Barbara, J. (1983). The Family Assessment Measure. *Canadian Journal of Community Mental Health, 2,* 91–105.

Spanier, G. (1976). Measuring dyadic adjustment: New scales for assessing the quality of marriage and similar dyads. *Journal of Marriage and the Family, 38* (1), 15–30.

Spitzer, R., & Endicott, J. (1977). *Research diagnostic criteria (RDC) for selected groups of functional disorders* (3rd ed.) Biometrics Research. New York: New York State Psychiatric Institute.

Steinglass, P. (1976a). Experimenting with family treatment approaches to alcoholism, 1950–1975: A review. *Family Process, 16,* 97–123.

Steinglass, P. (1976b). *Family interaction coding instrument.* Unpublished manuscript.

Steinglass, P. (1981a). The alcoholic family at home: Patterns of interaction in dry, wet, and transitional stages of alcoholism. *Archives of General Psychiatry, 38,* 578–584.

Steinglass, P. (1981b). The impact of alcoholism on the family. *Journal of Studies on Alcohol, 42,* 288–303.

Steinglass, P., & Robertson, A. (1983). The alcoholic family. In B. Kissin & H. Begleiter (Eds.), *The biology of alcoholism* (Vol. 6), *The pathogenesis of alcoholism: Psychosocial factors.* New York: Plenum.

Steinglass, P., Tislenko, L., & Reiss, D. (1985). Stability/instability in the alcoholic marriage: The interrelationships between course of alcoholism, family process, and marital outcome. *Family Process, 24,* 365–376.

Strodbeck, F. L. (1951). Husband-wife interaction over revealed differences. *American Sociological Review, 16,* 468–473.

Sugerman, A. A., Reilly, D., & Albahary, R. S. (1965). Social competence and essential-reactive distinction in alcoholism. *Archives of General Psychiatry, 12,* 552–556.

Tarter, R. E., Hegedus, A. M., Goldstein, G., Shelly, C., & Alterman, A. I. (1983). Adolescent sons of alcoholics: Neuropsychological and personality characteristics. *Alcoholism: Clinical and Experimental Research, 8,* 216–222.

Tarter, R., McBride, H., Buonpane, N., & Schneider, D. (1977). Differentiation of alcoholics: Childhood history of minimal brain dysfunction, family history, and drinking patterns. *Archives of General Psychiatry, 34,* 761–768.

Taylor, S. P., & Gammon, C. B. (1975). Effect of type and dose of alcohol on human physical aggression. *Journal of Personality and Social Psychology, 32,* 169–175.

Triandis, H. (1978). Some universals of social behavior. *Personality and Social Psychology Bulletin, 4,* 1–16.

Warner, R. H., & Rosett, H. L. (1975). The effects of drinking on offspring: An historical survey of the American and British literature. *Journal of Studies on Alcohol, 36* (11), 1395–1420.

Waxler, N., & Mishler, E. (1970). Sequential patterning in family interaction: A methodological note. *Family Process, 9,* 211–220.

Weiss, R. (1979). *Marital Interaction Coding Systems, MICS-II: Training and reference manual of coders.* Unpublished manuscript, University of Oregon.

Weiss, R. (1980). *The Areas of Change Questionnaire.* Marital Studies Program, University of Oregon, Department of Psychology.

Weiss, R. L., & Weider, G. B. (1982). Marital and family distress. In A. Bellack, M. Hersen, & A. Kazdin (Eds.), *International handbook of behavior modification* (pp. 767–809). New York: Plenum.

Wiggins, J. (1973). *Personality and prediction: Principles of personality assessment.* Reading, MA: Addison-Wesley.

Wilson, C. (1982). The impact on children. In J. Orford & J. Harwin (Eds.), *Alcohol and the family* (pp. 151–166). London: Croom Helm.

Wiseman, J. (1981). Sober comportment: Patterns and perspectives on alcohol addiction. *Journal of Studies on Alcohol, 42,* 106–126.

Wolin, S. J., Bennett, L. A., & Noonan, D. L. (1979). Family rituals and the recurrence of alcoholism over generations. *American Journal of Psychiatry, 136,* 589–593.

Biological Markers for Alcoholism: A Vulnerability Model Conceptualization[1]

Shirley Y. Hill, Stuart R. Steinhauer, and Joseph Zubin

University of Pittsburgh School of Medicine

Although the title suggests that biological factors are of central importance to the present discussion, we do not wish to ignore the psychosocial or sociocultural contributions to the development of alcoholism. There appears to be a clear need to merge biological and psychosocial theories of alcoholism to fully understand the complex phenomenon which we recognize as alcoholism. Consequently, we have been led to merge these rather diverse etiological theories by proposing a vulnerability model for alcoholism (Hill, 1981). The vulnerability model is not new in the area of psychopathology. In fact, Zubin and colleagues have proposed such a model for conceptualizing a multitude of factors that appear to be responsible for the development of schizophrenia (Zubin, Magaziner, & Steinhauer, 1983; Zubin & Spring, 1977; Zubin & Steinhauer, 1981).

Although the vulnerability model proposed here is a new one, the idea that there is a "vulnerability" to alcoholism was first suggested by Jellinek in 1960. Jellinek hypothesized that each individual is endowed with "psychological vulnerability" to alcoholism. Although every individual has this vulnerability, widely varying degrees of vulnerability may be seen. Jellinek's model was an important step, viewing alcoholism as it did as a result of both cultural factors and factors within the individual. Antecedents of the vulnerability mod-

1. This research was supported in part by National Institute on Alcohol Abuse and Alcoholism Grant #AA05909.

The authors wish to express their sincere gratitude to Mrs. Marilyn Glick for excellent editorial assistance. Jonathan Rightmyer deserves mention for his tireless efforts in recruiting families for the project.

els can be found in the diathesis-stress models promulgated by Meehl (1962), Rosenthal (1970), Falconer (1965), and Slater and Slater (1944). Zubin (1963) first formulated his version of the model at about the time Meehl's seminal articles appeared. Jellinek may have been influenced by these models, in his attempt to apply the model to alcoholism.

While Jellinek termed these individual differences in risk for developing alcoholism "psychological vulnerability," his formulation did not speculate about the particular conditions that might produce greater psychological vulnerability; the internal milieu of the individual prone to alcohol problems remained elusive and essentially a "black box." This was in part because the search for biological markers had hardly begun 25 years ago. Obviously, within the "black box" one can place a variety of predisposing variables which are biological in nature and which may include biochemical, genetic, and neurophysiological factors. Impinging on the "black box" are a variety of psychosocial and sociocultural factors, including beliefs about alcohol's effects, cultural and familial sanctions for drinking, as well as the relative availability of alcohol to particular individuals. For example, a person who has a biological vulnerability to developing alcoholism may never express this vulnerability if he or she is raised in a culture that prohibits drinking, as is the case for individuals who are members of certain religious groups (Moslems, Latter Day Saints). Similarly, the individual with minimal biological vulnerability may, nevertheless, develop alcohol abuse or alcoholism in environments where alcohol is freely available and the norm for excessive drinking is present. The high rate of alcohol and drug problems seen among military personnel during the Vietnam War typifies such a situation. Of particular interest was the fact that those who continued to have problems when they came back to the United States were those having a family history of alcoholism or drug abuse problems (Robins, Helzer, & Davis, 1975).

Our present conceptualization is depicted in Figure 1, and is intended as a pictorial representation of some of the central concepts of a vulnerability model. By emphasizing both the biological and psychosocial vulnerabilities, as well as their consequences, overcomes problems inherent in static models, allowing for changes to emerge in the individual as a result of drinking, which can then feed back into the "black box," and interact with the person's innate vulnerability.

Whether the feedback effects of drinking behavior should be regarded as a change in the innate vulnerability of the individual or

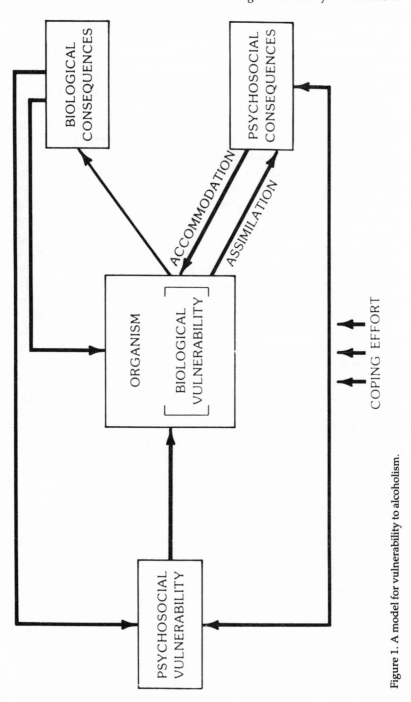

Figure 1. A model for vulnerability to alcoholism.

merely reflects the impact of drinking independent of the original vulnerability level is a moot point. The question cannot be answered until we eventually discover a way of measuring the original degree of vulnerability and then note whether drinking experience alters it. For the sake of the parsimony, we might propose that the innate level of vulnerability is unaltered by experience, thereby attributing changes in risk to the influence of subsequent drinking behavior. In this way we can at least theoretically separate out intrinsic vulnerability from the effects of the drinking experience.

Biological consequences of excessive drinking are included here not only as an end point in the drinking history but also to account for changes in the internal milieu (biological vulnerability) that may occur as a result of the individual's particular life course of drinking behavior. For example, it is now clear that alcohol affects sleep-stage regulation so that the chronic alcoholic is plagued by intermittent wakefulness, reduction in slow wave sleep, and subjective awareness of insomnia. These consequences will undoubtedly alter the biological vulnerability of the individual—a drink having more reward value because of its capacity to act temporarily as a sedative.

It is important to compare the present vulnerability model for alcoholism with the vulnerability model for schizophrenia as conceptualized by Zubin and colleagues. In the model for schizophrenia, vulnerability is not specified as either biological or psychosocial but rather is seen as a general vulnerability that is constant throughout life. Psychosocial factors are conceived of either as producing acquired vulnerability or as triggering events for the onset of episodes. In the present model, psychosocial variables are similarly seen as potential triggering conditions for an episode of heavy or abusive drinking. Unlike schizophrenia, development of alcoholism requires an eliciting agent, exposure to alcohol. Therefore, in the case of alcoholism, it is necessary to also consider psychosocial or sociocultural conditions which may be conceived of as psychosocial vulnerability factors.

For example, in most Western societies women tend to drink less than men. Evidence has been presented suggesting this difference exists in all cultures. Horton (1943), reporting on drinking customs of men and women in 30 cultures, found that in 16 of these men drank more than women, in 14 they drank equally, but in none of the cultures examined did women drink more than men. Similarly, Child, Barry, and Bacon (1965) found sufficient information for 89 societies to classify the drinking of its members by sex. In 53, sex differences were found, while in 36 drinking appeared to be equal, but again, none were found in which women drank more than men. It would appear, therefore, that women who reside in cultures that do not sanction drinking might have a different psychosocial vulnerability for developing alcoholism than those living in more permissive cultures. It is clear that all women do not have equal biological vulnerability. That adopted daughters of alcoholic biological mothers have an increased risk for developing alcoholism (Bohman, Sigvardsson, & Cloninger, 1981) has been observed among 913 Swedish adoptees. However, it would be impossible to detect such a biological difference in cultures where psychosocial vulnerability for women is very low owing to specific prohibitions against drinking for women.

Scientific Models of Etiology

The foregoing scheme is an attempt to draw together the various factors that contribute to the development of alcoholism. A brief overview of the etiological models that have been suggested for alcoholism may clarify the proposed conceptualization.

The field of psychopathology, in general, has two primary types of etiological models: biological and environmental. The biological models include the factors within the individual (genetic, internal environmental, neurophysiological, and neuroanatomical), while the environmental models include factors in the field surrounding the individual (ecological, developmental, and learning models) (Zubin, Steinhauer, Day, & van Kammen, 1985). It should be borne in mind that these models are not independent but interact with all others. In the field of alcoholism, the general etiological models can be regrouped as follows: genetic, ecological, and developmental. While some might argue for giving learning theory models a separate status, there is sufficient overlap between learning theory conceptualizations and both the ecological and developmental models, as they apply to alcoholism, to include them in a single model. The neurochemical and neurophysiological models tend to lean toward the genetic, whereas the ecological model emphasizes the environmental niche that the person occupies. From this general ecological model two specific types of environmental influences are proposed, each affecting the emergence of deviant drinking behavior: cultural influences in the form of nonfamilial environmental factors on the one hand, and familial influences on the other. Each of these models will be examined. We will begin by looking at the genetic model.

THE GENETIC MODEL

The genetic model is probably the most developed, drawing as it does on a variety of methodologies that have yielded results suggesting a genetic propensity for developing alcoholism. Though this propensity may perhaps not be both a necessary and sufficient condition, it may at least be a necessary condition for the development of alcohol-related problems. This might appear to overstate the case for genetics, given that some alcoholics appear to have a nonfamilial form (no first-degree biological relatives with alcoholism). We must remember, however, that not all individuals who carry a genotype express it.

Among the observations supporting a genetic vulnerability are greater concordance in drinking problems and in the greater similarity in quantity of alcohol consumed by monozygotic than dizygotic twins (Kaij, 1960; Partanen, Bruun, & Markkanen, 1966) and evidence from adoption studies that the risk for developing alcohol problems is elevated among adopted away offspring of alcoholics when contrasted with similar offspring of nonalcoholics (Goodwin, Schulsinger, Hermansen, Guze, & Winokur, 1973). Other work using the adoption strategy has confirmed a greater risk among adoptees of alcoholic biological parentage than those without such parentage (Bohman et al., 1981; Cadoret & Gath, 1978). A further refinement of this methodology has included the discovery of subtypes of alcoholism varying by the degree to which environmental factors confer greater or lesser amounts of risk or protection from developing alcohol problems. Bohman et al. (1981) have proposed a "milieu limited" type of alcoholism in which the alcoholic may be characterized as having milder alcohol abuse and minimal criminality. Further, no history of treatment for alcoholism can be noted among the biological parents of such individuals. In this form, the postnatal environment is important in determining the frequency and severity of alcoholism expressed in adopted away sons of alcoholics. The other form, termed by Bohman et al. (1981) as the "male limited" type, is characterized by severe alcohol abuse, severe criminality, history of frequent treatment for alcoholism among biological fathers, but normal alcohol use in mothers. In this form, the postnatal environment does not affect the risk for developing alcohol-related problems among offspring. The "male limited" form appears to carry a greatly increased risk to relatives of index cases, a reported tenfold increase in Bohman's study and a fourfold increase in the Danish adoption study reported by Goodwin et al. (1973). According to the genetic model, a genotype is transmitted from generation to generation either through a specific allele in a particular location on a specific chromosome, in the case of the single gene model, or through several alleles on the same or different chromosomes in the case of the polygenic model. Complicating the search for genetic markers is the fact that we presently cannot be certain about the genetic model which best describes the transmission of putative alleles. Thus, if we presume that a single gene is responsible, specific research strategies must be utilized (e.g., use of large extended pedigrees) and appropriate steps taken to ensure that the data collected will allow for testing this possibility. Similarly, if a polygenic model is presumed to be responsible, other strategies might be indicated. The multifactorial model of transmission is one such model that tests for polygenic influences as well as environmental transmission.

Briefly stated, the multifactorial model presumes that the liability to develop a disorder is the result of genetic factors, familial environmental factors and nonfamilial environmental factors (for example, cultural factors). From this model, predictions can be made about the mode of transmission of the disorder. For example, applying the multifactorial model to data collected for alcoholic and opiate abusing probands, including the assessment of these disorders in relatives of the probands, has previously allowed us to conclude that these two seemingly similar disorders (both involving addiction) are in fact transmitted independently within families (Hill, Cloninger, & Ayre, 1977). Familial transmission is demonstrated when a disorder tends to run in families. Genetic transmission is more difficult to demonstrate.

With regard to the genetic factors involved in the transmission of alcoholism, some geneticists have suggested that perhaps the combined effects of single genes against a background of polygenic influences would best describe the observed pattern of familial aggregation seen in alcoholic families. From this assumption a mixed-model approach has been offered. That is, the combined effect of single rare genes may contribute a significant proportion of the variance in some cases whereas polygenic influences may be more influential in others. This model would also account for the heterogeneity of phenotypes seen among alcoholics.

THE ECOLOGICAL MODEL

For some time now ecological explanations have been offered for alcoholism. The ecological model has not produced as much scientific evidence for etiology as the genetic model has, though use of an ecological framework has elucidated a number of factors clearly associated with alcoholism. For simplicity, these factors can be categorized as being of two types: familial and nonfamilial. Among those factors that might be characterized as nonfamilial environmental factors are such things as the socioeconomic status of the individual, characteristics of the social milieu, including the religious orientation of the culture he or she occupies, and the social norms of the culture or subculture that either proscribe drinking or encourage it. Familial environmental factors may well be of equal importance. Recently a number of researchers have begun to view the family as the social unit which directs the use of alcohol through family interaction patterns and use of alcohol within the family.

Familial environment. Wolin and colleagues have, for example, characterized families which transmit alcoholism from parents to children as differing from those families that do not, in terms of the degree to which the presence of an alcoholic in the family circle either disrupts the performance of family rituals, or owing to coping efforts of the family, appears to minimally affect the performance of these rituals, if at all (Wolin, Bennett, Noonan, & Teitelbaum, 1980). A family ritual is defined by these researchers as a "symbolic form of communication that, due to the satisfaction that family members experience through its repetition, is enacted out in a systematic fashion over time." Included among these "rituals" are typical behaviors displayed during holidays, mealtimes, vacations and so forth.

To evaluate the impact of drinking on these rituals, families in which an alcoholic parent was present were asked to describe in detail the families' interaction and behavior during periods preceding and following the parent's heaviest drinking. The study was designed to determine if some families protect their most cherished family rituals more effectively than others and to assess whether this has any influence on transmission of alcoholism. The authors' conclusion was that ritual protection does make a difference. Extreme ritual disruption was significantly related to increased transmission of alcoholism to children, whereas ritual protection was associated with less transmission.

In short, alcoholism can be transmitted through nongenetic means, here in the form of familial environmental factors, though of course cultural transmission can occur as well. The value of the multifactorial model of transmission, as we indicated earlier, is that it makes no assumptions about the relative contribution of environmental or genetic factors and therefore appears well suited for the task of assembling a diverse set of variables that affect transmission of alcoholism from generation to generation and ultimately making predictions about risk within and across families. Other models of transmission have also been developed that similarly assess multiple factors for the potential contribution of both genes and environment (Morton, 1974).

THE DEVELOPMENTAL MODEL

Studies that reflect the developmental model have focused primarily on rearing patterns of children that are associated with later adult adjustment. This work has failed to identify any particular pattern consistently associated with the development of alcoholism. Adult alcoholics have been described as experiencing minimal parental supervision as children (McCord & McCord, 1962) and as having been the target of lax or inconsistent discipline (Robins, Bates, & O'Neal, 1962). That 50% of alcoholics in treatment have an alcoholic father may explain the lenient discipline of these children who later become alcoholic noted by some. Parental alcoholism has a major impact on the children of alcoholics. Studies concerning rearing practices of nonalcoholic parents of children who later develop alcoholism are also needed to answer the question of whether or not particular rearing practices (e.g., lenient discipline) have significant developmental influence. The increased level of disruption observed in households of alcoholics may provide greater predictive power as a developmental influence than any other aspect of child rearing. More work is also needed to understand how characteristics of the social network of children of alcoholics may provide buffering effects for the child (e.g., presence of a supportive nonalcoholic friend or relative).

Other theories of how developmental influences are mediated include studies on infant care and on early separation from parents, neither of which appear to have much effect on long-term outcome for any particular psychopathology (Becker,1964; Caldwell, 1964; Yarrow, 1964). We suspect that, on the whole, Rosenthal's (1970) observation that child rearing is less important than genetic loading in producing psychopathology in general, may hold equally true for the development of alcoholism, though certainly having an alcoholic parent produces a distinct environment for the child.

Social learning theory. As mentioned previously, the social learning model has gained much acceptance as an etiological explanation for alcoholism. The basic tenet of the social learning theory is that the individual learns behavior, whether deviant or normative, through cognitive mediation (Bandura, 1969). Although the behavior may be maintained by external reinforcement, classical conditioning processes, or cognitive mediation, some of this learning occurs covertly in the form of modeling. From this theory one can predict that an individual will learn to become alcoholic by modeling the behaviors of alcoholics through a system of beliefs about the effects alcohol has on functioning.

In Bandura's early work he speaks of "no trial learning," in which new behaviors are most easily acquired through modeling. If the model has particular reward value, as parents certainly do, given their early ties to the emotional rewards of the child, learning of particular behaviors is facilitated. Further, in observing the parents' style of coping, the child learns to adopt similar modes of coping albeit maladaptive, in the case of the child who emulates an alcoholic parent.

For the child in an alcoholic home, communication patterns also are salient developmental factors since these homes are often characterized by the presence of disorders in the marital relationship as well as defects in the parent-child relationship. In fact, Jones (1968) has noted that the mothers of children who later became alcoholic, appeared uninterested in the child significantly more often than mothers whose children did not become alcoholic. Robins et al. (1962) has characterized children seen in a child guidance clinic who later became alcoholic as frequently experiencing parental cruelty or desertion and general parental inadequacy. Although the homes of these children have generally been described as inadequate, further work is needed to determine if protective factors may operate in these homes in the form of social network characteristics. For example, does the presence of one healthy parent or other supportive adult buffer the stress of living in an alcoholic household? While no one individual in the alcoholism field may readily be identified as a social learning theorist, research on the effects that beliefs have on the use and misuse of alcohol follow most closely this theoretical orientation (Marlatt, 1976).

Personality theory. Within this discussion of developmental theories we will include personality theories of alcoholism. Placing personality theory under the developmental model may be controversial for some, since recent studies show that at least some of the similarity in personality types within families may be under genetic control. At any rate, we have arbitrarily placed personality theory in the developmental domain for the present. As will be seen in later discussion of the vulnerability model, we view personality variables as premorbid characteristics of the individual that are orthogonal to symptomatic aspects of a particular psychopathology, whether schizophrenia or alcoholism, such that they may not "cause" alcoholism but rather may serve as moderating variables. Whether or not personality characteristics are vulnerability indicators or moderating variables is still a debatable issue awaiting further research.

Personality variables were not always accorded this role in the etiology of alcoholism. In fact the "addictive" personality at one time was considered the primary "cause" of alcoholism and substance abuse. This view not only attributed causality to personality but did so through a univariate explanation—one single personality type. This view probably emerged from psychoanalytic theory, which viewed the alcoholic as orally fixated, first dependent on the mother's breast, then excessively dependent on others for assistance, ultimately failing to get all the reassurance desired, finally turning to the bottle.

Recent research suggests that distinct personality types exist among alcoholics. Using the Minnesota Multiphasic Personality Inventory (MMPI) Nerviano and Gross (1983) have identified seven prominent subtypes: chronic severe distress, passive-aggressive sociopath, antisocial sociopath, reactive acute depression, severely neurotic psychophysiological, mixed character dysphoria, and paranoid alienated. Two of these subtypes, the passive-aggressive sociopath and the chronic severe distress type, have been replicated in a variety of studies (Morey & Blashfield, 1981; Skinner & Allen, 1982). Moreover, these subtypes appear to be correlated with different drinking styles and drinking problems, the distressed neurotics typically being heavier drinkers with more problems than the sociopathic alcoholics who drink more moderately and have fewer detrimental consequences (Skinner & Allen, 1982). The former sub-type appears to use alcohol to alleviate distress and cope with life problems, whereas alcoholics of the latter type appear to use alcohol simply because of poor impulse control.

Although a number of other personality tests exist, the MMPI has been most frequently administered clinically to alcoholic subjects. A number of MMPI profile configurations have been observed among alcoholics and certain scales appear to be more consistently elevated than others among alcoholics in treatment. These include elevations on Scale 4 (the Psychopathic Deviate Scale) with additional eleva-tions on Scale 2 (Depression) and Scale 7 (Psychasthenia) (see Owen & Butcher, 1979). Elevations on Scale 4 are thought to reflect impul-sivity and low frustration tolerance as well as disregard for social norms. Included in the Scale 4 elevation is a general tendency not to profit from past experience, especially negative reinforcement con-tingencies. The other two elevations, Scales 2 and 7, usually are taken as indicators of subjective distress, the former scale being associated with low mood, despair, and pessimism about the future whereas the latter is associated more with obsessive rumination and worry.

Particular scale elevations appear to be more characteristic of alco-holics in treatment than of prealcoholic individuals who will later become alcoholic though information is currently limited. A few longitudinal studies have been completed in which persons who la-ter became alcoholic were assessed before the possible confounding effects of drinking were manifest. Hoffmann, Loper, and Kammeier (1974) compared MMPI protocols of alcoholics undergoing treat-ment with their protocols obtained when they were college fresh-men. Next they compared the subjects' college protocols with those of their nonalcoholic classmates. From these comparisons they found that two of the clinical scales were elevated among the preal-coholics, Scale 4 (Psychopathic Deviate) and Scale 9 (Hypomania), suggesting that these individuals were more gregarious, impulsive, and nonconforming than their peers who did not become alcoholic. While no significant maladjustment in the form of subjective dis-tress was seen among the protocols of the prealcoholics, onset of alcoholism produced a different picture. The alcoholics now showed clear evidence of subjective distress, manifest as elevations on both the Psychasthenia and the Depression scales, as well as con-tinued elevations on Scale 4.

Other longitudinal studies have suggested that the potential alco-holic or drug abuser can be identified by a constellation of traits well before they begin to use these substances. The Oakland Growth Study (Jones, 1968, 1971), a prospective study of female and male adolescents who were followed into adulthood, revealed particular personality characteristics as a function of gender. The male adolescents who later became problem drinkers were described as "undercontrolled, impulsive and rebellious," while the females were described as "self-defeating, pessimistic, withdrawn, guilty, and depressive." Others, including Jessor and Jessor (1977, 1978) and Kandel (1978, 1980), have noted that adolescents could be identified as future users of addictive substances by their independence, rebelliousness, and failure to value conventional institutions. Although the MMPI was not administered in these studies, one wonders if the constellation of traits described by these observers might be the essence of what the Psychopathic Deviate scale measures. At any rate, it now appears that certain premorbid personality characteristics may accompany later development of alcoholism.

THE SEARCH FOR ETIOLOGY

As is abundantly clear from the foregoing review, each model makes a unique contribution to understanding the factors that may be responsible for the development of alcoholism. Each model fails, however, to explain why one individual bcomes an alcoholic and another does not. Even if alcoholism were completely determined by genetic factors, we could expect that some individuals would carry the genotype but not express the disorder because of incomplete penetrance. Clearly, there is a need to merge the various theories and models into a super-model to adequately explain the etiology of alcoholism. We propose that a vulnerability model similar to that previously proposed by Zubin and his colleagues for schizophrenia may offer greater explanatory power when considering the diverse expression of alcohol abuse patterns and outcome. Rather than postulating that alcoholism is a disease or at least a biological condition, on the one hand, or a defect in social learning on the other, the vulnerability model attempts to incorporate relevant findings from both the biological and psychosocial domains.

Though this view may seem heretical to those accustomed to viewing alcoholism as a chronic disease state, in which the alcoholic is considered to be, lifelong, a "recovering alcoholic," we propose that alcoholism is an episodic disorder, developing in the vulnerable individual when subjected to exogenous or endogenous stressors.

When the episode of drinking terminates the individual returns to his or her premorbid level of functioning. For those with good premorbid functioning, we consider the end of the episode and the return to their premorbid niche a recovery, or at least a remission. For those with poor premorbid functioning, it is difficult to know whether the effects of an episode have ended, since a return to the premorbid level still may not enable them to function as well as others. They may be mistakenly considered as persisting in their episode of drinking. However, a minority of individuals who are biologically vulnerable and undergo stressors necessarily develop episodes. In fact, some highly vulnerable individuals may never develop an episode of excessive drinking at all.

Among the moderating variables which may prevent development of an episode are: the individual's premorbid personality, characteristics of his/her social network, and the ecological niche which he/she occupies. That not all vulnerable individuals develop episodes is illustrated in the Danish adoption study. The majority (73%) of offspring of alcoholics adopted away shortly after birth (Goodwin et al., 1973) did not develop alcoholism as adults, though of course the risk was higher among this group than in a matched control group (18% versus 5%) by age 30 when they were assessed. The moderating variables of premorbid personality, supportive (perhaps nondrinking) social networks, and favorable ecological niches may cushion the impact of the stressor so that the episode is aborted.

Recent work by Marlatt and others who have examined the features of successful relapse prevention among treated alcoholics attests to the fact that triggering events play a major role in determining whether an individual who has displayed abusive drinking will relapse or go on to be symptom free. Marlatt and Gordon (1980) suggest that most relapses can be accounted for by four situational categories. Two of the categories are interpersonal and consist of situations in which the individual feels frustrated and angry and is unable to express these feelings, or feels incapable resisting the social pressure exerted by others to drink. The remaining two categories consist of situations in which the individual experiences negative emotional states such as anxiety, depression, or boredom. These observations have led Marlatt and Gordon to propose a cognitive behavioral model of relapse in which a person's expectations of competency interact with the availability and effectiveness of coping strategies to determine the response to situations in which drinking might occur.

Our present vulnerability model assumes that alcoholism is episodic. This assumption could be challenged in the case of the chronic alcoholic who does not achieve remission and goes on to progressively more entrenched drinking which may result in severe medical problems and sometimes death. In fact, one of the tenets of the disease model is that alcoholism is a progressive illness ending in death if not arrested once and for all. Yet recent epidemiological data suggest that not all alcoholics show a progressive course. A number of studies have examined in detail the drinking patterns of persons diagnosed as alcoholics at one point in time and followed them for periods of up to 20 years (Clark, 1974; Fillmore, 1974; Pettinati, Sugerman, DiDonato, & Maurer, 1982; Polich, Armor, & Braiker, 1981; Rohan, 1975). For example, a 1980 four-year follow-up of a subsample of persons who were part of the original Rand study (Polich et al., 1981) found that 18% of their subjects were drinking without problems or symptoms of dependence. The "typical" drinking pattern appeared to be one characterized by much changing back and forth between levels of consumption. They noted that some individuals when examined at multiple points in time continued to improve, while others deteriorated, with most alternating between relatively improved and unimproved status. Similar conclusions were reached by Fillmore (1974) in her 20 year follow-up; many drinkers with numerous and severe problems were later found either to have markedly improved or to have different problems. Clark (1974) suggests: "None of this fits with the disease model of alcoholism insofar as that model implies keeping early symptoms and early problems and adding others as time passes."

The Diagnosis of Alcoholism—Implications for Scientific Breakthroughs

When Jellinek first began to classify the types of alcoholisms which he had observed in the 1940s, systematic nomenclature for psychopathology had not been developed to the degree it has today. Jellinek's writing predated such classification systems as the Research Diagnostic Criteria (RDC) and the American Psychiatric Association's DSM-III by more than thirty years. Without the benefit of the large-scale epidemiological studies which were to take place much later, it is to Jellinek's credit that he was able to recognize so many different forms of alcoholism. Although RDC and DSM-III have their problems, they nevertheless represent considerable achievement for both psychology and psychiatry in making a systematic descriptive approach to diagnosis available to both clinicians and researchers.

The question then becomes, Have we come far enough in systematizing our diagnoses of alcohol-related problems? Probably not. To the same extent that Jellinek relied on his astute clinical judgment to describe the alpha, beta, and gamma alcoholic, DSM-III relied on the clinical judgment of a panel of experts in the alcohol field to come up with a definition of alcoholism. What then is the reliability and validity of the alcohol-related diagnoses using this classification system?

With the development of semistructured interviews such as the Schedule for Affective Disorders and Schizophrenia (SADS) and structured ones like the Diagnostic Interview Schedule, whose forerunner was the Renard Diagnostic Interview, it became possible to check the reliability of the diagnosis of alcoholism and following the advent of DSM-III, that of alcohol abuse and alcohol dependence. Reliability checks using these instruments suggest that clinicians can agree upon diagnoses of individuals having alcohol-related problems using the schema outlined in DSM-III.

The definition of alcoholism provided by the panel of experts convened by the American Psychiatric Association departed from earlier versions of the DSM by distinguishing between alcohol abuse and alcohol dependence (the latter probably most akin to alcoholism). The need to make this distinction undoubtedly came from the experts' clinical observations that some people can have a number of problems associated with alcohol use (e.g., job loss, marital difficulty) yet not be physically dependent on it. Prior to DSM-III the clinician had the choice of either placing a "case" for diagnosis into either an "alcoholic" or "not alcoholic" category. Obviously, if problems with alcohol fall along a continuum, this is a most unsatisfactory solution. Thus DSM-III overcame this problem, at least in part, by introducing a milder form of alcohol problems, namely, alcohol abuse.

According to DSM-III, an alcohol abuser is one who exhibits symptoms in two broadly defined categories: (A) pathological use, and (B) impairment in social or occupational functioning. The symptoms must also have been present for at least one month for a diagnosis of alcohol abuse to be correctly applied. Examples of pathological use listed are: need for daily use, drinking despite medical complications, binges, and blackouts. Impairment in social or occupational functioning due to alcohol use includes loss of job, legal difficulties, and arguments or violence with friends, family, or acquaintances while drinking.

The alcohol dependent person in DSM-III terminology is one who exhibits symptoms from either of the broad categories of pathological use or impairment in social or occupational functioning. In addition, to be labeled alcohol dependent, the individual must also display evidence that he or she has tolerance to the effects of alcohol or has experienced withdrawal symptoms.

Although these are far from perfect as definitions covering the vast spectrum of alcohol abuse problems, with or without dependence, nevertheless, we can describe the characteristics of people whom clinicians (the APA experts) have seen in their clinical practices and whom they know to be alcoholic. The emphasis is here placed on the word "know" because diagnosis of alcoholism, like diagnosis of all other psychiatric problems, is circular insofar as that clinicians diagnose the psychiatric disorder and then proceed to enumerate the characteristics of those individuals so labeled. Diagnosis becomes noncircular when the same diagnostic entity is observed over time and found to be consistent, that is, the alcoholic diagnosed at point A in time does not, for example, become schizophrenic at point B. To further validate a diagnostic entity, it is also useful to have information about treatment outcome and response to particular treatments. If, for example, a patient appears to be either severely depressed or possibly schizophrenic and shows no improvement after a course of antidepressants or ECT but responds well to one of the neuroleptic medications, our hunch that the patient was suffering from schizophrenia is further confirmed. So too, the various alcoholisms need to be studied with respect to treatment outcome and consistency across time. Finally, unraveling phenomenological aspects of the disorder associated with known markers for alcoholism would appear to be an important next step.

Markers

Since 1973, when the results of the Danish adoption study were released and the clear contribution of genetics to the development of alcoholism was fully realized, there has been increased attention to finding "markers" for alcoholism. While this is a laudable endeavor, the results of this search may turn out to be less fruitful than we had hoped because of our current lack of clarity in the alcoholism field as to what constitutes a "marker" and how to recognize one. It is our intent that the conceptualization provided by the present vulnerability model may direct our search in a more efficacious way.

The general parameters of our vulnerability model include the following variables: (1) the degree of vulnerability of the individual; (2) the necessary triggering events for eliciting an episode; (3) moderating factors that ameliorate or exacerbate the triggering event so that the episode is either aborted or actually experienced; (4) the time course of the episode; (5) the termination of the active episode; and (6) any residual effects of the episode.

The degree of vulnerability is gauged by measuring the indicators. The triggering events are the life events and endogenous events that impinge on the individual at the time of the development of the episode. Even though an individual may be highly vulnerable, based on the presence of the indicators, and even though he or she may have undergone considerable life event stressors, that person need not develop an episode if the social network, ecological niche and premorbid personality can absorb the stress the person is experiencing. However, once an episode begins, it will continue until there is intervention either by the individual or by some therapeutic agent. But episodes do not last forever, though the vulnerability tends to persist and even recovered alcoholics are still at high risk of relapse. Of course, after a chronic bout of alcoholism there is a tendency for residual effects to persist and these residual effects make it difficult to investigate the original premorbid vulnerability.

A vulnerability model allows for some individuals being at greater risk for a particular disorder though they have not ever developed the disorder and may never do so. Diabetes mellitus is one such condition that can now be characterized by biological "vulnerability markers." Specifically, juvenile onset diabetes has been found to be associated with particular HLA antigens. Obviously, when we speak of an association we mean that the frequency of a particular HLA variant is higher among the affected group; it does not mean that every case with the illness will have the marker nor that every person with the marker will have the illness. However, should two unaffected individuals who carry the marker have children, we can specify how much their children's risk is increased over population rates as a result of having such parentage.

Applying the vulnerability model to alcoholism requires that we find ways of identifying those who are vulnerable, regardless of whether they have ever displayed alcoholic behavior or even heavy drinking. This means finding indicators or "markers" of performance (neuropsychological, neurophysiological), measures of psychosocial functioning (e.g., participation in family and social networks), or other characteristics (profiles from personality tests). Ideally, these indicators would identify individuals who are either alcoholic and currently in an episode (drinking without significant periods of sobriety) or alcoholic and in remission (sobriety of six months duration), or unaffected individuals with a higher risk for developing alcoholism (persons with multiple blood relatives with alcoholism). The ideal marker is one that occurs only in alcoholics and not in normal controls or in other nonalcoholic psychiatric patients. Further, the marker or pattern of markers should be present in "high risk" individuals (blood relatives of alcoholics) more frequently than is seen in the normal population.

Specific cultural, ecological and social support or personality characteristics may modify the likelihood of developing an episode in the presence of a triggering event because they serve as buffering agents (i.e., they are moderating variables). Such variables can either amplify or diminish the immediate effects of stress and subsequent drinking behavior. Thus it is convenient to differentiate between the various types of indicators: vulnerability markers, episode markers, and moderating variables (Hill, 1981; Zubin et al., 1983; Zubin & Spring, 1977).

For some of the indicators we cannot yet state unequivocably that they are, for example, vulnerability markers rather than moderating variables. As one illustration of this, we have suggested earlier that individuals raised in certain religious environments may be imbued with such a persistent aversion to alcohol use such that throughout life and even in other environments that encourage drinking, these individuals will be more likely to remain abstinent. We have earlier denoted as psychosocial vulnerability this lifelong persistent psychological (attitudinal) stance. When similar kinds of environmental variables produce relatively transient modifications in the psychosocial environment of the individual, we prefer to classify them as moderating variables.

Before reviewing the evidence obtained thus far on a variety of putative markers for alcoholism, let us attempt to distinguish the various types of markers and the conditions under which they must be observed if they are to have even tentative value in terms of discovering the etiology of alcoholism. We in the behavioral sciences have extended the term "marker" beyond its usual more limited boundaries as used in genetics. In genetic studies the term marker usually refers to a characteristic or trait given at birth through one's genetic heritage that endures as for example, whether one has type O or B blood. Usually genetic markers have simple unequivocal patterns of inheritance and heritable variations common enough to be classified as genetic polymorphisms. Of course an enduring, heritable trait like type O or B blood is not necessarily a "marker" for a particular illness just because the frequency of the genetic marker is higher among a particular group of individuals having the illness. To be considered a "marker" the blood group or other variant should distinguish affected from nonaffected individuals, should distinguish relatives of affected individuals from individuals without such a family history, and additionally should show linkage with affected status. That is, within families there should be segregation of the marker with the disease status. Because the science of alcoholism is still in its infancy, we really have no markers as such. We have a number of indicators, however, which we will review.

First, we will look at the types of indicators that can be studied to clarify the etiology of alcoholism. We have outlined the conditions under which one would be able to distinguish a vulnerability indicator from an episode or residual indicator. We will here use the term "marker" because we are considering the idealized case at a point in time when marker status has been demonstrated for some of our more promising indicators. At present, a number of indicators appear to differentiate alcoholics from nonalcoholics (e.g., impaired performance on particular neuropsychological tests; elevations on MMPI subscales). All of these are candidates for status as vulnerability indicators, or perhaps markers; but because they are most often identified after the individual becomes an alcoholic, it is impossible to determine if these are indicators of an episode alone, disappearing when the person becomes sufficiently detoxified, or are persistent characteristics of the individual both during and after the episode, that is, they are vulnerability indicators or ultimately vulnerability markers.

We have outlined a number of strategies to enable us to differentiate between episode markers and vulnerability markers, as seen in Tables 1 and 2. The plus sign indicates that the marker is present; a minus sign means the marker is absent. But in order to properly classify the potential marker, we need to know its status both during and after the episode. Because the onset of alcoholism is insidious, it is sometimes difficult to know when the episode of alcoholism began. A period of heavy drinking lasting many years often precedes bona fide alcoholism. Also, since alcohol use may affect the marker

Table 1
Types of Markers by Episode and Postepisode Status

Marker	Status		Type of Marker
	Episode	Postepisode	
A	+	+	Vulnerability
B	+	−	Episode
C	−	+	Residual
D	−	−	Nondifferential

Note: (+) marker present; (−) marker absent

Table 2
Types of Markers by Preepisode, Episode, and Postepisode Status

Marker	Status			Type of Marker
	Preepisode	Episode	Postepisode	
A	+	+	+	Vulnerability
B	−	+	−	Episode
C	+	−	+	Vulnerability
D	+	−	−	Normalized by Episode
E	−	+	+	Residual
F	+	+	−	Normalized by Episode
G	−	−	+	Residual
H	−	−	−	Nondifferential

Source: Adapted from Zubin & Steinhauer, 1981
Note: (+) marker present; (−) marker absent

under study, even in quantities typically consumed by nonalcoholic individuals, more and more research designs utilize children who presumably have not begun to drink to get around this problem. The next step is to determine the status of the marker after the episode is over. If we didn't have enough problems defining the onset of the episode, we now must figure out when the episode ends! There certainly is no unanimity on this issue. While all can agree that an alcoholic off alcohol in a detoxification ward has ended his drinking episode, not all would agree about when the effects of drinking have passed. But if we can assume that the drinking episode has ended (the person is abstinent), and that the acute neurotoxic effects of the alcohol have subsided, then it may be reasonable to look at the marker at some arbitrary point, say, after approximately one month off alcohol.

In the schema we have outlined, A is definitely a vulnerability marker since it characterizes the person both during and after the episode whereas B is definitely an episode marker since it is present during the episode but disappears when the episode ends. C is normal during the episode but shows a residual effect in the postepisode period, indicating that it may reflect the effect of the episode rather than vulnerability to developing alcoholism. D indicates that the marker in question is absent both during and after the episode and hence is not a marker for alcoholism. It has been included here simply for logical clarity.

In order to determine whether C is merely present because of past alcohol consumption, that is, as a residual effect of the episode, we also need to know the status of the individual during the preepisode period. If the alcoholic exhibited the marker during the preepisode period, we could no longer regard it as a residual effect. Perhaps, we have here a vulnerable individual whose drinking during an episode alters the marker expression, but without the drinking we would see the marker throughout: pre, during, and following the episode.

In order to take into account the preepisode status, we have expanded the table (see Table 2). Here again A is a definite vulnerability marker and B is a definite episode marker. C is a vulnerability marker which changes toward control subject levels during an episode; at present this type of marker is purely speculative for alcoholism. However, one example of this type of marker can be seen in schizophrenia where homovanillic acid (HVA) appears to normalize during acute stages of schizophrenia (Post, Fink, Carpenter, & Goodwin, 1975). D reflects the normalization of the indicator as a result of an episode, the marker disappears in the postepisode period. Again, whether this type of marker will actually be found among alcoholics is yet to be determined.

E shows the residual effect of the episode since it was absent in the preepisode period but developed in the postepisode. An example of this is the disruption in sleep continuity and suppression of slow wave sleep mentioned earlier, which tends to develop during a drinking bout and can remain in evidence for as long as 1–2 years after the alcoholic achieves sobriety (Adamson & Burdick, 1973). F indicates that the episode normalized the marker, causing it to disappear in the postepisode period. One possible example of this would be a tendency for prealcoholics to exhibit higher levels of mania than those who never become alcoholic (elevation of Scale 9– MMPI). The mania levels could remain elevated during drinking, but as the person experiences withdrawal (subclinical withdrawal may go on for many months), it might be expected to normalize toward nonalcoholic levels. Because withdrawal is often associated with depression, increasing scores on the Depression scale may bring scores on the Mania scale more toward normal values. G, like E, demonstrates the residual effect of the episode. A good example of this is the lowered scores on the Category test of the Halstead Reitan battery which has now been reported in a number of studies (Goodwin & Hill, 1975; Parsons & Leber, 1982). H is a nondifferential marker.

Another way of determining the character of the marker is to examine the siblings of the probands. Because siblings have in common, on the average, 50% of their genes and share a common environment, study of the siblings aids us in determining whether the putative marker is a vulnerability marker, an episode marker, or possibly both. Table 3 shows the possibilities when the status of the sibling is considered. The heading "first degree relatives" is used because, in fact, one can also examine either the probands' natural parents or their children, since both share half of their genes on average. Two points need mentioned. First, we assume in this table that the sibling or parent is not affected by alcoholism. Secondly, when one speaks of a control group in this situation, we mean that the controls are free of alcoholism and other psychiatric disorders as are their first-degree relatives. Individuals who carry the genotype for alcoholism or psychiatric disorders, even though they are phenotypically healthy, must be excluded to avoid stacking the cards against finding markers among the alcoholic families even when they exist.

In Table 3, A remains a vulnerability marker, its character confirmed by its presence in siblings. AA is apparently a permanent characteristic of the proband but not of the sibling and hence might qualify as a nonfamilial marker. B remains an episode marker, while BB is not easy to explain and may be an impossible marker. C and CC are vulnerability indicators which change during an episode, C being more likely a familial marker while CC is not. D is definitely a

Table 3
Types of Markers Based on Presence in Probands and Their First-Degree Relatives

Marker	Status				Type of Marker
	Preepisode	Episode	Postepisode	First-degree Relatives	
A	+	+	+	+	Vulnerability
AA	+	+	+	–*	Vulnerability
B	–	+	–	–	Episode
BB	–	+	–	+	?
C	+	–	+	+	Vulnerability
CC	+	–	+	–	Vulnerability, Nonfamilial
D	+	–	–	+	Vulnerability, Change by Episode
DD	+	–	–	–	Vulnerability, Nonfamilial, Change by Episode
E	–	+	+	–	Residual Effect of Episode
EE	–	+	+	+	?
F	+	+	–	+	Vulnerability, Change by Episode
FF	+	+	–	–	Vulnerability, Nonfamilial, Change by Episode
G	–	–	+	–	Residual Effect of Episode
GG	–	–	+	+	?
H	–	–	–	–	Nondifferential for Alcoholism
HH	–	–	–	+	Invulnerability

Note. (+) marker significantly more frequent in alcoholics and/or their first-degree relatives than in normal controls during designated period; (–*) marker significantly less frequent in alcoholics and/or their first-degree relatives than in normal controls during the period; (–) marker not differential during the period; (?) doubt whether the pattern across the periods occurs in nature.

vulnerability marker which disappears during and after an episode, so that siblings who develop an episode would lose the marker. DD on the other hand shows the effect of the episode only. E may be regarded as representing a residual effect of the episode but is not a vulnerability marker. EE is absent during the preepisode but present during and after the episode and also occurs in siblings. Only a follow-up of the siblings can reveal the significance of this type of marker. It is also possible that this pattern will not emerge in a real data set. F represents a marker of vulnerability that disappears in the proband who develops an episode but that may have a familial basis, since the siblings also exhibit the marker as well. FF is similarly a vulnerability marker that changes during an episode and presumably is nonfamilial since siblings do not exhibit it. G shows the residual effect of the episode and might be further elucidated by follow-up of the siblings. GG is a bit of a puzzle since it seems to appear only after an episode and is present in the siblings. H is nondifferential for alcoholism while HH can be examined only by follow-up.

MARKERS FOR ALCOHOLISM

Heterogeneous etiology. The search for markers for alcoholism is a complicated one, owing to the heterogeneity of the disorder and the fact that alcoholics and their first-degree relatives show higher rates for a number of psychiatric illnesses than those expected in the general population. Families of alcoholics show increased rates of affective disorders (Behar & Winokur, 1979; Dunner, Hensel, & Fieve, 1979) and anorexia nervosa (Eckert, Goldberg, Halmi, Casper, & Davis, 1979). Increased rates of sociopathy and Briquet's Syndrome have also been reported. However, there does appear to be a tendency for alcoholism to "run true to type" in the sense that alcoholics appear to have higher rates of alcoholism in their families than any other psychopathology (Cotton, 1979; Hill et al., 1977). Nevertheless, we cannot ignore the increased rates of other psychopathology. These increased rates of other psychopathology may be due to the fact that persons with psychiatric problems may drink in an attempt to modify psychiatric symptons or it may simply reflect the heterogeneous nature of alcoholism. (There may be different forms.) To date, we have not come very far in specifying the subtypes of the disorder. Two systems frequently referenced are: (1) the primary/secondary distinction, originating with the St. Louis group (Goodwin & Guze, 1979), and (2) the familial/nonfamilial distinction described by many investigators (Frances, Timm, & Bucky, 1980; Goodwin, 1983). Little is currently known about the reliability and validity of these distinctions. Even when such data are available, we suspect that improved diagnostic typologies will have limited value unless we can identify trait-related markers. At any rate, armed with more precise typologies for diagnosing more homogeneous groups of alcoholics, we can now proceed to search for markers in accordance with the hypotheses emanating from the model we have outlined for understanding the etiology of alcoholism. Several of the potential markers available to us will be discussed.

Metabolism. Because alcohol is a drug, it is understandable that the search for what might be genetically transmitted has included studies looking at the metabolism of alcohol. Alcohol is eliminated from the body predominantly by metabolism in the liver. Oxidation of ethanol to acetaldehyde by alcohol dehydrogenase (ADH) is followed by nicotinamide-adenine dinucleotide (NAD)-dependent oxidation by aldehyde dehydrogenase (ALDH) to acetate. The enzyme alcohol dehydrogenase has received attention in recent years (Li, Bosron, Dafeldecker, Lange, & Vallee, 1977; von Wartburg, 1979) because three gene loci have been identified: ADH-1, ADH-2, ADH-3. Two common alleles occurring at two of the loci have particular polypeptides associated with them (B-1, B-2, and gamma-1, gamma-2). Depending on the genotype, isoenzymes can be formed by a combination of these subunits. Isoenzymes containing an "atypical" subunit, B-2, have higher enzymatic activity than those composed of "normal" subunits. The atypical subunit is far more common among Orientals who, because of their lower rates of alcoholism, appear to be protected in some way. The higher enzymatic activity of the "atypical" isoenzyme could increase elimination rates and lead to production of greater amounts of acetaldehyde, a substance associated with physiological discomfort.

Wolff has demonstrated that increased vasomotor response to alcohol can be elicited in over 80% of Orientals and American Indians (Wolff, 1972, 1973) as contrasted with 5% of Caucasians. The differential response appears to be present independent of alcohol exposure since Oriental infants show greater peripheral dilation than Caucasian infants following parenteral administration of ethanol. This increased vasomotor response includes flushing, abdominal discomfort, muscle weakness, dizziness, tachycardia, and hypotension. These aversive symptoms have together been implicated as a "protective factor." This factor may indeed be a vulnerability marker which is changed by an episode of drinking, similar to the situation previously outlined for marker D. The high rates of alcoholism among North American Indians and increasing rates of alcoholism among the Japanese suggest that if the "flush reaction" is a protective factor, it can easily be modified through drinking.

Behavioral markers. For convenience, we have placed the Oriental "flush" among the behavioral markers because identification of this marker was by incidental behavioral observations. Obviously it has biochemical underpinnings as previously noted in our discussion of "atypical" ALDH. A second behavioral marker that has received much attention is the statistically significant difference in the subjective "high" experienced by individuals receiving alcohol in a laboratory setting as a function of whether or not they had a positive family history for alcoholism (Schuckit, 1980). College students were sent questionnaires soliciting participation in a study concerning alcohol use. The questionnaire included questions about drinking behavior of first-degree relatives. Using this information, Schuckit set out to contrast the response to alcohol administration in two groups of individuals: (1) those without a first-degree relative with alcohol problems (Family History Negative) and (2) individuals with such a history (Family History Positive). Students who were themselves alcohol abusers were carefully excluded from the study. The two groups were matched on demographic variables and drinking history. Two significant findings emerged: Those with a positive family history of alcoholism rated themselves lower on a global rating scale of intoxication despite comparable blood alcohol levels and had significantly higher blood acetaldehyde levels. The acetaldehyde findings (Schuckit & Rayses, 1979) remain somewhat controversial due to the difficulties which a number of investigators have had in measuring acetaldehyde accurately (Eriksson, 1980).

That Family History Positive (FHP) subjects rated themselves lower on the subjectively experienced "high" produced by alcohol ingestion than the Family History Negative (FHN) ones, suggested to Schuckit that the seeds of abuse could be found in this phenomenon. Due to the fact that more alcohol would need to be consumed for the FHP individual to feel high, it would be expected that these individuals might develop alcohol tolerance sooner. Also, because one biological variant, acetaldehyde, appeared to be linked to a genetic predisposition to alcoholism (FHP), Schuckit proposed that alcohol could have a differential effect on reward centers in the central nervous system of FHP and FHN subjects. We were intrigued by these findings and wondered if they could be replicated. Secondly, if replicated, would they be due to the pharmacological effects of alcohol on brain tissue, a result of beliefs about alcohol learned only in the families of alcoholics, or perhaps due to both? As his dissertation research Jonathan Rightmyer undertook in our laboratory the task of designing an experiment that would allow replication of Schuckit's study and test these alternative explanations of FHP/FHN differential responsivity. Ultimately we chose the balanced-placebo design, a design frequently used in studies in which the relative contribution of the subjects' beliefs about alcohol effects are pitted against its actual pharmacological effects. This called for four experimental cells, a two-by-two design in which the subject either received alcohol or did not and was told either that he would receive alcohol or that he would receive only the mixer (tonic water).

The Subjective High Assessment Scale (SHAS) was administered to both FHP and FHN young men (mostly college students) both before and after they consumed the appropriate beverage (tonic or 0.5 g/kg alcohol). All subjects were interviewed extensively about their drinking experience to rule out any potential differences in alcohol tolerance. No significant effects on the individual's subjective assessments of the alcohol induced "high" as a function of family history were found using the SHAS. However, a number of other interesting findings emerged. The Mood Adjective Checklist (MACL) (Nowlis & Green, 1964) assessments and other scales from the SHAS used in Rightmyer's study revealed a number of family history effects. Some of these were interactions between family history and beliefs (instruction/expectancy) while others were interactions between family history and beverage consumed (pharmacological effects). For one scale, "Concentration," from the MACL, both beverage and expectancy effects were noted as a function of family history of alcoholism (Rightmyer & Hill, unpublished). Because of the potential importance of finding biological differences in the way alcohol affects brain reward systems, further work on the subjective effects of alcohol appears indicated in families with varying levels of vulnerability.

Currently we are studying vulnerability to alcoholism using multiplex families evaluated for performance on a number of variables. A multiplex family is one in which, after ascertaining an affected proband, one selects families who have at least one other affected sibling and one other unaffected sibling. In this way the acute effects of episodes of illness can be partialed out using a cross-sectional design. The advantages are clear given the time required to conduct a prospective study of prealcoholic individuals and wait for some to become alcoholics. Also included in our study were control families chosen because of an absence of psychopathology in the index case or in first- and second-degree relatives.

As mentioned previously, elevation in the Psychopathic Deviate scale (Pd) of the MMPI is a common finding in the profiles of alcoholic subjects. Whether this elevation in Pd is an episode marker or vulnerability marker is an important question. If it is only an episode marker, then it would be useful in predicting relapse among alcoholics, perhaps, but not discriminating as a marker among nonalcoholics for the purpose of determining who will later become alcoholic. On the other hand, if the Pd scale is a vulnerability marker, it might ultimately be used as a screening tool, to channel those with higher scores into prevention programs of some sort, particularly if other risk factors are present as well. As mentioned previously, Hoffmann et al. (1974) found Pd elevations in individuals who later became alcoholics. Our own data appear to confirm these findings for Pd as a possible vulnerability marker.

Like others, we found significant elevations in clinical scales when we contrasted our affected (alcoholic) subjects with the nonalcoholic, nonpathological control group. Five significant differences were observed (see Figure 2). The affected individuals were significantly higher on Pd, Ma, Pt, Sc, and Pa than the normal controls. To determine whether any of these scale elevations might be vulnerability markers, we chose to contrast the unaffected siblings of the alcoholics with the normal controls. Because in neither group were there alcoholics, we reasoned that any differences observed would be due to some personality characteristic of individuals at high risk for becoming alcoholics. Three significant differences were found (see Figure 3). The high-risk individuals had significantly greater Pd, Hy, and Sc scale scores. Because Pd and Sc were higher in the alcoholics than in normals, it would appear that these two characteristics may prove to be vulnerability markers. Because of the convergence between our data and those of Hoffmann et al. (1974), we are most confident about the Pd finding as a marker. It is not yet known whether elevations in the Psychopathic Deviate scale will eventually turn out to be a vulnerability marker for alcoholism or simply a moderating variable present in families of alcoholics, in the terminology of the multifactorial model, a familial-environmental factor.

Concordance for drinking. Although not a marker as such, concordance in drinking behavior among genetically related individuals should follow some predictable pattern if drinking behavior has a genetic basis. The evidence suggests a fairly high concordance. Kaij (1960) studied 174 Swedish twin pairs selected because one member of the pair had appeared on the national register of alcohol abusers. Using a five-point scale from abstention to chronic alcoholism, he found about twice the concordance in monozygotic twins (Mz) (53%) as in dizygotic twins (Dz) (28%) in terms of having the same grade of drinking (1–5). He also found greater concordance when the chronically alcoholic proband was a member of a monozygotic twin pair (70%) than a member of a dizygotic pair (32%). Partanen et al. (1966) in Finland failed to find greater concordance in monozygotic than dizygotic twins for "out of control"

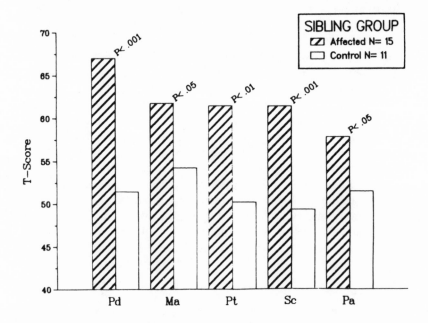

Figure 2. Mean scores for affected versus control sib pairs on the Psychopathic Deviate (Pd), Mania (Ma), Psychasthenia (Pt), Schizophrenia (Sc), and Paranoia (Pa) subscales of the MMPI.

drinking or "consequences of drinking." These twins were drawn from a general population sample, whereas Kaij's sample was chosen from the registry of alcohol abusers. However, in both frequency and quantity per occasion, there was greater concordance in the monozygotics than the dizygotics Partanen studied, suggesting a genetic influence in drinking. Heritability estimates were 0.39 for frequency and 0.36 for quantity per occasion.

Two other twin studies are worthy of mention. One was a sample of twins gleaned from among the 600,000 juniors who took the National Merit Scholarship Questionnaire Test (Loehlin, 1972). Greater concordance was found among Mz twins than among Dz twins for questions related to heavy drinking among the 850 twins identified in this sample. Jonsson and Nilsson (1968), in their study of 1500 Swedish twin pairs, also found greater concordance among the Mz twins than the Dz twins in the quantity consumed.

All of these findings taken together suggest that genetic influences operate to make concordance of drinking patterns more similar among relatives, with those sharing the greater proportion

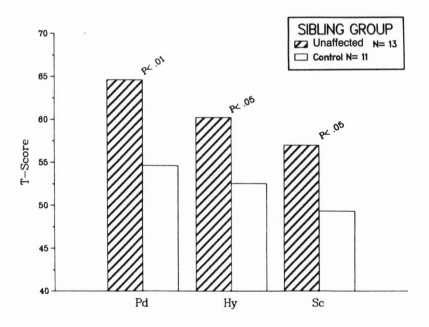

Figure 3. Mean scores for unaffected sibs of probands versus control sib pairs on the Psychopathic Deviate (Pd), Hysteria (Hy), and Schizophrenia (Sc) subscales of the MMPI.

of their genes even more similar. It should be noted that environmental factors play an important role as well. Harburg, Davis, and Caplan (1982) have noted that children of alcoholics are less often social drinkers than children of nonalcoholics because they either model the affected parent, becoming heavy drinkers, or shun the negative aspects of drinking altogether by becoming abstainers. Once again, the vulnerability model proposed here would explain these two seemingly contradictory sets of data. That is, a certain proportion of highly vulnerable individuals will never develop an episode of heavy drinking or alcohol abuse because of moderating variables that cushion the impact of the stressful life event.

NEUROLOGICAL, NEUROPSYCHOPHYSIOLOGICAL, AND NEUROPSYCHOLOGICAL MARKERS

We will begin by discussing the evidence that neurological dysfunction may predict the development of alcoholism. This theory has received increasing attention in recent years largely because a number of investigators have pointed to a possible relationship between childhood hyperactivity and later development of alcoholism. The studies have either begun looking at the family histories of children in treatment for hyperactivity (Cantwell, 1972; Morrison & Stewart, 1971) or started with alcoholic probands and assessed their hyperactivity retrospectively (Goodwin, Schulsinger, Hermansen, Guze, & Winokur, 1975; Tarter, McBride, Buonpane, & Schneider, 1977). Only two studies have looked at drinking in hyperactive adolescents. In one the assessment was made cross-sectionally (Mendelson, Johnson, & Stewart, 1971) where hyperactive children were found to use greater amounts of alcohol, and in the other where prospective data were collected. In the latter no significant relationship was found except for those who persisted in antisocial behavior (Gittelman, Mannuzza, Shenker, & Bonagura, 1985). At present the association between hyperactivity and alcoholism appears to be no greater than it is for any other psychiatric disorder. Thus, while hyperactivity was previously considered a marker for alcoholism, it now appears to be a nonspecific marker for psychiatric illness. Such has been the fate of other markers such as the Dexamethasone Suppression Test (DST). While responsivity on this test was originally thought to be specific for depression, it was later found to be present in other psychiatric states.

Another indicator of neurological functioning that has received attention recently is static ataxia. The report by Lipscomb, Carpenter, and Nathan (1979) that measures of static ataxia differentiated young men with or without a family history of alcoholism was based on somewhat of a serendipitous finding. The design of that study included administering alcohol to young men and determining their tolerance to ethanol using a variety of behavioral assessments both before and after the alcohol administration. The use of static ataxia measures to determine alcohol tolerance had been anticipated several years before by Goldberg (1943) in Sweden who made extensive tests of alcohol tolerance in alcoholics, heavy users, and controls. The serendipity was in finding that persons with a family history of alcoholism differed, at baseline, from those without such a history. A number of attempts to replicate this work have largely been successful. A study of 1200 school children who were administered the static ataxia test show clear differences as a function of family history (Lester & Carpenter, 1985). In our first investigation of this phenomenon, children of alcoholics, normal controls, and children of depressives were found to differ on static ataxia using an apparatus patterned after Lipscomb's setup (Hegedus, Tarter, Hill, Jacob, & Winsten, 1984). These results were quite encouraging because they suggest a specificity of this marker for alcoholism. Further work is currently in progress in our laboratory assessing children of affected and unaffected siblings from our highly selected multiplex families described earlier.

Neuropsychological differences between family history positive and negative subjects have been reported by Schaeffer, Parsons, and Yohman (1984) suggesting that some of the neuropsychological deficits seen in alcoholics and previously considered a consequence of drinking, may in fact be vulnerability markers. Neuropsychological tests performed on children whose biological fathers were alcoholic have revealed a number of deficits when their performance is contrasted with children without alcoholic biological parents (Drejer, Theilgaard, Teasdale, Schulsinger, & Goodwin, 1985). These include a greater number of errors on the Category Test (Halstead-Reitan Battery), lower WAIS Vocabulary scores, and poorer performance on the Porteus Maze Test among the children of alcoholics. Our ongoing study of multiplex families is assessing the replicability of the Category Test data.

Neurophysiological markers. The ensuing discussion will focus on the neurophysiological model as one approach to understanding the etiology of alcoholism. Our premise is that observation of overt behavior alone may not be sufficient for understanding why some individuals persist in behaviors that appear to us to be maladaptive. A neurophysiological analysis may provide insights into which systems may be involved in particular psychopathologies and how information in those systems is processed. Information processing demands may vary over a wide range of complexity, from minimal processing activity to tasks that require a great deal of attention and interpretation by subjects, and the level of the demands may aid us in the detection of neurophysiological markers.

Many different task demands have been placed on alcoholic subjects varying from those that passively record resting heart rate or EEG to those that measure heart rate changes or EEG characteristics during a problem-solving task while the subject is actively processing information. The latter results in a group of electrical potentials that can be recorded from the scalp and which are collectively known as Event-Related Potentials (ERPs). These should be distinguished from brain-stem evoked responses which have provided a major neurological tool for detecting intact or deviant reactivity of the nervous system at very early (1–10 msec) stages of processing. These are elicited under relatively passive conditions, whereas the ERP is elicited when relatively more complex processing is required. Certain psychophysiological measures are especially useful for studying ongoing information processing activities because they occur with relatively short latency (approximately 1000 msec or less). These may be contrasted with the temporal resolution of other recently developed techniques for understanding brain functioning (e.g., PET scan, cerebral blood flow), each of which provides an indication of metabolic activity, but integrate activity over much longer periods of time, and are thus not capable of monitoring reactions to discrete types of events, as can be accomplished with ERPs.

Among the variety of measures available, the long-latency components of the ERP have proven to be the most closely related to information processing activity across different experiments. The most prominent aspects include the P300 component, a scalp-recorded positivity with a latency of approximately 300 msec, which was first noted by Sutton, Braren, Zubin, and John in 1965, and related long-latency activity such as slow-wave and processing negativity, as well as the contingent negative variation (CNV) which precedes an expected imperative stimulus. A number of earlier components have been identified and studied including N100, which is clearly related to selective attention.

Brain function has been studied in alcoholics by conventional

EEG and by computer averaged Event-Related Potentials (ERPs). The EEGs of chronic alcoholics have been described as poorly synchronized and deficient in alpha activity (Docter, Naitoh, & Smith, 1966). Also, it has been shown that 12-year-old sons of alcoholics show an excess of high frequency activity (Gabrielli et al., 1982). Further, there is evidence that alpha activity is genetically determined (Vogel, Schalt, Kruger, Propping, & Lehnert, 1979) and that persons at higher risk for alcoholism may be deficient in alpha activity (Propping, Kruger, & Mark, 1981). Because alcohol consumption elicits alpha activity in normals (Propping, Kruger, & Janah, 1980), particularly those with low baseline levels, it has been suggested that alpha activity may be a marker for alcoholism (Pollock et al., 1983). Pollock and colleagues have shown that high risk individuals (sons of male alcoholics) display greater increases in slow alpha energy following alcohol administration than individuals from a matched control group. Propping et al. (1981) similarly found alcohol to have a greater synchronizing effect on individuals with borderline alpha EEG, all of whom were either alcoholics or their relatives.

Event-Related Potentials. Neville, Snyder, and Bloom (1982) were the first to observe that alcohol administration has different effects on ERP in individuals with a first-degree relative who is alcoholic (Family History Positive) than those without such a history. Because these subjects were not matched for drinking habits, the results could not be interpreted unambiguously. Therefore, in their second study this variable was more closely monitored in 10 subjects, 5 each who were either Family History Positive (FHP) or Family History Negative (FHN) (Elmasian, Neville, Woods, Schuckit, & Bloom, 1982). Subjects with a positive family history showed significantly reduced amplitudes for the P300 component of the ERP when making decisions about task relevant stimuli. Also, the latency of the positive component and reaction times to correctly detected targets were significantly later in individuals with a positive family history. Recently a visual discrimination task was administered to children of alcoholics and children of nonalcoholics with differences being seen primarily in the amplitude of the P300 component (Begleiter, Porjesz, Bihari, & Kissin, 1984). This was the first demonstration of changes in information processing in a high risk group of subjects without the confounding effects of current or previous alcohol consumption. All of the subjects were preadolescent and had been screened for having never used alcohol. The second aspect of this study that should be emphasized is that these results were found without the necessity of administering alcohol to the subjects.

This study was a seminal contribution to the alcoholism literature, pointing out as it did the potential usefulness of Event-Related Potentials for uncovering a possible biological risk for developing alcoholism. Two other studies have looked at the P300 responding of adult children of alcoholics. In one of these (O'Connor and Hesselbrock, 1985), two visual tasks were used while subjects were either sober or mildly intoxicated. The amplitude of P300 was reported to be smaller for young men at greater risk (all had alcoholic fathers) than those with minimal risk (fathers and other first degree relatives were not alcoholic). These results are in accord with Begleiter's findings for younger children of alcoholics. In the second study Polich and Bloom (1985) compared normal subjects and individuals at risk for developing alcoholism using an auditory oddball task. In all, 24 male subjects were evaluated, 12 with a family history of alcoholism and 12 without. A positive history was defined as having a father who met DSM-III criteria for alcoholism. No significant differences for either latency or amplitude of the P300 were found between the two family history groups. A significant correlation between P300 amplitude and the quantity of alcohol consumed on any one occasion was also observed. This effect appeared to be greater for the family history positive as contrasted with the family history negative subjects and was elicited only when task difficulty was increased.

Utilizing our highly selected multiplex families, we have investigated the possibility that ERP characteristics may be markers for vulnerability to alcoholism. In our laboratory, a modification of the "oddball" task is used. Normally, when subjects are asked to count a rare auditory or visual stimulus embedded in a sequence of different but more frequent stimuli, a large P300 response is evoked by the rare event (Donchin, 1977). Our subjects are informed that two "rare" stimuli (high-pitched tones) never occur in a row, so that every high tone is followed by a frequent stimulus, a low-pitched tone. Thus, the frequent tone which follows a rare, counted tone is predictable (probability = 1.00), while after a frequent tone, either another frequent tone may occur (probability = .67) or a rare tone may be presented (probability = .33). The subject's task is to report the number of rare target tones at the end of every block of trials. Normal subjects show a large amplitude P300 response to the rare tone, a smaller P300 to the unpredictable frequent tone (i.e., the repeated frequent tone, probability = .67), and the smallest response to the predictable frequent tone which follows each rare tone (probability = 1.00).

Some comments are needed regarding the task requirements. All subjects are required to count rare tones, but are not required to pay attention to sequences, even though some information is made available to them at the outset. In the analyses of the data, only blocks of trials for which the subject has counted accurately (within 3 counts) are included, so that in general all subjects considered have been performing adequately. Insuring adequate performance is a necessity before inferring that P300 is reduced because of processing difficulty. Some reports of reduced P300 amplitude in demented patients have also noted that performance was poor in those subjects. Thus the reduced P300 may merely reflect poor performance on the task in such experimental paradigms that allow inattention. We also used a reaction task in which subjects are asked to make a response on either of two switches, either "right" or "left," which is counterbalanced over blocks for the rare and frequent tones.

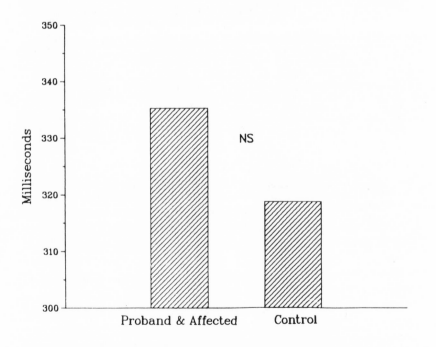

Figure 4. Latency of P300 for the .67 probability condition in the auditory Counting Task: means of probands and affected brothers versus control sibs.

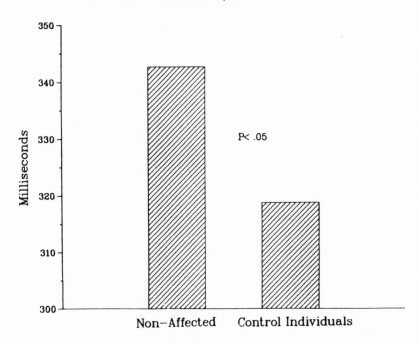

Figure 5a. Latency of P300 for the .67 probability condition in the auditory Counting Task: means of unaffected sibs of probands versus controls.

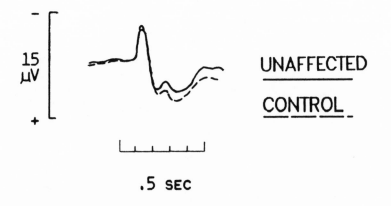

Figure 5b. Superaverages for ERPs obtained from Pz electrode site for each group during the auditory Counting Task (.67 probability condition).

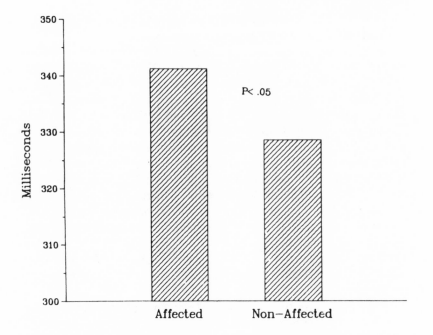

Figure 6a. Latency of P300 for the .33 probability condition in the Choice Reaction Task: means of probands and affected brothers versus unaffected brothers.

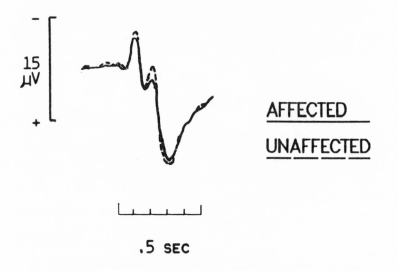

Figure 6b. Superaverages for ERPs obtained from Pz electrode site for each group during the auditory Choice Reaction Task (.33 probability condition).

As in Figure 4, we observed longer latency for P300 in the counting task (though here nonsignificant) between alcoholics and controls. Were we to stop here we could only conclude that we have
suggestive evidence for an episode marker; that is, alcohol exposure
may be providing cognitive changes that are reflected in neurophysiological responding. As seen in Figure 5, we also found significant
latency differences when the unaffected siblings were compared
with normal nonalcoholic controls, suggesting that we may have a
vulnerability marker. Of course the nonaffected siblings might have
been drinking more than controls indicating merely an episode
marker. However, two aspects of our methodology suggest alternatives: (1) we asked all subjects to refrain from using alcohol or drugs
for 48 hours before testing; (2) extensive alcohol-use questions were
determined for both groups and verified by liver enzyme measures.
The liver enzymes SGOT, SGPT and GGPT are elevated in heavy
drinkers, particularly GGPT. We rejected from analysis any subject
whose self-report did not match expectations about alcohol effects
on liver functioning.

When we made the same comparison with the choice-reaction

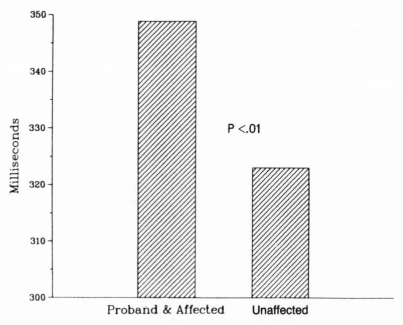

Figure 7a. Latency of P300 for the .67 probability condition in the auditory Choice
Reaction Task: means of probands and affected brothers versus unaffected brothers.

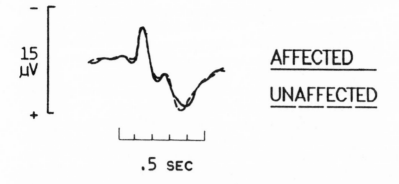

Figure 7b. Superaverages for ERPs obtained from Pz electrode site for each group during the auditory Choice Reaction Task (.67 probability codition).

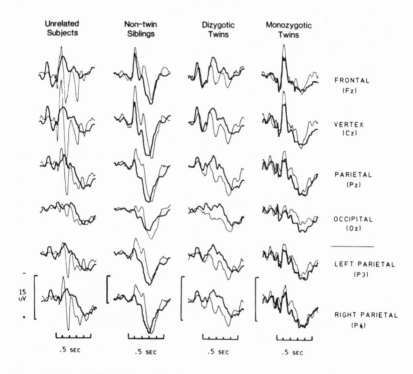

Figure 8. Event-Related Potentials elicited at six electrode sites by an infrequent auditory stimulus (.33 probability condition) during the Counting Task. P300 is the positive (downward-going) wave, which is most prominent at the Cz and Pz locations, at approximately 300 msec. Data are presented for four pairs of subjects varying in their degree of familial relationship. (Note that the data for both of the nontwin siblings are scaled down relative to the other subjects.)

task, we saw the same significant differences between the two affected siblings and their unaffected siblings in both the .33 and the .67 probability conditions, lending further support to our hypothesis that latency of P300 may be a vulnerability marker (see Figures 6 and 7).

To further assess the meaning of the finding, it is useful to examine the possibility that the marker is under genetic control. There is evidence that ERP waveforms are heritable. An example is provided by data obtained in our laboratories for the .33 probability condition of the counting task (see Figure 8). Four pairs of subjects are displayed who vary in their genetic similarity to each other. The unrelated individuals are least congruent in the wave forms elicited, whereas the nontwin siblings show more resemblance, which is similar to the dizygotic twin pair, with monozygotic twins showing the greatest congruity. This is what one would expect based on the shared genes of these groups. Dizygotic twins are no more closely related genetically than siblings, sharing as they do half of their genes on average, whereas monozygotic twins share all their genes.

Summary

As the foregoing review indicates, we have made considerable progress in identifying a number of promising metabolic, behavioral, and neurophysiological markers for assessing risks for developing alcoholism. As previously noted, the term "marker" has been extended beyond its current usage in genetic marker studies where typically a blood marker has been used to elucidate the genetic transmission of particular diseases. In these studies the "ideal" marker is one which is itself an inherited characteristic that is polymorphic (there exist two or more discrete forms that are commonly found in the population), has an established mode of inheritance, is unaffected by the presence of the episode (e.g., the ABO system is unaffected by presence of a disorder), and is localizable to a particular chromosome. Few potential markers satisfy all these requirements, yet it is important to keep this in mind as we search for "markers" for vulnerability to developing alcoholism.

We have proposed a vulnerability model for alcoholism in an attempt to sort out which potential markers hold promise for identifying individuals who are at risk. We have chosen to look at vulnerability from both biological and psychosocial perspectives realizing that some people may carry biological markers as part of their genetic heritage yet never develop episodes of abusive drinking because they lack psychosocial vulnerability. For example, women appear less likely to develop alcoholism than men because of cultural factors that reduce the chance that they will become heavy drinkers. The greater risk for heavy drinking among men than women appears, however, to be independent of the particular cultures. As mentioned earlier, among the 30 cultures assessed for male and female drinking practices, in no instance did women drink more than men, and in 16 men drank more than women.

In the vulnerability model proposed, we assume that alcoholism is not a continuous disorder but that vulnerability, whether biological or psychosocial, is. This vulnerability may remain latent throughout life or may become manifest when triggers sufficient to produce an episode occur. These triggers may be life events or changes in the internal milieu. For example, biological changes may well produce a major affective disorder which in turn may lead to alcohol abuse. That some individuals have only one major episode of abusive drinking and never return to excessive use of alcohol attests to the fact that alcoholism should not be conceived of as a lifelong disease. Therapeutic intervention should be aimed at preventing its initial occurrence or its recurrence.

We view the identification of markers for vulnerability as essential to achieving this goal. Each of the models of alcoholism should be investigated to provide markers by which the etiological factors can be determined. Once such markers are available, it may be possible to identify individuals prone to alcoholism even before episodes of heavy drinking occur. Although intervention efforts designed to reach all segments of the population might be desirable, they may be impractical owing to inevitable limitation of resources. Therefore, identifying those at greatest risk would make it possible to design intensive intervention for those who might benefit most.

By establishing the various indicators of vulnerability, episode, and postepisode characteristics, it may become possible to detect the presence of vulnerability long before alcoholism develops and through educational procedures perhaps forestall the development of even the first episode or relapses in recovered individuals. Unlike other mental disorders, we can actually hope to prevent alcoholism since there is no endogenous disease process without alcohol consumption.

It is our hope that presenting the current status of the "marker" movement in the alcoholism field and noting the gaps in our present knowledge may encourage others to search for vulnerability mark-

250
NEBRASKA SYMPOSIUM ON MOTIVATION, 1986

ers for alcoholism. Ultimately, this can be of measurable benefit to
the well-being of individuals at high risk for developing alcoholism.
Armed with risk markers, we may be able in the future to identify
those who should be cautioned, perhaps, never to drink alcohol.
Only then can the high risk individual wage his or her personal war
against multigenerational transmission of alcoholism.

Adamson, J., & Burdick, J. A. (1973). Sleep of dry alcoholics. *Archives of
General Psychiatry, 28,* 146–149.
Bandura, A. (1969). *Principles of behavior modification.* New York: Holt, Rinehart & Winston.
Becker, W. C. (1964). Consequences of different kinds of parental disci-
pline. In M. L. Hoffman & L. W. Hoffman (Eds.), *Review of child develop-
ment research* (Vol. 1). New York: Russell Sage Foundation.
Begleiter, H., Porjesz, B., Bihari, B., & Kissin, B. (1984). Event-related brain
potentials in boys at risk for alcoholism. *Science, 225,* 1493–1496.
Behar, D., & Winokur, G. (1979). Research in alcoholism and depression: A
two-way street under construction. In R. W. Pickens & L. L. Heston
(Eds.), *Psychiatric factors in drug abuse.* New York: Grune and Stratton.
Bohman, M., Sigvardsson, S., & Cloninger, C. R. (1981). Maternal inheri-
tance of alcohol abuse. *Archives of General Psychiatry, 38,* 965–969.
Cadoret, R. J., & Gath, A. (1978). Inheritance of alcoholism in adoptees.
British Journal of Psychiatry, 132, 252–258.
Caldwell, B. M. (1964). The effects of infant care. In M. L. Hoffman & L. W.
Hoffman (Eds.), *Review of child development research* (Vol. 1). New York:
Russell Sage Foundation.
Cantwell, D. P. (1972). Psychiatric illness in the families of hyperactive chil-
dren. *Archives of General Psychiatry, 27,* 414–417.
Child, I. L., Barry, H., III, & Bacon, M. K. (1965). A cross-cultural study of
drinking. III. Sex differences. *Quarterly Journal of Studies on Alcohol* (Suppl.
3), 49–61.
Clark, W. B. (1974). Distinction needed between alcoholism as a disease and
"problems." *Family Practice News, 4,* 39.
Cotton, N. S. (1979). The familial incidence of alcoholism: A review. *Journal
of Studies on Alcohol, 40,* 89–116.
Docter, R. F., Naitoh, P., & Smith, J. C. (1966). Electroencephalographic
changes and vigilance behavior during experimentally induced intoxication with alcoholic subjects. *Psychosomatic Medicine, 28,* 605–615.

Donchin, E. (1977). Event-related brain potentials: A tool in the study of human information processing. In H. Begleiter (Ed.), *Evoked brain potentials and behavior* (pp. 13–88). New York: Plenum Press.

Drejer, K., Theilgaard, A., Teasdale, T. W., Schulsinger, F., & Goodwin, D. W. (1985). A prospective study of young men at high risk for alcoholism: Neuropsychological assessment. *Alcoholism: Clinical and Experimental Research, 9,* 498–502.

Dunner, D. L., Hensel, B. M., & Fieve, R. R. (1979). Bipolar illness: Factors in drinking behavior. *American Journal of Psychiatry, 136,* 583–585.

Eckert, E. D., Goldberg, S. C., Halmi, K. A., Casper, R. C., & Davis, J. M. (1979). Alcoholism in anorexia nervosa. In R. W. Pickens & L. L. Heston (Eds.), *Psychiatric factors in drug abuse.* New York: Grune and Stratton.

Elmasian, R., Neville, H., Woods, D., Schuckit, M., & Bloom, F. (1982). Event-related brain potentials are different in individuals at high and low risk for developing alcoholism. *Proceedings of the National Academy of Sciences of the United States of America, 29,* 7900–7903.

Eriksson, C. J. (1980). Elevated blood acetaldehyde levels in alcoholics and their relatives: A reevaluation. *Science, 207,* 1383–1384.

Falconer, D. S. (1965). The inheritance of liability to certain diseases, estimated from the incidence among relatives. *Annals of Human Genetics, 29,* 51–76.

Fillmore, K. M. (1974). Drinking and problem drinking in early adulthood and middle age. *Quarterly Journal of Studies on Alcohol, 35,* 819–840.

Frances, R. J., Timm, S., & Bucky, S. (1980). Studies of familial and nonfamilial alcoholism. *Archives of General Psychiatry, 37,* 564–566.

Gabrielli, W. F., Mednick, S. A., Volavka, J., Pollock, V. E., Schulsinger, F., & Itil, T. M. (1982). Electroencephalograms in children of alcoholic fathers. *Psychophysiology, 19,* 404–407.

Gittelman, R., Mannuzza, S., Shenker, R., & Bonagura, N. (1985). Hyperactive boys almost grown up. I. Psychiatric status. *Archives of General Psychiatry, 42,* 937–947.

Goldberg, L. (1943). Quantitative studies on alcohol tolerance in man: The influence of ethyl alcohol on sensory, motor and psychological functions referred to blood alcohol in normal and habituated individuals. *Acta Physiological Scandinavica, 5* (Suppl. 16), 1–128.

Goodwin, D. W. (1983). *Familial alcoholism: A separate entity?* Paper presented at the International Symposium on the Psychobiology of Alcoholism, January 16–18, 1983, Beverly Hills, CA.

Goodwin, D. W., & Guze, S. B. (1979). *Psychiatric diagnosis* (2nd ed., pp. 118–144). New York: Oxford University Press.

Goodwin, D. W., & Hill, S. Y. (1975). Chronic effects of alcohol and other psychoactive drugs on intellect, learning and memory. In J. G. Rankin (Ed.), *Alcohol, drugs and brain damage*. Toronto: Addiction Research Foundation of Ontario.

Goodwin, D. W., Schulsinger, F., Hermansen, L., Guze, S. B., & Winokur, G. (1973). Alcohol problems in adoptees raised apart from alcoholic biological parents. *Archives of General Psychiatry, 28*, 238–243.

Goodwin, D. W., Schulsinger, F., Hermansen, L., Guze, S. B., & Winokur, G. (1975). Alcoholism and the hyperactive child syndrome. *Journal of Nervous and Mental Disease, 160*, 349–353.

Harburg, E., Davis, D. R., & Caplan, R. (1982). Parent and offspring alcohol use: Imitative and aversive transmission. *Journal of Studies on Alcohol, 43*, 497–516.

Hegedus, A. M., Tarter, R. E., Hill, S. Y., Jacob, T., & Winsten, N. E. (1984). Static ataxia: A possible marker for alcoholism. *Alcoholism: Clinical and Experimental Research, 8*, 580–582.

Hill, S. Y., Cloninger, C. R., & Ayre, F. R. (1977). Independent familial transmission of alcoholism and opiate abuse. *Alcoholism: Clinical and Experimental Research, 1*, 335–342.

Hill, S. Y. (1981). A vulnerability model for alcoholism in women. *Focus on Women: Journal of Addictions and Health, 2*, 68–91.

Hoffmann, H., Loper, R. G., & Kammeier, M. L. (1974). Identifying future alcoholics with MMPI alcoholism scales. *Quarterly Journal of Studies on Alcohol, 35*, 490–498.

Horton, D. (1943). The function of alcohol in primitive societies: A cross-cultural study. *Quarterly Journal of Studies on Alcohol, 4*, 199–320.

Jellinek, E. M. (1960). *The disease concept of alcoholism*. Highland Park, NJ: Hillhouse Press.

Jessor, R., & Jessor, S. (1977). *Problem behavior and psychosocial development: A longitudinal study of youth*. New York: Academic Press.

Jessor, R., & Jessor, S. (1978). Theory testing in longitudinal research on marijuana use. In D. Kandel (Ed.), *Longitudinal research on drug use*. Washington, DC: Hemisphere.

Jones, M. C. (1968). Personality correlates and antecedents of drinking patterns in adult males. *Journal of Consulting and Clinical Psychology, 32*, 2–12.

Jones, M. C. (1971). Personality antecedents and correlates of drinking patterns in women. *Journal of consulting and Clinical Psychology, 36*, 61–69.

Jonsson, F., & Nilsson, T. (1968). Alkoholkonsumption hos monozygota och dizygota tvillingar. *Nordisk Hygienisk Tidskrift, 49*, 21–25.

Kaij, L. (1960). *Studies on the etiology and sequelae of abuse of alcohol*. Lund: University of Lund.

Kandel, D. B. (1978). *Longitudinal research on drug use: Empirical findings and methodological issues*. Washington, DC: Hemisphere.

Kandel, D. B. (1980). Drug and drinking behavior among youth. In A. Inkeles, N. J. Smelser, & R. H. Turner (Eds.), *Annual review of sociology* (Vol. 6). Palo Alto, CA: Annual Reviews.

Lester, D., & Carpenter, J. A. (1985). Static ataxia in adolescents and their parentage. *Alcoholism: Clinical and Experimental Research, 9,* 212. (From RSA abstracts No. 171.)

Li, T.-K., Bosron, W. F., Dafeldecker, W. P., Lange, L. G., & Vallee, B. L. (1977). Isolation of II-alcohol dehydrogenase of human liver: Is it a determinant of alcoholism? *Proceedings of the National Academy of Sciences of the United States of America, 74,* 4378–4381.

Lipscomb, T., Carpenter, J., & Nathan, P. (1979). Static ataxia: A predictor of alcoholism? *British Journal of Addiction, 74,* 289–294.

Loehlin, J. C. (1972). An analysis of alcohol-related questionnaire items from the National Merit Twin Study. *Annals of the New York Academy of Science, 197,* 117–120.

Marlatt, G. A. (1976). Alcohol, stress, and cognitive control. In C. Spielberger and I. Sarason (Eds.), *The series in clinical and community psychology: Stress and anxiety* (Vol. 3). Washington: Hemisphere.

Marlatt, G. A., & Gordon, J. R. (1980). Determinants of relapse: Implications for the maintenance of behavior change. In P. O. Davidson & S. M. Davidson (Eds.), *Behavioral medicine: Changing health lifestyles.* New York: Brunner/Mazel.

McCord, W., & McCord, J. (1962). A longitudinal study of the personality of alcoholics. In D. J. Pittman & C. R. Snyder (Eds.), *Society, culture and drinking patterns.* New York: Wiley.

Meehl, P. E. (1962). Schizotaxia, schizotypy, schizophrenia. *American Psychologist, 17,* 827–838.

Mendelson, W., Johnson, N., & Stewart, M. A. (1971). Hyperactive children as teenagers: A follow-up study. *Journal of Nervous and Mental Disease, 153,* 273–279.

Morey, L. C., & Blashfield, R. K. (1981). Empirical classifications of alcoholism: A review. *Journal of Studies on Alcohol, 42,* 925–937.

Morrison, J. R., & Stewart, M. A. (1971). A family study of the hyperactive child syndrome. *Biological Psychiatry, 3,* 189–195.

Morton, N. E. (1974). Analysis of family resemblance. I. Introduction. *American Journal of Human Genetics, 26,* 318–330.

Nerviano, V. J., & Gross, H. W. (1983). Personality types of alcoholics on objective inventories. *Journal of Studies on Alcohol, 44,* 837–851.

Neville, H., Snyder, E., & Bloom, F. (1982). *Twelfth Annual NCA AMSA/RSA Conference.* New Orleans, LA.

Nowlis, V., & Green, R. (1964). *Factor analytic studies of mood.* Technical Report Contract No. Nonr-668 (12), Office of Naval Research.

O'Connor, S., & Hesselbrock, V. (1985). Neuroelectric correlates of increased risk for alcoholism in men. In *Abstracts, Fourth World Congress of Biological Psychiatry* (p. 436). Philadelphia.

Owen, P., & Butcher, J. (1979). Personality factors in problem drinking: A review of the evidence. In R. Pickens & L. Heston (Eds.), *Psychiatric factors in drug abuse.* New York: Grune and Stratton.

Parsons, O. A., & Leber, W. R. (1982). Alcohol cognitive dysfunction, and brain damage. (1982). *Biomedical processes and consequences of alcohol use* (pp. 213–229). In Alcohol and Health Monograph 2. National Institute on Alcohol Abuse and Alcoholism. Rockville, MD.

Partanen, J., Bruun, K., & Markkanen, T. (1966). *Inheritance of drinking behavior.* New Brunswick, NJ: Rutgers Center of Alcohol Studies.

Pettinati, H. M., Sugerman, A. A., DiDonato, N., & Maurer, H. S. (1982). The natural history of alcoholism over four years of treatment. *Journal of Studies on Alcohol, 43,* 201–215.

Polich, J. M, Armor, D. J., & Braiker, H. B. (1981). *The course of alcoholism: Four years after treatment.* New York: Wiley.

Polich, J., & Bloom, F. (1985). P300 reflects the degree of cognitive decline from the residual effects of alcohol consumption in normals and individuals at risk for alcoholism. In *Abstracts, Fourth World Congress of Biological Psychiatry* (p. 436), Philadelphia.

Pollock, V. E., Volavka, J., Goodwin, D. W., Mednick, S. A., Gabrielli, W. F., Knop, J., & Schulsinger, F. (1983). The EEG after alcohol administration in men at risk for alcoholism. *Archives of General Psychiatry, 40,* 857–861.

Post, R. M., Fink, E., Carpenter, W. T., & Goodwin, F. K. (1975). Cerebrospinal fluid amine metabolites in acute schizophrenia. *Archives of General Psychiatry, 32,* 1063–1069.

Propping, P., Kruger, J., & Janah, A. (1980). Effect of alcohol on genetically determined variants of the normal electroencephalogram, *Psychiatry Research, 2,* 85–98.

Propping, P., Kruger, J., & Mark, N. (1981). Genetic disposition to alcoholism: An EEG study in alcoholics and their relatives. *Human Genetics, 59,* 51–59.

Rightmyer, J., & Hill, S. Y. (1986). Subjective effects of acutely administered alcohol in family history positive and family history negative subjects using a balanced placebo design. Manuscript submitted for publication.

Robins, L. N., Bates, W. M., & O'Neal, P. (1962). Adult drinking patterns of former problem children. In D. J. Pittman & C. R. Snyder (Eds.), *Society, culture and drinking patterns.* New York: Wiley.

Robins, L. N., Helzer, J. E., & Davis, D. H. (1975). Narcotic use in Southeast

Asia and afterward—An interview study of 808 Vietnam returnees. *Archives of General Psychiatry, 32,* 955–961.

Rohan, W. P. (1975). Drinking behavior and "alcoholism." *Journal of Studies on Alcohol, 36,* 908–916.

Rosenthal, D. (1970). *Genetic theory and abnormal behavior.* New York: McGraw-Hill.

Schaeffer, K. W., Parsons, O. A., & Yohman, J. R. (1984). Neuropsychological differences between male familial and nonfamilial alcoholics and nonalcoholics. *Alcoholism: Clinical and Experimental Research, 8,* 347–351.

Schuckit, M. A. (1980). Self-rating of alcohol intoxication by young men with and without family histories of alcoholism. *Journal of Studies on Alcohol, 41,* 242–249.

Schuckit, M. A., & Rayses, V. (1979). Ethanol ingestion: Differences in blood acetaldehyde concentrations in relatives of alcoholics and controls. *Science 203,* 54–55.

Skinner, H. A., & Allen, B. A. (1982). Alcohol dependence syndrome: Measurement and validation. *Journal of Abnormal Psychology, 91,* 199–209.

Slater, E., & Slater, P. (1944). A heuristic theory of neurosis. *Journal of Neurology, Neurosurgery and Psychiatry, 7,* 49–55.

Sutton, S., Braren, M., Zubin, J., & John, E. R. (1965). Evoked potential correlates of stimulus uncertainty. *Science, 150,* 1187–1188.

Tarter, R. E., McBride, H., Buonpane, N., & Schneider, D. U. (1977). Differentiation of alcoholics: Childhood history of minimal brain dysfunction, family history, and drinking pattern. *Archives of General Psychiatry, 34,* 761–768.

Vogel, F., Schalt, E., Kruger, J., Propping, P., & Lehnert, K. F. (1979). The electroencephalogram (EEG) as a research tool in human behavior genetics: Psychological examination in healthy males with various inherited EEG variants. *Human Genetics, 47,* 1–45.

von Wartburg, J. P. (1979). Pharmacogenetic aspects of alcohol use and abuse. *Drug and Alcohol Dependence, 4,* 103–104.

Wolff, P. H. (1972). Ethnic differences in alcohol sensitivity. *Science, 175,* 449–450.

Wolff, P. H. (1973). Vasomotor sensitivity to alcohol in diverse mongoloid populations. *American Journal of Human Genetics, 25,* 193–199.

Wolin, S., Bennett, L. A., Noonan, D., & Teitelbaum, M. (1980). Disrupted family rituals: A factor in the intergenerational transmission of alcoholism. *Journal of Studies on Alcohol, 41,* 199–214.

Yarrow, L. J. (1964). Separation from parents during early childhood. In M. L. Hoffman & L. W. Hoffman (Eds.), *Review of child development research* (Vol. 1). New York: Russell Sage Foundation.

Zubin, J. (1963). Behavior concomitants of the mental disorders: A biometric view. In B. Wigdor (Ed.), *Recent advances in the study of behavior change*. Montreal: McGill University.

Zubin, J., Magaziner, J., & Steinhauer, S. R. (1983). The metamorphosis of schizophrenia: From chronicity to vulnerability. *Psychological Medicine, 13*, 551–571.

Zubin, J., & Spring, B. (1977). Vulnerability—A new view of schizophrenia. *Journal of Abnormal Psychology, 86*, 103–126.

Zubin, J., & Steinhauer, S. R. (1981). How to break the logjam in schizophrenia: A look beyond genetics. *Journal of Nervous and Mental Disease, 169*, 477–492.

Zubin, J., Steinhauer, S. R., Day, R., & van Kammen, D. P. (1985). Schizophrenia at the crossroads: A blueprint for the 80's. *Comprehensive Psychiatry, 26*, 217–240.

The Motivation to Use Drugs: A Psychobiological Analysis of Urges

Timothy B. Baker, Elsimae Morse, and Jack E. Sherman

University of Wisconsin–Madison

*A*ny young clinician who attempts to do both applied and research work with substance abusers will probably notice a curious anomaly. Although researchers pay very little attention to urges, they are a chief topic when addicts discuss their addiction. In fact urges might be viewed as the principal phenomenological manifestation of addiction, and some theorists have viewed them as a sine qua non (Jellinek, 1960; Ludwig & Wikler, 1974).

The reluctance of addiction researchers to investigate urges can be attributed to a variety of factors. First, operantly or behaviorally oriented researchers have had a general philosophical disinclination to countenance mental constructs. If urges or cravings are merely "mental way stations" on the road to drug ingestion, why not study drug self-administration per se rather than a hypothesized, intangible construct (e.g., Mello, 1972)? Another reason the concept of urge may have fallen into disfavor is that some authors equated urges with "loss of control" (e.g., Mello, 1972). Therefore, as data accumulated showing that intoxicated drug users could in certain circumstances control their drug self-administration (Gottheil, Corbett, Grasberger, & Cornelison, 1972), the concept of urges became less compelling.

We would like to revive interest in urges because we believe their analysis will foster a clearer understanding of motivational processes important to addiction. We view urges as affects that, like other affects, have prototypic phenomenological, behavioral, and physiological correlates. If one adopts the notion that affects reflect the processing of motivationally significant stimuli—that affects and emotions are "readouts" of activity levels in motivational systems

(Buck, 1985)—then urges should reflect important information about the nature of drug use motivation. We believe the motivational significance of urges is clear; they occupy the position relative to approach behavior that fear occupies with respect to avoidance.

Viewing urges as affects helps one avoid problems that might otherwise plague urge research. First, it makes clear that they need not share functional equivalence with drug consumption. Just as fear does not necessarily lead to avoidance or escape, an urge does not necessarily lead to drug use approach or self-administration. That urges and drug consumption are not functionally equivalent means that analyzing urges might yield unique information. Although alcohol or cocaine *consumption* might be of great social, legal, or medical relevance, we suggest that urges may have greater psychological relevance (Wiggins, 1973). One reason is that drug use behavior is so obviously multidetermined, and thus susceptible to psychologically uninteresting variables—for example, drug cost and the opportunity for use. We see urges as being more directly related to psychologically significant variables and processes because of the intimate connection we believe exists between affects such as urges and associated motivational states. Thus an urge dependent measure may reflect psychological factors important to addiction more sensitively than does self-administration.

Viewing urges as affects suggests a strategy for conceptualizing and assessing urges—a three-system approach similar to that used with affects such as fear (e.g., Lang, Levin, Miller, & Kozak, 1983). If urges do indeed have physiological, attitudinal/verbal, and behavioral response properties, only a three-system assessment approach will adequately characterize the urge construct. In this chapter we adopt an urge construct assuming that urges should be associated with increased drug self-administration (e.g., relapse), operant work for the drug, increased positive evaluations of the drug, and characteristic physiological response patterns (type as yet unspecified). Because these response elements may be loosely organized and integrated, their covariation may be imperfect.

The urge to use drugs is assumed to reflect the presence of a drug-acquisitive motivational state. Several motivational models have been forwarded to account for drug urges. In the following section we present three such models—the withdrawal, compensatory response, and opponent-process models—and review some of the evidence offered in support of them.

Drug Urges: Motivational Models

WITHDRAWAL MODEL

The withdrawal model, identified primarily with Abraham Wikler, Arnold Ludwig, and Charles O'Brien, is based on the notion that a primary motivating influence in compulsive drug use, and relapse to drug use, is escape from or avoidance of unconditioned and conditioned withdrawal symptoms and signs (e.g., Ludwig & Wikler, 1974; O'Brien, Ternes, Grabowski, & Ehrman, 1981; Wikler, 1980). Although the avoidance or amelioration of withdrawal has long been recognized as a potent motivator of drug use, the important contribution made by Wikler and the others is that withdrawal can be conditioned, and therefore withdrawal escape may be an important motivational factor even in the nonintoxicated organism.

Basic tenets of the conditional withdrawal model are that withdrawal symptoms or signs (*a*) are aversive, (*b*) are relieved rapidly and efficiently by drug use, (*c*) can become conditioned to a range of exteroceptive and interoceptive cues, and (*d*) when elicited, serve as a discriminative stimulus for drug self-administration. According to this model, the precipitants of drug self-administration, perceived as cravings or urges, are often unconditioned or conditioned drug withdrawal responses (e.g., Ludwig, Wikler, & Stark, 1974; Ternes, O'Brien, Grabowski, Wellerstein, & Jordan-Hayes, 1980).

A schematic of the proposed conditioning model is presented in Table 1, which shows that a variety of drug-associated cues or states (affects) have been proffered as possible conditioned stimuli (CSs). Table 2 lists stimuli or situations that one patient reported as eliciting *both* craving and withdrawal "sickness"—suggesting a link between the two (O'Brien, 1976). While it may seem incongruous that drug administration stimuli (e.g., someone's "works," Table 2) would be associated with withdrawal, research shows that addicts may be in withdrawal, or "partial withdrawal," during much of a drug use episode (Mello & Mendelson, 1970, 1972). Thus there are ample opportunities for withdrawal to be associated with signals of drug delivery. That withdrawal symptoms often precede rather than follow drug administration may not be a serious impediment to a withdrawal conditioning account, since research reveals the occurrence of significant backward conditioning with pharmacologic unconditioned stimuli (USs) (e.g., Domjan & Gregg, 1977).

The withdrawal model, including its conditioning elements, has

Table 1
Withdrawal: Pavlovian Paradigm

Conditioned stimuli (CS) + Drug paraphernalia Drug cues Withdrawal-associated affects Cues signaling declining blood drug levels	Unconditioned stimulus (US) (withdrawal of drug)
after CS-US pairings	
Conditioned response (CR) = withdrawal response	Unconditioned response (UR) = withdrawal syndrome

Table 2
Hierarchy of Stimuli Provoking Withdrawal "Sickness" and "Craving"

1. Being offered a "taste" by an old copping buddy
2. Seeing a friend in the act of "shooting up"
3. Talking about drugs on copping corner
4. Standing on copping corner
5. Seeing a successful pusher—making lots of money, envy
6. Socially awkward situations: job interview, family criticism, feeling like an outsider at a party
7. Talking about drugs in group therapy
8. Seeing a few bags of heroin
9. Seeing someone's "works"
10. Seeing pictures of drugs and "works"
11. Seeing antidrug poster with "good veins" and somebody "shooting up"

Note. Ranked from most potent down to least potent.

Source. O'Brien, 1976.

received considerable direct and indirect support. For instance, addicts often list withdrawal as an important reason for drug use. Rankin, Stockwell, and Hodgson (1982) found that problem drinkers listed withdrawal symptoms as being likely to increase their desire to drink.

These authors also found that severely dependent drinkers were more likely than moderately dependent drinkers to cite withdrawal symptoms as important reasons for drinking. The results of Rankin et al. (1982) are fairly consistent with the results of numerous other studies, indicating that alcohol use, or the urge to use alcohol, is associated with withdrawal symptoms in addition to negative affects, social pressure, and alcohol-associated cues (e.g., Deardorff, Melges, Hoyt, & Savage, 1975; Edwards, Hensman, Chandler, & Peto, 1972). To support the association between withdrawal and urges, Ludwig and his associates have shown that craving incidence or severity is positively related to the severity of previous withdrawal episodes (Ludwig & Stark, 1974; Ludwig et al., 1974). There are also data and clinical observations linking opiate urges to opiate withdrawal symptoms (e.g., Wikler, 1953).

There is considerable evidence that withdrawal reactions can be conditioned. For instance, Wikler and his colleagues have performed studies showing that rats can acquire conditioned abstinence signs if environmental stimuli are paired with opiate withdrawal (e.g., Wikler & Pescor, 1967; Wikler, Pescor, Miller, & Norrell, 1971). Moreover, O'Brien and his colleagues have conducted studies suggesting that opiate withdrawal symptoms in humans can be classically conditioned. In one study, eight heroin addicts maintained on methadone received 12 withdrawal-conditioning sessions. In these trials the CS (a tone plus peppermint odor) was paired with naloxone-precipitated withdrawal. Results showed that conditioned subjects displayed the following pre- to postconditioning changes in response to the compound CS: increased heart rate, increased respiration, and decreased skin temperature. Since all these changes are present during opiate withdrawal, the authors concluded that elements of the opiate withdrawal were classically conditioned. This conclusion was buttressed by an increase (though not significant) in behavioral signs of opiate withdrawal that accompanied the physiological increase: for example, ptosis, yawning, and sniffing.

Although it is true that both Wikler and O'Brien have proposed that withdrawal, and conditioned withdrawal effects, may serve as the principal substrate of drug urges/cravings, it would be incorrect to suggest that they proposed this as the sole motivational influence on drug taking or drug seeking (e.g., O'Brien et al., 1981).

COMPENSATORY RESPONSE MODEL

The compensatory response model, proposed by Siegel and his colleagues (e.g., Siegel, 1983), is very similar to the conditioned withdrawal model. It arises from tolerance research, conducted by Siegel, showing that animals acquire drug tolerance more rapidly when drug delivery is signaled than when it is unsignaled. Siegel conceives of a drug administration episode as a Pavlovian conditioning trial in which the drug constitutes the US and signals of drug delivery (e.g., drug administration paraphernalia, gustatory drug cues, initial drug actions) constitute the CS. The unconditioned response (UR) in this paradigm is the direct (agonist) effect of the drug, while the conditioned response (CR) is a homeostatic adjustment that counters the agonist effect of the drug. Table 3 depicts this basic compensatory response model. In this table the taste of alcohol serves as the CS, alcohol constitutes the US, the hypothermic effect of alcohol is the UR, and hyperthermia is the CR. This model accounts quite nicely for tolerance development; as the CR increases in magnitude over iterative conditioning trials, it reduces the agonist effect of the drug.

One advantage of the compensatory response is that it accounts elegantly for the contextual specificity of drug tolerance. Le, Poulos, and Cappell (1979) provided an example of this phenomenon. Alcohol produces hypothermia, and these investigators explored the extent to which an environmental context could elicit tolerance to this effect. In this research (Experiment 2), rats were injected with alcohol (2.5 g/kg) in a distinctive context over the course of nine tolerance-development days. After the last tolerance-development session, rats were assigned to two groups and given a tolerance test. One group was given alcohol in the distinctive context, while the other group received alcohol in the home cage environment. Rectal temperature served as the dependent measure. Figure 1 shows that rats tested in the distinctive context (DC) showed a hypothermic response of about 1°C, while rats given alcohol in the home cage (HC) environment showed a hypothermic response of about 1.6°C. An initial alcohol dose in either the home cage environment or the distinctive context produced a hypothermic response of about 2°C. Thus, though both groups had acquired some tolerance to alcohol's

Table 3
Compensatory Response Model

Conditioned stimulus +	Unconditioned stimulus
(Taste of alcohol)	(Alcohol dose)
after pairings CS-US	
Conditioned response/	Unconditioned response/
compensatory response	agonist drug effect
(hyperthermia)	(hypothermia)

hypothermic actions, only rats with a consistent predrug signal (the DC) displayed maximum levels of tolerance.

If contextually mediated tolerance is caused by the acquisition of a drug compensatory response (a response opposite in direction to initial drug effects), then it should be possible to elicit a compensatory response in an animal not given the drug (Siegel, 1975). To test this possibility, Le et al. (1979) administered saline solution to animals that had previously received alcohol in the distinctive context. Half of these animals were given the saline in the distinctive context and half were given it in the home cage environment. Figure 2 shows that rats exposed to the distinctive context showed significant *hyper*thermia, whereas rats exposed to the home cage environment (which had not previously been paired with alcohol) showed little thermic change. Thus these results support the hypothesis that contextually mediated tolerance is produced by the acquisition of responses that oppose or counter agonist drug actions.

This theory has major implications for conceptualizations about the addictions. One is that agonist drug effects to which animals become tolerant will be greatest when the drug is administered in a context not previously associated with drug administration. Siegel has, in fact, argued that heroin overdose may be caused, at least in part, by addicts' self-administering the drug in either an unusual manner or an unusual context. Siegel has supported this hypothesis in two ways. First, he conducted an interview investigation in which survivors of heroin overdoses reported that the overdose was associated with an unusual heroin administration procedure or location. To test this overdose hypothesis experimentally, Siegel

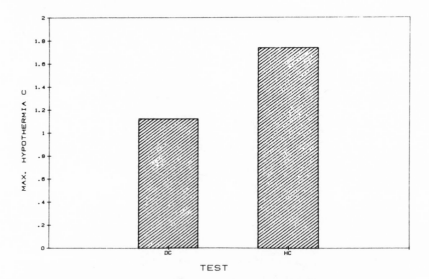

TEST

Figure 1. Rats given alcohol (EtOH) in a distinctive context (DC) displayed more toler-
ance to alcohol's hypothermic actions than did rats given alcohol in the home cage
(HC) when both groups had previously received alcohol in the DC. Presumably the
DC served as a CS for alcohol (Le, Poulos, & Cappell, 1979).

(Siegel, Hinson, Krank, & McCully, 1982) administered gradually
increasing doses of heroin to rats in one of two environments during
the course of 15 tolerance-development sessions. A control group
received vehicle-alone injections in both environments. On the test
day, rats were administered 15 mg/kg heroin in the same environment as the one in which tolerance development occurred or in a
different environment. Of the control group, 96.4% died when
given the 15 mg/kg dose (their first dose of the drug), while 64.3% of
the rats died that were given heroin in different environments on
the test and tolerance-development days. Consistent with the compensatory response model, when rats were given heroin in the same
environment during both the test and tolerance development, only
32.4% died.

Another way compensatory responses are relevant to addictions
is that, according to Siegel, such responses may be the major basis of
the withdrawal syndrome. Siegel (1983) argued that withdrawal
symptoms are often opposite in direction to the agonist effects of a
drug, thereby making it possible that they are produced by compensatory responses that overwhelm the agonist effects or persist
long after agonist effects have dissipated. Examples of drug ago-

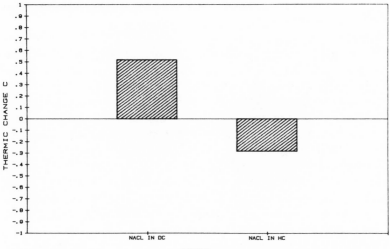

Figure 2. All animals had received alcohol in the distinctive context (DC). On the test, half of these animals received saline solution (NaCl) in the DC while the other half received NaCl in the home cage (HC) environment. According to Siegel's compensatory response model, animals given NaCl in the DC were hyperthermic relative to other animals because the DC, previously paired with alcohol, elicited a compensatory response of hyperthermia (Le, Poulos, & Cappell, 1979).

Table 4
Agonist Effects and Withdrawal Reactions

Agonist Effect	Withdrawal Reaction
Opiates	
Euphoria	Dysphoria
Constipation	Diarrhea
Hyposensitivity to external stimuli	Hypersensitivity to external stimuli
Ethanol	
Sedation	Hyperexcitability
Hypothermia	Hyperthermia
Nicotine	
Tachycardia	Bradycardia
Arousal	Fatigue, lethargy

266
NEBRASKA SYMPOSIUM ON MOTIVATION, 1986

nist effects and antagonistic withdrawal reactions are presented in Table 4.

Finally, Siegel (1983) has suggested that compensatory responses are relevant to addiction in that they constitute the basis of urges or craving. According to the compensatory response theory, some subset of direct drug effects is appetitive, a conclusion supported by considerable data (e.g., Sherman, Pickman, Rice, Liebeskind, & Holman, 1980; Van Der Kooy, Mucha, O'Shaughnessy, & Bucenieks, 1982). However, organisms develop at least partial tolerance to appetitive drug effects (e.g., the "euphoric" effects of opiates; Haertzen, & Hooks, 1969), suggesting that organisms acquire dysphoric compensatory responses that neutralize the direct appetitive actions of a drug. Siegel hypothesizes that it is these dysphoric or aversive compensatory responses that constitute the basis of drug use urges.

Although the compensatory response model enjoys considerable support, it does face discrepant data. For example, Baker and Tiffany (1985) have recently argued that, at least in the case of opiate drugs, contextually mediated tolerance effects are not produced by compensatory responses (see Tiffany, Petrie, Baker, & Dahl, 1983). Another difficulty for the compensatory response model is that withdrawal symptoms are frequently not antagonistic to direct drug effects (e.g., Ludwig, Cain, Wikler, Taylor, & Bendfeldt, 1977; Ludwig et al., 1974; cf. Newlin, 1986a, 1986b).

OPPONENT-PROCESS MODEL

The opponent-process model introduced by Solomon in the early 1970s (Solomon & Corbit, 1973, 1974) is predicated on the notion that the central nervous systems of mammals are organized to oppose spontaneously diverse types of affective or hedonic states. Opponent processes are mobilized by events or stimuli that can serve as effective Pavlovian USs or operant reinforcers. According to this theory, an effective US (one that motivates learning) elicits a primary affective or hedonic reaction that is determined by US quality, magnitude, and duration. For instance, in the case of a shock US, the primary affective reaction would be negative (fear) and would increase as a function of shock magnitude and duration. Likewise, in the case of a food US, the characteristics of the primary affective process are determined by the amount and type of food, and since food is an appetitive US, it would give rise to a positive affective process. Solomon labeled the primary affective responses to a US a-processes. A-processes are thought to be phasic and show little habituation over iterative elicitations.

Owing to the operating principles of CNS organization, an a-process is automatically opposed by a secondary b-process that suppresses or opposes the hedonic state yielded by the a-process. Thus, if a shock US activates a primary affective reaction of fear, the fear per se will automatically activate or elicit a countervailing b-process. In this case the b-process will reduce fear and fear-related behaviors. In contrast to the a-process, the b-process has a longer latency to onset, grows over repeated US exposures, and decays slowly, thereby persisting long after the direct effects of the US (a-processes) have dissipated.

The characteristics of a- and b-processes are depicted in Figures 3 and 4. As Figure 3 shows, the features of the a-process are largely invariant across repeated elicitations. The b-process, however, grows in size and duration each time it is elicited. The affective state of the organism is determined by which state is predominant. As Figure 4 shows, in early applications of the US the a-process predominates, causing the organism to remain primarily in an "a-state." However, after b-processes have grown in magnitude over US exposures, "b-states" tend to predominate.

Solomon (Solomon & Corbit, 1973) recognized that his opponent-process model was consistent with major features of addictive disorders. He noted that drugs certainly are effective USs; thus their direct (agonist) actions can be considered a-processes. Therefore we can consider all sorts of direct drug actions, such as the euphoric effects of opiates, the tachycardic effects of alcohol, and the vasoconstrictive effects of nicotine, to reflect a-processes. Theoretically, we should find evidence that organisms develop opponent processes to such direct drug actions.

Solomon (1977) was particularly interested in the affective consequences of drug use because he believed they are vital in motivating drug ingestion and addiction. For example, he recognized that opiates can produce intense pleasure in individuals (often labeled as "euphoria") and that such appetitive effects probably motivate initial drug use. However, he argued, as have others (e.g., Haertzen & Hooks, 1969), that such pleasurable effects disappear with repeated use and are replaced by aversive counterreactions that Solomon identifies as withdrawal symptoms. Of course Solomon attributes such aversive counterreactions (i.e., withdrawal) to opponent processes:

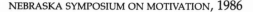

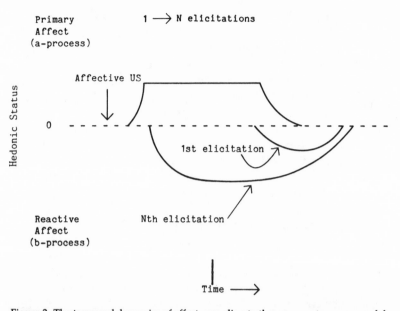

Figure 3. The temporal dynamics of affect according to the opponent-process model. With each activation, b-processes become larger and more persistent; a-processes, however, remain the same, given that the conditions of activation do not change (e.g., the magnitude of the US does not change).

the intense pleasure of the opiate "rush" for an opiate user reflects an a-process and the aversive withdrawal symptoms, both physiological and psychological, reflect the b-process, the opponent. Should in-strumental self-dosing occur during or at the peak of magnitude of withdrawal agony, the user will usually discover a very dramatic effect: the new dose produces complete cessation of craving and dis-comfort, and at the same time it reinstates the pleasurable attribute of the hedonic state aroused during the previous self-dosage. (Solomon, 1977, p. 95)

By the time addiction has developed, a-processes, the direct appetitive effects of drug use, exert little influence on the course of addiction. Solomon suggests that the addict has probably become completely tolerant to appetitive drug effects, and the raison d'être for continued drug use is amelioration of the withdrawal syndrome. In fact, for Solomon the amelioration of withdrawal craving is the sine qua non of addiction: "Addiction is the use of a specific drug for the effective alleviation of craving and withdrawal discomfort" (p. 96).

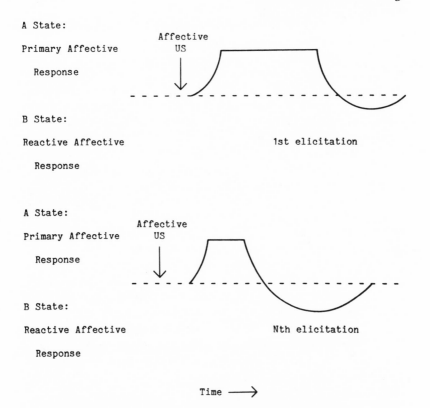

A State:

Primary Affective
Response

B State:

Reactive Affective
Response

A State:

Primary Affective
Response

B State:

Reactive Affective
Response

Time ⟶

Figure 4. Because b-processes get larger with succeeding elicitations, the affective state produced by the b-process (the b-state) gets larger each time the affective US is presented. Because the b-state is opposite in direction from the a-state, the affective state produced by the a-process, the a-state, necessarily becomes smaller (see Figure 3).

While Solomon has usually emphasized the nonassociative aspects of his theory, he does recognize that associative factors influence drug motivation. Solomon (1977) assumes that environmental stimuli may become associated with either a- or b-processes, depending on the temporal contingencies between CS occurrence and the onset and peaks of the associated a- and b-processes. Presumably, CSs associated with US delivery will become associated with a-processes. Therefore Solomon's theory is consistent with data showing that CSs paired with drug administration can elicit appetitive CRs (e.g., Sherman et al., 1980). The person trying to quit smoking will strain to sniff the smoke from someone else's cigarette because the smell of smoke elicits a-processes, which presumably reduce the quitter's aversive withdrawal syndrome. However, these a-process elicitations exact a price—even though they are associative in origin. Associatively based a-process elicitations are followed by b-processes just as drug-induced a-processes are. Thus the smoker who temporarily alleviates his or her withdrawal syndrome by sniffing smoke will be plunged further into withdrawal when the a-process has dissipated.

THREE MODELS OF DRUG USE MOTIVATION:
A COMPARISON

The reader has no doubt observed that despite their different theoretical bases, all three addiction models arrive at the same destination. For all three theories, the substrate of urges or cravings for drugs is produced by withdrawal-related processes. For all three, once addiction has developed, the euphoric effects of opiates or the anxiolytic properties of alcohol are inconsequential apart from their ability to alleviate withdrawal or withdrawal-like states.

Although the three theories are absolutely congruent with respect to the importance of withdrawal in motivating compulsive drug use once it has begun, they do differ on other issues. Some of these differences are:

1. Both the compensatory response and the opponent-process models demand that withdrawal symptoms be counterdirectional to direct drug effects. Thus organisms should acquire tolerance to some set of drug effects (not necessarily all), and during withdrawal the organism should display responses antagonistic to the drug effect in question. The withdrawal model does not require that withdrawal responses be antagonistic to direct drug effects.

2. The withdrawal model does not require that tolerance magnitude, urge magnitude, and magnitude of withdrawal responses be correlated. The compensatory response and opponent-process models, however, both stipulate that tolerance and withdrawal are produced by the same underlying processes and thus should be closely related.

3. The opponent-process model holds that the rate of development and magnitude of tolerance responses (b-processes) should be a function of the characteristics of the preceding drug effects (a-processes). This theory therefore has difficulty accounting for why tolerance develops much more rapidly when drug delivery is sig-

naled than when it is not, given that the signaling does not necessarily affect the magnitude of the direct effects of a drug (e.g., Le et
al., 1979). The faster development of tolerance in signaled, as
opposed to unsignaled, conditions is quite congruent with the compensatory response model, however. According to this model,
tolerance is due largely to associative processes and therefore
should occur most rapidly when drug delivery is reliably signaled.

4. The opponent-process and withdrawal models are both compatible with the notion that tolerance may occur through nonassociative routes. The opponent-process model especially is clear about
the processes involved in such tolerance development and about its
determinants. Although Siegel recognizes that tolerance can occur
via nonassociative routes (e.g., tissue tolerance; Rezvani, Huidobro-Toro, Hu, & Way, 1983), his theory is silent on the nature of
nonassociative tolerance processes.

5. Both the opponent-process and the compensatory response
models predict that if a drug signal elicits enhanced tolerance in a
drugged organism, that signal should elicit a drug-antagonistic response when the organism is drug free. The withdrawal model is
silent on this issue.

It is not our goal to appraise the general empirical support en-
joyed by the various theories reviewed. We will point out, however,
that both the opponent-process and compensatory response models are faced with discrepant data. For example, both models are
opposed by data showing that some withdrawal signs are isodirectional to direct drug effects (e.g., alcohol increases both respiration
and heart rate, and both are associated with alcohol withdrawal).
Also, both models are opposed by data showing that tolerance and
withdrawal can accrue at different rates (e.g., Majchrowicz & Hunt,
1976) and can be experimentally dissociated (Ritzmann & Tabakoff,
1976). Moreover, while the compensatory response model accounts
nicely for the rapid contextual enhancement of tolerance, the opponent process model does not. Solomon (e.g., 1977, 1980) recognizes
that the rapid recruitment of tolerance (b-processes) by drug signals
is not predicted by the opponent-process model and suggests that
unusual features of the tolerance conditioning paradigm contribute
to this finding. Siegel's compensatory response model, on the other
hand, is not intended to account for nonassociative tolerance and
dependence phenomena and therefore was not intended to be a
"complete" account of motivational factors in addiction.

The withdrawal model has the narrowest scope of the three models, being intended to account only for the nature and occurrence of

drug urges/cravings. Importantly, all three models largely agree on the nature of urges; they reflect the associative or nonassociative elicitation of withdrawal processes. For the opponent-process and compensatory response models, withdrawal responses should be counter to the direct effects of drug use and should be seen in response systems reflecting tolerance development. The withdrawal model makes no such claims.

We will now present an empirical review of data relevant to urges and motivational processes important to addiction. To anticipate the conclusion of our review, we suggest that a new motivational model of urges is needed to account for the extant data. In contrast to the models described above, however, this model is based not solely on withdrawal processes but also on the appetitive motivational effects of drugs. Stewart, de Wit, and Eikelboom (1984) have recently ascribed a primary role to the unconditioned and conditioned appetitive incentive effects of drugs in the maintenance of drug use. According to their model, drug use may be initiated and maintained by conditioned drug agonist effects on appetitive motivational systems. Borrowing from these notions, we suggest that a primary route to urge elicitation is the activation of appetitive motivational systems and associated affect networks. We believe that urges may be elicited associatively and nonassociatively by cues, pharmacologic and nonpharmacologic, that have motivational effects similar to the agonist effects of drug—for example, cues that induce positive affective states.

Data on the Nature of Urges

RELAPSE DATA

We believe, as do others (e.g., Ludwig & Wikler, 1974), that urges are affects that increase the probability of concomitant or subsequent drug use. Indeed, there is empirical and experimental evidence linking drug self-administration with self-report of urges. For instance, Ludwig et al. (1974) found that craving ratings were accurate predictors of the alcohol use patterns of alcoholics. Brandon, Tiffany, and Baker (1985) found that self-report of bothersome urges was associated with early relapse among smokers. Because urges are associated with drug self-administration, we may be able to

learn something about the conditions that elicit urges by characterizing the situations that lead to relapse episodes.

Marlatt (e.g., Marlatt, 1978; Marlatt & Gordon, 1980) was one of
the first investigators to characterize carefully the events surrounding and preceeding relapse. In one study 137 smokers, heroin
addicts, and alcoholics were questioned about the circumstances
surrounding their relapse episodes. A classification schema was
used (Marlatt & Gordon, 1980) that assigned relapse episodes to 12
discrete categories as a function of instigating circumstances (see
Table 5). Three-quarters of the relapse episodes fell into the following categories: coping with negative emotional states, social pressure, and coping with interpersonal conflict (see Table 6). These
findings point out the importance of negative emotional states to re-

Table 5
Classification Scheme for Relapse Situations

I. Intrapersonal/environmental determinants
    A. Coping with negative emotional states
        1. Coping with frustration and anger
        2. Coping with other negative emotional states (e.g., fear, anxiety)
    B. Coping with negative physical physiological states
        1. Coping with physical states associated with prior sub-stance use (e.g., withdrawal)
        2. Coping with other negative physical states (e.g., ill-ness, headache)
    C. Enhancement of positive emotional states
    D. Testing personal control
    E. Giving in to temptations or urges
II. Interpersonal determinants
    A. Coping with interpersonal conflict
        1. Coping with frustration and anger
        2. Coping with other interpersonal conflict
    B. Social Pressure
        1. Direct social pressure
        2. Indirect social pressure
    C. Enhancement of positive emotional states

Source. Marlatt & Gordon, 1980.

Table 6

Characteristics of Relapse Situations: Relapse Episodes of Alcoholics, Smokers, and Heroin Addicts

Situation	Alcoholics (n = 70)	Smokers (n = 35)	Addicts (n = 32)	All Subjects (n = 137)
Intrapersonal determinants	61%	57%	53%	58%
Negative emotional states	38	43	28	37
Negative physical states	3	—	9	4
Positive emotional states	—	8	16	6
Testing personal control	9	—	—	4
Urges and temptations	11	6	—	7
Interpersonal determinants	39%	43%	47%	42%
Interpersonal conflict	18	12	13	15
Social pressure	18	25	34	24
Positive emotional states	3	6	—	3

Source. Marlatt & Gordon, 1980.

lapse. Other important findings were that negative physical states (including drug withdrawal) were associated with a relatively small proportion of relapses, as were urges and temptations and positive emotional states.

Marlatt (1978) viewed these data as being in conflict with theories of addiction that emphasize conditioned withdrawal (e.g., O'Brien, 1976) or the importance of urges per se (e.g., Ludwig et al., 1974). In addition, very few of the relapse episodes seemed to be accounted for by individuals pursuing the positive incentive properties of drugs. In general the results seemed most compatible with a relapse model in which subjects use drugs because the reinforcing value of drugs is enhanced when the subject is in a negative affective state or because a negative affective state may decrease the addict's ability to cope with preexisting urges (Marlatt & Gordon, 1980).

It is important to note that in Marlatt's research, urge occurrence was scored only if no other salient antecedent (e.g., interpersonal conflict) occurred before relapse. This scoring procedure presumably underestimated urge occurrence, since it is likely that urges occurred in the context of social pressure, negative affects, and so forth.

Shiffman (1982) has gathered a great deal of information on smoking relapse that is congruent with aspects of Marlatt's data. Shiffman used an advertised "Stay-Quit" hotline to collect data from smokers who were experiencing a relapse crisis (they either had smoked or feared they would).

Shiffman, like Marlatt, found that negative affect and stress were associated with a large percentage of relapse episodes. However, he also discovered that a sizable proportion of relapses were associated with positive emotional states (28.8%) or were precipitated (in the opinion of respondents) by stimuli other than negative affects: smoking stimuli, eating or drinking, and feelings of relaxation. In fact, about 60% of relapse crises occurred shortly after food, beverage, or drug intake (see Table 7). These precipitants were likely to be accompanied by positive affect. Only about half the subjects reported experiencing withdrawal symptoms at the time of the reported crisis.

Shiffman's results are extremely valuable. However, like the results of other relapse studies (e.g., Brandon et al., 1985), they must be interpreted with caution. Such studies are prey to self-presentation, memory, and selection biases. Moreover, they depend upon subjects' and researchers' coding self-reports into meaningful categories. For example, in Shiffman's research, physical complaints of headache, nausea, and diarrhea were coded as withdrawal symptoms, as were anxiety and irritability. Although these symptoms may accompany withdrawal (Shiffman & Jarvik, 1976), they may also be unrelated to smoking and smoking withdrawal. Additionally, although Shiffman included irritability and anxiety as withdrawal symptoms, he excluded urges and cravings and negative affects such as depression, even though these are hallmarks of withdrawal (Shiffman & Jarvik, 1976). Thus it is difficult to interpret Shiffman's data relating withdrawal symptoms to relapse crises.

Table 7
Precipitants of Relapse Crises

Stimulus	Percentage of Subjects
Negative affect, stress	52.0
Smoking stimuli	31.8
Eating or drinking	20.9
Feelings of relaxation	10.8
Other stimuli	8.1

Source. Shiffman, 1982.

Note. Multiple codings result in totals over 100%; $N = 148$.

Table 8
Percentage of Respondents Reporting Consumption before Relapse

Consumption	Percentage of Respondents
None	30.2
Food	11.3
Alcohol	45.3
Caffeinated coffee/tea	24.5
Caffeinated soft drink	1.9
Recreational drug	5.6

Source. Brandon, Tiffany, & Baker, 1985.

Note. Multiple codings result in totals over 100%; 98.1% of 54 smokers responded to this question.

In our laboratory we have examined the role of urges in the relapse process (Brandon et al., 1985). We characterized the relapse contexts of 54 smokers and our results are consistent with those of Marlatt and Shiffman. For example, over half of responding relapsers reported experiencing negative affect before relapse. However, about 20% of subjects reported positive, and 12% neutral, affect before relapse. Also, in agreement with Shiffman, Brandon et al. found that consumption frequently preceded relapse (see Table 8). In response to questions about urge incidence and severity before relapse about 80% of respondents reported having one or more urges per day before their relapse, and slightly fewer than half reported that urges disrupted their lives. This commonly took the form of a disruption of thinking or functioning or a negative mood. Subjects who reported that they had bothersome urges relapsed more quickly than did other subjects.

One of the goals of the Brandon et al. research was to study the *process* of relapse; that is, we were concerned about individuals' behavior both before and after their initial drug ingestion (a "lapse"). Results showed that of subjects who smoked one cigarette during the two-year follow-up period, 94.4% went on to smoke a second cigarette and 90.7% returned to daily smoking. Thus this research agrees with other reports showing that drug addicts (alcoholics and smokers) are at great risk for excessive drug use if any drug is sampled (e.g., Marlatt & Gordon, 1980). Moreover, regression analyses revealed no correlation between the length of time between quitting and a subject's first cigarette (the lapse) and the time between this first cigarette and a return to regular smoking; r (47) = $-.02$. We examined the correlations between a host of subject characteristics or behaviors at the time of the lapse and the length of the lapse-relapse interval. We found that neither subjects' affect before the lapse, their affective or cognitive reaction to the lapse, nor their use of coping responses after the lapse was significantly related to the lapse-relapse interval. The one variable that was most closely related to this interval was subjects' level of smoking before cessation, r = $-.46$, $F(1,43)$ = 11.62, $p < .01$. These data suggest that factors that affect likelihood of initial postwithdrawal drug use (e.g., coping-response execution; Shiffman, 1982, 1984) may not be potent determinants of readdiction once the drug has entered the body. Once ingested, readdiction may be influenced more by the same pharmacologic motivational systems that determined precessation drug self-administration.

McAuliffe and his colleagues (McAuliffe, Feldman, et al., 1985) also performed a follow-up investigation intended to reveal the role of urges in the relapse process. Subjects in this study were 184 opiate addicts who had completed or nearly completed opiate treatment programs. These subjects participated in a two-hour interview before treatment discharge and were then followed up for six months.

The authors determined that addicts' predischarge craving ratings were sigificantly correlated with their views of themselves as being psychologically dependent on ($r = .64$), or addicted to ($r = .49$), opiates, and that postdischarge craving accounted for a significant proportion of variance in relapse incidence ($R^2 = .31$, $p < .001$).

Summary. Investigations of relapse data suggest that urge self-report does predict later relapse. Moreover, although most relapses occurred after stress or in the context of negative affect, a substantial portion of relapse episodes (or relapse crises) occurred while subjects were in positive affective states. Many subjects reported eating or drinking before relapse or relapse crises, and such reports were frequently associated with self-reports of positive affect. Also, one study revealed that the rate of readdiction to cigarettes (the lapse-relapse interval) was related to prior smoking rates.

Elicitors of Urges and Drug Self-Administration: Results of Interview and Questionnaire Investigations

ALCOHOL

Questionnaire studies have shown that problem drinkers report drinking in response to such factors as physical arousal/withdrawal, negative emotions, social situations/pressure, and drug-related stimuli (Rankin et al., 1982). Other investigations reveal that urges are elicited by similar stimuli or feelings (e.g., Hore, 1971; Ludwig & Stark, 1974). For instance, Ludwig and Stark (1974) found that a majority of alcoholics reported having urges when depressed, nervous, or worried. A smaller but still sizable group also reported having urges when successful, happy, or feeling good (35%, 30%, and 23%, respectively). Ludwig and Stark's data also revealed a relationship between the strength of craving and the nature of the eliciting stimuli. Mild or moderate craving was related to mild nervousness or anxiety, tiredness, a desire to be sociable, or physical stimuli associated with alcohol. Intense craving was associated with intense negative emotions (extreme anger, fear, or depression), a catastrophic event, or physical symptoms reminiscent of alcohol withdrawal.

OPIATES

McAuliffe and his colleagues have conducted several interview studies in an effort to characterize the factors associated with compulsive opiate use and urge elicitation. In an initial study, McAuliffe and Gordon (1974) found that virtually all opiate addicts sampled had experienced intense pleasurable effects from opiate injection (euphoria), that almost half experienced such effects daily, and that addicts continued to experience such effects after many years of drug use. In a subsequent study, McAuliffe (McAuliffe, Feldman, et al., 1985) examined the importance of euphoria in addicts' decisions to use opiates and explored differences between addicts who did and did not rate euphoria as an important factor in their drug use.

McAuliffe et al. showed that the importance of achieving opiate-induced euphoria varied greatly with addict characteristics. Among addicts who had become addicted iatrogenically (through the use of opiates under medical supervision), attaining euphoria ("to get high," "to be more energetic") was rated as fairly unimportant. These addicts had rated ameliorating physical or psychological discomfort as a more important reason for using drugs. However, among addicts who began using drugs primarily for recreational purposes (e.g., street addicts, addicted medical personnel), drug-induced euphoria was rated as a very important reason for using opiates. In addition to attaining euphoria, recreational drug users also rated alleviating withdrawal illness as a major reason for taking opiates.

Ratings of the importance of euphoria as a determinant of drug use appeared to be related to drug-use patterns as well as to motivation for initial drug use. In particular, individuals rating euphoria as an important reason for using drugs tended to use greater amounts and appeared to be more insouciant about the hazards or costs of excessive drug use. The following two quotations illustrate the different drug use patterns that characterize the addicts for whom euphoria was and was not important. Both are taken from so-called street addicts:

> Case #1. This 24-year-old white male is probably the hardest of the "hardcore addicts," a term used by McAuliffe and Gordon (1974) to describe addicts who achieve euphoric [sic] from opiates on a daily basis. "I'm trying to get high" was his goal for shooting opiates. When interviewed, he had been out of prison nine months and had been using heroin on a daily basis since his discharge. He said he would have

to spend $12 a day on heroin just to avoid withdrawal, but was actually using between $25 and $30 each day. When asked how much he would use if he had twice the amount he needed, he replied, "As much as I could hold . . . to get loaded." His explanation for relapsing since getting out of jail illustrates the key place euphoria occupies in his opiate use: "I like it. I just really like shooting dope. That's why I'm on it. I don't like having a habit or anything. That's just, you know, you try not to get it, but eventually, you know, you do."

Quarrels with his wife over drugs, loss of his job, and his shoplifting and dealing drugs led to divorce; he now lives alone. Asked about his sex life, he replied, "I don't have any use for it. No craving for it . . . I'd rather shoot dope." The interviewer asked, "You prefer drugs to sex?" He answered emphatically, "Definitely. I'd rather nod. . . . I like to shoot dope better than anything else in the world."

Case #3. This black male had the lowest interest in euphoria in the sample of active street addicts. When asked whether he was using drugs to feel normal or to get high, he said, "Just trying to get normal." Describing his daily dosage, he said, "I try to keep it down now on account of being married. I get along on $5 (per day)." He was using only $2 per day when he first began, and despite five years of continuous daily use, he needs only $5 worth. When asked how much he would use if he had $10 worth of heroin, he answered, "Same thing. $5 once a day." He attributed his very modest escalation over the years to his inability to stay normal on less. . . .

A remarkably conventional lifestyle accompanies his indifference to drug euphoria. During the entire period of his dependence, he has been working full-time, living with his wife and child, and supporting them along with his habit out of his salary. He likes his current job, and says he would not want to be high while working for fear he might be fired. (McAuliffe, Rohman, Feldman, & Launer, 1985, pp. 214–215)

As part of the relapse study reported earlier (McAuliffe, Feldman, et al., 1985), McAuliffe and his colleagues asked the 184 opiate addicts in that study to list, and rate the importance of, factors that affected their craving.

Reasons for craving included such things as anger control, need for the drug in order to feel normal, recollection of withdrawal, the presence of withdrawal symptoms, the need to relax, the need to mitigate negative affects such as depression and anxiety, and the desire to experience drug-induced euphoria ("to feel good"). The top reasons addicts listed for taking drugs were to cope with negative affect (anxiety or depression) and to experience drug-induced euphoria. Among their least important reasons for craving was the experience or recall of withdrawal illness. McAuliffe, Feldman, et al. (1985) also asked addicts to rate the effectiveness of various brief vignettes in eliciting urges. The most highly rated vignettes were ones comprising the notions of the sudden availability of opiates, the presence of cues previously paired with opiate use, or the recollection of opiate-induced euphoria. Addicts rated withdrawal-related vignettes as quite ineffective in eliciting craving (see Table 9).

Table 9
Vignettes Reported by Opiate Addicts to Be Effective and Ineffective in Eliciting Craving to Use Opiates

Effective Vignettes	Ineffective Vignettes
You are in a situation in which you have often used opiates before.	You are watching a movie or a television show depicting the story of a person who is about to use opiates after being in a cold sweat and yawning.
You remember really enjoying how good the feeling of being under the influence of opiates was.	There is an empty bottle of drugs on the table, and you start to think that you'll soon be feeling drug sick.
You open the medicine cabinet at a friend's house, and there is a bottle of opiates on the shelf.	You catch a cold, your nose is running, and you're really feeling bad.
Your dentist offers to give you a prescription of opiates for a toothache.	You read a book or magazine article about someone going through severe withdrawal.

Source. McAuliffe, Feldman, et al., 1985.

NICOTINE

Numerous studies have been conducted in an effort to sample smokers' reasons for smoking. In fact, such efforts led to the development of a "Reasons for Smoking" questionnaire (Ikard, Green, & Horn, 1969). Through factor analysis, researchers have identified seven factors or mechanisms that are thought to account for motivation to smoke: Pleasure-Taste, Addiction, Habit, Anxiety, Stimulation, Social Reward, and Fiddle (handling the cigarette, oral habit). There are data indicating that subjects' responses to this questionnaire predict how they will respond to environmental manipulations; for example, high Taste-Pleasure smokers show greater reductions in smoking rates if forced to smoke vinegar-adulterated cigarettes than do smokers low in Taste-Pleasure motivation (Leventhal & Avis, 1976). Using this Reasons for Smoking Questionnaire, researchers have generally found the following scales to be the most highly endorsed by smokers: Pleasure-Taste, Stimulation, and Anxiety (Green, 1977; Ikard et al., 1969; Kozlowski, 1979). The Pleasure-Taste scale taps smoking for taste, for undifferentiated pleasure, and for relaxation. Therefore these results suggest that smokers report the management of affect as an important global reason for smoking. They smoke to achieve direct, pleasurable effects of nicotine (Stimulation and Pleasure-Taste scales) or to ameliorate negative affects (e.g., to reduce anxiety).

Appropriately enough, these results are very consistent with predictions yielded by Tomkins's model of smoking—the model upon which the Reasons for Smoking Questionnaire is based (Tomkins, 1966). Tomkins proposed that smokers smoke largely to produce or enhance positive emotional states or to reduce negative ones.

SUMMARY: INTERVIEW AND QUESTIONNAIRE STUDIES

Interview and questionnaire studies suggest that for the three drugs studied, namely, alcohol, opiates, and nicotine, a variety of factors were associated with urges (or with estimates of likelihood of self-administration): withdrawal symptoms, negative affects, and positive affects. For all three addict types, negative affective states were highly associated with urges. Positive affective states and information on drug availability were also associated with urges, but perhaps less consistently than were negative affects. McAuliffe and his colleagues found that many opiate addicts reported that appetitive, agonist opiate effects were important to their drug self-administration, and that those who reportedly took opiates for appetitive effects engaged in a particularly virulent and compulsive form of self-administration. Heavy drinkers were especially likely to associate drug (alcohol) use with withdrawal symptoms. It is unclear why withdrawal might be a more potent elicitor for alcoholics than for other addict groups.

Laboratory Investigations of Conditioned Drug Responses and Urges

ALCOHOL

Characterization of conditioned drug responses. We will first review research designed to characterize the directionality of conditioned alcohol effects and then will examine data on the laboratory-based elicitation of urges as assessed through attitudinal, behavioral, and physiological assays.

Newlin has conducted a series of alcohol studies (Newlin, 1985, 1986a, 1986b) designed to show that cues paired with alcohol ingestion later elicit compensatory responses. In one (Newlin, 1986a), seven male social drinkers received alcohol in a distinctive drinking room while another seven received a placebo in that same room. After both groups received two such drinking trials in the distinctive room, both groups were given a placebo in that environment. Newlin's results showed that the group that had previously received alcohol in the distinctive room showed decreased pulse transit time and finger skin temperature relative to the placebo group. He contended that the distinctive environment had come to serve as a CS for alcohol and that it had elicited CRs that were compensatory for, or antagonistic to, direct alcohol effects. Newlin notes that such compensatory responses might subserve craving in alcoholics.

Although Newlin's results are intriguing, a number of considerations cast doubt on their relevance to urges. First, Newlin's research has not yet included complete control conditions for nonassociative effects of alcohol. Second, it is difficult to accept some of the placebo responses he obtains as compensatory responses when the alcohol dose used in conditioning does not produce a significant agonist effect on the measure in question or there is no tolerance development during conditioning. Finally, the placebo responses he obtained (decreased pulse-transit time, decreased finger temperature, and increased heart rate; e.g., Newlin, 1985, 1986a, 1986b), could be produced by nonpharmacological factors: subjects' surprise at not receiving alcohol in placebo tests, by anticipation, and so forth.

Urge elicitation. There have been about a half-dozen laboratory investigations designed to characterize urge-eliciting stimuli or urge correlates or both. In one recent study, Eriksen and Gotestam (1984) examined the psychophysiological, attitudinal, and behavioral responses of 16 alcoholics to alcohol-relevant and neutral photographic slides. The behavioral and attitudinal measures used in this study indicated that the alcohol-relevant slides produced greater anxiety and craving than did the neutral slides. Psychophysiological measures revealed no differences as a function of slide type. Because alcoholics typically evidence great craving and anxiety during alcohol withdrawal, the authors interpreted their results to mean that the alcohol slides elicited conditioned withdrawal. These results are amenable to other interpretations; for example, the alcohol-related slides may have elicited strong urges, and the strong urges may themselves have increased subjects' anxiety. There was no independent evidence of alcohol withdrawal.

Pomerleau and his associates have conducted several studies aimed at characterizing alcohol urges. In one (Pomerleau, Fertig, Baker, & Cooney, 1983) the authors presented the smell of alcoholic beverages and cedar chips to 8 alcoholics and 10 nonalcoholic controls. In addition to psychophysiological measures, dependent measures included ratings of desire to drink and number of sniffs.

Alcoholics showed more swallowing and craving in response to the alcohol odor than did nonalcoholic controls but did not differ on psychophysiological measures. The authors suggest that swallowing might serve as a sensitive measure of the incentive value of alcohol, but their data show that swallowing was only modestly related to desire-to-drink ratings (see Figure 3 in Pomerleau et al., 1983).

In another study (Kaplan et al., 1985; also see Kaplan, Meyer, & Stroebel, 1983), the authors investigated the psychophysiological correlates of "desire-to-drink" ratings made by nonproblem drinkers ($N = 26$) and alcoholics ($N = 59$). As in the Pomerleau et al. research, the authors exposed subjects to the odor of both cedar chips and alcoholic beverages. The physiological measures revealed that alcoholics showed higher skin conductance level (SCL) and heart rate (HR) during alcohol exposure than did controls. Moreover, only for alcoholics was psychophysiological responding related to desire-to-drink ratings: SCL was positively correlated with ratings ($r = .39$). As opposed to the results of Pomerleau et al. (1983), alcoholics and control subjects were not distinguished on the basis of swallowing in response to alcohol.

The authors noted that their data are consistent with the proposition that alcohol cues elicit a subclinical withdrawal syndrome and that this serves as a cue for alcoholics' instrumental self-administration of drug. They also noted that both elevated SCL and HR reflect autonomic nervous system arousal, and that alcohol withdrawal is characterized by autonomic hyperactivity (e.g., Gross & Lewis, 1973; Gross, Lewis, & Hastey, 1974). Further support of the conditioned withdrawal explanation comes from the finding that SCL during alcohol exposure was positively related to alcoholics' self-report of both the number of heavy drinking days and the severity of withdrawal symptoms in the 30 days before admission for treatment. Presumably, the greater the prior drinking and resultant withdrawal symptoms, the stronger the elicited withdrawal CR.

The authors' interpretation of their findings is a reasonable one. Their findings are, however, susceptible to competing interpretations; for example, autonomic arousal might reflect anxiety, worry, or tension independent of conditioned withdrawal. It makes sense that subjects with a more severe drinking problem would experience the greatest anxiety—and hence the greatest autonomic arousal—because alcohol has been associated with more severe, inappetitive consequences for these subjects. Moreover, alcoholics' desire-to-drink ratings were not associated with the number of prior heavy drinking days or withdrawal severity self-reports. This is a problem if we are to assume that heavy drinking and withdrawal should both lead to greater conditioned withdrawal reactions and hence greater craving.

The landmark research on urges was performed by Ludwig and his associates. In an initial study, Ludwig and his colleagues sought to determine whether: (1) a low dose of alcohol would stimulate alcohol withdrawal symptoms more than a high dose (which would suppress withdrawal) and hence would elicit greater craving; (2) a realistic drinking setting ("Label" condition) would elicit greater craving and greater alcohol acquisitive behavior than a neutral ("Nonlabel") context; (3) conditions producing greater craving would be associated with physiological responses associated with the alcohol withdrawal syndrome; and (4) maximum expression of craving would be produced by the joint occurrence of interoceptive (low dose) and exteroceptive (Label) urge elicitors.

Subjects in this research were 24 detoxified alcoholics randomly assigned to either the Label or the Nonlabel condition. A within-subjects factor was dose level as subjects participated in three sessions, each at a different dose level: 0 ml/kg; 0.6 ml/kg 100% EtOH ("low dose"); or 1.2 ml/kg 100% EtOH ("high dose"). Subjects were blind as to the dose level they received each session, and an attempt was made to disguise the placebo session (a small amount of alcohol was floated on top of the mixer). Dependent measures in this research included craving rating (0–100), two operant work schedules—one for alcohol and one for money—and a variety of psychophysiological assessments.

Results showed that subjects receiving alcohol with alcohol signals present (Label condition) reported greater craving than subjects getting alcohol without signals. When the Label and the Nonlabel conditions were collapsed, both high and low doses resulted in greater craving ratings than the placebo condition. In addition, the influence of alcohol and signaling appeared to be additive. When both alcohol signals and alcohol were presented concomitantly, subjects tended to report greater craving than when either was presented singly.

The pattern of results obtained with operant responding for alcohol also indicated the importance of both alcohol effects and alcohol signals for urge elicitation (assuming operant responding can be viewed as a behavioral manifestation of an urge). Administered alcohol (especially the low dose) resulted in increased operant responding, as did the Label condition. Also, as was the case with urge ratings, the greatest operant responding was found when the low dose was administered in the Label condition.

One interesting analysis the authors presented concerned "relapse" to alcohol drinking. At the beginning of each session, some subjects voiced their intent not to respond for alcohol. However, some of these same subjects eventually decided to work for alcohol sometime after dose administration (placebo, low, or high) and before the session's end. Such "relapses" were most common in the Label and alcohol administration conditions

Not only did alcohol and the alcohol signal ("Label") conditions produce greater urge ratings and operant responding, but the joint presence of these conditions resulted in higher correlations between the urge rating and operant measures. That is, when subjects were given alcohol in the Label condition, their urge ratings and operant

Table 10
Intercorrelations of Urge Ratings and Operant Work for Alcohol as a Function of Alcohol Dose and Label Condition

Condition	Placebo	Low Dose	High Dose
Label	.66	.92	.90
Nonlabel	.56	.43	.69

Source. Ludwig, Wikler, & Stark, 1974.

responding for alcohol showed greater concordance (see Table 10).

In terms of physiological effects, the high dose effected large increases in heart rate, respiration, and alpha-wave activity and a large decrease in systolic blood pressure (SBP). The low dose produced similar but weaker effects. In addition, the high dose produced a significant decrease in hand tremor amplitude whereas the low dose produced a small increase. The Label condition also affected physiological activity. When subjects were collapsed across the three dose levels, it was determined that the Label condition was associated with reduced heart rate but increased elicited skin potential response (SPR) and alpha-wave activity.

In a second study, Ludwig and his colleagues (Ludwig et al., 1977) compared the urge responses of "binge" and "steady" types of alcoholics. Forty-four alcoholics were randomly assigned to "Label" and "Nonlabel" conditions. In addition to the label factor, subjects participated in either "Success" or "Failure" trials after a baseline measurement period. In the Success condition, subjects were told that they had solved a proverb labeling task; in the Failure conditioning, they were given failure feedback on 75%–85% of trials. As in the 1974 study, dependent measures comprised craving and arousal ratings, operant responding for alcohol, and a host of psychophysiological measures.

The results of this research showed that, relative to the Nonlabel condition, the Label condition resulted in greater craving ratings, greater operant work for alcohol, and greater skin conductance levels but declines in systolic and diastolic blood pressure. However, these significant Label effects obtained only for steady drinkers. The authors also examined the correlates of operant responding for

alcohol. Consistent with the notion that urges are affects that increase the likelihood of drug-approach behavior, the most consistently accurate predictor of subjects' operant responding for alcohol
was their craving ratings. Other measures that were significantly related to operant responding for alcohol were increased alpha-wave
activity, diastolic blood pressure (DBP), and respiration. If the Label
condition activates urge response systems, then it should result in
greater urge-response concordance, just as the Label and alcohol
conditions did in the 1974 study. This was what was found. In the
baseline session in the Label condition, 68.8% of variance in operant
work for alcohol was accounted for by arousal and craving ratings,
alpha-wave activity, respiration, and blood pressure. The same
measures accounted for only 22.3% of the variance in the baseline
session in the Nonlabel condition.

The physiological responses associated with urge elicitation in
Ludwig's research are presented in Table 11. All these responses
either were associated with operant work for alcohol or were produced by a condition that significantly increased alcohol urge ratings (i.e., a dose or "Label" condition).

A final line of research directly relevant to alcohol urges or craving
was conducted by Hodgson and Rankin and their colleagues. An
early investigation by these authors concerned whether craving for
alcohol is increased or elicited by alcohol per se. They administered
low and high "priming" doses of alcohol (8 and 48 g, respectively) to
moderately ($n = 9$) and severely ($n = 11$) dependent alcoholics
abstinent at the time of priming-dose administration (Hodgson,
Rankin, & Stockwell, 1979). Three hours after receiving their priming doses, subjects were allowed to drink additional alcohol, and
their self-rated desire for a drink and speed of drinking were measured. The high priming dose resulted in an increased drinking rate
among severely, but not moderately, dependent alcoholics, and
rate of drinking was positively related to rated desire to drink.

In a subsequent study, Stockwell, Hodgson, Rankin, and Taylor
(1982) examined the effects of both the pharmacologic action of alcohol and the expectancy of alcohol effects on urge-relevant ratings,
physiological measures, and actual alcohol consumption. Urge-
relevant ratings included ratings of desire to drink, tension, pleasure from alcohol, and difficulty in resisting available alcohol. In this
study each subject ($N = 20$) participated in four conditions described by the four cells of a two-by-two "balanced placebo" design
(Marlatt, Demming, & Reid, 1973; see Table 12). The two factors involved in this design were what subjects were told a drink contained

Table 11
Physiological Responses Associated with Urge Elicitation

Ludwig et al. (1974)			Ludwig et al. (1977)	
Low Dose	High Dose	Label Effect	Label Effect	Work Correlate
↑Alpha wave	↑↑Alpha wave	↑Alpha wave	↑Skin resistance	↑Alpha wave
↑Respiration	↑↑Respiration	↓Heart rate	↓SBP	↑DBP
↑Heart rate	↑↑Heart rate		↓DBP	↑Respiration
↓SBP	↓↓SBP			
↑Hand tremor	↓Hand tremor			

Note. Physiological correlates both of responding for alcohol and of variables positively associated with urge self-report across Ludwig's two experiments. An upward-pointing arrow indicates increased magnitude, and a downward-pointing arrow indicates decreased magnitude. The double arrows under the high-dose condition of Ludwig et al. (1974) indicate that the associated physiological effects were greater than in the low-dose condition of that study.

and what the drink actually contained. Subjects participated in a different experimental condition on each day of the experiment. Half the subjects in this study were severely dependent alcoholics and the other half moderately dependent alcoholics.

Subjects were administered a "priming" drink, with stated and actual content depending upon their experimental condition (Table 12). Fifteen and 60 minutes after the priming drink, the following assessments were made: desire-to-drink ratings, hand tremor and pulse measurement, and affect ratings. After the 60 minute assessment, subjects were given access to an alcoholic drink in a "drinking test," and their drinking rate was recorded.

Results revealed that the false labeling appeared to be effective; few subjects even suspected that the drink labels were ever inaccurate.

Much recent psychological research has shown that manipulating subjects' expectations can significantly influence the behavioral,

Table 12
Experimental Design Used by Stockwell et al.

What the Drinks Actually Contained	What Subjects Were Told Their Drinks Contained	
	Alcohol	Tonic
Alcohol		
Tonic		

Source. Stockwell et al., 1982.

cognitive, or affective impact of a drug dose (e.g., Marlatt et al., 1973). Therefore it is unremarkable that labels significantly influenced performance in this study. For instance, moderately dependent subjects drank more quickly in the drinking test if they had been *told* the priming drink contained alcohol (regardless of actual drink content). In addition, the Told Alcohol condition resulted in both groups' having higher expectations of pleasure from drinking. Finally, 15 minutes after the priming drink, severely dependent alcoholics expected to have a greater desire to drink if they were in the Told Alcohol condition.

An especially interesting finding of this study was that the actual content of the drinks affected subjects' behavior and attitudes. For instance, when severely dependent subjects actually received alcohol (regardless of the label), they drank faster in the subsequent drinking test, even though alcohol content did not influence subjects' desire-to-drink ratings. Also, both groups reported greater pleasure in the postpriming ratings if they were in the Told Alcohol/ Received Alcohol condition as opposed to the Told Alcohol/Received Tonic condition.

Finally, severely dependent subjects displayed greater urge-response concordance than moderately dependent subjects. The speed of drinking of only the first group was positively related to their pulse level ($r = .24$) and their rated desire to drink ($r = .30$). Interestingly, hand tremor, a component of the alcohol withdrawal syndrome, was unrelated to speed of drinking in both groups.

Summary. Experimental investigations revealed that effective cues for eliciting urges in the laboratory are alcohol signals, such as bottles (Eriksen & Gotestam, 1984; Ludwig et al., 1977), and alcohol consumption per se. In fact, alcohol consumption appeared to be an extremely effective elicitor of urges (Ludwig et al., 1974). Research by Stockwell et al. (1982) showed that the effectiveness of the drug in eliciting urges or alcohol self-administration can be attributed in part to alcoholics' expectations about the effects of alcohol. However, the research of both Stockwell et al. and Ludwig et al. (1974) suggests that the motivational impact of the alcohol stimulus cannot be attributed to expectancy effects per se; the pharmacologic actions of alcohol appear to foster urges and increased self-administration.

A number of studies have reported evidence of psychophysiological correlates of urges or alcohol self-administration. Kaplan et al. (1985) found that the alcohol stimulus produced increases in HR and SCL among alcoholics, with SCL being related to desire-to-drink ratings. Ludwig and his associates found that work for alcohol, or urge-eliciting stimuli, was associated with psychophysiological changes such as heart rate increases and respiration increases (see Table 11). Theoretically, SCL and HR in the Kaplan study and the variables displayed in Table 11 may be urge-response components. Both Kaplan et al. and Ludwig et al. (1974, 1977) suggest that these urge correlates reflect conditioned withdrawal reactions. Thus their results could be viewed as consistent either with the withdrawal or with one of the homeostatic motivational models.

We find it difficult to attribute these urge-related responses to subclinical withdrawal syndromes. First, as noted previously, responses such as increased HR and SCL may reflect a variety of states such as fear, excitement, or anxiety, and we cannot at present discount the possible role of these states in the results obtained. Second, the observed psychophysiological responses do not share an unambiguous relationship with drug effects. For example, although increases HR and SCL as observed in the Kaplan study are often associated with withdrawal, they also may be direct effects of alcohol (e.g., Dafters & Anderson, 1982; Newlin, 1985; Peris & Cunningham, 1985). Similarly, Ludwig et al. (1974) note that such responses as increased heart rate, respiration, and hand tremor (see Table 11) are all components of the alcohol withdrawal syndrome. This led these authors to conclude that the low dose of alcohol in their study elicited withdrawal signs, including craving. However, there is copious evidence that increased heart rate and respiration both are also agonist effects of alcohol (e.g., Docter & Bernal, 1964;

Docter & Perkins, 1960). Therefore the increased heart and respiration rates observed in the low and high dose conditions might merely represent direct drug effects, a hypothesis buttressed by the fact that both effects increased as a positive function of dose. Another reason for suspecting that elevated heart rate and respiration do not represent conditioned withdrawal responses subserving urges is that they tended to occur only in response to the alcohol doses; that is, they were not elicited by the Label condition even though it prompted increased urge self-reports. Respiration was positively correlated with work for alcohol (Table 11), but this may have been due to the metabolic requirements of the operant task.

The two most consistent urge correlates in Ludwig's research were alpha-wave activity and decreased systolic blood pressure (Table 11). As Ludwig et al. (1974) recognized, the systolic blood pressure finding is discordant with their withdrawal hypothesis, because alcoholics are typically hypertensive during withdrawal (Feuerlein, 1980). Moreover, the relation between alpha-wave activity and urges is also at variance with a withdrawal model. Alcohol withdrawal has consistently been found to be associated with decreased alpha power/frequency (Begleiter & Platz, 1972; Kaplan et al. 1985; see also Zilm, Huszar, Carlen, Kaplan, & Wilkinson, 1980), whereas the direct effects of alcohol increase both the percentage of time in alpha and alpha-wave abundance (Begleiter & Platz, 1972). Here we have a response that has been related to work for alcohol, has been consistently prompted by urge elicitors, is clearly *not* a withdrawal sign, and clearly is a direct effect of alcohol. In sum, when the physiological responses associated with urges, or urge-eliciting stimuli, are closely examined, there is stronger evidence that such responses reflect agonist, as opposed to withdrawal or antagonist, drug effects.

Therefore considerable self-report and laboratory research shows that alcohol withdrawal is a potent elicitor of urges (e.g., Edwards et al., 1972; Rankin et al., 1982). However, there is little unimpeachable evidence implicating conditioned withdrawal, or alcohol-antagonistic responses, in urge elicitation.

Finally, the alcohol data show that concordance of urge responses is associated with two factors: severity of physical dependence (Kaplan et al., 1985; Stockwell et al., 1982) and adequacy or completeness of the eliciting stimuli (Ludwig et al., 1974, 1977). Apparently, as is the case with affects such as fear, the threshold for activating an affect response network is a function of a match between the stimuli present and prototypic stimulus information coded into the affect network (Lang, 1984). In theory, the closer the match between the stimuli impinging on the organism and prototypic stimulus information encoded, the more complete is network activation and the greater the concordance of affect-relevant responding. Because severity of dependence may be positively related to coherence of the affect response network, severely dependent alcoholics may show stronger, more concordant urge responses than less dependent alcoholics (Kaplan et al., 1985; Rankin et al., 1982). Similar relationships hold with respect to severity and concordance of fear across fear response measures (Rachman & Hodgson, 1974; Sartory, Rachman, & Grey, 1977).

OPIATES

Characterization of conditioned drug responses. O'Brien and his associates have attempted to show, in a variety of studies (O'Brien, 1976; O'Brien et al., 1981;Ternes et al., 1980), that opiate withdrawal signs can be conditioned to arbitrary environmental stimuli (e.g., O'Brien, Testa, O'Brien, Brady, & Wells, 1977) and that naturalistic stimuli (e.g., syringes), paired with direct drug effects or withdrawal, appear to elicit components of the opiate withdrawal syndrome (e.g., Ternes et al., 1980).

Although O'Brien's research has concentrated on the conditioning, or elicitation, of withdrawal symptoms/signs, he and his coworkers have also consistently obtained evidence of the elicitation of direct drug effects. For instance, in one study (O'Brien, Greenstein, Ternes, McLellan, & Grabowski, 1980) where drug-free opiate addicts were permitted to engage repeatedly in the opiate-injection ritual, patients reported that before injection they experienced an increase in drug craving and feelings of withdrawal. However, after injecting themselves (with saline solution or hydromorphine, the agonist effects of the latter being blocked by the long-acting antagonist, naltrexone), addicts typically reported experiencing weak opioid agonist effects (e.g., mild pleasure). Over several self-administration trials, these agonist effects decreased while opiate antagonist or withdrawal effects appeared to increase. The latter comprised dysphoria, cravings for opiates, and a fall in skin temperature.

In sum, the research of O'Brien and his colleagues suggests that opiate signals may elicit both drug agonist and withdrawal responses. Conditioned agonist and withdrawal responses were associated with positive and negative affective states, respectively.

Urge elicitation. Employing a within-subjects design, Sherman, Zinser, and Sideroff (1985) compared the effects of anxiety provoking (A), boring (B), and explicitly heroin-related (H) stimuli on self-ratings of mood, heroin craving, and physical withdrawal sickness in 35 male, drug-free heroin addicts. Each stimulus condition consisted of an eight-minute videotape followed by exposure to an object relevant to the stimulus condition for an additional minute. For example, for the H stimulus condition, following exposure to video scenes depicting heroin administration and its acute effects, addicts viewed actual drug-administration paraphernalia. Self-ratings on all measures were taken at baseline, that is, before the stimulus presentations, and immediately following each stimulus presentation. Additionally, a continuous measure of drug craving was obtained during stimulus presentations by having addicts turn a dial to indicate their degree of craving.

The authors found that, relative to baseline, all three stimulus conditions evoked negative affect. The A stimulus condition increased anxiety, tension, and arousal and decreased pleasure. The B stimulus condition decreased vigor and pleasure. These mood changes were congruent with the authors' characterization of the A and B stimulus conditions as anxiety-provoking and boring, respectively. In response to the H stimulus condition, addicts reported an increase in anxiety and tension and a decrease in pleasure and vigor. The only measure on which all three stimuli produced statistically significant changes in the same direction was pleasure—all evoked a decrease. The A stimulus evoked greater displeasure than the other two stimuli, which did not differ from one another.

Sherman et al. were interested in whether negative affect might be sufficient to elicit symptoms of craving and withdrawal in heroin addicts. Although previous studies suggested that heroin-related stimuli elicit craving (Sideroff & Jarvik, 1980) and withdrawal symptoms (e.g., O'Brien et al., 1980), such stimuli also had been shown to elicit negative affect (e.g., Teasdale, 1973). Because drug craving may be elicited by situations promoting negative affect (e.g., Marlatt & Gordon, 1980; Shiffman, 1982), Sherman et al. considered the possibility that negative affect per se might be sufficient to elicit urges (Ludwig & Wikler, 1974).

Self-ratings of drug craving obtained during the stimulus presentations with the dial measure and those obtained shortly afterward with a paper-and-pencil test were slightly discrepant. While both measures showed that the H stimulus significantly increased the degree of drug craving above baseline, the paper-and-pencil measure also showed a small but significant elevation in craving in response to the A and B stimuli. With regard to withdrawal sickness, addicts reported significant increases above baseline in response to all three stimulus conditions. As with the craving measures, significantly more withdrawal was reported to the H stimulus condition than either of the other two stimuli.

Clearly, drug-related affective responses were most congruent in the H stimulus condition, which produced the largest increases in drug craving and withdrawal sickness. However, the results indicate that nonpharmacologic stimuli that elicit negative affects may also elicit self-reports of urges and withdrawal responses.

Last, the authors assessed the relation between craving and withdrawal sickness. Although the H stimulus condition elicited increases in self-reports of craving and withdrawal sickness, increases in withdrawal sickness were not a necessary condition for the elicitation of craving: 44% (12/27) of the addicts reporting increased craving above baseline did not report increased withdrawal sickness. If we assume that the self-rating measure of withdrawal is valid, this result suggests that the elicitation of withdrawal sickness is not the only factor mediating drug craving. However, their results also suggest that increased withdrawal sickness may have been sufficient to elicit craving: 94% (15/16) of those addicts reporting increased withdrawal sickness also reported an increase in drug craving.

O'Brien's data suggest that urges or cravings for opiates are related to the presence of withdrawal signs and dysphoria and that when conditioned drug agonist effects occur, they are small in magnitude and transient. The data of Sherman and his colleagues also suggest that urges are typically characterized as negative affective states and that, though urges are not necessarily accompanied by reports of withdrawal symptoms, withdrawal is invariably accompanied by urges.

In contrast to the picture presented by O'Brien's data, Mirin, Meyer, McNamee, and McDougle (1976) found that strong craving was frequently associated with drug access, not withdrawal, and that it was often characterized by positive, rather than negative, affect. Mirin and his colleagues studied the self-administration of heroin by six addict volunteers. The authors found that simple knowledge of drug availability was sufficient to produce strong craving in subjects, and this was accompanied by excitement and anticipation. Moreover, the authors noted that actual injection of heroin, even at a high dose, had relatively little effect on craving levels. The authors noted that "it appears that regular heroin administration does little to alter craving for the drug" (p. 542). Finally, they reported that with long-term self-administration subjects gradually became increasingly dysphoric (anxious, belligerent), while maintaining high craving levels similar to those reported at the inception of self-administration.

Summary. O'Brien's data suggest that components of the opiate withdrawal syndrome can be elicited either by stimuli paired with opiate administration during the natural course of opiate addiction (e.g., Ternes et al., 1980) or by arbitrary stimuli that are contingent upon opiate administration (O'Brien et al., 1977). However, it is difficult to distinguish between some elements of the opiate withdrawal syndrome and the physiological concomitants of anger, anxiety, and frustration. Therefore it is not clear to what extent the conditioned effects obtained by O'Brien and his colleagues predominantly reflect withdrawal. In sum, it is likely but not certain that opiate signals, and cues paired with withdrawal, can elicit withdrawal signs in humans. It is also likely that conditioned withdrawal is associated with increased urges.

The data of Sherman et al. support the notion that elicited withdrawal responses lead to increased urges, since 94% of addicts reporting withdrawal sickness in response to the heroin film also reported increased urges. Moreover, Sherman's data suggested that, though negative affects per se may produce increased urges, the combination of negative affect plus a drug stimulus results in significantly greater urge elicitation.

Finally, data of Mirin et al. (1976) characterize urges as associated with positive affects that are sustained for relatively long periods during the course of addiction and that are associated with the receipt of a drug or the anticipation of drug receipt. A crucial distinction between the studies of O'Brien and Sherman, on the one hand, and that of Mirin on the other is that opiate addicts were abstinent in the former and the drug was actually available in the latter.

NICOTINE

Baker and Morse (1985) recently conducted two studies designed to gather data on the nature of nicotine urges: 60 subjects (40 smokers and 20 nonsmokers, with an equal number of males and females in each group) participated in the first study and 36 (24 smokers and 12 nonsmokers, all female) participated in the second. Both studies consisted of an orientation session and two psychophysiological assessment sessions. In the assessment sessions, subjects were presented with cigarette smoke (taking a puff without inhaling), water (2 ml squirted into the subject's mouth as a control stimulus), and noise blasts (105 dB, 2-second duration). Half the smokers were asked to abstain from smoking between the two assessment sessions, which were 24 hours apart. Carbon monoxide level (CO; in ppm) was assessed to ensure that withdrawing subjects had, in fact, not smoked. During each session, subjects filled out mood questionnaires (Mood Adjective Checklist [MACL]; Nowlis, 1965), Withdrawal Symptoms Questionnaires (WSQ; Shiffman & Jarvik, 1976), and ratings of their urge for a cigarette, the pleasantness of the stimulus presented, and their arousal level. (Multiple urge ratings were collected only in Experiment 2.) In addition, heart rate (HR; in interbeat intervals), skin conductance level (SCL), and respiration were monitored during baseline periods and during stimulus presentations.

Because cigarettes accelerate heart rate (at doses produced by smoking; Henningfield, 1984; Henningfield, Miyasato, Johnson, & Jasinski, 1981), because smokers become tolerant to this tachycardic effect (Benowitz, Peyton, Jones, & Rosenberg, 1982; Henningfield, 1984; Jones, Farrell, & Herning, 1978), and because withdrawal from cigarettes is characterized by bradycardia (Knapp, Bliss, & Wells, 1963), all three urge models reviewed earlier (the withdrawal, compensatory response, and opponent-process models) predict that self-reported urges should be positively related to bradycardia. Moreover, because cigarettes tend to produce positive affects in smokers, or to decrease negative affects (e.g., Henningfield, 1984; Jasinski, Johnson, & Henningfield, 1984), the three urge models suggest that urges should be positively related to negative-affect ratings (responses opposite to agonist drug effects) and negatively related to positive-affect ratings. Finally, both the compensatory response and the opponent-process models strongly predict that the sight and taste of cigarettes should yield a conditioned bradycardia among smokers, or at least less tachycardia than observed among nonsmokers, because smokers acquire tolerance to nicotine's tachycardic actions.

Cardiac data. Results of both studies showed that, compared with nonsmokers, smokers had higher baseline HRs and CO levels in Session 1. However, once smokers had withdrawn from cigarettes for 24 hours (i.e., the "withdrawn" smokers in Session 2), their CO and HR levels resembled those of nonsmokers.

Presenting cigarettes generated a complex cardiac waveform comprising both accelerative and decelerative components. Compared with nonsmokers, smokers showed significantly reduced acceleration and enhanced deceleration. Withdrawn smokers, though, showed greater acceleration to cigarettes than either continuing smokers or nonsmokers. The most parsimonious explanation for these findings is that the effect of smoking on phasic HR is largely a function of its effect on tonic HR. That is, smoking enhances baseline HR, and consistent with the law of initial values (Benjamin, 1963), this constrains the magnitude of further accelerations. The high baseline HR levels of smokers might also foster their relatively large HR decelerations. Thus, even though the phasic HR responses of smokers were superficially consistent with predictions of homeostatic models of addiction (e.g., smaller HR accelerations to cigarettes, indicating tolerance to tachycardia), it appears that these phasic HRs are not compensatory in nature but instead merely reflect the direct pharmacologic actions of nicotine on baseline HR.

Mood and craving. In addition to decreases in CO and HR levels, withdrawing smokers were distinct from continuing smokers in Session 2 in that they reported more negative affect and greater craving. For instance, withdrawing smokers had higher scores on the Aggression scale of the MACL, and lower scores on the Surgency (lively, witty, talkative), Elation, Social Affection, and Nonchalance scales. In addition to these differences, continuing smokers were higher than nonsmokers on the following MACL scales: Surgency, Elation, and Nonchalance. This suggests that the differences in MACL scores between continuing and withdrawing smokers might be as much a function of the mood-elevating effects of smoking as of the dysphoric effects of withdrawal. Finally, withdrawing smokers scored higher than continuing smokers on the Craving, Psychological Symptoms, and Appetite scales of the WSQ.

Of greatest relevance to the present chapter are data on the correlates of smoking urges among smokers. In Experiment 1, smokers' ratings after the noise blasts revealed that among withdrawing smokers (Session 2), urges were positively associated with MACL ratings of Aggression and Anxiety and negatively associated with Elation, Social Affection, and Surgency. Moreover, urge magnitude was positively correlated with phasic HR decreases in response to noise blasts ($r = .317, p < .10$). The correlation between mean HR decrease over noise blasts and Aggression was positive ($r = .435, p < .05$), whereas the correlation between mean HR decreases and Nonchalance was negative ($r = -.388, p < .05$).

In contrast to data yielded by withdrawing smokers, among continuing smokers phasic HR decreases tended to be *negatively* related to craving magnitude. Moreover, phasic HR showed a different pattern of mood correlates among continuing smokers. Phasic HR decreases were associated with decreased Sadness, while HR increases were associated with greater Social Affection and Nonchalance and reduced Aggression and Anxiety.

The data of Experiment 1 suggested that urge ratings made by continuing and withdrawing smokers were characterized by distinct mood and HR correlates. As opposed to the urges of continuing smokers, the urges of withdrawing smokers were associated with HR decreases and negative affect ratings.

The data of Experiment 2 show that, before withdrawal (data of Session 1), urge magnitude was consistently, negatively related to phasic HR decreases. An examination of mood data shows that when smokers were smoking (all smokers in Session 1, and continuing smokers in Session 2), urge ratings were inversely related to negative affect ratings and directly related to positive affect ratings. (Table 13 lists representative affect-urge relationships for Session 1, and Table 14 lists such relationships for continuing smokers in Session 2.)

Once smokers entered withdrawal (Session 2), a very different pattern of urge correlates emerged. As in Experiment 1, the urge ratings of withdrawing smokers were consistently, directly related to phasic HR decreases (decreases to cigarettes especially; see Table 15 for representative correlations), were positively related to negative affect ratings, and were negatively related to positive-affect ratings (see Table 16). When mood ratings were dichotomized into positive and negative categories (Social Affection, Elation, Surgency vs. Sadness, Aggression, and Anxiety) and correlated with urge ratings from the beginning and end of Session 2, we discovered that the correlations representing the two smoker groups were opposite in sign to one another on 75% of the rating occasions.

Table 13
Mood and Urge Correlations:
Experiment 2, Session 1, Urge-Rating Occasion

MACL Scale	Control	First H_2O	First Cigar- ette	Last Cigar- ette	Last H_2O	After Smoking
Aggression			−.387*	−.375*		
Anxiety			−.368*	−.355*		
Surgency	.435*	.379*	.374*			
Elation	.413*	.368*			.422*	
Fatigue				−.409*		
Sadness	−.405*	−.376*	−.563**	−.567**	−.599***	−.462*
Skepticism		−.353*	−.431*	−.569**	−.603***	−.345*

Source. Baker & Morse, 1985.

Note. **p < .05; **p < .01; ***p < .001; one-tailed tests.

Summary. The data just reviewed are amenable to various interpretations, and they require replication before their external validity can be gauged (e.g., relatively few smokers were studied; they were young and had smoked for relatively brief periods of time; they had been smoking daily for about six years). However, the data suggest that active and withdrawing smokers experience urges that possess distinct physiological and affective correlates. That is, there are distinct urge setting events for continuing versus withdrawing smokers. For example, the urges of withdrawing smokers were associated with negative affect, whereas the urges of continuing smokers were associated with positive affect. Thus the mood correlates of urges of withdrawing smokers were consistent with a homeostatic model, but those of continuing smokers were not. Moreover, very different phasic cardiac response patterns were associated with urges in the two smoker groups. Consistent with a homeostatic model, among withdrawing smokers urges were *positively* associated with bradycardic responses, while urges were *negatively* associated with bradycardia among continuing smokers. This difference in cardiac correlates of urges is somewhat difficult to interpret, however, because there was some evidence (not presented) that

Table 14
Mood Correlates of Urge Ratings: Experiment 2, Session 2, Continuing Smokers

---

Initial urges
Skepticism = −.57
Sadness = −.51

Urges in H_2O trials
Concentration= +.50
Social Affection = +.50
Aggression = −.43

Urges in cigarette trials
Aggression = −.55
Anxiety = −.48
Sadness = −.47
Social Affection = +.31

Urges after noise trials
Aggression = −.50
Fatigue = −.44
Sadness = −.51
Anxiety = −.43
Concentration = +.64
Social Affection = +.32

Source. Baker & Morse, 1985.

among continuing smokers the nature of HR-urge correlations differed as a function of initial HR level.

Overview. We believe these data on urges provide some support for homeostatic models, but we also believe they suggest that such models tell only half the story with respect to drug motivation in addiction. In short, such models appear to ignore the importance of the direct, appetitive effects of a drug in determining addictive drug use. We reach this conclusion not only because of our nicotine research, but also because of previously reviewed findings such as the following:

Table 15

Correlations Between Phasic Heart Rate Responses and Urge Rating Magnitudes Among Withdrawing Smokers: Experiment 2, Session 2

Heart Rate Response	Urge-Rating Occasion			
	Initial	First H_2O	First Cigarette	Session End
First cigarette block				
Foreperiod decrease		.564		.547
Foreperiod increase		−.540		−.500
Poststimulus decrease	.620	.607	.571	.790
Second cigarette block				
Foreperiod decrease		.672		
Poststimulus decrease	.567	.654	.541	
Poststimulus increase		.515		

Source. Baker & Morse, 1985.

1. Addicts report having urges while in positive affective states, states not compatible with withdrawal.
2. Some addicts report relapsing in positive affective states.
3. Among the most powerful elicitors of urges are the presence of the drug and information on drug availability.
4. High doses of the drug may result in little diminution of urge magnitude.
5. Urges may be associated with physiological responses isodirectional to drug agonist effects, not with responses characteristic of withdrawal.

Some of the findings could be incorporated into a withdrawal or homeostatic model, but such an incorporation would be tortuous and post hoc.

We shall now discuss a model of addiction motivation that we believe can account for the importance of direct drug effects in the motivation of compulsive drug use.

Table 16
Mood Correlates of Urge Ratings: Experiment 2, Session 2, Withdrawing
Smokers

Initial urges
Aggression = +.56
Anxiety = +.56
Sadness = +.32

Urges after H_2O trials
Anxiety = +.40
Fatigue = +.49
Elation = −.62
Sadness = +.34
Social Affection = −.46

Urges after noise trials
Anxiety = +.41
Surgency = −.76
Elation = −.58
Sadness = +.34
Social Affection = −.66

Source. Baker & Morse, 1985.

A Two-Affect Model of Urges and Drug Motivation

As noted earlier, we view urges as affects. Therefore, we believe
that it is appropriate to evaluate data on urges using a bioinforma-
tion-processing paradigm developed to model affective information
processing (see Lang, 1984; Leventhal & Mosbach, 1983). According
to this paradigm, affects are represented in neural networks that
comprise information on stimulus features or setting events, affect-
related responses, and anticipated consequences of potential response options. In short, the networks constitute propositionally
coded data structures that provide meaning or interpretations for
affect-relevant stimuli and responses. We believe that the particular
information coded into an urge network will vary with drug, drug-
history variables, and urge type. Also, the threshold of activation of
the network is reduced, and the network becomes more articulated

and extensive, as a function of associative and nonassociative learning produced by iterative drug exposures.

POSITIVE-AFFECT URGE NETWORK

We believe that there are at least two distinct, incompatible (mutually inhibitory) urge networks. We will discuss the positive-affect urge network first. Coded into this network is information on direct drug actions; especially, but not exclusively, information regarding the direct actions of drugs on drug-sensitive motivational systems. Also coded into the network is information on signals of drug availability, stimuli previously paired with the drug and nonpharmacologic appetitive stimuli, and cognitions concerning anticipated effects of the drug. We posit that a critical action of addictive drugs is the direct stimulation, at supraphysiological levels, of an appetitive motivational system; its activation results in increased behavioral and physiological activation, increased attention to dominant response options, a strong tendency to pursue previously rewarded operants, and positive affect. In essence, we believe that a principal motivational effect of drugs is to stimulate a "GO" motivational system that mediates pursuit of appetitive consequences; cf. Panksepp's foraging/expectancy system (Panksepp, 1982), Gray's behavioral activating system (Fowles, 1980; Gorenstein & Newman, 1980; Newman, Widom & Nathan, 1985), and Young's positive affective reaction model (Young, 1961). Compulsive drug use is a natural consequence of the operative characteristics of this motivational system (see Stewart, 1984; Stewart et al., 1984).

Although much evidence currently suggests that for opiates and stimulants this critical motivational system involves the dopaminergic ventral tegmental system (Bozarth & Wise, 1981; Stewart, 1984; van Wolfswinkel & van Ree, 1985), it is possible that different drugs activate different motivational systems (Wise & Bozarth, 1982; although see Clarke & Pert, 1985; Glessa, Muntoni, Collu, Vargin, & Mereu, 1985). It is not important that diverse addictive agents activate the same motivational system, but it *is* important that the motivational systems involved mediate the same effects; namely, positive affect and the pursuit of appetitive consequences (incentives).

Because a cardinal effect of activating the "GO" motivational system is positive affect, we label the urge network coding direct drug effects the "positive-affect network." The "GO" motivational system constitutes the "hardware" of the positive-affect network, while learned associations, expectations, and so forth, constitute its "software." The activation of the network is a function of a match between internal and external stimuli and the prototypic eliciting stimulus complex. In theory, when enough stimulus features of the prototype are matched by prevailing stimulus configurations, the motor or efferent elements of the network are processed en masse. In the case of positive-affect urges, the following factors would match the coded prototype: information that the drug is available, feedback of either the direct effects of the drug or the effects of non-pharmacologic activation of the motivational substrate, stimuli previously associated with the drug, and anticipated pleasurable consequences of drug use. As the stimulus configuration approaches the prototype, diverse measures of urge magnitude will reflect greater coherence of urge response systems. Greater coherence of urge responding might also be expected as the urge network becomes more highly articulated, for example, with increased drug experience. We do not believe that operant drug-seeking behaviors are coded into the urge network; that is, they are not necessarily processed as a consequence of network activation. However, drug seeking is more likely if a network is activated, and stimulus features of drug seeking may activate the network to the extent that they signal drug availability.

The most potent elicitor of positive-affect urges is no doubt the presence of the drug itself. Only the receipt of the drug per se can match the prototype. However, we believe the prototype can be activated nonpharmacologically, for example, by the induction of positive affect, by information that the drug is available.

One other important characteristic of the positive-affect urge network merits mention. Partial activation of the network reduces the threshold for additional activation or reactivation. Because the network is activated by appetitive stimuli and because activation of the relevant motivational system stimulates the pursuit of appetitive consequences, activation of the positive-affect network can produce a positive feedback loop as described in control systems theory. Thus the drug activates the urge network (and its underlying motivational substrate), and this activation decreases the threshold for reactivation of the network so that each drug dose increases the likelihood of drug craving, seeking, and self-administration.

Positive feedback loops are fairly common in nature; they are especially important in sustaining an organism's pursuit of appetitive, biologically significant goals. For example, sugar detectors on a fly's feet cause it to lower its proboscis. The fly then eats until nerves in its gut signal distention. If these nerves are severed, the fly will feed till it bursts (Dethier, 1976). This example illustrates an important attribute of naturally occurring positive feedback systems—an intrinsic braking mechanism that prevents unceasing pursuit of the goal object. It may be that the compulsive pursuit of addictive drugs is due, in part, to the absence of intrinsic braking mechanisms that inhibit appetitive motivational systems (i.e., there are no '"gut distention" nerves with respect to drug effects). Thus the drug user relies upon general toxic effects of a drug, to which he or she may become partially tolerant, to inhibit drug pursuit. Indeed, the gradual *development* of a braking mechanism (feedback regarding a negative effect of the drug) may be critical in many instances where drug use is reduced or ceases. Developing a physical symptom attributable to drug use is frequently cited by former smokers as a reason for quitting (Pechacek & Danaher, 1979). Also, it is well documented that persons who have recently experienced a drug-related disease are especially likely to reduce or cease substance use (Burt et al., 1974; Lichtenstein & Danaher, 1978). The slow development of drug-related disease or symptoms could explain why the proportion of drug users in the general population does not decline until the age of 50 or so (1976 Gallup Poll).

What drug effects are most likely to be critical in activating the positive-affect urge network? As would be expected, the euphoric and activating, or energizing, effects of drugs seem likely candidates. These drug effects are consistent with the expected effects from activating a "GO" motivational system, and activating effects are relatively unlikely to reflect substantial or complete tolerance (e.g., Mansky, 1978; Peris & Cunningham, 1985; Stewart et al., 1984). Thus they could conceivably influence drug self-administration and pursuit across iterative drug exposures.

How does our characterization of the positive-affect urge network map onto extant data? Below we list findings or observations consistent with the major features of the model we have outlined:

1. The model is consistent with the fact that "priming" doses of the drug increase rates of self-administration of that drug (e.g., Davis & Smith, 1976; Stewart, 1984; Stewart et al., 1984). We suggest the effectiveness of the drug stimulus in activating the positive-affect network, which results in increased pursuit of the appetitive drug stimulus, accounts for this effect. Drugs with strong sedative effects at high doses, such as alcohol, may produce greater urge activation at low doses than at high doses (e.g., Ludwig et al, 1974).

The same may be true for opiates, since these drugs also yield depressant-sedative effects at high doses (e.g., Baker & Tiffany, 1985).

2. The positive feedback properties of the positive-affect urge network can also account for the high rate of readdiction once an abstinent addict uses a drug (e.g., Brandon et al., 1985; Marlatt & Gordon, 1980) and is consistent with addict folklore that any drug use greatly increases the likelihood of compulsive drug use (Anonymous, 1939).

3. That the induction of positive affect can activate the positive-affect urge network can explain why relapse often occurs in positive affective states (e.g., Brandon et al., 1985). Moreover, eating or drinking is often associated with relapse (Brandon et al., 1985) or with relapse crises characterized by positive affect (Shiffman, 1982) suggest that the positive affect instated by nonpharmacologic appetitive stimuli can prime the positive-affect urge network. This hypothesis is consistent with the finding that training to respond for a water reward facilitates later operant responding for morphine among previously dependent rats (Weeks & Collins, 1986). Cross-priming between pharmacologic and nonpharmacologic appetitive stimuli is also borne out by recent findings that heroin self-administration increases self-administration of rewarding brain stimulation by rats (Gerber, Bozarth, Spindler, & Wise, 1985). Also, opiate administration stimulates food seeking and consumption in rats (Gosnell, Levine, & Morley, 1986; Woods & Leibowitz, 1985), an effect perhaps partly due to the activating effects of opiates on dopaminergic systems resulting in lowered thresholds for the pursuit of incentive stimuli and increased nonregulatory ingestive behaviors (Mittleman, Castañeda, Robinson, & Valenstein, 1986; White, 1986).

4. The model is consistent with the facts that both positive affect and signals of drug availability serve as potent elicitors of urges (Baker & Morse, 1985; McAuliffe, Rohman, Feldman, & Launer, 1985) and that negative affects can be associated with decreased urge magnitude (Baker & Morse, 1985). We believe the latter occurs because strong activation of one network inhibits activation of the other network. To the extent that the negative-affect network is activated, it will inhibit activation of the positive-affect network. This incompatibility between positive- and negative-affect urge systems is, we believe, due to an intrinsic feature of the processing of motivational/affective information. Owing to the functional properties of our nervous systems—our motivational system "hardware"—we are incapable of processing simultaneously intense positive and

negative emotional information (e.g., Diener & Ivan-Nejad, 1986). Because direct drug effects are potent activators of the positive-affect network, negative-affect responses would be more likely to reduce urge magnitude during periods of intoxication than during periods of withdrawal or sobriety.

5. In general, a dose of one addictive drug serves to prime self-administration of a second addictive drug; this occurs both in animals (Pfeffer & Samson, 1985) and in humans (Henningfield, 1984). Our model holds that such cross-drug priming should occur at the same extent as the priming drug activates the positive-affect urge network. This is at least in part a function of the extent to which the priming drug induces positive affect. Consistent with this, Henningfield (1984) has reported that how much priming doses of a variety of drugs enhance smoking rates is a function of how much the priming drug enhances the subject's score on the MBG scale of the Addiction Research Center Inventory (a scale thought to tap a sense of pleasure, or well-being, often labeled the "Euphoria" scale).

6. Because an addictive drug activates a positive feedback loop, a drug dose should produce only a transitory diminution in urge magnitude. This is consistent with findings in both the opiate and the smoking research literature (Baker & Morse, 1985; Mirin et al., 1976). A transitory diminution in urge magnitude following drug ingestion might be due to the aversive, toxic effects of a high drug dose or to its sedative-depressant effects.

7. According to our model, the positive-affect network is activated by direct drug effects. Therefore it is not surprising that urges, especially among intoxicated subjects, may be positively related to associatively or nonassociatively elicited physiological, agonist drug actions (Baker & Morse, 1985; Ludwig et al., 1974).

8. Data from various laboratories show that as the number, or type, of cues of drug presence increases, subjects display stronger and more coherent urge-response patterns (Ludwig et al., 1974, 1977; Stockwell et al, 1982). Also, there is evidence that coherence of urge responding increases with severity or duration of the addiction (Kaplan et al., 1985). We attribute these findings to the approximation of stimuli to the network prototype and to the tighter associative organization of the affect network that occurs through repeated learning opportunities, respectively.

NEGATIVE-AFFECT URGE NETWORK

We expect that the positive-affect urge network may be largely responsible for the compulsive use of a drug during a protracted course of self-administration. However, there is little doubt that as dependence develops the emergence of withdrawal symptoms and signs can yield drug urges (Baker & Morse, 1985; Rankin et al., 1982; Sherman et al., 1985). We believe that withdrawal-based urges occur owing to the activation of a neural network into which is coded the following sort of information: information on withdrawal-associated physiological and behavioral responses; cues previously associated with withdrawal; expectations regarding the course of withdrawal; the outcomes of various potential response options; stimuli signaling drug unavailability; nonpharmacologic stimuli that elicit negative affect; and so forth. Principal among the phenomenological characteristics of associatively or nonassociatively primed activation of the withdrawal network is negative affect (anxiety, anger, depression). Hence we have labeled the withdrawal-based urge network a "negative-affect urge network."

While the prototypical stimulus configuration that can activate the negative-affect network is produced by withdrawal, we believe it can also be activated via other routes; for example, the conjoint occurrence of negative affect with drug cues, or the exposure to nonpharmacologic aversive stimuli (e.g., Sherman et al., 1985). In Baker and Morse (1985), urges reported following aversive noise blasts, even by subjects actively smoking, tended to be associated with cardiac deceleration and negative affect. This suggests that a sufficiently potent stressor can induce negative-affect urges even among intoxicated individuals.

Potent activation of the positive-affect network suppresses activation of the negative-affect network and reduces coherence among urge response systems. This is consistent with the fact that positive affect was negatively related to urge magnitude among withdrawing smokers (Baker & Morse, 1985).

Although our model holds that strong negative-affect urges should be accompanied by withdrawal responses, it does not demand that withdrawal responses associated with urge self-report be compensatory for initial drug effects. For example, heart rate increases may be associated with negative-affect urges among alcoholics, even though tachycardia is a direct effect of alcohol. Presumably, heart rate increases might be associated with positive- or negative-affect alcohol urges, depending on the nature of concomitant stimuli (e.g., positive-affect responding, withdrawal cues).

As is the case with positive-affect urges, we presume that the magnitude and coherence of negative-affect urge responding increases with duration and level (severity) of dependence. Although few data support this directly, there are some suggestive findings. For instance, severely dependent alcoholics are more likely to report a desire to drink in response to physical withdrawal symptoms than are less dependent alcoholics (Rankin et al., 1982). With increasing drug exposure, the threshold for activation of the negative-affect urge network may decrease relative to that for the positive-affect network. This may be a natural function of the lengthy course of development of maximum dependence/withdrawal. This might account for why long-term smokers reported the greatest urge increases in response to a stressor in Experiment 2 of the Baker and Morse studies and why these stress-induced urges were associated with a withdrawal-like psychophysiological response (bradycardia). Younger smokers, with shorter smoking histories, reported experiencing the greatest increases in urges over cigarette exposures, as opposed to stress exposures, and such increases were associated with drug-isodirectional physiological responses (tachycardia) and high pleasure ratings of cigarettes.

Why does activation of the negative-affect urge network actually increase the probability of drug self-administration and pursuit? In the case of positive-affect urges, this is accounted for by the consequences of activating the "GO" motivational system. With respect to negative-affect urges, we make the same assumptions previously made by incentive motivation theorists: "deprivation increases the incentive value of the goal object" (Bolles, 1967, p. 349). In simple terms, positive affective state yielded by the drug becomes increasingly desirable as the drug addict's negative affective state increases, either because of withdrawal or because of nonpharmacologic aversive events. We presume that coded into the negative-affect network is information concerning the probable consequences of drug use—expectations of desirable drug effects. We believe that this incentive model of negative-affect urges is consistent with increased urge magnitude and drug self-administration that occurs as a positive function of withdrawal interval magnitude (e.g., Baker & Morse, 1985; Henningfield & Griffiths, 1979; Wikler, 1953) and the frequency with which relapse occurs in negative affective states (Marlatt & Gordon, 1980).

Our model suggests reasons why urges may have traditionally

been associated with negative-affect and withdrawal states (e.g., Solomon, 1977). First, most studies have used either abstinent or withdrawing addicts as subjects. Since the drug stimulus is part of the prototypical eliciting context of positive affect urges, it is possible that for the abstinent or withdrawing addict there is a reduced likelihood of positive-affect urge elicitation. Second, many studies have used very chronic addicts as subjects. This may also reduce the likelihood of observing positive-affect urges or positive-affect-induced drug self-administration. Where subjects with less chronic addiction histories have been used, it is frequently found that urges and drug self-administration are associated with positive affect (e.g., Baker & Morse, 1985; Sobell, 1985).

The positive/negative-affect urge model we have outlined is consistent with independent evidence that nonpharmacologic appetitive stimuli activate the same neural systems as are directly activated by opiates, and that nonpharmacologic aversive stimuli activate the same neural systems activated in withdrawal (Panksepp, Siviy, & Normansell, 1985). Such evidence is important because it affords insight into the nature of the intrinsic motivational systems opportunistically activated by the drug and withdrawal, and into the nature of urge-associated affective states. In an impressive series of studies, Panksepp and his colleagues have shown that young animals suffering from separation distress are exquisitely sensitive to opiates; for example, doses as low as 0.5 mg/kg were effective in completely eliminating separation-induced distress vocalizations (Panksepp, Herman, Connor, Bishop, & Scott, 1978). (Nicotine also is effective in reducing separation-induced vocalization; Panksepp et al., 1985). Moreover, there is some interchangability between morphine and an appetitive social cue. Young rats were trained to run a T-maze to return to an antechamber of their home environment. Later the rats underwent extinction of this response; neither arm of the maze led to the home environment. Subjects that received morphine during extinction never showed any decrement in the learned response, whereas rats that received naloxone showed accelerated extinction (DeEskinazi, Panksepp, 1979; Panksepp & DeEskinazi, 1980). Panksepp et al. (1985, p. 20) note that one interpretation of these results is that opiate "prevents the animal from appreciating the affective consequences of social loss."

A link between opiate withdrawal and negative-affect response systems is indicated by data showing that naloxone significantly increases distress behaviors of separated animals, clonidine reduces both separation distress and withdrawal, and opiate withdrawal potentiates separation-induced distress (Panksepp et al., 1985). Moreover, Panksepp notes response similarities between separation-induced distress and depression and the opiate-withdrawal syndrome.

Panksepp suggests his research shows that opioid neural systems mediate social rewards and that opiate receptor blockade or withdrawal stimulates a negative affective state, among the phenomenological manifestations of which is social need.

We believe that Panksepp's model of the opioid mediation of social reward and separation distress is analogous to our two-affect model of drug urges. The reason for this similarity should be clear—in our model and in Panksepp's, the same or similar motivational systems are being activated, in the former by drugs, in the latter by social stimuli. We assume that all addictive drugs activate motivational systems with the same or similar properties.

PREDICTIONS

The proposed model of urges yields several predictions that are vulnerable to experimental analysis:

1. Strong negative affective stimuli of a nonpharmacologic nature should elicit withdrawal-like responses (e.g., psychophysiological changes) in abstinent addicts because they activate the negative-affect network. Conversely, appetitive, nonpharmacologic stimuli should elicit drug-agonist responses in abstinent addicts because they activate the positive-affect urge network. In short, addicts should show different responses than nonaddicts to nonpharmacologic, hedonically valenced stimuli as a function of drug agonist and withdrawal responses to which they have been exposed. However, activation of the two urge networks should be greatest when pharmacologic stimuli are present.

2. Relapse prevention programs will be successful to the extent that they reduce dysphoric mood swings and inculcate in subjects alternative strategies for dealing with dysphoric mood states.

3. Urge magnitude among active drug users should be reduced by mild stressors that reduce addicts' positive affective states. Conversely, appetitive stimuli should temporarily reduce urge magnitude among withdrawing addicts.

Summary

Traditionally, theories of addiction have stressed that drug urges are characterized by dysphoria, occur in response to decreasing levels of drug or drug effect, and are associated with withdrawal symptoms/signs or drug-antagonistic responses arising from a homeostatic mechanism. However, recent research has shown that urges, drug self-administration, and relapse all occur concomitant with both positive and negative affect, rising and falling levels of drug, and with drug-agonistic responses, as well as antagonistic/withdrawal responses.

In keeping with recent theorizing about motivation and emotions, we believe that affective responding provides a readout of the motivational status of an organism (e.g., Buck, 1985). We conceive of urges as affects, whose activation mediates drug pursuit and self-administration. Moreover, we believe that affects are represented in neural networks comprising information on affect-relevant stimuli, responses, and meaning/expectancy. We believe that there are two types of urge networks. One, a "positive-affect" network, is activated, associatively and nonassociatively, by appetitive stimuli, especially appetitive drug actions that activate "GO" motivational incentive systems. Activation of this network is characterized by positive affect, drug isodirectional responding, attentional focus on a dominant response, and enhanced pursuit of appetitive stimuli — especially the drug. The operating characteristics of the positive-affect network, and the associated motivational systems, result in a drug's instating a positive feedback loop. Appetitive drug actions increase the likelihood of the pursuit of appetitive stimuli, and additional drug constitutes a prepotent candidate from among the available appetitive stimuli. This positive feedback loop may account in part for cardinal features of addiction: for example, the great relapse likelihood once any drug is sampled, the attainment of very high blood levels of a drug, and the pursuit of adjunctive appetitive stimuli while using a drug.

The second type of urge network we have labeled a "negative-affect" network, and we believe it is activated, associatively and nonassociatively, by inappetitive stimuli or consequences (punishment, signals of punishment, frustrating lack of reward, etc.) and by withdrawal and signals of withdrawal (e.g., drug cues, which during the course of addiction are associated with both direct drug effects and withdrawal). Activation of the network is characterized by withdrawal symptoms and signs, negative affect, and drug seeking. We believe that drug seeking occurs because the induction of negative affect through network activation enhances the incentive value of a drug.

Moreover, in this chapter we attempt to characterize the general operating principles of affect information processing (Lang, 1984; Leventhal & Mosbach, 1983) as they relate to urge-network development and activation. For example, we note that urge-network activation may yield more coherent response patterns with increases in matches between internal and external stimulus configurations and stimulus information coded into the network.

Finally, there are relatively few data to support some elements of the proposed model (e.g., aversive stimuli per se can induce "withdrawal-like" urges). Also, we recognize that we have largely ignored data that point to the very different characteristics of different drugs—for example, different sites of actions and different types of direct appetitive effects. Because some elements of our model are based primarily on research with one type of drug, it lacks a desirable level of external validity. Our model is not intended to be a complete model of addiction. For example, it cannot account for why some drug users do not become addicted. Despite these caveats, we believe it is consistent with a great many experimental data and empirical observations on addictions. Moreover, the theoretical perspective on urges that we have described, and its associated research strategies, may be useful in revealing where our working model of urges is wrong or lacking.

REFERENCES

Anonymous. (1939). *Alcoholics Anonymous*. New York: Works.
Baker, T. B., & Morse, E. (1985). *The urge as affect*. Paper presented at the convention of the Association for the Advancement of Behavior Therapy, Houston.
Baker, T. B., & Tiffany, S. T. (1985). Morphine tolerance as habituation. *Psychological Review, 92*, 78–108.
Begleiter, H., & Platz, A. (1972). The effects of alcohol on the central nervous system in humans. In B. Kissin & H. Begleiter (Eds.), *The biology of alcoholism: Physiology and behavior* (Vol. 2). New York: Plenum.
Benjamin, L. S. (1963). Statistical treatment of the Law of Initial Values (LIV) in autonomic research: A review and recommendation. *Psychosomatic Medicine, 25*, 556–566.
Benowitz, N. L., Peyton, J., Jones. R. T., & Rosenberg, J. (1982). Interindivi-

dual variability in the metabolism and cardiovascular effects of nicotine in man. *Journal of Pharmacology and Experimental Therapeutics, 221,* 368–372.

Bolles, R. C. (1967). *Theory of motivation.* New York: Harper and Row.

Bozarth, M. A., & Wise, R. A. (1981). Intracranial self-administration of morphine into the ventral tegmental area in rats. *Life Sciences, 28,* 551–555.

Brandon, T. H., Tiffany, S. T., & Baker, T. B. (1986). The process of smoking relapse. In F. Tims & C. Leukefeld (Eds.), *Relapse and recovery in drug abuse.* National Institute of Drug Abuse Research Monograph. Washington, DC: U.S. Government Printing Office.

Buck, R. (1985). Prime theory: An integrated view of motivation and emotion. *Psychological Review, 92,* 389–413.

Burt, A., Illingworth, D., Shaw, T. R. D., Thornley, P., White, P., & Turner, R. (1974). Stopping smoking after myocardial infarction. *Lancet, 1,* 304–306.

Clarke, P. B. S., & Pert, A. (1985). Autoradiographic evidence of nicotine receptors in nigrostriatal and mesolimbic dopaminergic neurons. *Brain Research, 348,* 355–358.

Dafters, R., & Anderson, G. (1982). Conditioned tolerance to the tachycardic effect of ethanol in humans. *Psychopharmacology, 78,* 365–367.

Davis, W. M., & Smith, S. G. (1976). Role of conditioned reinforcers in the initiation and extinction of drug seeking behavior. *Pavlovian Journal of Biological Science, 11,* 222–236.

Deardorff, C., Melges, S., Hoyt, C., & Savage, D. (1975). Situations related to drinking alcohol. *Journal on Alcohol, 36,* 1184–1195.

DeEskinazi, F., & Panksepp, J. (1979). Opiates lead to persistence of spatial habits with social rewards. *Society for Neuroscience Abstracts, 5,* 315.

Dethier, V. G. (1976). *The hungry fly.* Cambridge: Harvard University Press.

Diener, E., & Iran-Nejad, A. (1986). The relationship in experience between various types of affect. *Journal of Personality and Social Psychology, 50,* 1031–1038.

Docter, R. F., & Bernal, M. E. (1964). Immediate and prolonged psychophysiological effects of sustained alcohol intake in alcoholics. *Quarterly Journal of Studies in Alcohol, 25,* 438.

Docter, R. F., & Perkins, R. B. (1960). The effects of ethyl alcohol on autonomic and muscular responses in humans. *Quarterly Journal of Studies on Alcohol, 22,* 374.

Domjan, M., & Gregg, B. (1977). Long-delay backward taste-aversion conditioning with lithium. *Physiology and Behavior, 18,* 59–62.

Edwards, G., Hensman, C., Chandler, J., & Peto, G. (1972). Motivation for drinking among men: Survey of a London suburb. *Psychological Medicine, 3,* 260–271.

Eriksen, L., & Gotestam, K. G. (1984). Conditioned abstinence in alcoholics: A controlled experiment. *International Journal of the Addictions, 19,* 287–294.

Feuerlein, W. (1980). Alcohol withdrawal syndromes. In M. Sandler (Ed.), *Psychopharmacology of alcohol.* New York: Raven Press.

Fowles, D. C. (1980). The three arousal model: Implications of Gray's two-factor learning theory for heart rate, electrodermal activity, and psychopathy. *Psychophysiology, 17,* 87–104.

Gerber, G. J., Bozarth, M. A., Spindler, J. E., & Wise, R. A. (1985). Concurrent heroin self-administration and intracranial self-stimulation in rats. *Pharmacology, Biochemistry and Behavior, 23,* 837–842.

Glessa, G. L., Muntoni, F., Collu, M., Vargin, L., & Mereu, G. (1985). Low doses of ethanol activate dopaminergic neurons in the ventral tegmental area. *Brain Research, 348,* 201.

Gorenstein, E. E. & Newman, J. P. (1980). Disinhibitory psychopathology: A new perspective and a model for research. *Psychological Review, 87,* 301–315.

Gosnell, B. A., Levine, A. S., & Morley, J. E. (1986). The stimulation of food intake by selective agonists of mu, kappa, and delta opioid receptors. *Life Sciences, 38,* 1085–1088.

Gottheil, E., Corbett, L. O., Grasberger, J. C., & Cornelison, F. S. (1972). Fixed interval drinking decisions. 1. A research and treatment model. *Quarterly Journal of Studies on Alcohol, 33,* 311–324.

Green, D. E. (1977). Psychological factors in smoking. In M. E. Jarvik (Ed.), *Research on smoking behavior.* National Institute of Drug Abuse Research Monograph 17. Washington, DC: U.S. Government Printing Office.

Gross, M. M., & Lewis, E. (1973). Observations on the prevalence of the signs and symptoms associated with withdrawal during continuous observation of experimental intoxication and withdrawal in humans. In M. M. Gross (Ed.), *Alcohol intoxication and withdrawal: Experimental studies.* Advances in Experimental Medicine and Biology, Vol. 35. New York: Plenum.

Gross, M. M., Lewis, E., & Hastey, J. (1974). Acute alcohol withdrawal syndrome. In B. Kissin & H. Begleiter (Eds.), *The biology of alcoholism: Clinical pathology* (Vol. 3). New York: Plenum.

Haertzen, C. A., & Hooks, N. T. (1969). Changes in personality and subjective experience associated with the chronic administration and withdrawal of opiates. *Journal of Nervous and Mental Disease, 148,* 606–614.

Henningfield, J. E. (1984). Behavioral pharmacology of cigarette smoking. In T. Thompson, P. B. Dews, & J. E. Barrett (Eds.), *Advances in behavioral pharmacology* (Vol. 4). New York: Academic Press.

Henningfield, J. E., & Griffiths, R. R. (1979). A preparation for the experimental analysis of human cigarette smoking behavior. *Behavioral Research Methods and Instrumentation, 11,* 538–544.

Henningfield, J. E., Miyasato, K., Johnson, R. E., & Jasinski, D. R. (1981). Nicotine: Behavioral and physiological effects and self-administration in humans. *Pharmacology, Biochemistry and Behavior, 15,* 830.

Hodgson, R. J., Rankin, H. J., & Stockwell, T. R. (1979). Alcohol dependence and the priming effect. *Behaviour Research and Therapy, 17,* 379–387.

Hore, B. D. (1971). Factors in alcoholic relapse. *British Journal of the Addictions, 66,* 89–96.

Ikard, F. F., Geen, D. E., & Horn, D. (1969). A scale to differentiate between types of smoking as related to the management of affect. *International Journal of the Addictions, 4,* 649–659.

Jasinski, D. R., Johnson, R. E., & Henningfield, J. E. (1984). Abuse liability assessment in human subjects. *Trends in Pharmacological Sciences, 5,* 196–200.

Jellinek, E. M. (1960). *The disease concept of alcoholism.* Highland Park, NJ: Hillhouse Press.

Jones, R. T., Farrell, T. R., & Herning, R. I. (1978). Tobacco smoking and tolerance. In N. A. Krasnegor (Ed.), *Self-administration of abused substances: Methods for study.* National Institute of Drug Abuse Research Monograph 20. Washington, DC: U.S. Government Printing Office.

Kaplan, R. F., Cooney, N. L., Baker, L. H., Gillespie, R. A., Meyer, R. E., & Pomerleau, O. F. (1985). Reactivity to alcohol-related cues: Physiological and subjective responses in alcoholics and nonproblem drinkers. *Journal of Studies on Alcohol, 46,* 267–272.

Kaplan, R. F., Meyer, R. E., & Stroebel, C. F. (1983). Alcohol dependence and responsivity to an ethanol stimulus as predictors of alcohol consumption. *British Journal of the Addictions, 78,* 259–267.

Knapp, P. H., Bliss, C. M., & Wells, H. (1963). Addictive aspects in heavy cigarette smoking. *American Journal of Psychiatry, 119,* 966–972.

Kozlowski, L. T. (1979). Psychosocial influences on cigarette smoking. In N. A. Krasnegor (Ed.), *The behavioral aspects of smoking.* National Institute of Drug Abuse Research Monograph 26. Washington, DC: U.S Government Printing Office.

Lang, P. J. (1984). Cognition in emotion: Concept and action. In C. Izard, J. Kagan, & R. B. Zajonc (Eds.), *Emotions, cognition, and behavior.* New York: Cambridge University Press.

Lang, P. J., Levin, D. N., Miller, G. A., & Kozak, M. J. (1983). Fear behavior, fear imagery, and the psychophysiology of emotion: The problem of affective response integration. *Journal of Abnormal Psychology, 92,* 276–306.

Le, A. D., Poulos, C. X., & Cappell, H. (1979). Conditioned tolerance to the hypothermic effect of ethyl alcohol. *Science, 206*, 1109–1110.

Leventhal, H., & Avis, N. (1976). Pleasure, addiction, and habit: Factors in verbal report or factors in smoking behavior? *Journal of Abnormal Psychology, 85*, 478–488.

Leventhal, H., & Mosbach, P. (1983). A perceptual-motor theory of emotion. In J. T. Cacioppo & R. Petty (Eds.), *Social psychophysiology: A sourcebook*. New York: Guilford.

Lichtenstein, E., & Danaher, B. G. (1978). What can the physician do to assist the patient to stop smoking? In R. E. Brashear & M. L. Rhodes (Eds.), *Chronic obstructive lung disease: Clinical treatment and management*. St. Louis: Moseley

Ludwig, A. M., Cain, R. B., Wikler, A., Taylor, R. M., & Bendfeldt, F. (1977). Physiologic and situational determinants of drinking behavior. In M. M. Gross (Ed.), *Alcohol intoxication and withdrawal*. Studies in alcohol dependence, Vol. 111b. New York: Plenum.

Ludwig, A. M., & Stark, L. H. (1974). Alcohol craving: Subjective and situational aspects. *Quarterly Journal of Studies on Alcohol, 35*, 899–905.

Ludwig, A. M., & Wikler, A. (1974). "Craving" and relapse to drink. *Quarterly Journal of Studies on Alcohol, 35*, 108–130.

Ludwig, A. M., Wikler, A., & Stark, L. H. (1974). The first drink: Psychobiological aspects of craving. *Archives of General Psychiatry, 30*, 539–547.

Majchrowicz, E. & Hunt, W. A. (1976). Temporal relationship of the induction of tolerance and physical dependence after continuous intoxication with maximum tolerable doses of ethanol in rats. *Psychopharmacology, 50*, 107–112.

Mansky, P. A. (1978). Opiates: Human psychopharmacology. In L. L. Iversen, S. D. Iversen, & S. H. Snyder (Eds.), *Handbook of psychopharmacology* (Vol. 12). New York: Plenum.

Marlatt, G. A. (1978). Craving for alcohol, loss of control, and relapse: A cognitive-behavioral analysis. In P. E. Nathan, G. A. Marlatt, & T. Loberg (Eds.), *Alcoholism: New directions in behavioral research and treatment*. New York: Plenum.

Marlatt, G. A., Demming, B., & Reid, J. B. (1973). Loss of control drinking in alcoholics: An experimental analogue. *Journal of Abnormal Psychology, 81*, 233–241.

Marlatt, G. A., & Gordon, J. R. (1980). Determinants of relapse: Implications for the maintenance of behavior change. In P. Davidson & S. Davidson (Eds.), *Behavioral medicine: Changing health lifestyles*. New York: Brunner/Mazel.

McAuliffe, W. E., Feldman, B., Friedman, R., Lannes, E., Mahoney, C., Magnuson, E., Santangelo, S., & Ward, W. (1986). Explaining relapse to opiate addiction following completion of treatment. In F. Tims & C.

Leukefeld (Eds.), *Relapse and recovery in drug abuse*. National Institute of Drug Abuse Research Monograph. Washington, DC: U.S. Government Printing Office.

McAuliffe, W. E., & Gordon, R. A. (1974). A test of Lindesmith's theory of addiction: The frequency of euphoria among long-term addicts. *American Journal of Sociology, 79*, 795–840.

McAuliffe, W. E., Rohman, M., Feldman, B., & Launer, E. K. (1985). The role of euphoric effects in the opiate addictions of heroin addicts, medical patients and impaired health professionals. *Journal of Drug Issues*, Spring, 203–224.

Mello, N. K. (1972). Behavioral studies of alcoholism. In B. Kissin & H. Begleiter (Eds.), *Biology of alcoholism* (Vol. 2, pp. 219–291). New York: Plenum.

Mello, N. K., & Mendelson, J. H. (1970). Experimentally induced intoxication in alcoholics: A comparison between programmed and spontaneous drinking. *Journal of Pharmacology and Experimental Therapeutics, 173*, 101–116.

Mello, N. K., & Mendelson, J. H. (1972). Drinking patterns during work-contingent and non-contingent alcohol acquisition. *Psychosomatic Medicine, 34*, 139–164.

Mirin, S. M., Meyer, R. E., McNamee, H. B., & McDougle, M. (1976). Psychopathology, craving, and mood during heroin acquisition: An experimental study. *International Journal of the Addictions, 11*, 525–544.

Mittleman, G., Castañeda, E., Robinson, T. E., & Valenstein, E. (1986). The propensity for nonregulatory ingestive behavior is related to differences in dopamine systems: Behavioral and biochemical evidence. *Behavioral Neuroscience, 100*, 217–220.

Newlin, D. B. (1985). Human conditioned compensatory response to alcohol cues: Initial evidence. *Alcohol, 2*, 507–509.

Newlin, D. B. (1986a). Conditioned compensatory response to alcohol placebo in humans. *Psychopharmacology, 88*, 247–251.

Newlin, D. B. (1985b). The antagonistic placebo response to alcohol cues. *Alcoholism: Clinical and Experimental Research, 9*, 411–416.

Newman, J. P., Widom, C. S., & Nathan, S. (1985). Passive avoidance in syndromes of disinhibition: Psychopathy and extraversion. *Journal of Personality and Social Psychology, 48*, 1316–1327.

Nowlis, V. (1965). Research with the mood adjective checklist. In S. S. Tomkins & C. E. Izard (Eds.), *Affect, cognition and personality*. New York: Springer.

O'Brien, C. P. (1976). Experimental analysis of conditioning factors in human narcotic addiction. *Pharmacological Reviews, 27*, 533–543.

O'Brien, C. P., Greenstein, R., Ternes, J., McLellan, A. T., & Grabowski, J.

(1980). Unreinforced self-injections: Effects on rituals and outcome in heroin addicts. In L. S. Harris (Ed.), *Problems of drug dependence, 1979*, National Institute of Drug Abuse Research Monograph 27. Washington, DC: U.S. Government Printing Office.

O'Brien, C. P., Ternes, J. W., Grabowski, J., & Ehrman, R. (1981). Classically conditioned phenomena in humn opiate addiction. In T. Thompson & C. E. Johnson (Eds.), *Behavioral pharmacology of human opiate addiction*. National Institute of Drug Abuse Research Monograph 37. Washington, DC: U.S. Government Printing Office.

O'Brien, C. P., Testa, T., O'Brien, T. J., Brady, J. P., & Wells, B. (1977). Conditioned narcotic withdrawal of humans. *Science, 195*, 1000–1002.

Panksepp, J. (1982). Toward a general psychobiological theory of emotions. *Behavioral Brain Science, 5*, 407–467.

Panksepp, J., & DeEskinazi, F. G. (1980). Opiates and homing. *Journal of Comparative and Physiological Psychology, 94*, 650–663.

Panksepp, J., Herman, B., Connor, R., Bishop, P., & Scott, J. P. (1978). The biology of social attachments: Opiates alleviate separation distress. *Biological Psychiatry, 13*, 607–618.

Panksepp, J., Siviy, S. M., & Normansell, L. A. (1985). Brain opioids and social emotions. In M. Reite & T. Field (Eds.), *The psychology of attachment and separation*. New York: Academic Press.

Pechacek, T. F., & Danaher, B. G. (1979). How and why people quit smoking: A cognitive-behavioral analysis. In P. C. Kendall & S. D. Hallon (Eds.), *Cognitive-behavioral interventions: Theory, research and procedures*. New York: Academic.

Peris, J., & Cunningham, C. L. (1985). Dissociation of tolerance to the hypothermic and tachycardic effects of ethanol. *Pharmacology, Biochemistry and Behavior, 22*, 973–978.

Pfeffer, A. O., & Samson, H. H. (1985). Oral ethanol reinforcement in the rat: Effects of acute amphetamine. *Alcohol, 2*, 693–697.

Pomerleau, O. F., Fertig, J., Baker, L., & Cooney, N. (1983). Reactivity to alcohol cues in alcoholics and nonalcoholics: Implications for a stimulus control analysis of drinking. *Addictive Behaviors, 8*, 1–10.

Rachman, S., & Hodgson, R. J. (1974). Synchrony and desynchrony in fear and avoidance. *Behaviour Research and Therapy, 12*, 311–318.

Rankin, H., Stockwell, T., & Hodgson, R. (1982). Cues for drinking and degrees of alcohol dependence. *British Journal of Addiction, 77*, 287–296.

Rezvani, A., Huidobro-Toro, J. P., Hu, J., & Way, E. L. (1983). A rapid and simple method for the quantitative determination of tolerance development to opiates in the guinea pig ileum *in vitro*. *Journal of Pharmacology and Experimental Therapeutics, 199*, 158–170.

Ritzmann, R. F., & Tabakoff, B. (1976). Dissociation of alcohol tolerance and dependence. *Nature, 263,* 418–420.

Sartory, G., Rachman, S., & Grey, S. (1977). An investigation of the relation between reported fear and heart rate. *Behaviour Research and Therapy, 15,* 435–438.

Sherman, J. E., Pickman, C., Rice, A., Liebeskind, J. C., & Holman, E. W. (1980). Rewarding and aversive effects of morphine: Temporal and pharmacological properties. *Pharmacology, Biochemistry and Behavior, 13,* 501–505.

Sherman, J. E., Zinser, M. C., & Sideroff, S. (1985). Subjective reports of craving, withdrawal sickness and mood induced by boring, anxiety-provoking, or heroin-asociated stimuli among drug-free addicts in treatment. Paper presented at the American Psychological Association Meetings, Los Angeles.

Shiffman, S. M. (1982) Relapse following smoking cessation: A situational analysis. *Journal of Consulting and Clinical Psychology, 50,* 71–86.

Shiffman, S. M. (1984). Coping with temptations to smoke. *Journal of Consulting and Clinical Psychology, 52,* 261–267.

Shiffman, S. M. & Jarvik, M. E. (1976). Trends in withdrawal symptoms in abstinence from cigarette smoking. *Psychopharmacology, 50,* 35–39.

Sideroff, S. I., & Jarvik, M. E. (1980). Conditioned heroin response as an indication of readdiction liability. In L. S. Harris (Ed.), *Problems of drug dependence, 1979.* National Institute of Drug Abuse Research Monograph 27. Washington, DC: U.S. Government Printing Office.

Siegel, S. (1975). Evidence from rats that morphine tolerance is a learned response. *Journal of Comparative and Physiological Psychology, 89,* 498–506.

Siegel, S. (1983). Classical conditioning, drug tolerance, and drug dependence. In R. G. Smart, F. B. Glaser, Y. Israel, H. Kalant, R. E. Popham, & W. Schmidt (Eds.), *Research advances in alcohol and drug problems* (Vol. 7). New York: Plenum.

Siegel, S. Hinson, R. E., Krank, M. D., & McCully, J. (1982). Heroin "overdose" death: The contribution of drug-associated environmental cues. *Science, 216,* 436.

Sobell, L. C. (1985). *Recent advances in the treatment of alcohol problems.* Paper presented at the convention of the Association for the Advancement of Behavior Therapy, Houston.

Solomon, R. L. (1977). An opponent-process theory of acquired motivation: The affective dynamics of addiction. In J. D. Maser & M. E. P. Seligman (Eds.), *Psychopathology: Experimental models.* San Francisco: W. H. Freeman.

Solomon, R. L. (1980). The opponent-process theory of acquired motivation: The cost of pleasure and the benefits of pain. *American Psychologist,* 35, 691–712.

Solomon, R. S., & Corbit, J. D. (1973). An opponent-process theory of motivation. 2. Cigarette addiction. *Journal of Abnormal Psychology, 81,* 158–171.

Solomon, R. S., & Corbit, J. D. (1974). An opponent-process theory of motivation: 1. Temporal dynamics of affect. *Psychological Review, 81,* 119–145.

Stewart, J. (1984). Reinforcement of heroin and cocaine self-administration behavior in the rat by intracerebral application of morphine in the ventral tegmental area. *Pharmacology, Biochemistry and Behavior, 20,* 917–923.

Stewart, J., de Wit, H., & Eikelboom, R. (1984). Role of unconditioned and conditioned drug effects in the self-administration of opiates and stimulants. *Psychological Review, 91,* 251–268.

Stockwell, T. R., Hodgson, R. J., Rankin, H. J., & Taylor, C. (1982). Alcohol dependence, beliefs and the priming effect. *Behaviour Research and Therapy, 20,* 513–522.

Teasdale, J. (1973). Conditioned abstinence in narcotic addicts. *International Journal of the Addictions, 8,* 273.

Ternes, J. W., O'Brien, C. P., Grabowski, J., Wellerstein, H., & Jordan-Hayes, J. (1980). Conditioned drug responses to naturalistic stimuli. In L. S. Harris (Ed.), *Problems of drug dependence, 1979.* National Institute of Drug Abuse Research Monograph 27. Washington, DC: U.S. Government Printing Office.

Tiffany, S. T., Petrie, E. C., Baker, T. B., & Dahl, J. (1983). Conditioned morphine tolerance in the rat: Absence of a compensatory response and cross-tolerance with stress. *Behavioral Neuroscience, 97,* 335–353.

Tomkins, S. (1966). Psychological model of smoking behavior. *American Journal of Public Health, 56,* 17–27.

Van Der Kooy, D., Mucha, R. F., O'Shaughnessy, M., & Bucenieks, P. (1982). Reinforcing effects of brain microinjections of morphine revealed by conditioned place preference. *Brain Research, 243,* 107–117.

van Wolfswinkel, L., & van Ree, J. M. (1985). Site of rewarding action of morphine in the mesolimbic system determined by intracranial electrical self-stimulation. *Brain Research, 358,* 349–353.

Weeks, J. R., & Collins, R. J. (1968). Patterns of intravenous drug self-injection by morphine-addicted rats. In A. Wikler (Ed.), *The addictive states* (pp. 288–298). Research Publication of the Association for the Advancement of Nervous and Mental Disease, Vol. 46, Baltimore: Williams and Wilkins.

White, N. M. (1986). Control of sensorimotor function by dopaminergic nigrostriatal neurons: Influence on eating and drinking. *Neuroscience and Biobehavioral Reviews, 10,* 15–36.

Wiggins, J. (1973). *Personality and prediction* . New York: Addison-Wesley.

Wikler, A. (1953). *Opiate addiction.* Springfield, IL: Charles C. Thomas.

Wikler, A. (1980). Conditioning processes in opioid dependence and in relapse. In A. Wikler (Ed.), *Opioid dependence: Mechanisms and treatment.* New York: Plenum.

Wikler, A., & Pescor, F. T. (1967). Classical conditioning of a morphine abstinence phenomenon, reinforcement of opioid drinking behavior and "relapse" in morphine-addicted rats. *Psychopharmacologia, 10,* 255–284.

Wikler, A., Pescor, F. T., Miller, D., & Norrell, H. (1971). Persistent potency of a secondary (conditioned) reinforcer following withdrawal of morphine from physically dependent rats. *Psychopharmacologia, 20,* 103–117.

Wise, R. A., & Bozarth, M. A. (1982). Action of drugs of abuse on brain reward systems: An update with specific attention to opiates. *Pharmacology, Biochemistry and Behavior, 17,* 239–243.

Woods, J. S., & Leibowitz, S. F. (1985). Hypothalamic sites sensitive to morphine and naloxone: Effects on feeding behavior. *Pharmacology, Biochemistry and Behavior, 23,* 431–438,

Young, P. T. (1961). *Motivation and emotion.* New York: Wiley.

Zilm, D. H., Huszar, L., Carlen, P. L., Kaplan, H. L., & Wilkinson, D. A. (1980). EEG correlate of alcohol-induced organic brain syndrome in man. *Clinical Toxicology, 16,* 345–358.

Subject Index

abstention/abstinence, 113, 127, 225, 238
  temporary, 100–101
abstinence violation effect, 5
addiction
  homeostatic models of, *see* drug urges
  Solomon's definition of, 268
  theories of, 313
  urge research on, 257. *See also* urges
"addictive" personality, 217
adolescent drinking, 33–34, 36, 58, 69, 88, 219, 238
adolescents, hyperactive, 238
adoption studies, 11, 196, 211, 212–213, 220, 223
affective disorder alcoholism, 70
age factors
  in alcoholism, 58, 68–70
  in drinking behavior (1971–1981), 104
  in drinking onset, 33–34, 105
  in substance abuse, 30–31
  in women's drinking, 58, 97, 101–102, 104, 105–106, 122, 123
  See also life stages
Al-Anon, 15
Alateen, 15
alcohol
  conditioned effects and urge data on, 283–293
  depressive effects of, 8
  hypothermic effects of, 262–263
  metabolism of, 3–4, 9, 11, 232

"priming dose" of, 5, 288–290
  subjective "high" effects of, 233–234
  vasomotor response to, 232–233
alcohol abuse
  according to DSM-III, 196, 222
  ECA data on, 29–32
alcohol consumption
  dose/response relationships in, 182
  as elicitor of urges, 291
  in hospitals, 13
  See also drinking behavior; drinking levels
alcohol cues, 261, 283–285, 291
alcohol dehydrogenase, 3, 232
alcohol dependence
  according to DSM-III, 223
  ECA data on, 29–32
  in 1981 survey, 104
  urge responses and, 292–293, 310
  withdrawal symptoms and, 261
  in women, 90, 94, 97, 100, 101, 104, 105, 110, 111, 112, 120, 122, 127
alcohol detoxification, 13, 15, 16
alcohol education programs, 19–20
alcoholic beverages
  advertising of, 19–20
  availability of, 66, 115, 123, 127, 208
  children's conceptions of, 44–48
  restrictions on, 18–19
alcoholic relapse, *see* relapse, alcoholic
alcoholics
  diversity/heterogeneity of, 6–7

in substance abuse disorders, 29–31
sex norms for drinking, children's
   awareness of, 47–48
sexual dysfunction, 99–100, 126
sexual experience, 99–100, 126
Shoo Fly Powders, 13
Short Michigan Alcohol Screening
   Test (SMAST), 42
significant others, drinking by, 103
sleep, alcohol and, 210, 228
Smell Recognition Task, 44, 46
Smoking urges
   of active vs. withdrawing smokers,
      297–300
   cardiac data and, 298
   mood data on, 298–299
   questionnaire findings, 282
   relapse and, 272–273, 275, 276–277,
      278
   withdrawal and, 270, 297–300
      passim, 310
social class, alcoholism and, 7, 55–56,
   66, 67–68, 70–71
social learning perspective, 12, 15, 16
social learning theory, 165, 216
social norms for alcohol use,
   children's awareness of, 46–48,
   51
spouses' drinking, in women's
   survey, 103
spouses of alcoholics, 160–162, 176.
   See also marital interaction of
   alcoholic couples; marital
   stability, drinking and stages of
   variables, in women's drinking
   study, 107–110
static ataxia, 239
steady drinkers, 185, 188–191, 193–
   198 passim, 287
stress, alcohol use and, 10, 67, 71,
   125–126, 167–168
Structural Analysis of Social Behavior
   (SASB), 48
Subjective High Assessment Scale
   (SHAS), 234
substance use disorders, ECA data

on, 29–32
suicide, 98
survey of women's drinking (1981), 89–
   113, 115, 117, 119–120, 122–128
System Organization, 178
systems theory, 165

teacher ratings, 174
temporary abstention, 100–101
tension-reduction theory, 10, 12
"time out," 179–180
time-series analyses, 182, 189
tolerance
   behavorial (to alcohol), 2–4, 11, 233
   in compensatory response theory,
      262–264, 266, 270–271
   contextually-mediated, 263, 266
   to opiates, 266
   in opponent-process model, 268,
      270–272
   research on, 4, 262
   static ataxia and, 239
   subjective "high" and, 233
   in withdrawal model, 270–272
treatment of alcoholism
   approaches to (1935 vs. 1985), 13–
      17
   cognitive factors in, 12
   family-oriented, 159, 165
   life-grid perspective on, 73
   outcome predictors in, 17, 20
   programs for, 14, 15–17
   recovery rates, 16–17
   women's experiences with, 9, 15,
      86
triggering events, 210, 220, 224, 225,
   249
twin studies, 212, 236–237, 248

urge elicitation
   alcohol and, 278, 284–293
   cues and, 272
   Ludwig's work on, 285–288
   opiates and, 279–281, 294–296
urge networks
   negative affect, 309–312, 313

334

Author Index